THE
SHAKESPEARIAN TEMPEST

By the same Author

★

ON SHAKESPEARE
The Wheel of Fire (Tragedies)
The Imperial Theme (Tragedies and Roman Plays)
The Crown of Life (Final Plays)
The Sovereign Flower (Royalism; General Index)
The Mutual Flame (Sonnets)
Shakespearian Production

ON OTHER POETS
The Burning Oracle (Spenser, Milton, Pope, Byron)
The Starlit Dome (Wordsworth, Coleridge, Shelley, Keats)
Chariot of Wrath (Milton, Prose and Poetry)
Laureate of Peace (Pope)
Lord Byron: Christian Virtues
Lord Byron's Marriage
The Golden Labyrinth (on British Drama) Ibsen

POETRY AND RELIGION
The Christian Renaissance (The New Testament, Dante, Goethe)
Christ and Nietzsche (on Poetic Doctrine)
Hiroshima

GENERAL
Atlantic Crossing
The Dynasty of Stowe

DRAMA
The Last of the Incas

The
Shakespearian Tempest

With a Chart of Shakespeare's Dramatic Universe

by

G. WILSON KNIGHT

Emeritus Professor of English Literature in the University of Leeds
Formerly Chancellors' Professor of English at
Trinity College, Toronto

From lightning and tempest; from plague, pestilence, and famine; from battle and murder, and from sudden death, good Lord, deliver us.   THE LITANY

Which is the best of Shakespeare's plays? I mean in what mood and with what accompaniment do you like the Sea best?   KEATS, Letter to Jane Reynolds
14 Sept. 1817

METHUEN & CO. LTD. LONDON
11 New Fetter Lane · E.C.4

Originally published by Oxford University Press in 1932
First published (Third Edition) by Methuen & Co. Ltd., 1953
Reprinted 1960 and 1964

TO

W. F. JACKSON KNIGHT

PREFATORY NOTE

(In this note references to *The Wheel of Fire* (1949 edition), *The Imperial Theme*, *The Crown of Life* and *The Shakespearian Tempest* are given under the headings *WF*, *IT*, *CL* and *ST*)

THE reissue of this volume may profitably be made the occasion of a few remarks on recent developments in Shakespearian study. We have lately seen a number of works and articles stressing the intellectual 'background' of Shakespeare's plays, Elizabethan world-pictures, and so on. I have already pointed out that the significances adumbrated, in so far as they are Shakespearian at all, were first discovered not by any reading of medieval or Elizabethan philosophies, but by a simple inspection of the poetry. A new layer of symbolic meaning was unearthed by direct interpretation; of this certain elements were abstracted by scholarship and equated with medieval philosophy; and finally the philosophy—not even the Shakespearian elements—is arbitrarily applied to the poetry *from outside* as the one sure canon of judgment and necessary implement of interpretation. The illogicality is patent. Let us inspect the dangers.

That Shakespeare's work contains a high proportion of medieval thought is not strange; but the drama itself is more important than the thought. *Hamlet* and *Antony and Cleopatra* could not have been composed and acted in the age of Chaucer. Now, whereas Shakespeare's thought may often be related to a philosophy of 'order' (and other hierarchies), his *action* functions regularly as a challenge to such concepts. Though the philosophies themselves may be either medieval or contemporary, we can certainly relate the challenge itself to Renaissance humanism, and, beyond that, to poetic and dramatic genius. Anyone can understand the necessity of order; we all know how salutary it is, in any age, to pray for 'the squire and his relations', or their equivalents. What only genius can do is to set going an action which comes near to toppling over the universe whilst simultaneously engaging our sympathies. It is, moreover, fatal to suppose that any great genius is necessarily bound by the current thought-forms of his, or any, age; in nine instances it may be so, but in every tenth vital exception it is not. The problem of Isabella's testing—that pinnacle of human insight—will not be solved by a whole library of moral textbooks, however Elizabethan (or medieval) they may be.

But must not my own interpretations, so closely entwined from the start with symbolisms of order, share the responsibility for such developments? The essay 'Brutus and Macbeth' in *The Wheel of Fire* might, indeed, be called their originator. But 'order' was not there regarded as a simple concept; it was even remembered that the assassinations concerned were ultimately not disorderly actions at all, being part of the natural universe; rather as Pope places Catiline and Borgia within the harmonies of the *Essay on Man*; 'disorder' was shown to be a relative concept, dependent on the viewpoint taken (*WF*, pp. 137–8; *IT*, pp. 94–5). The whole essay was concerned primarily not with concepts, but with symbols; and, as I was at pains to argue in *The Christian Renaissance*, where the central theory of all these interpretations is set out, the symbol is richer than its compacted meanings (*ST*, pp. 13–17; and see *IT*, p. 29). Though concepts must be used as an interpretative medium, they must never be allowed to dominate the thing interpreted. After all, 'order', usually under the form of 'the moral order', has always been an implement of Shakespearian commentary; what was new was the surveying of the symbols and the exact relating of them to the persons and the action. And so, variously, with my other interpretations: my essay on *Timon of Athens* thrilled to the protagonist's curses *against* society; and with *Macbeth*, though one essay laid a primary emphasis on 'order', it nevertheless hinted that our valuations might be reversed in death (*IT*, p. 152); while another came near to asserting Macbeth's achievement of spiritual stature through a life of crime (*WF*, pp. 155–7, 159). Order-symbols may be doing little more than defining what the protagonist is up against: they are certain most important items in our bag of tricks, but no more than that. With any particular interpretation we need not all agree; but, when faced by a Falstaff, a Macbeth, or Milton's Satan, we must all at least be left free to follow our dramatic or poetic experience, *wherever it may lead us.* Otherwise we are reducing these titanic creations to the level of a moral tract, and that is tantamount to a denial of great literature, at least one essential element of which is, from age to age, a challenge to established systems.

Our argument may be assisted by a few words on Prof. G. I. Duthie's most excellent introduction to modern Shakespearian studies (*Shakespeare*, 1951). For Prof. Duthie's comments on my own labours I am deeply grateful; he is one of the few living writers who has seen the nature and importance of what I call the 'spatial' approach to literature. He does, however, find himself in serious disagreement with my interpretation of *Troilus and Cressida;* and the nature of that disagreement is interesting.

My own treatment, it will be remembered, regarded the Trojans as people of religious faith, intuition and romance; and the Greeks as people of reason, cynicism and stupidity; the Trojans being considered as the more pleasant party. The central incident in our tragic love-story—for we must never forget that it *is* primarily a love-story—was the handing over of Cressida from the Trojan side to the Greek, where she succumbs to the blandishments of Diomedes. Prof. Duthie, who takes 'order' as his interpretative key, observes that on *both* sides there are persons of orderly behaviour and of disorder. But, though I certainly regarded the Trojans as the more harmonious society, he is surely wrong in supposing that I would totally disagree with this analysis; even with my own, different, antithesis, I observed that both sorts existed on both sides; if they did not, you could have no dialogue.

But in *Troilus and Cressida* 'order' does not seem to me to take us very far, and we are really at cross-purposes, since Prof. Duthie is thinking of an order–disorder antithesis where I was thinking of intelligence and intuition (or reason and faith). The validity of my own emphases and sympathies might be urged—though I am a little ashamed of such an argument—by remembrance of the idealized association of Troy and Britain in Elizabethan thought. When Prof. Duthie—and other writers have felt the same —appears surprised at my Trojan sympathies, he is perhaps being governed by the thought that the greatest order-speech in Shakespeare is spoken by Ulysses on the Greek, that is—in my scheme—the rational, side. But what of our emotions? Is it enough to write off Troilus' impetuous love as rash and disorderly and therefore to be reproved? Does it not, especially at the climax ('This is, and is not, Cressid', v. ii. 143), channel in the highest degree our dramatic sympathy? Again, we are back at our old problem: it is the *business* of our dynamic protagonists to challenge the hierarchies, as with Romeo's 'Then I defy you, stars!' (*Romeo and Juliet*, v. i. 24). Any Shakespearian hero worth his place is expected to speak like that. We are not shocked; on the contrary, we demand it of him.

We have, moreover, to consider various *kinds* of order —personal, social political, spiritual, cosmic—any of which may conflict with others (*IT*, pp. 9, 16–18, 29; *ST*, 291). It is important to realize that, though a cosmic symbolism may be related to political order, it may equally well be found supporting some individualistic assertion at odds with that order.

In a recent article 'The Northern Star' (*Shakespeare Quarterly*, II, 4) Mr. Roy Walker—the worth of whose Shakespearian studies I have often saluted—takes a line similar to that of *The Olive and the Sword* and *The Crown of Life* in relating Shakespeare's Roman interests, including *Titus Andronicus*, through the union of Rome and Britain in *Cymbeline*, to Cranmer's prophecy in

Henry VIII. All this is most ably argued; but it nevertheless appears to me necessary to question Mr. Walker's
handling of the symbols.

His key-symbol is 'star', though he also uses 'moon'.
These he tends to range with affairs of state, relating
them to Julius Caesar, Octavius and Coriolanus, with their
opponents denied approval. But Caesar's self-comparison
with 'the Northern Star' grows from a highly complex
and in part ironic study, as I have shown elsewhere (in
The Imperial Theme); and directly after his assertion of
eternal constancy, he is a bleeding corpse. Again, Cassius' fearlessness in tempest is counted against him as
impious, whereas surely it registers, dramatically at
least, in his favour? We must remember, too, that from
Cassius' view the tempest and Caesar are to be equated
('a man most like this dreadful night', *ST*, p. 186; see also
WF, pp. 131–2; *IT*, pp. 84, 95); to him it is Caesar who
represents disorder. Moreover, the play's grandest cosmic symbolism is the association of the setting sun with
Cassius' death, Cassius being 'the Sun of Rome' (*IT*, pp.
60, 91). That last honour is, however, accorded him less
as a republican than as a man of *emotional* integrity, and as
lover (*IT*, pp. 91–2): which points us on to *Antony and
Cleopatra*. Here a vast cosmic imagery is associated almost
wholly with the lovers (*IT*, pp. 240–3). Some of it (e.g.
Antony's 'stars' deserting their 'orbs'; iii. xi. 145) is
tragically toned, but the massed effect serves very clearly
to aureole *them*, and not Caesar the politician, with cosmic
meaning. When Antony is said to 'outstare the lightning'
(iii. xi. 194), and threatens to 'lodge Lichas on the horns
of the moon' (iv. x. 58), we note the bravado, but recognize a mighty passion; and so on. With Antony we have,
of course, a clear sense of practical and political failure;
he is a tragic figure; but the aura lingers. With Cleopatra
the positive impact is greater. When she passes beyond
the 'fleeting moon' (v. ii. 239) to a marble constancy,
politics are *not* involved by the imagery; and when her
dying is heralded by 'O Eastern Star!' (v. ii. 310) we are

aware both of Christian associations and of rising life. This victorious intuition is counted by Mr. Walker against her: 'That star, too,' he says, 'is fallen'. I cannot believe it.

To pass to *Coriolanus*. Mr. Walker, noting that Coriolanus strikes Corioli 'like a planet' (ii. ii. 119), gives him an almost complete political approval involving an equivalent repudiation of the mob. The mob certainly *is* scorned; but Coriolanus' true opposers are the Tribunes; and in the political context Coriolanus is far from completely justified. His main fault, however, is personal, a crushing of all softer emotions by military pride; and that is, precisely, why the cosmic imagery never burns out in full glory till the moment when he subdues his pride to a mother's plea—*not* to the Tribunes, or the mob. Throughout Mr. Walker attempts to maintain the political-cosmic association; but 'the moon of Rome' (v. iii. 65) applies to Valeria's chastity, not to her political integrity; and, as for the cosmic cluster of 'stars', 'sun', 'heavens' (v. iii. 59–60, 183; v. iv. 55; discussed *IT*, pp. 192–7, and *ST*, pp. 209–10) that accompanies the surrender, one cannot properly re-engage politics by saying that the three women are now the 'last embodiment' of Rome's 'imperishable spirit'. It is a victory pre-eminently for the *feminine principle* as against all statecraft, and therefore the 'ladies' are said to deserve 'to have a temple' (not statues) 'built' for them (v. iii. 206). It is a victory for the domestic and familial values against military prowess and class wrangling. Hence the cosmic justification.

Mr. Walker is right in insisting on the magical radiations of Shakespeare's Rome; but his emphasis appears to be unduly limited to state affairs; and this seems dangerous. Cosmic symbolism, in its positive aspect, only holds communal reference when politics touch royalty (*IT*, p. 25; *CL*, pp. 318, 334). Julius Caesar has his rather insecure star; Octavius is scarcely 'royal' and given no stellar support to speak of outside a single reference to shining (ii. iii. 28); and Coriolanus, though great with a sort of blind planetary force, is denied cosmic sanction until his surrender to love. Cosmic symbolism in its *positive aspect* is, indeed, naturally a love-accompaniment, as with the sun-imagery of *Love's Labour's Lost*, the 'patines of bright gold' in Lorenzo's music-speech (*The Merchant of Venice*, v. i. 59), and the outstanding use of the star in Sonnet cxvi: 'It is the star to every wandering bark'. If the argument be still in doubt, let us face one final example. There are in *Antony and Cleopatra* no fine cosmic images on Caesar's side at all; there are masses of it tossed about on the other side; and these culminate—rather as we found with the death of Cassius—in *Cleopatra's extended dream-description of her cosmic Antony, with sun and moon for eyes* (*IT*, pp. 258–9). Where, then, is our thesis of cosmic symbolism set against Antony because Caesar is the symbol of political order?

The truth is, 'order'—which must not be limited to the 'moral order'—can have various connotations; by itself, it is an insubstantial concept. With Prof. Duthie Coriolanus is denied approval because his behaviour is egotistic, anti-social, and therefore against 'order'; with Roy Walker he is regarded as a figure of leadership and strength upholding order against the mob. Who is right? Both are right, and both, in part, wrong: for disorder only exists as a relation (*WF*, p. 139; *IT*, pp. 54, 176, note).

What, then, is our solution? This: that our only safe course is to keep our eyes unwaveringly fixed not on concepts, but on the living symbols, from which any concepts we choose to draw must be regarded as provisional derivatives only. We must always be more interested in the symbols themselves than in our own interpretation of them. And this brings us to my present study.

On its first appearance a reviewer in *The Times Literary Supplement* suggested that the principle of unity revealed might be better defined in terms of disorder and order than by Tempests and Music; and I replied that that would be to reduce Shakespeare's world to a philosophic thesis, whereas the unity of a great poet's work must be poetic. Though the lesser concepts are used throughout the following pages—and I admit that my phraseology in such brief sketches may sometimes leave room for misconception—it will be found that the necessary reservations are, in all the key-passages, clearly made. The selection of these symbols for primary attention is itself admitted to be an arbitrary action undertaken for a specific purpose; no claim is made for them, *and much less for any concepts*, as independent entities (p. 15); and the danger of remaining content with a conceptual translation is duly recorded (p. 16). The opposition of tempests and music is itself regarded as provisional, since tempests are part of 'great creating nature', and indeed themselves a music (pp. 290–1). They are thus (p. 292) more ultimate than 'disorder' or 'death', which remain negative and provisional—you cannot use the words without some sense of the deplorable, or the bad (disorder always sounds nasty)—while the Shakespearian heart is, and must be, a grand positive, beyond all moral or metaphysical negations. Such are the necessary reservations, foreshadowed by my first plea in the introduction to *The Wheel of Fire* (p. 11; see also pp. 45–6) that even such concepts as 'death' and 'evil' should as far as possible be handled and understood as positive powers.

To clarify our discussion, I offer a simple chart (pp. xvi–xvii) devised to form a kind of *vade mecum* for the Shakespearian expert. Since these are pre-eminently 'spatial' matters, they will be the clearer from a spatial formulation.

The 'line of poetic insight' running through the chart from eternity to eternity signifies that the whole area is poetically impregnated and holds eternal significance. Eternity may, however, vary from dark to light, with extremes shown at either end; the phrase 'bright eternity' being justified by the 'bright faces' and 'thousand beams' of Queen Katharine's vision in *Henry VIII* (iv. ii. 88). Dark eternity is mysterious, covering variously Hecate as interpreted in Appendix B of this volume, and

Timon's sea-shore grave, and perhaps most adequately defined by the 'caverns measureless to man' and 'sunless sea' of *Kubla Khan*.

On the right we have personal qualities; on the left, social and political. In the centre is a creative 'conflict' (not exactly 'disorder') related to the clash of individual and society. This conflict is nevertheless mainly inward and spiritual, and most fully experienced within the protagonist. It next tends, like a cyclone or hurricane, to move *down* the chart, developing into 'armed opposition', with the area columns showing a strong divergence of personal and communal symbolism as the rift widens; and so on to a tragic resolution.

Let us now look upwards. 'Human passions' aspire to 'love'; and 'political order', itself merely rational, desires consummation under the magic properties of 'royalty'; both these higher values holding cosmic sanction. 'Religious grace' is given a comparatively humble position, since it denotes passages of Christian toning that scarcely dominate outside *The Merchant of Venice*, *Measure for Measure*, *Macbeth* and *Henry VIII*, while its more dramatic realization is illustrated above. Here it may be called a leavening of passion. Balancing it, we have 'warrior honour', a high value yet liable, as with Hotspur and Coriolanus, to excess. About love and true, that is magical, royalty—as with the royal boys in *Cymbeline* and their sun-worship—there is no question. Still higher are the supreme entities: the 'youth eternal' passages of *The Winter's Tale*, and the resurrections there and in *Pericles*, on the one side; and Prospero (whose stature is politically important) as 'superman' and the 'royal child' Elizabeth, on the other. The high placing of the 'London crowd' is forced by *Henry VIII* (*CL*, pp. 303–6, 328–9); it also covers more widely the general challenge of Shakespeare's broad humanity and humour in relation to kings (we remember Falstaff and Bottom), and its position among the hierarchies makes a necessary point. 'Gods' and 'angels' (Diana, Apollo, Jupiter, and the angels of Queen Kathar-

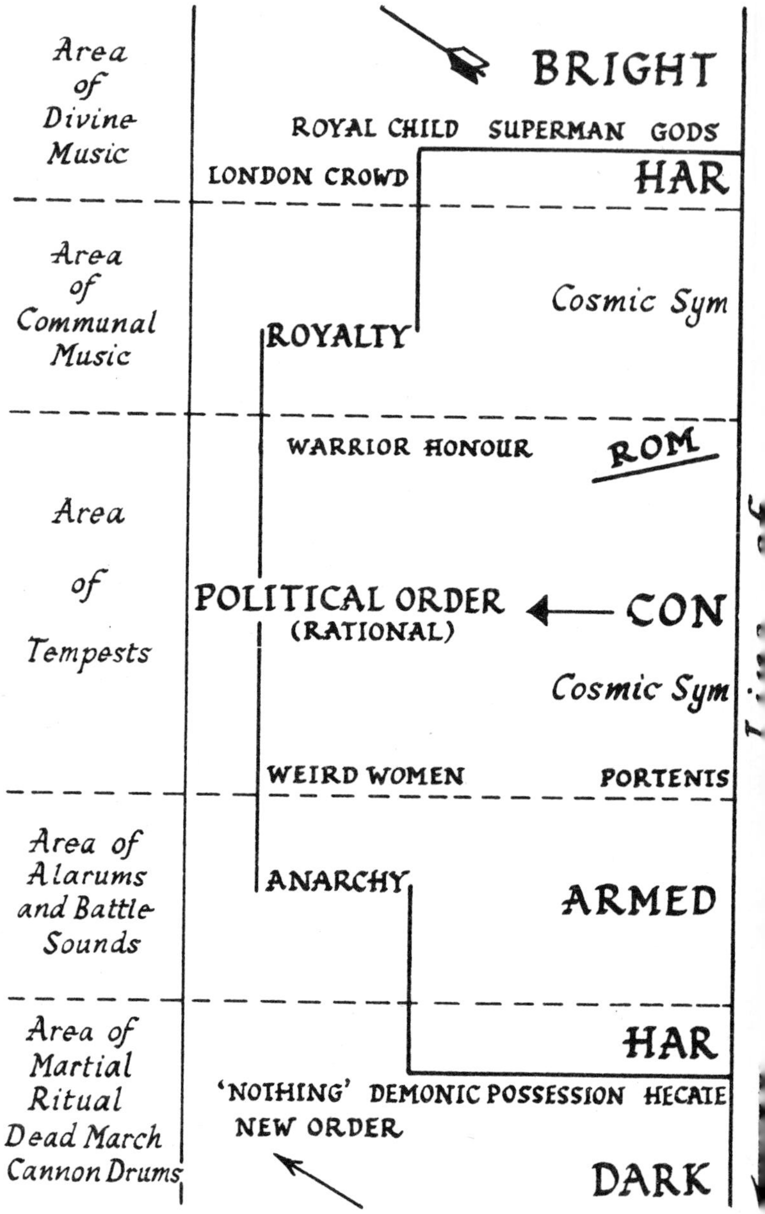
Area of Divine Music
Area of Communal Music
Area of Tempests
Area of Alarums and Battle Sounds
Area of Martial Ritual Dead March Cannon Drums
BRIGHT
ROYAL CHILD
SUPERMAN
GODS
LONDON CROWD
HAR
Cosmic Sym
ROYALTY
WARRIOR HONOUR
ROM
POLITICAL ORDER (RATIONAL)
CON
Cosmic Sym
WEIRD WOMEN
PORTENTS
ANARCHY
ARMED
HAR
'NOTHING'
DEMONIC POSSESSION
HECATE
NEW ORDER
DARK

ETERNITY ←		Area of Spiritual Music
ANGELS RESURRECTION YOUTH ETERNAL		
MONY	SACRAMENTAL NATURE	
bols Bright		Area of Personal Music
ANTIC COMEDY →	LOVE	
RELIGIOUS GRACE		
		Area of Tempests
FLICT →	HUMAN PASSIONS (RHETORICAL)	
bols Blurred		
GHOSTS	MADNESS	
OPPOSITION	NIHILISM	Area of Broken Music
MONY		Area of Evil Music Surf and Silence
MONUMENTS GRAVES DEATH		
	Sea = Infinity ⤦	
ETERNITY		

2

ine's vision) function as visitations only, and scarcely deserve a higher position than that accorded them, while their status precludes a lower: they are shown close to the line of poetry, or eternity.

The marginal areas denote effects discussed in this volume. 'Spiritual music' refers to Pericles' 'music of the spheres', the resurrection music of *Pericles* and *The Winter's Tale*, the Apparition in *Cymbeline*, *The Tempest*, and Queen Katharine's angelic vision (pp. 228, 223, 231, 239, 251–65, 243 below); the communal correspondence being whatever divinely suggestive music we choose for the Coronation and Christening in *Henry VIII* (e.g., pealing church bells). 'Personal music' needs little comment (pp. 58–63). 'Communal music' refers to Caesar's first entry in *Julius Caesar*, Duncan's feasting in *Macbeth*, the feast in *Timon of Athens* (pp. 185, 191, 201–2) and similar occasions. 'Broken music' occurs often in the fourth act (see especially p. 216; also pp. 57–8, 61, 176, 178, 183, 187, 198–9, 215). 'Evil music' refers to Hecate (pp. 329–31), and 'surf' (as a necessary stage effect) to the concluding scenes of *Timon of Athens*. Martial ritual, with dead march or other appropriate sounds, occurs powerfully in *Hamlet*, *Timon of Athens* and *Coriolanus* (pp. 216–17); and less vividly elsewhere (or ritual may be civic, as at the conclusion to *Romeo and Juliet*).

'Romantic Comedy' exists mainly in an area of 'personal music', aspiring directly to love, though its origins are in a 'tempest' area, and usually communal: hence our arrow, starting just inside the area of communal interests. Its comparative triviality is marked by its small area of action and lack of other relations: it is differentiated from the Final Plays by its failure to touch the area of 'spiritual music'.

The top half of our chart shows what might be called the settled values of Shakespeare's world; it corresponds roughly to what recent academic study calls 'the chain of being', though it is necessarily different too, since it relies entirely on powers drawn from Shakespearian drama. As the eye moves up, we see what Shakespeare's people aspire to.

The lower half is fairly clear. The separation of 'warrior honour' and 'armed opposition' will appear the more reasonable when we remember that the one is a fine value and the other a fearful event. Both Witches, or Weird Women, and Ghosts, are shown to be disorder forces (or effects) as *no human person ever is*.[1] Dark powers are ranged below corresponding to the group on top: for 'nothing' as a psychic or spiritual experience in *Macbeth* and elsewhere see *WF*, pp. 153, 231, 257–69; *IT*, pp. 137, 152, 357–8; *CL*, pp. 81–3 and note; 'demonic possession' applies to Lady Macbeth, and related examples; for Hecate and 'evil music' see Appendix B; and for sea as dark infinity, see *WF*, pp. 230–1, 245 (note); and *ST*, pp. 205–6; also pp. 51–3. Some of these may appear early in a play's action, but their place is here. They are all absolutes (e.g., see *WF*, pp. 152, 157), and so harmonious entities, though those on the left threaten social implications. Ghosts, being dramatically violent, are placed elsewhere. In placing Hecate and Death on different sides of the chart from their corresponding music, we illustrate Hecate's complaint that she has been forced from personal artistry into a position of human and social reference. Our dark entities, being Dionysian, are really all *one*, while their corresponding figures under 'bright eternity' necessarily show the Apollonian individuation.

But our chart illustrates not merely entities and positions; it is showing us powers and directions, and must be felt dynamically. We have accordingly to consider not only aspiration, but also action; otherwise we shall have interpreted Shakespeare's 'thought' while forgetting his drama. Now, though the people aspire upwards, yet the dramatic movement is normally—except for romantic comedy—not up, but *down*. So we must next imagine our

---

[1] For Witches in relation to disorder, see pp. 188 and 330 below; also *2 Henry VI*, i. iv., and *Richard III*, iii. iv. 58–71. Compare also *Cymbeline*, i. v. 1–45; and Sycorax in *The Tempest*.

sheet bent over till the dark and light eternities touch. We now have not just a rectangle, but a *cylinder*. We can next trace Shakespeare's progress downwards from the Romantic Comedies, Histories and Tragedies to Timon's 'nothing brings me all things' (v. i. 193; see *WF*, p. 246; *IT*, pp. 357–8; *CL*, p. 12)—the promise denoted by our arrow pointing from sea-infinity towards 'bright eternity' —and, through the *coincidence* of the two eternities in *Antony and Cleopatra* (*IT*, pp. 262, 286, 320; *CL*, pp. 12–13), to the area of the Final Plays.[1] We achieve our goal by an apparent loss of it, recalling the New Testament. You can accordingly see how dangerous it may be to force a rigid application of even Shakespeare's own apparent values on to his dramatic action; for what we find with Shakespeare's whole progress is true also of the great tragedies in isolation, which tend to move from communal music, through tempest, to a tragic resolution. New order is established for the community (this is shown by an arrow from 'bright eternity'); but the tragedy is also in itself creative and conceived less as failure than as achievement. The central conflict *unleashes power*; what was human becomes Titanic; Hamlet, Macbeth, Lear, Timon, Prospero, all in key-speeches touch eternal recognition; and we must assume some indefinable purpose. *The positive thrust of Shakespearian tragedy must at all costs, and in morality's despite, be unequivocally asserted.*[2]

We can use our chart in various ways, provided that we always think dynamically in terms of directions, oppositions, or conflicts. No single entity is to be valued in isolation; or, if it is, it must be recognized as a *power*,

---

[1] For the metaphysical implications of this transition, see *The Christian Renaissance*, X ('Immortality'): e.g., 'The moment a negation becomes absolute, it swiftly becomes, next, positive' (p. 255; cp. *IT*, p. 153).

[2] The problems raised by tragedy are very difficult. Agamemnon, Nestor and Ulysses discuss them in *Troilus and Cressida*; see pp. 170–1 below and *WF*, pp. 49–50; the discussion significantly occurring not in a tragedy, but in a 'problem play'. The most profound explanation hitherto advanced of the tragic enigma is probably Nietzsche's in *The Birth of Tragedy*.

radiating lines of force. Here are a few examples. *Love's Labour's Lost* can be indicated by using our comedy-arrow in *reverse* direction, to show it contradicting the movement of other comedies (*ST*, p. 82); *A Midsummer Night's Dream* will adventure slightly into the area of 'spiritual music', before curving back to 'love'; and for *The Merchant of Venice* we may substitute a simple line rather than an arrow, with a greater proportion within the area of tempests to indicate a balanced opposition of two worlds rather than a simple direction. *Richard II* can be shown as a triangle with 'royalty', 'human passions' and 'political order' as its corners, the first two—though separated on the chart—in conflict with the third; or, more simply, as a conflict of 'royalty' and 'order'. For *Troilus and Cressida* you can imagine the great order-speech, which is in essence rational, under 'political order', with Troilus on the right aspiring vertically to 'love', but dragged laterally towards Ulysses. Hamlet moves during most of his play within the quadrilateral made by 'ghosts', 'madness', 'death' and 'graves', touching thoughts of 'armed opposition,' and with a kind of antenna feeling up to 'angels' (*WF*, p. 312); while an accusing arrow can be shown pointing from his dark area towards Claudius, himself rather insecurely based on 'political order', and trying frantically to escape upwards within the ratification of that 'royalty' which he never properly attains. Othello in his last act is deep within the tragic area, but shafts of light slant *down* from 'love' to match the cosmic lights ('stars', 'moon', 'chrysolite') of his love-burdened *recollection*; Lear's reunion with Cordelia will be touched by beams from both 'love' and 'religious grace', coming round *from beneath*, to indicate more of a promise from *beyond*; and something similar, only with a far greater blaze shooting from *both* cylindrical directions, will illustrate Cleopatra's dream of her cosmic Antony. The repentant Leontes with Paulina will be among the absolutes of 'dark eternity', moving round—it is only a step—to the 'resurrection'. For *The Tempest*, you can imagine 'superman', with controls going in all directions, especially on to 'tempests' and 'music'.

Most important of all, the true nature and purpose of *Henry VIII* can be vividly and expansively illuminated. Here we have three persons (Buckingham, Wolsey, and Queen Katharine) in the tragic area, with delicate lines from 'religious grace' slanting across their blessings, and Katharine receiving lines also from 'love' and 'angels'. But both the stories and *last thoughts* of these three persons are offered in service to the King; and therefore strong lines of devotion must slant from them to 'royalty'. The King himself from his own 'royal' position (he is, of course, given sun-equivalence in the text) offers a yet stronger line of devotion to the 'royal child'; and so do 'political order', 'love' (the King's for Anne Boleyn), 'religious grace' (Cranmer), the 'London crowd', 'ritual', and perhaps 'romantic comedy'. We have thus a great web of lines, including the tributaries first noticed, *all* finally offered, directly or circuitously, to the royal child as their final home and centre. The limit of 'dark eternity' is never quite touched; and the great drama's general movement is up; *the dramatic action at last points direct to the hierarchies.*

Our chart illustrates the real lines of force in Shakespeare, while taking into exact account the various powers and purposes of his world. It is mapped from a view beyond moral good and evil; the tragic progress is shown as an achievement—as Nestor suggests (*ST*, p. 170) in *Troilus and Cressida*—rather than a failure; the darker powers enjoy an harmonious area; and the word 'evil' only occurs for a music (Hecate's) *outside the moral order* (*ST*, p. 329). We do not claim to cover everything; humour, which would require a different sort of diagram, is not adequately illustrated. But our chart should at least serve to indicate the danger of saddling Shakespeare's world with any static scheme whatsoever. Only when these various powers are recognized shall we understand the true process of harmonization at work.

The basic symbols of tempest and music in vital opposition unify Shakespeare's world; but also—and how well this points the rights of human passion in all its grades as *against* the cosmos—Prospero himself finally dominates and uses these symbols, turning tempests and music on and off like a tap. But there is also, as I showed at the conclusion of *The Olive and the Sword*, another subtly related principle of unity: Elizabethan patriotism. This is *not just an equivalent to 'order'*. Indeed, we must accord full sympathy to Macbeth, Falstaff and all the other great disrupters, before we attain that specific and exactly located harmony celebrated throughout *Henry VIII* (*CL*, p. 307). That is precisely why the raw, rough and *disorderly* London crowd (*CL*, pp. 303–6, 328, 335) is set among the hierarchies, as the long story reaches fulfilment and peace under, not a concept, but the royal child; a particular human being at a definite point in history, conceived as the defender not only of 'the Faith', but also of all the humanities and profundities of Shakespeare's world; for great poets put slight trust in abstractions.

And that is another story. I hope soon to complete my work on Shakespeare in this definitive edition with a fifth and last volume, using and expanding my earlier contributions during the war, on the stage and in books, towards a full recognition of Shakespeare's national statement; and to include in it an index covering the whole sequence.

My original preface contained acknowledgments to Colin Still in regard to the symbolic nature of the 'filthy-mantled pool' in *The Tempest*; to Caroline Spurgeon, who had already observed the bird-imagery of *Much Ado*; and to F. C. Kolbë, who first drew attention to the moon in *A Midsummer Night's Dream*. After completing my study, I discovered that Mr. Cumberland Clark's *Shakespeare and Science* (1929) contained passages on Shakespeare's tempest poetry; and that some of my material had been collected by Miss Anne Treneer in *The Sea in English Literature* (1926).

For a concrete argument on the question of sources as discussed on pp. 8–13 below, I would point to my letter (in answer to a review of *The Imperial Theme*) in *The Times Literary Supplement*, 25th February, 1932.

My old Globe references have been altered to come within three or four lines of the Oxford Shakespeare. I regret not having been able to change the recurring 'wreck' to the more Shakespearian 'wrack'. I have added a note (on p. 325) concerning *The Pheonix and the Turtle*.

LEEDS, 1952

G. W. K.

The Olive and the Sword now forms part, under the title 'This Sceptred Isle', of *The Sovereign Flower* (1958).

I have tidied my Conclusion (pp. 267–92 below), adding references, correcting some errors and removing a few mannerisms.

EXETER, 1963

G. W. K.

CONTENTS

I

INTRODUCTION

IN any intellectual study we expect first some principle of unity; but it is exactly this that has been lacking to our understanding of Shakespeare. If no unity be apprehended, the result will be an intellectual chaos such as has surely emerged throughout recent Shakespearian investigation. My purpose here is to replace that chaos by drawing attention to the true Shakespearian unity: the opposition, throughout the plays, of 'tempests' and 'music'.

My analysis is drawn from and appeals to that particular emotional and rational complex known as literary criticism or interpretation. Now it may be argued that such an interpretative faculty is irrelevant to the unique reality known as art. True, I have already suggested that the intelligence must needs find its unity: yet it is possible that the work of art is not intellectual in the ordinary sense, and demands an especial intuition which transcends all reasoning. Very likely there may be a higher and more direct mode of purest intuition to which it is theoretically possible that my conclusions are irrelevant; and I am therefore content to pluck out the heart of the Shakespearian mystery without claiming to reveal its soul. My interpretations in these essays may thus add nothing to the immediate enlightenment of a reader, if such exists, who has already experienced the Shakespearian universe—including *Titus Andronicus* and *Pericles*—as a single and harmonious whole, even though he may not have consciously given attention to Shakespeare's tempests. But the tortuous paths and 'indirect crook'd ways'—to say nothing of the blind alleys—trodden by much past commentary certainly show that Shakespeare has met with intellectual misrepresentation; and may suggest a corresponding error in our intuitive understanding. The ideal reader with a perfectly tuned poetic receptivity may indeed have often existed.

He has left no record of himself. Nor is there any reason why he should do so. My interpretations, however, are justified by the fact that those whose business it is to leave records of their findings have clearly, at certain important points, misrepresented Shakespeare. Even if we grant their intuitive understanding to be correct, their intellectual formulations have certainly proved, very often, erroneous. The transition from the one mode to the other has been improperly performed. And this inexactitude has been dangerous and harmful. For the general reader is not quite independent of the higher scholarship. If the authorities tell him that a large part of *Timon of Athens*, or the Vision of Jupiter in *Cymbeline*, is not authentic, he will, very likely, believe them: certainly his enjoyment will be sullied. How many readers outside the ranks of scholarship would ever have suspected as spurious the noble soliloquies of Wolsey and his dialogue with Cromwell in *Henry VIII*? Yet, once told they are by Fletcher, the unexpert reader may rule them out of his imaginative repertory. My point is that, even if true commentary adds little or nothing to the enjoyment of the average sensitive reader, certainly a false commentary may detract from that enjoyment. And my purpose here is in part to safeguard Shakespeare for the general reader from the disintegration of misguided scholarship. While a right interpretation is not offered, many wrong ones will continue to appear. The human mind is an active and sometimes a dangerous force. If it cannot discover its unity, it will speak loud its discovery of chaos. That is what has happened in recent Shakespearian study.

The disagreement often noticeable to-day among experts on many fundamental points is but a sign that Shakespearian commentary has left solid fact in pursuit of abstractions. We are in sore need of unity. Chaos and conflict are rampant. And, where there is chaos, there is, necessarily, no limit set to the extravagances of individual opinion. Each commentator is a law to himself. Any one is at liberty to credit any Elizabethan with the authorship of those passages or plays in Shakespeare which he, personally, feels inclined to reject. Even though he gives reasons for his rejection, such as metrical tests, the value of such tests yet remains a matter of opinion. 'Metre' is clearly a dangerous quicksand. Any poet can vary his metre at will, and Shakespeare appears to have done so continually. Again, intensive study has tried to discover reasons for what may appear faults or eccentricities in Shakespeare by crediting such to other and lesser writers, or to the 'old play' on which Shakespeare was at work. Or we are reminded that the unrefined Elizabethan audience demanded such 'faults' from its playwrights. Or we make random shots in the dark, hoping to bring down one of Shakespeare's 'intentions'. But all this is surely hypothetical. We should never have found ourselves involved in it, were it not that commentary has long broken free from its cables, storm-driven from the objective basis of an imaginative understanding, and tossed on the tumultuous seas of personal prejudice. Antagonism can go too far. Where there is no sure basis of agreement, no foundation, the conflicts of scholars cease to be a sign of health. And the cause is simple. We have failed to focus correctly the Shakespearian unity. Thus, there being no common starting-point for our inquiry, indeed no purely objective element at all in our subject-matter to which we are all equally responsive, we have become involved in pure emotionalism, individualism, and anarchy. Nor shall we find safety and surety till we give primary attention to the imaginative solidities of Shakespeare; since only then shall we see his work as a unity rather than a chaos.

This tendency to neglect the Shakespearian imagination has wrecked our understanding. Perhaps it is but the natural result of the excessive importance attached to Shakespeare's psychology and 'characterization' by the criticism of the last century. While we view the plays primarily as studies in character, abstracting the literary person from the close mesh of that poetic fabric into which he is woven, we shall, by continually over-emphasizing certain qualities in each play and attending closely to no others, necessarily end by creating a chaos of the whole. If, however, we give attention always to poetic colour and suggestion first, thinking primarily in terms of symbolism, not 'characters', we shall find each play in turn appear more and more amazing in the delicacy of its texture, and then, and not till then, will the whole of Shakespeare's work begin to reveal its richer significance, its harmony, its unity. In place of that unity, we have, to-day, chaos; in place of that music, tempest. Confronted with this amazing collection of plays formulating the grandest intuitions in terms of intellectual chaos, we have been able neither to rest, nor move to any safety. The mind must have an object for its inquiry; and we have long ceased to know the Shakespearian imagination as an objective fact. Hence our difficulties have further objectified themselves beyond the plays to the identity of their author. Chaos has disintegrated even that primary unity which the name 'Shakespeare' gives. Now I do not wish to make any derogatory suggestion about either the Baconian or Oxfordian school of research. I adhere to neither. But I think both have done valuable work, if only to press home to us that there is a problem to be solved. That problem may well turn out to be, after all, no problem of historical personality: though I am convinced that from a careful study of the plays will surely emerge a William Shakespeare as different from that smug mixture of platitudinizing moralist and beery yokel which is our conventional 'Bard of Avon' as any Lord Bacon or Edward de Vere might be from 'Shaksper'. All these, and other, questions, however, must be considered afresh in the light cast upon Shakespeare's work by a careful consideration of its purely imaginative qualities. Then we shall, I think, also cease to hand over large quantities of Shakespeare to minor Elizabethan dramatists.

But I do not suggest that the tempests which I here trace prove anything directly as to the authorship of 'doubtful' plays. Any poet is at liberty to use the tempest symbol. It possesses a universal appeal and may be found in the Bible, the Classics, and throughout English Literature; strongest, perhaps, in our hymn books. So, too, with music. Shakespeare's use of it is very straight-forward. No author would give directions for soft music whilst Duncan is being murdered: the music-love asso-ciations in Shakespeare are as natural as his tempests. The most universal of poets has clearly but employed the most universal of symbols. Any one who valued this tem-pest-imagery alone as evidence for authorship might well be quickly disillusioned by a search for tempests in other writers. In any one instance, a tempest is poor evidence. And yet the tempest-music opposition is indirectly rele-vant to the question of authorship. It is so precisely and consistently used by Shakespeare, that, if we regard his work as a whole from this view, we focus an especial Shakespearian unity unlike that of any other poet. Shake-speare is differentiated from other poets by his peculiarly consistent use of images and symbols common to all. He has no private and esoteric system of impressions. Now we tend to forget that, failing very strong evidence, we are bound to assume the editors of the First Folio to have made good their very decisively worded claims. Moreover, once we feel the massive unity of Shakespeare, we shall begin to understand the separate plays as contributing to this single harmony; and, understanding, we shall be less and less inclined to raise questions of authorship. Many doubtful passages will be seen to have been doubtful only because not understood. Therefore, though I think the recurrence of certain highly complex triple or quadruple associations in similar tempest-passages might certainly be used as direct evidence for authorship in certain cases, I prefer here to insist primarily on the absolute necessity for a pure poetic understanding as a preliminary to all such discus-sions. The imaginative study of Shakespeare has not yet properly begun. For any such understanding must surely start by consideration of the hitherto neglected Shakespearian essence: the tempest-music opposition.

Tempests are thus all-important. Taken in opposition with music they form the only principle of unity in Shakespeare. 'Characterization', plots, metre, even typical 'values', change; plays are tragical, historical, comical, or pastoral, light as Plautus or heavy as Seneca; but all may be shown to revolve on this one axis. Therefore, by seeing each in turn as a new aspect, a new presentation, of this one theme, we unify the whole of Shakespeare's work; nor could that work be so unified in any other fashion. But this unity has been hitherto ignored. I shall next, therefore, make some suggestions as to why so important an element in Shakespeare has failed to receive recognition and understanding.

A Shakespearian play is, indeed, mysterious. It is not life, though it is very life-like; and our normal waking consciousness, which we may call the intellectual, is not readily and instinctively[1] adapted to understand this poetic reality, which demands and awakens an especial intuition. The intellect may, however, be unaware of its own limitations, and lay claim to an understanding for which it is not equipped: then it becomes very dangerous. This normal intellectual consciousness is, clearly, accustomed to traffic daily with a limited human rather than a universal reality; therein is its chief interest. Moreover, it has itself given birth to our ethical systems, which will be found ever to reflect the more 'common-sense' view of human conduct, rejecting the impassioned, the visionary, or the nihilistic, and all immediate intuitions, whose fine frenzies of delight or agony cannot be justified by considerations of cause and effect. True, this common-sense view may well be an excellent thing in life; though it knows little of love's bright and careless unreason without which there would be few marriages and life itself thus quickly be impoverished. But this intellectual consciousness is ill adapted to analysis of poetry. A Shakespearian play

---

[1] We must always remember that the intellect-instinct distinction is not final. 'Instinct' is often based on intellectual reasoning, intellect often, perhaps always, instinctive.

certainly has elements both psychological and ethical, but it has much else, of more universal suggestion, besides. Moreover, those other elements are exactly those which constitute our poetic enjoyment. They are received intuitively, enjoyed, and swiftly forgotten: the memory, or intellect, is as a sieve which lets the precious liquid escape and preserves only those stones which are fitted to its own practical purposes. What remains is what interests the memory, the intellect, and common sense. Thus our imaginative reaction to a poem is a succession of intuitive states, each forgotten in its unique quality as it passes, and, save for a minute residuum of the richer essence, which fortunately accumulates slowly on every fresh acquaintance, handing on to its successor only those elements which the intellect and memory happen to like. After reading *Macbeth*, we tend to remember the chief persons, and the story: all the rest, the child-symbolism, the varied atmospheric suggestion, the tempests and strange screams of death, all this is only appreciated after years of study. And yet it is there, staring at us. But it is extraordinarily difficult to force the intellect into any activity alien to its instinct. The memory will always try to reject the imagination, and has to be rigidly schooled into humility. Otherwise the gold-dust escapes and the stones remain.

Throughout Shakespeare the tempest-symbol is heavily emphasized. When pointed out, it is very clearly important; and yet it has never been properly observed. Though most readers are conscious of the tempest in *Lear*, comparatively few appear to be aware that there is also a significant tempest in *Othello*. Commentary has not appreciated the exquisite interweaving of sea and tempest thoughts in *Twelfth Night* with themes of music; and all that this implies. As for *The Merry Wives of Windsor*, the very suggestion of a symbolic content in the ducking of Falstaff appears ludicrous: yet, from a comprehensive understanding of Shakespeare's work, it certainly is symbolically important, and very necessary to an inclusive analysis of tempests, and the closely related

3

thought of drowning. These are a few random instances.
But they are typical. And this failure in appreciation has
been harmful. It has led to an entirely false view of Shakespeare's work as a whole, and the final phase of that work
in particular. But, though these tempests have not been
duly observed and correlated by the critical and interpretative intelligence, they may well have—indeed must
have—been regularly understood by the intuition. The
Othello tempest carries its own conviction as we read or
listen in the theatre. So does the narrow escape from a
ludicrous drowning experienced by Falstaff. There is an
imaginative appeal and conviction; and it is exactly, and
only, this imaginative appeal and conviction which, on the
plane of intellectual interpretation, constitutes symbolism.
But these separate intuitions are isolated, marooned, after
their first immediate effect, in the waters of forgetfulness;
but vaguely remembered till another reading visits them,
only to leave them once more again marooned. Memory,
which is close-twined with the intelligence, is ever reluctant to store the treasures of intuition. The normal
consciousness does not understand the imagination.

It is truly remarkable how, even when one is alert to
discover certain expected imaginative effects, one may well
pass over a particularly glaring instance, probably because
it occurs in a passage so well known that it is soaked in
alien associations.[1] And to-day we are peculiarly unfortunate in respect to these false associations. For years
Shakespearian study has been clouded by consideration of
'sources'. We immediately associate the mysterious music
in *Antony and Cleopatra* with its source in Plutarch. Now
that step alone is not directly to be blamed. There is certainly a very clear relation between Plutarch and *Antony
and Cleopatra*. But the moment consideration of this
source is allowed to barrier our understanding from the

[1] Mr. Franklin Gary compares certain arguments of mine with those
of Mr. I. A. Richards concerning 'the critical preconceptions which hinder
readers from appreciating lyric poems'. (Towards the Integration of
Shakespeare, *The Symposium*, April 1931.) This has helped me here.

immediate symbolic or aesthetic value of this effect, the source has clearly overflowed its proper limits—or, rather, it has ceased to fill its river, and becomes the source of nothing but itself. We cannot reason that the existence of a source necessarily drains the significance of an artistic unit, or any part of such a unit. This reasoning is quite puerile and dissolves at once before the simplest examination. It is really extraordinary that any trained intelligence should employ it. But the cause is not hard to find. We are faced in reality not by any dangerous aesthetic philosophy—since such source-arguments have nothing in common with any reputable aesthetic theory—but by a simple habit of false association which masquerades as a considered theory. The process is curious. We are accustomed to associate a certain artistic effect with its source, because we are taught to. This association becomes most powerful. Therefore it will not allow us to associate that effect with any especial meaning or any other artistic effects, either in the same play, or other plays. Finally we are inevitably forced to deny this lonely excellence, thus cut off from all possible relations but its own source, any artistic effect whatsoever. The source has killed it. And each Shakespearian beauty for which we can unearth a source undergoes this paralysing process, leaving us only a few derelict and now unrelated fragments in each play for imaginative analysis—these we at once relate, of course, to Shakespeare's 'intentions'—until we are faced by a Shakespeare which is, to the intelligence, a mere hotch-potch of puerilities, imitations, and vulgarities; which same Shakespeare nevertheless continues to sound the orchestrations of great poetry, no whit silenced by any criticism, to the receptive intuition of the average reader.

I do not deny that sources exist, nor would I be thought to decry the scholarship that finds them. I only wish them not to encroach on our imaginative appreciation. There is no good reason why they should. Now I claim that Shakespeare's play *The Tempest* is strongly impregnated with

mysticism. I regard its tempest as symbolical. But it is
universally considered that *The Tempest* derives its name
and action primarily from Sir George Somers's shipwreck.
It is clearly impossible to prove that Shakespeare did not
owe something to that event. It is, indeed, extremely
probable that he knew as much about it, and probably
more, than we do. For, if one certain biographical fact can
be deduced from the material collected here, it is, surely,
this: that the Shakespearian imagination reacts with extreme sensitivity to all sea tempests. Therefore we may
conclude that not many sea adventures with which his
mind may have come into contact would have been rejected. Rather, he would, in all probability, have learned
all he could with avidity. That much is probably certain
and will hardly be denied. It might even be further urged
that Shakespeare himself must on one occasion, at least,
have actually seen the sea, and perhaps a ship; or, even,
have undertaken a passage, however short, in a boat:
across the Thames, for example. That, however, is entirely hypothetical—a matter for fancy, not for scholarship—and quite beyond my immediate purpose. Here I
would emphasize only that my present argument, which
is based on Shakespeare's imaginative infatuation with
tempests in general, does not preclude the possibility
that he may have been also interested in a certain actual
tempest in particular; and, conversely, that his having
heard with interest about an actual tempest need not
necessarily have paralysed his imaginative development
and control.

It may, perhaps, appear unnecessary to labour this point.
Yet it is not. As I have already argued, the mind is only
too accustomed to banish one association because a certain
poetic effect is already strongly charged with another. If
the tempest in *The Tempest* is Sir George Somers's tempest, it cannot, we feel, be Shakespeare's too; if Cleopatra
is Plutarch's, she cannot be properly Shakespeare's; if the
Weird Sisters are Holinshed's, they cannot be vivid imaginative creations in the realm of poetry. One association

crowds out the other. Of course, we can continue such an argument very far. It has been done. And then, failing to find sources for everything, and finding ourselves quite derelict and adrift from all poetic solidities, we are forced to find more hypothetical originals, and still more, in order to fit Shakespeare out with a complete list of sources. I do not, however, suggest that all work on sources is wasted; and I am far from denying both its interest and, when carefully carried out, its value. But when such 'realistic' arguments are directed against an imaginative interpretation, I maintain that we are in danger of committing imaginative suicide. To return to Sir George Somers. Certainly if the tempest in *The Tempest* be wholly his—the actual one—it is not Shakespeare's. But Shakespeare's tempest is primarily a literary one: therefore it is not wholly Sir George Somers's. But perhaps it is neither. Poetry is a mystery. Possibly *The Tempest*, or the tempest in *The Tempest*, is not in any valuable sense either Sir George Somers's nor even Shakespeare's. A man may be divinely inspired when writing poetry. Then we can only say the tempest is, at the most, to be associated or indirectly related to both. And here we see clearly how, at the root of the matter, we have one legitimate association forbidding entrance to another. But meanwhile, having attributed the true origin to Divinity, we shall not be now surprised to find profound meanings in the result. No one can safely argue from sources to poetic truth without first steadying himself firmly on some clear aesthetic philosophy which claims to be able to expose an exact relation subsistent between the minutest details of the poet's life adventures (or his interest in others' life adventures) and his written poetry. And that philosophy or science will not be readily forthcoming. Therefore it will be clear that not one of my quotations in the following pages can be lightly denied one fraction of imaginative significance on the grounds that it is found in Shakespeare's source. I can hardly be expected to subtract all tempests that might have a close parallel in a book read by Shakespeare, or an event of which he might have heard. This will probably be granted. But, again, the mind is most recalcitrant in this matter of association. Rationally, it may be convinced; and the next moment it is back at its old perversity. What of Shakespeare's description of Cleopatra on her barge at Cydnus? It paraphrases Plutarch closely. I have—here and in my more detailed examination of *Antony and Cleopatra*—considered it as most important in point of imaginative detail. But again I am awkwardly aware that the whole incident is in Plutarch. However clearly we see the rational inconsequence in a destructive 'source' philosophy, we yet instinctively feel that sources cannot be blended with imaginative interpretation. This is a trick of the mind, a complex, a form of abnormal neurosis, perhaps, from which, like most types of abnormal neurosis, we all suffer. Again, we will try to clarify our issue; though, of course, no rational arguments will ever drive out a really powerfully rooted prejudice.

If it be granted that Plutarch's description suits Shakespeare's usual imaginative method remarkably well, we can say: (i) that this very incident is the one which first stimulated Shakespeare's imagination concerning calm waters, soft airs, and music; or (ii) that chance favoured the poet and, elsewhere altering what he chose, he found this particular incident too exactly appropriate to his manner to reject it; or (iii) that Shakespeare reads and rereads Plutarch especially because the Plutarchan and Shakespearian imagination have much in common. So, too, with tempests. With any one, throughout the long list, we may be prepared, if a source is shown us, to argue that this was the very one which first set him writing about tempests; with the next, we could say that this or that plot was, perhaps, chosen for the sake of its tempest. And if we are confronted with a long list of tempest sources we shall then conclude that Shakespeare invariably looked first for a tempest when selecting material for a play. Or again, we may say that the tempest is so

universal a symbol that you are likely to find it in most
stories; and that Shakespeare only gave it prominence
and a more exact significance than his originals. There
is really no sound argument against the importance of
these tempests. Prejudiced criticism can—and no doubt
will—ignore them; but it cannot delete them from the
collected works, much as it may wish to do so; they are
there, and they cannot be argued away. But surely we
might profitably return to simplicities. No poet in his
senses, nor any imaginative historian, would have placed
Cleopatra on a dirty and bedraggled ship, awkwardly
steering its course on a raw and gusty day, Cleopatra
drenched with rain, and her nose red with the cold wind;
nor would he have accompanied her progress with the
howls of jackals in place of soft music. Nor, indeed, would
the real Cleopatra have been so stupid as to choose such a
day for a pleasure trip at the end of which she hoped to
make an amatory conquest. The effects I am analysing
are ever simple, obvious, and universal. There is nothing
esoteric nor, in any recondite sense, mystical in them.
True, they are used with exceptional precision. But that
is Shakespeare's habit: his work is always characterized
by remarkable control of the simple, the obvious, and the
universal. Most writers find these of all the most intract-
able material. And yet, in another sense, these tempests
become indeed mystic symbols. *The Tempest* is, if ever
there was one, a profound mystic vision; its tempest is
its primary symbol; and tempests are, imaginatively, very
simple things to understand. Pure mysticism is, we must
conclude, only complicated to a perverted vision. Therefore our understanding of *The Tempest* is to be a matter of
excessive and growing importance, now and in the future.

That is to say, we are to give conscious attention to
Shakespeare's symbolic effects. But the very term 'symbolism' is apt to mislead and repel the unsympathetic and
reluctant inquirer. I have already hinted that any immediate appeal to the imagination constitutes a symbolic
force to the intelligence. Thus there is nothing rigid about

a symbol. It is not a sign which 'stands instead of' something else. Any one symbol is not a symbol of any one
thing in particular but holds rather a number of suggestions. It might be said to have infinite relations: it is
both infinite and yet closely defined. Everything in the
art-form that is momentarily associated with it undergoes
a dynamic change; while it, too, undergoes a dynamic
change with every fresh association. We cannot say about
any one symbol that it means anything more or less than
it must mean in its particular context. All we can, ultimately, say is that it has dynamic relations: it receives and
radiates power. Such is the tempest or the sea in Shakespeare. And the variable nature of the symbol can be
well illustrated from the passages I quote in the following pages. The sea is usually impregnated with tragic
power. Often it holds a 'death' suggestion; it is often a
formless chaos; and yet it may, if imaged as calm, suggest
peace. Again, its infinite expanse may suggest the in-
finities of either guilt or glory; its raging contest with
rocks may indicate either nobility or savagery; its fathom-
less depths are rich with the piled treasuries they have
filched from navigation. And the implications extend
indefinitely. Where the sea is kind, we may find the
thought of tragedy absent from the play's integral statement, as in *Henry V*; or, again, we may find the thoughts
of death and tragedy themselves pleasant, as in *Antony and
Cleopatra*. The Dauphin in *Henry V* speaks aptly of the
'sea':

> Nay, the man hath no wit that cannot, from the rising of the
> lark to the lodging of the lamb, vary deserved praise on my
> palfry: it is a theme as fluent as the sea: turn the sands into
> eloquent tongues, and my horse is argument for them all. . . .
>
> (III. vii. 33)

So Shakespeare varies his praise of the sea, which ever
elicits his finest eloquence. We thus, clearly, cannot finally
say the sea in Shakespeare has any one persistent meaning
as a symbol but only as itself, as the sea. It becomes a
symbol only when we start to interpret. It is the same

with tempests. In *Othello* the tempest suggests not Fortune's cruelty but rather Fortune's favour; yet, by contrast, it throws forward to another, spiritual, tempest, wherein Fortune's favour is withdrawn. In *Lear* the tempest, though cruel, is yet kind in comparison with man's cruelty. The tempest in *Macbeth* is, as near as may be, wholly cruel, destructive, impregnated with death. A poet's symbol has thus queer propensities. It may often be equivalent to its opposite in the sense that any contrast is a comparison. Thus physical tempests are primarily cruel in Shakespeare; yet often their presence serves to indicate a tempestuous reality even more cruel in terms of spiritual experience. The tempest is kind by comparison and is, apparently, introduced primarily that we may be aware of this kindness. Tempests thus vary from play to play. We cannot finally say that tempests are to be absolutely and always equated with tragedy when they are as likely to be contrasted with it.

And yet, from a comprehensive view of Shakespeare's work, we are forced to regard tempests and sea-imagery as less flexible than other fictional realities. As I have observed, the symbol and its environment are inter-significant, interaffective. But, if we are to pursue analysis at all, we must regard something as fixed. Motion itself demands a static base of reference. The Ptolemaic system said that the sun revolved round the earth; the Copernican, the earth round the sun. Both are right and both are wrong in terms of modern understanding: since, in an absolute sense, motion must be relative. Yet, whilst we confine our attention to the solar system, it is clear that we do well to regard the sun as fixed, because by so doing we can the more readily unify our facts. Therefore, in the Shakespearian system, we shall be forced to regard either the sea in all its variations or the tempest-music opposition (these being equivalent since the sea, variably rough and calm, tends to include the modes suggested by the other terms) as fixed; and we shall say that plots are built round tempests—or, to be more exact, round

the tempest-music opposition—rather than that tempests
are inserted into plots. Plots vary, tempests persist.
It is always the same tempest; and, indeed, it is continually given almost exactly repetitive phrases in description. Ultimately, we must call the Shakespearian tempest
something like this: 'Shakespeare's intuition of discord
and conflict.' But even that is to translate the symbol:
therefore we should improve it to 'Shakespeare's intuition
of tempestuousness at the heart of existence'. That, too,
is a concession to the intelligence. But so much is to be
allowed or we shall get no farther than 'tempests are tempests'. Perhaps, however, that is best. Certainly in *Lear*
we must not consider that the physical tempest is merely
a poetic device to assist our response to the conflict in
Lear's mind: if that were the ultimate truth, we should be
justified in relegating tempest-symbolism to secondary
consideration. The truth is more complex, yet simpler.
The tempest on the heath and the tempest in Lear's
mind ('the tempest in my mind') are one tempest; or
rather facets of one tempest. The real tempest is composed of both, and other elements of conflict too—such
as the Fool's plaintive incompatibilities of humour and
Edgar's jarring discord of mock-lunacy; and, too, the
numerous 'divisions' between France and England,
Albany and Cornwall, Goneril and Regan, Edmund and
Edgar, and so on; in fact, the whole play. The play is
a vision of conflict, or tempest. The tempest-conflict-
division complex, or unity, is at the heart of the play: the
rest is its outward trappings. This, I mean, to the intelligence. The pure and perfect intuition, wherever it exists,
is beyond analysis and outside the scope of my—or any—
language. Therefore in *Lear* the essence is to be considered the tempest, not the 'character' of the protagonist. So throughout Shakespeare. The poet's intuitions of conflict and disorder, and, again, of concord and
love, are ultimate. Seeking expression, he gives them one
form after another, comic or tragic, historical or pastoral.
But they remain ultimates: tempests and music opposed

or interwoven. Even at the extreme of interpretative scepticism we shall, I think, be forced to admit that throughout Shakespeare tempests and music occur significantly; and that that significance constitutes the only final unity in Shakespeare.

In abstracting this opposition from Shakespeare's work I have shown that work to possess an imaginative unity which can be submitted to intellectual formulation. For my immediate purpose this abstraction has been necessary. Nor do we falsify our understanding by such an arbitrary act. To isolate such a symbol clarifies our perception of the whole play, whereas to isolate a 'character' distorts it: this symbol partaking more directly of the quality of the whole. But it has not been always easy to disentangle a pure tempest–impression from its context. Moreover, tempest-imagery is only one very obvious and recurrent thread in a wider pattern of 'disorder' thought, often bodied into imagery of universal disorder: comets and meteors, earthquakes, and such like: which again may blend with 'disease' imagery. Conversely music is enmeshed in other pleasant suggestion, especially delicate airs (to be contrasted with tempests), flowers, gold, jewels, and all rich stones. On the purely human plane, these groups are associated with disorder, conflict, and all fierce passions on the one side; and love, concord, peace, on the other. Tempests, also, are to be related to all Shakespeare's 'weather' thought, blending with rain, clouds, fog, all dark or wintry effects; whereas music harmonizes with spring and summer, light and warmth. Moreover, as I observe in the following pages, tempests are often associated with trees, especially the cedar, oak, and pine, and rough beasts; also we find gentle beasts —especially birds—suggesting the opposite, though birds may in turn be evil, as in *Macbeth*. So that our tempest-symbolism cannot be finally abstracted from all Shakespeare's imagery, suggestion, symbolism, stage-directions, or dramatic events, reflecting impressions of man's physique, flowers and beasts, earth, water, air and fire; sun, moon, and stars; light and dark. If, then, our tempest-music opposition is to be our starting-point in Shakespearian study, we are clearly involved at once in a mass of intricacies which will need years of careful analysis and sensitive appreciation before they yield their full significance. It may, perhaps, seem that I should have expanded the scope of this essay to include such adjacent effects; and yet that would have prevented the tempests themselves from receiving proper emphasis. On the other hand, the thesis of my essay would certainly have appeared more striking had I restricted my notice to the purest forms of this symbol, neglecting altogether such plays as *As You Like It* and *Timon*, where nature's roughness is presented without any actual tempests, apart from minor imagery. But that, again, would result in too rigid a schematic and would not show the true place of tempests in Shakespeare's poetry. I have tried to steer a middle course. The rest must eventually follow. And many of our conventional views on Shakespeare will then be quickly reversed. It might therefore appear that this essay rather creates but a new chaos in place of the old. But that is not so. There is nothing to fear from any series of complexities in a study which obeys the laws of its object, recognizing first that object's peculiar unity and individuality. Such a study will be progressively interesting, progressively valuable. It may be difficult, but it will never be chaotic. And that is why I urge the importance of understanding the true unity of Shakespeare. In this way only will the tempests of professional discord be resolved in the music of understanding.

In the following pages I present, in Chapter II, a collection of river, sea, and tempest references, relating them to the concept 'tragedy'; next referring them to music, jewels, and love-themes. Here I draw primarily on the early Tragedies, Historical Plays, and Poems, occasionally, however, quoting from the early Romances. In Chapter III I trace the tempest-music opposition through those Romances, and in Chapters IV and V through the Tragedies and Final Plays respectively. Chapter VI is devoted to some concluding remarks. I have been content with amassing direct evidence, without attempting more than the barest running commentary. At the start I would urge the extreme importance of actually reading the quotations and carefully observing the numerous similarities in phrase, idea, poetic colour, and poetic feeling, which render these tempest passages so remarkably consistent. The words 'fortune', 'split', 'rage', 'chafe', 'tops' (applied to trees, mountains, or waves) are recurrent. Especially important is the tempest-beast association, the beasts being usually fierce: the lion, tiger, wolf, bear, boar. These animals are interesting when associated together, even though the tempest idea is absent: though it is then, however, often implicit. But, though I observe a few such instances, that is really outside my present inquiry. A monograph on the Shakespearian Menagerie would, however, be of the greatest value to scholarship.

Finally, I would again emphasize that Shakespeare's imaginative effects are not peculiar to his work. They occur throughout Elizabethan literature, though elsewhere not so consistently and artistically employed. By analysis of the Shakespearian imagination we thus put ourselves in direct contact with Shakespeare's contemporaries and the Elizabethan mind in general. An intensive study of the literature of a period is often likely to cast light on the age of its composition; though facts about that age as recorded in modern histories are seldom of help to evaluate the meanings of its literature. And not only will we thus widen our knowledge of Elizabethan England. Shakespeare's effects are universal. We shall therefore be widening our knowledge of the human mind in whatever time or place. By this study we open out new and splendid tracts in the human consciousness for inspection, enjoyment, and use.

THE HISTORIES, EARLY TRAGEDIES, AND POEMS

I

THE sea in Shakespeare is often strongly impregnated with tragic significance. England derives strength from her sea-setting; she is a 'precious stone set in the silver sea', and that sea is a 'moat' to protect her (*Richard II*, II. i. 46). But there is suggestion that the sea is savagely dangerous to foes: which is explicit in a similar passage, to be observed later, in *Cymbeline*. England's strength is imaged as a sea strength. Her 'white-faced' cliffs 'spurn back the ocean's roaring tides' (*King John*, II. i. 23). Her story is a proud conquest of crashing waves, a survival of hostile attacks, a persistence amid peril and adversity. So she is

> England, bound in with the triumphant sea
> Whose rocky shore beats back the envious siege
> Of watery Neptune.   (*Richard II*, II. i. 61)

The sea is 'triumphant', 'envious'; relentless and cruel. The contest of waves and rocks is stern and pitiless, a ceaseless war of elements, the ebb and flow of time itself washing on the shore of existence. So the chances and changes of life are as the continual alteration of sea and land:

> O God! that one might read the book of fate,
> And see the revolution of the times
> Make mountains level, and the continent,
> Weary of solid firmness, melt itself
> Into the sea! and, other times, to see
> The beachy girdle of the ocean
> Too wide for Neptune's hips; how chances mock,
> And changes fill the cup of alteration
> With divers liquors! O, if this were seen,
> The happiest youth, viewing his progress through,

What perils past, what crosses to ensue,
Would shut the book, and sit him down to die.
                    (*2 Henry IV*, III. i. 45)

Such is the tragic literature of human life. Sorrow 'ebbs
and flows' like a vast current (*Lucrece*, 1569). Mortality
is subject to the waves of time:

Like as the waves make toward the pebbled shore,
So do our minutes hasten to their end.   (Sonnet LX)

For Time's ravage is like the ever-running interchange of
sea and land:

When I have seen by Time's fell hand defaced
The rich proud cost of outworn buried age;
When sometime lofty towers I see down-razed,
And brass eternal slave to mortal rage;
When I have seen the hungry ocean gain
Advantage on the kingdom of the shore
And the firm soil win of the watery main,
Increasing store with loss and loss with store;
When I have seen such interchange of state,
Or state itself confounded to decay;
Ruin hath taught me thus to ruminate,
That Time will come and take my love away.
     This thought is as a death, which cannot choose
     But weep to have that which it fears to lose.
                              (Sonnet LXIV)

The 'hungry ocean'; a usual thought. So is the word
'rage'. Or again,

Since brass, nor stone, nor earth, nor boundless sea,
But sad mortality o'ersways their power,
How with this rage shall beauty hold a plea,
Whose action is no stronger than a flower?
O how shall summer's honey breath hold out
Against the wreckful siege of battering days,
When rocks impregnable are not so stout,
Nor gates of steel so strong, but time decays?
                              (Sonnet LXV)

'Rage' and 'wreckful' are usual ideas; and flowers and

summer airs are usual as a contrast. Notice 'siege' and 'battering', a metaphor which points to a close sea-war association. So rocks and sea oppose each other, in embittered and age-long strife. Human battling is like wind and sea opposed:

> This battle fares like to the morning's war,
> When dying clouds contend with growing light,
> What time the shepherd, blowing of his nails,
> Can neither call it perfect day nor night.
> Now sways it this way, like a mighty sea
> Forced by the tide to combat with the wind;
> Now sways it that way, like the selfsame sea
> Forced to retire by fury of the wind:
> Sometime the flood prevails, and then the wind:
> Now one the better, then another best;
> Both tugging to be victors, breast to breast,
> Yet neither conqueror nor conquered:
> So is the equal poise of this fell war.
>
> *(3 Henry VI, II. v. 1)*

Sea and wind and land all provide images of tragic significance, suggesting the chances and changes suffered by mortality. Thus weak men are as feathers to the wind:

> Look, as I blow this feather from my face,
> And as the air blows it to me again,
> Obeying with my wind when I do blow,
> And yielding to another when it blows,
> Commanded always by the greater gust;
> Such is the lightness of you common men.
>
> *(3 Henry VI, III. i. 84)*

Such are those whose integrity is no match for the shifting play of fortune. These images may serve as an introduction. Next I shall observe the many variations played on these 'water' and 'wind' ideas. Provisionally, we may equate winds and waves with 'time', 'fickle fortune', and especially tragic 'chance'.

II

Since the sea is so tragically apprehended, its war with land so powerfully visualized, it is clear that any image of water breaking its bounds is an apt symbol for 'disorder'. 'Disorder' and 'tragedy' are in Shakespeare practically synonymous. Disorder in man or state is like a flood over-flowing its limits. Passion may often be considered to swell higher than the bounds imposed by reason. Tears are imaged as 'a flood' (*1 Henry VI*, iii. iii. 56); as 'currents' to 'drown the world' (*Richard III*, ii. ii. 70); or 'floods' to drown speech (*Titus Andronicus*, v. iii. 90); 'envious floods' that o'errun the face (*Taming of the Shrew*, Ind. ii. 67). Again, tears are associated with drowning in *All's Well*, iv. iii. 79. We have 'rivers of remorse' (*King John*, iv. iii. 110). Tears may be a 'crystal tide' (*Venus and Adonis*, 957), or 'brinish current' (*A Lover's Complaint*, 284). So Tarquin's passion rises:

> My uncontrolled tide
> Turns not, but swells the higher by this let.
>
> (*Lucrece*, 645)

The sighs of Lucrece's husband in his 'rage' are like a 'violent roaring tide' rushing through an 'arch' (*Lucrece*, 1667–73); Adonis's anger is like a river that overflows its banks (*Venus and Adonis*, 72); sorrow concealed is as a 'river stay'd' which thus 'swelleth with more rage' (*Venus and Adonis*, 331–2); and 'sighs' are said to 'stream' at *All's Well*, ii. iii. 82. Excessive tears are like a 'proud river peering o'er his bounds' (*King John*, iii. i. 23). Tears are rivers again at *Richard III*, i. iii. 176; and like mountain streams at *Lucrece*, 1077–8. Sweat is 'like bubbles on a late-disturbed stream' (*1 Henry IV*, ii. iii. 62). Words are too weak to express sorrow. Therefore:

> Deep sounds make lesser noise than shallow fords,
> And sorrow ebbs, being blown with wind of words.
>
> (*Lucrece*, 1329)

There is Venus's 'swelling passion' (*Venus and Adonis*, 218).

4

'Swell' is continually used for rising emotion, often with water-imagery; often, too, 'swell' occurs in sea-storm descriptions only indirectly describing emotion. Richard uses the word:

> And these external manners of laments
> Are merely shadows to the unseen grief
> That swells with silence in the tortur'd soul.
>
> (*Richard II*, iv. i. 296)

A vast sea of grief. Again, in a fine description of calamity:

> Glad am I that your highness is so arm'd
> To bear the tidings of calamity.
> Like an unseasonable stormy day,
> Which makes the silver rivers drown their shores,
> As if the world were all dissolved to tears,
> So high above his limits swells the rage
> Of Bolingbroke, covering your fearful land
> With hard bright steel and hearts harder than steel.
>
> (*Richard II*, iii. ii. 104)

We may recall another line from this play: 'The swelling difference of your settled hate' (i. i. 201); so Bolingbroke's rage here 'swells'. This is a usual tempest-word. And here our image suggests insurrection. Our other images indicated emotional disorder. They may equally be used for political disorder, just as music may suggest either the joys of love for the individual—the 'state of man'—or the concord of states political. The flood-disorder association is important:

> Let heaven kiss earth! Now let not Nature's hand
> Keep the wild flood confined! Let order die!
> And let this world no longer be a stage
> To feed contention in a lingering act;
> But let one spirit of the first-born Cain
> Reign in all bosoms, that, each heart being set
> On bloody courses, the rude scene may end,
> And darkness be the burier of the dead!
>
> (*2 Henry IV*, i. i. 153)

In truth a 'stormy passion' (i. i. 165). Such passages show

how darkly tragic all ruthless floods and sea-tempests are
in Shakespeare. 'Sedition' is such a 'flood' (*3 Henry VI*,
II. ii. 141, 157–8). So is rebellion:

> We will untread the steps of damned flight,
> And like a bated and retired flood,
> Leaving our rankness and irregular course,
> Stoop low within those bounds we have o'erlooked
> And calmly run on in obedience,
> Even to our ocean, to our great King John.
>   (*King John*, v. iv. 52)

Another similar passage occurs in the same play:

> France, hast thou yet more blood to cast away?
> Say, shall the current of our right run on?
> Whose passage, vex'd with thy impediment,
> Shall leave his native channel and o'erswell
> With course disturb'd even thy confining shores,
> Unless thou let his silver water keep
> A peaceful progress to the ocean.
>   (*King John*, II. i. 334)

Floods are so impregnated with war-feeling that we find
them blending their water with blood. So Simois's waters
are incarnadined till they 'imitate the battle' (*Lucrece*,
1438) and Lucrece in her blood

> . . . like a late-sack'd island, vastly stood
> Bare and unpeopled in this fearful flood.
>   (*Lucrece*, 1740)

So, too, nobles lie 'drown'd' in 'mercenary blood' (*Henry V*,
IV. vii. 79); and we find 'a sea of blood' in *1 Henry VI*,
IV. vii. 14. But more often we have the simple thought of
unruly waters. 'A tide of woes' comes 'rushing' on England in *Richard II*, II. ii. 98. The Scot 'came pouring like
a tide' into England (*Henry V*, I. ii. 149); and Henry V's
warlike approaches are 'fierce as waters' (*Henry V*, II. iv. 9).
But the French king can claim the same image:

> Rush on his host, as doth the melted snow
> Upon the valleys, whose lowly vassal seat
> The Alps doth spit and void his rheum upon.
>   (III. v. 50)

So the ocean, elsewhere, 'spits in the face of heaven'—I quote the passage later. Such virulent human imagery is usual.

Unruly floods in river or sea are caused by storms and tempests. We have, in fact, been analysing one element in Shakespeare's tempest-imagery. Personal emotion is as often given direct storm or tempest expression as it is compared to floods. 'Cares and joys' are thus like the seasons (2 Henry VI, ii. iv. 1–4). The association of tears with rain and sighs with wind is especially frequent. Tears are compared with dew and rain at 2 Henry VI, iii. ii. 340, 341. Again,

> Why only, Suffolk, mourn I not for thee,
> And with the southern clouds contend in tears,
> Theirs for the earth's increase, mine for my sorrows?
> (2 Henry VI, iii. ii. 383)

There are Mortimer's lovely lines:

> . . . that pretty Welsh
> Which thou pour'st down from these swelling heavens
> I am too perfect in.   (1 Henry IV, iii. i. 201)

'Swelling' again. We hear of the 'weeping clouds' at 2 Henry IV, i. iii. 61; and the standers-by 'had wet their cheeks', we hear, 'like trees bedash'd with rain' at Richard III, i. ii. 163. This is typical:

> One hour's storm will drown the fragrant meads;
> What will whole months of tears thy father's eyes?
> (Titus Andronicus, ii. iv. 54)

Tears are rained or rain at Love's Labour's Lost, v. ii. 819, and Venus and Adonis, 83; and they are 'silver rain' at Venus and Adonis, 959, and 'showers of silver brine' at Lucrece, 796. Eyes are as 'two suns cloud eclipsed' by grief and 'overwash'd with woe' (Lucrece, 1224–5). Tears are rain again at Lucrece, 1271, and storms at line 1589. Sighs are 'windy' at Venus and Adonis, 51. Again,

> Aumerle, thou weep'st, my tender-hearted cousin!
> We'll make foul weather with despised tears;
> Our sighs and they shall lodge the summer corn . . .
> (Richard II, iii. iii. 160)

Therefore 'sorrow' is naturally like 'clouds' (*Richard III*,
II. ii. 112). A fine passage occurs in *King John*:

Lewis. A noble temper dost thou show in this;
 And great affections wrestling in thy bosom
 Do make an earthquake of nobility.
 O, what a noble combat hast thou fought
 Between compulsion and a brave respect!
 Let me wipe off this honourable dew,
 That silverly doth progress on thy cheeks:
 My heart hath melted at a lady's tears,
 Being an ordinary inundation;
 But this effusion of such manly drops,
 This shower, blown up by tempest of the soul,
 Startles mine eyes, and makes me more amazed
 Than had I seen the vaulty top of heaven
 Figured quite o'er with fiery meteors.
 Lift up thy brow, renowned Salisbury,
 And with a great heart heave away this storm:
 Commend these waters to those baby eyes
 That never saw the giant world enraged;
 Nor met with fortune other than at feasts,
 Full of warm blood, of mirth, of gossiping. (v. ii. 40)

A passage full of characteristic elements. Notice the sense
of discord and conflict in the soul compared with an
earthquake (as in the symbolism of *Macbeth*); the heart
'melting', as often elsewhere; the 'tempest of the soul';
the thought of meteors associated with tempests, both
being natural disorder-symbols in Shakespeare; the idea
of the world 'enraged', the very word usually given to the
sea, which is not strange since here the world stands for
fortune and the troubles of mortal existence in general,
realities which are more often thought of as a stormy sea;
the word 'fortune' itself; and the contrast of feasts with
tragic events. Often rain and wind imagery are twined
into a complex pattern of emotion. York reviles Margaret,
saying she has 'a tiger's heart wrapped in a woman's hide'
(*3 Henry VI*, I. iv. 137)—the tiger and other beasts are
important as symbols of ferocity often blending with
'tempests'—and he continues:

Women are soft, mild, pitiful, and flexible;
Thou stern, obdurate, flinty, rough, remorseless.
Bid'st thou me rage? Why, now thou hast thy wish:
Would'st have me weep? Why, now thou hast thy will:
For raging wind blows up incessant showers,
And when the rage allays, the rain begins.
These tears are my sweet Rutland's obsequies:
And every drop cries vengeance for his death,
'Gainst thee, fell Clifford, and thee, false Frenchwoman.

                                    (*3 Henry VI*, I. iv. 141)

Notice the characteristic word 'flinty', and the reiterated word 'rage'. So Queen Margaret may be said to cause 'tempests'. She is 'more inexorable' than 'tigers of Hyrcania' (I. iv. 155): which is important, since Hyrcania is, in *The Merchant of Venice*, associated with rough sea-imagery; and the 'Hyrcan tiger' in *Macbeth* is vividly mentioned in a context suggesting ruthless savagery and ferocity. The tempest-beast association is always to be noted. Here is another grief-tempest passage:

Ah, no, no, no, it is mine only son!
Ah, boy, if any life be left in thee,
Throw up thine eye! see, see what showers arise,
Blown with the windy tempest of my heart!
O, pity, God, this miserable age!
What stratagems, how fell, how butcherly,
Erroneous, mutinous, and unnatural,
This deadly quarrel daily doth beget!

                                    (*3 Henry VI*, II. v. 83)

Such are the tempests of civil war. 'Stratagems' may be related to the stratagems which we may expect from a man who has no music in him, in *The Merchant of Venice*: whereby we may observe how music and tempests are true opposites in Shakespeare. Again, with more 'sighs', we have another tempest passage describing grief:

Q. *Margaret.* This is it that makes me bridle passion
And bear with mildness my misfortune's cross;
Ay, ay, for this I draw in many a tear
And stop the rising of blood-sucking sighs,

Lest with my sighs or tears I blast or drown
King Edward's fruit, true heir to the English crown.
(3 Henry VI, iv. iv. 19)

More sighs and storms occur in *Venus and Adonis*:

O, how her eyes and tears did lend and borrow!
Her eyes seen in the tears, tears in her eye;
Both crystals, where they view'd each other's sorrow,
Sorrow that friendly sighs sought still to dry;
　　But like a stormy day, now wind, now rain,
　　Sighs dry her cheeks, tears make them wet again.

Variable passions throng her constant woe,
As striving who should best become her grief;
All entertain'd, each passion labours so,
That every present sorrow seemeth chief,
　　But none is best: then join they all together,
　　Like many clouds consulting for foul weather.
(961)

'Variable passions' suggest Cleopatra. Passionate sorrow
is frequently thus given weather-imagery. Tense passion
is as a 'windy tempest', ready to 'blow up rain', which only
holds back 'sorrow's tide', to make it more strong, till 'at
last it rains and busy winds give o'er' (*Lucrece*, 1786–90).
Another fine passage occurs in *Lucrece*, full of 'sighs' and
'groans', and blending with sea-imagery:

My husband is thy friend; for his sake spare me:
Thyself art mighty; for thine own sake leave me:
Myself a weakling; do not then ensnare me:
Thou look'st not like deceit; do not deceive me.
My sighs, like whirlwinds, labour hence to heave thee:
　　If ever man were moved with woman's moans,
　　Be moved with my tears, my sighs, my groans.

All which together, like a troubled ocean,
Beat at thy rocky and wreck-threatening heart,
To soften it with their continual motion;
For stones dissolved to water do convert.
O, if no harder than a stone thou art,
　　Melt at my tears, and be compassionate!
　　Soft pity enters at an iron gate.
(582)

A fine example of rocks, stone, and iron suggesting hard cruelty. Here the emotion of Lucrece is the sea, Tarquin the rocks. But it is our usual image of tragic conflict. Notice the 'wreck': we shall have more to say of wrecks later. Lucrece's passage has a reflection in *A Lover's Complaint*:

> But with the inundation of the eyes
> What rocky heart to water will not wear?   (290)

Perhaps the finest passage of all in the tempest-grief tradition is one from *Titus Andronicus* where the protagonist and Lavinia are grandly imaged in terms of the mighty sea and sky themselves as they face each other in immeasurable, tempestuous grief:

> If there were reason for these miseries,
> Then into limits could I bind my woes:
> When heaven doth weep, doth not the earth o'erflow?
> If the winds rage, doth not the sea wax mad,
> Threatening the welkin with his big-swoln face?
> And wilt thou have a reason for this coil?
> I am the sea; hark, how her sighs do blow!
> She is the weeping welkin, I the earth:
> Then must my sea be moved with her sighs;
> Then must my earth with her continual tears
> Become a deluge, overflow'd and drown'd;
> For why my bowels cannot hide her woes,
> But like a drunkard must I vomit them.
> Then give me leave, for losers will have leave
> To ease their stomachs with their bitter tongues.
>
> (III. i. 220)

Notice the typical word 'rage'; and the vivid personal imagery—characteristic of tempest-passages—of 'big-swoln face'. But not only sorrow—any violent passion can be a storm or tempest, or may be compared with the sea. Anger is often 'thunder'. Constance in anger wishes herself a Jove:

K. Philip. O fair affliction, peace!
Constance. No, no, I will not, having breath to cry:
   O, that my tongue were in the thunder's mouth!

Then with a passion would I shake the world;
And rouse from sleep that fell anatomy
Which cannot hear a lady's feeble voice,
Which scorns a modern invocation.
                              (*King John*, iii. iv. 36)

Shakespeare's thunder-imagery is always interesting: its most powerful later personifications being Coriolanus in *Coriolanus* and Jupiter in *Cymbeline*. Again:

And that engenders thunder in his breast
And makes him roar these accusations forth.
                              (*1 Henry VI*, iii. i. 39)

And:

If Talbot do but thunder, rain will follow.
                              (*1 Henry VI*, iii. ii. 59)

Human moods may be given weather-imagery:

I am not a day of season,
For thou may'st see a sunshine and a hail
In me at once: but to the brightest beams
Distracted clouds give way; so stand thou forth;
The time is fair again.   (*All's Well*, v. iii. 32)

With which we might compare a passage from *A Lover's Complaint*:

His qualities were beauteous as his form,
For maiden-tongued he was, and thereof free;
Yet, if men moved him, was he such a storm
As oft 'twixt May and April is to see,
When winds breathe sweet, unruly though they be. (99)

The word 'May' recalls Kent's description of Cordelia's tears towards the end of *Lear*; that is, if we read 'May' for 'way':

                              You have seen
Sunshine and rain at once: her smiles and tears
Were like a better way; those happy smilets,
That play'd on her ripe lip, seem'd not to know
What guests were in her eyes; which parted thence,
As pearls from diamonds dropp'd. In brief,
Sorrow would be a rarity most beloved,
If all could so become it.   (*Lear*, iv. iii. 19)

So the Globe edition. 'May' would suit the style of such passages fairly well. But to return. We hear of Adonis

> ... with a heavy, dark, disliking eye,
> His louring brows o'erwhelming his fair sight,
> Like misty vapours when they blot the sky ...
> (*Venus and Adonis*, 182)

Or again, human rage may be compared to the sea:

> High-stomach'd are they both, and full of ire,
> In rage deaf as the sea, hasty as fire.
> (*Richard II*, i. i. 18)

'Rage' again, a word continually present in such tempest passages. 'Deaf' recalls Pericles' speech on board ship, when the seaman's whistle is 'as a whisper in the ears of death, unheard': I quote the passage later. 'Fire' sometimes occurs as here in this association; but it is not so frequent as the sea. Wrath is 'cloudy' (*Richard III*, i. iii. 268). Or human rage may be compared to both sea monster and foul weather:

> We may as bootless spend our vain command
> Upon the enraged soldiers in their spoil
> As send precepts to the leviathan
> To come ashore. Therefore, you men of Harfleur,
> Take pity of your town and of your people,
> Whiles yet my soldiers are in my command;
> Whiles yet the cool and temperate wind of grace
> O'erblows the filthy and contagious clouds
> Of heady murder, spoil, and villany.
> (*Henry V*, iii. iii. 24)

The 'leviathan' blends Shakespeare's beast and tempest imagery. Strangely, at first sight, he recurs as a natural image for Oberon (*A Midsummer Night's Dream*, ii. i. 174). But, as I note later, there is a gnomish fearsomeness within the atmosphere of that play, however delicate and sweet be the final effect.

III

Now storms and tempests are regularly symbols of disorder and tragedy—terms practically synonymous in Shakespeare—in a wide sense:

> The sun sets weeping in the lowly west,
> Witnessing storms to come, woe and unrest.
>   (*Richard II*, II. iv. 21)

This is spoken in a scene powerful with disorder symbols of the usual Shakespearian kind: meteors, a blood-coloured moon, dismal prophecies of woe. Storms are things of disorder and disunion, often leaguing with the sea to 'disperse' societies or disorganize states. Buckingham's army 'by sudden floods' is 'dispersed and scatter'd' (*Richard III*, IV. iv. 512). Again, in *King John* King Philip says:

> So by a roaring tempest on the flood,
> A whole armado of convicted sail
> Is scatter'd and disjoin'd from fellowship.
>   (*King John*, III. iv. 1)

This 'dispersing' nature of tempests is important. The Dauphin's supplies are 'wreck'd on Goodwin Sands' (*King John*, v. iii. 11), and the Bastard's forces 'taken by the tide' and 'devour'd' in the Lincoln Washes (*King John*, v. vi. 40–1). Such is the part played by the sea and by tempests in Shakespeare: forces of dispersion, destruction, and death. Hence, the 'ill-dispersing wind of misery' at *Richard III*, IV. i. 53. This idea is finely expressed in *Titus Andronicus*:

> You sad-faced men, people and sons of Rome,
> By uproar sever'd, like a flight of fowl,
> Scatter'd by winds and high tempestuous gusts,
> O let me teach you how to knit again
> The scatter'd corn into one mutual sheaf,
> These broken limbs again into one body.   (v. iii. 67)

Notice how the 'harvest' reference suggests the opposite of disunion and tempestuous weather. Thunder and lightning accompany the evil spirits raised by black magic in

2 *Henry VI*. 'It thunders and lightens terribly; then the spirit riseth' (I. iv. 25). We remember *Macbeth*. Tempests and thunder are forces of tragedy, of evil and disorder. Civil strife is a 'tempest'; the thought is recurrent in *Richard II*. So we hear of 'this louring tempest of your home-bred hate' (I. iii. 187); the tragic recklessness of the King is a 'storm' (II. i. 35); Bolingbroke says he would not 'bedrench' England with the 'crimson tempest' of war (III. iii. 46); heaven will 'rain hot vengeance on offenders' heads' (I. ii. 8), and God muster in the 'clouds' his pestilence on Richard's behalf, pestilence which will strike 'children yet unborn' in vengeance for the disorderly act whereby Richard is dethroned (III. iii. 85–90). The tears of the sorrowing are here 'foul weather' (III. iii. 161), and treachery like 'clouds' (I. i. 42). King Richard, as his authority fails, is as a dimmed sun:

> See, see King Richard doth himself appear,
> As doth the blushing, discontented sun
> From out the fiery portal of the east
> When he perceives the envious clouds are bent
> To dim his glory . . .   (III. iii. 62)

This play is throughout tempestuous. Its heart is exposed and finely expressed in Bolingbroke's words:

> Methinks King Richard and myself should meet
> With no less terror than the elements
> Of fire and water, when their thundering shock
> At meeting tears the cloudy cheeks of heaven:
> Be he the fire, I'll be the yielding water:
> The rage be his, whilst on the earth I rain
> My waters: on the earth, and not on him.   (III. iii. 54)

Again, our vivid personal imagery: 'cheeks of heaven'. So Bolingbroke grows by the 'sprinkling' rain of Richard's blood (V. vi. 46). At the birth of Richard III 'dogs howled and hideous tempest shook down trees' (*3 Henry VI*, V. vi. 46). All personal or civil vice is evil weather, Tarquin's lust a 'black-faced cloud' (*Lucrece*, 547), 'craft and perjury', 'black-faced storms' (*Lucrece*, 1517–18). So, too, civil wars are 'clouds' at *Richard III*, i. i. 3. Revolution is 'a tempest of commotion', like the 'south' with its 'black vapour' (*2 Henry IV*, ii. iv. 397). Which recalls distressed Silvius in *As You Like It*, 'like foggy south puffing with wind and rain' (iii. v. 50). So Pandulf, in *King John*, caused a 'tempest':

> It was my breath that blew this tempest up,
> Upon your stubborn usage of the Pope,
> But since you are a gentle convertite,
> My tongue shall hush again this storm of war,
> And make fair weather in your blustering land.
>
> (v. i. 17)

A 'home-bred marriage' will not strengthen the common-wealth against 'foreign storms' (*3 Henry VI*, iv. i. 38). Civil wars are, indeed, tempestuous:

> Whiles I in Ireland nourish a mighty band,
> I will stir up in England some black storm
> Shall blow ten thousand souls to heaven or hell;
> And this fell tempest shall not cease to rage
> Until the golden circuit on my head,
> Like to the glorious sun's transparent beams,
> Do calm the fury of this mad-bred plan.
>
> (*2 Henry VI*. iii. i. 348)

Again, in *2 Henry VI*, Clifford and Warwick have an interesting dialogue:

> *King.* Call Buckingham, and bid him arm himself.
> *York.* Call Buckingham, and all the friends thou hast,
>   I am resolved for death or dignity.
> *Clifford.* The first I warrant thee, if dreams prove true.
> *Warwick.* You were best to go to bed and dream again,
>   To keep thee from the tempest of the field.
> *Clifford.* I am resolved to bear a greater storm
>   Than any thou canst conjure up to-day;
>   And that I'll write upon thy burgonet,
>   Might I but know thee by thy household badge.
> *Warwick.* Now, by my father's badge, old Nevil's crest,
>   The rampant bear chain'd to the ragged staff,
>   This day I'll wear aloft my burgonet,

> As on a mountain top the cedar shows
> That keeps his leaves in spite of any storm,
> Even to affright thee with the view thereof.
> *Clifford.* And from thy burgonet I'll rend thy bear,
> And tread it under foot with all contempt,
> Despite the bear-ward that protects the bear. (v. i. 192)

A most valuable passage. Observe the tempest-battle association. Next, we have a 'bear', such beasts being found often in tempest passages, owing to their suggestion of ferocity. Here the bear is, as it were, pitted against the tempest, as in *Lear* later. Again the cedar (or pine) on the mountain-top is a recurrent image in tempest poetry. Tempests battle often with such trees. 'Top' is a usual word, applied to waves, mountains, and trees, in these passages. This is a remarkable instance of typical images close-knit. So civil unrest is a tempest. Citizens moralize on the civil dangers threatening in *Richard III*:

> *Third Citizen.* When clouds appear, wise men put on their
>   cloaks;
>   When great leaves fall, the winter is at hand,
>   When the sun sets, who doth not look for night?
>   Untimely storms make men expect a dearth.
>   All may be well; but, if God sort it so,
>   'Tis more than we deserve, or I expect.
> *Second Citizen.* Truly, the souls of men are full of dread:
>   Ye cannot reason almost with a man
>   That looks not heavily and full of fear.
> *Third Citizen.* Before the times of change, still is it so:
>   By a divine instinct men's minds mistrust
>   Ensuing dangers: as, by proof, we see
>   The waters swell before a boisterous storm.
>   But leave it all to God.   (ii. iii. 32)

Thus are contrasted the tragic throes of change with the changeless providence of God.

Any tragic or unfortunate event is, to its subject, as a tempest or storm. These storms are, indeed, explicitly associated with the literary concept 'tragedy'. We may remember the 'book of Fate' given sea-imagery in a

passage I have already quoted.´ A murderer is a 'sea'
imaged as 'swallowing up' the life of his victim, and the
tale of his deed a 'tragic history' (*3 Henry VI*, v. vi. 24–8).
Gloucester suggests his own death to be merely the 'prologue to the play' of his enemies' 'plotted tragedy', and
continues:

> Beaufort's red sparkling eyes blab his heart's malice;
> And Suffolk's cloudy brow his stormy hate.
> > (*2 Henry VI*, iii. i. 147–55)

Ill news is thus received:

> Yea, this man's brow, like to a title leaf,
> Foretells the nature of a tragic volume:
> So looks the strand whereon the imperious flood
> Hath left a witness'd usurpation.   (*2 Henry IV*, i. i. 59)

A tempest is implied here, the strand imaged as strewn
with sea-weed, drift-wood, and shells, all dirtied and
disarranged by the storm. Any distressing story is a
'storm':

> Men judge by the complexion of the sky
> > The state and inclination of the day:
> So may you by my dull and heavy eye,
> > My tongue hath but a heavier tale to say.
> > > (*Richard II*, iii. ii. 194)

This messenger-thought recurs again in *King John*:

> A fearful eye thou hast: where is that blood
> That I have seen inhabit in those cheeks?
> So foul a sky clears not without a storm:
> Pour down thy weather: How goes all in France?

The news is heard. Then:

> Bear with me, cousin; for I was amazed
> Under the tide: but now I breathe again
> Aloft the flood.   (iv. ii. 106, 137)

Thus we may see that any kind of ill fortune is, to its subject, a tempest. Henry IV, approaching death, says that
this 'cloud of dignity', being held up 'by so weak a wind'

of life, will 'quickly drop'; so his 'day is dim' (*2 Henry IV*,
IV. v. 99). Ill fortune in battle is a 'tempest':

> *King.* How bloodily the sun begins to peer
>   Above yon busky hill! the day looks pale
>   At his distemperature.
> *Prince.*   The southern wind
>   Doth play the trumpet to his purposes,
>   And by his hollow whistling in the leaves
>   Foretells a tempest and a blustering day.
> *King.* Then with the losers let it sympathise,
>   For nothing can seem foul to those that win.
> <div align="right">(<i>1 Henry IV</i>, v. i. 1)</div>

The problem is acute and interesting. If disorder is a
'tempest', objectively, the tempest relates ultimately to
neither party, but only to their antagonistic relation; and
yet, without a subject to experience the sense of disorder,
there is no proper tempest or, indeed, any real disorder.
There will only be a sense of disorder and tragedy to the
loser. This difficulty is at the root of the complex pattern
of *Julius Caesar*. So Henry V is to his enemies as a
'tempest':

> Therefore in fierce tempest is he coming,
> In thunder, and in earthquake, like a Jove . . .
> <div align="right">(<i>Henry V</i>, II. iv. 99)</div>

A fine Jove-thunder association. 'O that I were a god
to shoot forth thunder', cries Suffolk at *2 Henry VI*, IV. i.
104. Another passage wherein ill fortune is given storm-
imagery occurs in *3 Henry VI*:

> *K. Edward.* Thus far our fortune keeps an upward course,
>   And we are graced with wreaths of victory.
>   But, in the midst of this bright-shining day,
>   I spy a black, suspicious, threatening cloud,
>   That will encounter with our glorious sun,
>   Ere he attain his easeful western bed:
>   I mean, my lords, those powers that the queen
>   Hath raised in Gallia have arrived our coast,
>   And, as we hear, march on to fight with us.

Clarence. A little gale will soon disperse that cloud,
　　And blow it to the source from whence it came:
　　The very beams will dry those vapours up,
　　For every cloud engenders not a storm.　　　(v. iii. 10)

A fine speech of Aaron in *Titus Andronicus*, ii. i. 1–25, is
full of important imagery recalling Sonnet xxxiii. Here
tempests suggest ill fortune, but, as in Sonnet xxxiii, the
sun in sovereign brilliance suggests happiness:

　　Now climbeth Tamora Olympus' top,
　　Safe out of Fortune's shot; and sits aloft,
　　Secure of thunder's crack, or lightning flash;
　　Advanced above pale envy's threatening reach.
　　As when the golden sun salutes the morn,
　　And having gilt the ocean with his beams,
　　Gallops the zodiac in his glistering coach,
　　And overlooks the highest-peering hills;
　　So Tamora.

Then, hearing sounds of a quarrel, Aaron continues:

　　Holloa! What a storm is this?

Which recalls a speech of Juliet's:

　　What storm is this that blows so contrary?

she cries (*Romeo and Juliet*, iii. ii. 64). Often the dangers
or sorrows encompassing the individual are imaged as
winds or waves. Hastings in *2 Henry IV* suggests that the
rebels shall make peace with the King and stand as firm
'as rocky mountains': a usual tempest thought. Mowbray
disagrees:

　　We shall be winnow'd with so rough a wind
　　That even our corn shall seem as light as chaff
　　And good from bad find no partition.

Then the Archbishop of York insists that foes are too
close 'enrooted' with friends and may not easily be 'un-
fixed': that the King is in the position of a man who is
'enraged' with his wife but dare not strike her when she
holds out 'his infant' in her arms (*2 Henry IV*, iv. i. 188–
214). All these thoughts of wind, firm mountains, rooted

5

trees, and—if we remember Katharina in *The Taming of the Shrew*—angry women, are in the 'tempest' tradition.

Winds and waves are in Shakespeare usually things cruel and relentless. We hear of a corpse which 'against the senseless winds shall grin in vain' (*2 Henry VI*, IV. i. 77); the 'perilous' ocean (*Henry V*, Pro. I, 22); of 'a galled rock swilled with the wild and wasteful ocean' (*Henry V*, III. i. 11–14). All are things, like Queen Elizabeth's emotional conflict, of 'tragic violence' (*Richard III*, II. ii. 34–9), and so tragic events are associated with them. A fall from power is like a 'day o'ercast' (*Richard III*, III. ii. 88), the beard of an old man 'like to the summer's corn by tempest lodged' (*2 Henry VI*, III. ii. 176), the face of age as a 'grained' tree hid 'in winter's drizzled snow' (*Comedy of Errors*, v. i. 311). This last is an important image: the 'tree' and 'winter'[1] ideas are closely related to 'tempests'. Prince Henry, when incensed, is said to be 'humorous as winter' (*2 Henry IV*, IV. iv. 34), and Westmoreland is compared to 'a summer bird' singing after 'winter' (*2 Henry IV*, IV. iv. 91). The 'stream of time and rough torrent of occasion' forces men from quiet (*2 Henry IV*, IV. i. 70–2). 'No common wind, no customed event' (*King John*, III. iv. 155) is a natural Shakespearian association. Misfortunes are 'blasts' (*Richard III*, I. iii. 259). All the pains and woes that flesh is heir to may be equated with storms, tempests, and sea-grief, though rain by

---

[1] Wintry effects in Shakespeare naturally blend with tempests. Yet, in so far as they may be picturesque and of pleasant suggestion, they are charged with optimistic force. Hence snow is usually a happy image. See *Lucrece*, 1009–12; *Othello*, v. ii. 4; *Coriolanus*, v. iii. 65–6; *Macbeth*, IV. iii. 53; *The Winter's Tale*, IV. iv. 372–5; *Cymbeline*, II. v. 13; *A Midsummer Night's Dream*, III. ii. 141–3. In such passages snow, ladies' hands or skin, and moral purity are associated. Hence snow is, on the whole, an optimistic impression, and occurs in *Antony and Cleopatra* (I. iv. 65). It may, of course, suggest too much of a good thing as when it is applied to Angelo's purity (*Measure for Measure*, I. iv. 57–8).

Hence we may observe the simplicity of Shakespeare's effects. 'Drizzled snow', or a 'thaw' (in *Much Ado*) is unpleasant; so, usually, are frosts, cold winds, &c. But snow itself, in all its white purity, is a delight. It is the same with us all. Any one can understand Shakespeare's symbolism.

itself may have a gentler association, mercy being like the
'gentle rain from heaven' (*Merchant of Venice*, IV. i. 185).
The Bastard speaks of the 'thorns and dangers of this
world' and 'vast confusion' to come:

> Now happy he whose cloak and cincture can
> Hold out this tempest.   (*King John*, IV. iii. 140–59)

Lucrece is like a swimmer drowning in a 'sea of care' and
maddened by the bird's morning 'melody' which interrupts her passion with music (*Lucrece*, 1096–1108).
Throughout Shakespeare music and tempests are contrasted. A perilous adventure is like walking on a spear
over a 'roaring current' (*1 Henry IV*, I. iii. 190–3), and
Hotspur would rescue 'drowned Honour' from the bottom
of the deep (*1 Henry IV*, I. iii. 205): an extreme boast, if
we remember the tragic significance of the sea. Misery is
often as a sea surrounding the sufferer, as when King
Henry's heart is 'drown'd with grief' and his 'body round
engirt with misery' (*2 Henry VI*, III. i. 198–200). Again,

> The sea enraged is not half so deaf,
> Lions more confident, mountains and rocks
> More free from motion, no, not Death himself
> In mortal fury half so peremptory . . .
>   (*King John*, II. i. 451)

Notice the word 'enraged'. 'Rage' is a usual tempest
word, so is 'fury'. As often elsewhere, the sea is here
associated with death. Notice, too, the 'lions' and the
'mountains': beasts, mountains, and sea tempests being
usual associations. But civilization is the opposite of tempestuous, unruly passions, and cruel beasts. Hence King
Henry fears his kingdom will 'reel back into the beast', to
use Tennyson's phrase, under the careless rule of his son:

> O thou wilt be a wilderness again,
> Peopled with wolves, thy old inhabitants!
>   (*2 Henry IV*, IV. v. 137)

Beasts are especially frequent. Young Talbot is said to
have commenced 'deeds of rage' and is compared to 'a

hungry lion'; he showed 'dizzy-eyed fury and great rage
of heart' (*1 Henry VI*, iv. vii. 7–14). Henry V tells his
soldiers to 'imitate the action of the tiger', and put on
'hard-favour'd rage' (*Henry V*, iii. i. 6–8). So, too, Romeo
cries:

> The time and my intents are savage wild
> More fierce and more inexorable far
> Than empty tigers or the roaring sea.
>
> (*Romeo and Juliet*, v. iii. 37)

So human anger and its grim effects may be compared to
beasts and tempests: and tempests, especially sea tempests, are ever the symbols and accompaniments of human
passion and tragic events. The sea is usually fierce, and
cruel: when it is not, the contrast is especially important.
The full force of the sea as a tragedy symbol is apparent
in a passage from *Titus Andronicus* which holds as concentrated an agony as any in Shakespeare:

> For now I stand as one upon a rock
> Environ'd with a wilderness of sea,
> Who marks the waxing tide grow wave by wave,
> Expecting ever when some envious surge
> Will in his brinish bowels bury him.   (iii. i. 93)

So, too, Henry's army before Agincourt are 'even as men
wrecked upon a sand, that look to be wash'd off next tide'
(*Henry V*, iv. i. 100).

IV

Since sea storms are so constantly the poetic image
correspondent to human tragedies, the party or individual
which suffers disaster is continually thought of as a boat
or 'bark'. I will next notice such images, first regarding
the themes of party and political, then those of private,
tragedy. 'The commonwealth hath daily run to wreck'
(*2 Henry VI*, i. iii. 127) is typical. Or again, 'the general
wreck and massacre' (*1 Henry VI*, i. i. 135) is a natural
association. So, too, the Duke of Burgundy writes that
he is 'moved with compassion of my country's wreck'

(*1 Henry VI*, iv. i. 56). Fate is to be equated with the
elements, any human enterprise with the ship, as in:

> What fates impose, that men must needs abide;
> It boots not to resist both wind and tide.
> > (*3 Henry VI*, iv. iii. 58)

A rash act of King John's is like a 'shifted wind' to a 'sail'
making his followers' thoughts 'fetch about' (*King John*,
iv. ii. 23–4). His queen led Henry VI:

> As doth a sail, fill'd with a fretting gust,
> Command an argosy to stem the waves.
> > (*3 Henry VI*, ii. vi. 35)

Conspirators 'venture on dangerous seas' (*2 Henry IV*,
i. i. 181); soldiers fly from battle 'like ships before the
wind' (*3 Henry VI*, i. iv. 4), or charge like a swan swimming against the tide 'with bootless labour' (*3 Henry VI*,
i. iv. 19–20). The thought is vivid in *Richard II*:

> *Northumberland.*   . . . Most degenerate king!
> But, lords, we hear this fearful tempest sing,
> Yet seek no shelter to avoid the storm;
> We see the wind sit sore upon our sails,
> And yet we strike not, but securely perish.
> *Ross.* We see the very wreck that we must suffer;
> And unavoided in the danger now,
> For suffering so the causes of our wreck.   (ii. i 262)

Talbot tells his son to fly for safety in order to avenge his
own death:

> O too much folly is it, well I wot,
> To hazard all our lives in one small boat!
> > (*1 Henry VI*, iv. vi. 32)

The image is carried to an extreme by Queen Margaret in
a long speech in *3 Henry VI*:

> *Q. Margaret.* Great lords, wise men ne'er sit and wail their loss,
> But cheerly seek how to redress their harms.
> What though the mast be now blown overboard,
> The cable broke, the holding-anchor lost,
> And half our sailors swallow'd in the flood?
> Yet lives our pilot still. Is't meet that he

Should leave the helm, and like a fearful lad
With tearful eyes add water to the sea,
And give more strength to that which hath too much,
While, in his moan, the ship splits on the rock,
Which industry and courage might have saved?
Ah, what a shame! ah, what a fault were this!
Say Warwick was our anchor; what of that?
And Montague our topmast; what of him?
Our slaughter'd friends the tackles; what of these?
Why, is not Oxford here another anchor?
And Somerset another goodly mast?
The friends of France our shrouds and tacklings?
And, though unskilful, why not Ned and I
For once allow'd the skilful pilot's charge?
We will not from the helm to sit and weep,
But keep our course, though the rough wind say no,
From shelves and rocks that threaten us with wreck.
As good to chide the waves as speak them fair.
And what is Edward but a ruthless sea?
What Clarence but a quicksand of deceit?
And Richard but a ragged fatal rock?
All these the enemies to our poor bark.
Say you can swim; alas, 'tis but a while!
Tread on the sand; why there you quickly sink:
Bestride the rock; the tide will wash you off,
Or else you famish; that's a threefold death.
This speak I, lords, to let you understand,
In case some one of you would fly from us,
That there's no hoped-for mercy with the brothers,
More than with ruthless waves, with sands and rocks.

(v. iv. 1)

This is an interesting speech, full of characteristic phrases and words: weeping 'adding water' to a sea or river—a thought found again in *Twelfth Night, As You Like It* (in Jaques' description of the weeping stag), and *Hamlet*; and the 'pilot', 'bark', 'fatal rock', 'ruthless sea', and 'ruthless waves', the 'rough wind', the 'quicksand', the thought of being marooned on a rock and washed off by the tide—all are typical.

The sea-wreck is a recurrent image in Shakespeare. It

applies also to the individual, as well as the party. Throughout Shakespeare individual and communal disorder or tragedy are interdependent and receive similar poetic colourings. Thus Romeo speaks of his 'betossed soul' (*Romeo and Juliet*, v. iii. 76) and, on the point of death, cries:

> Thou desperate pilot, now at once run on
> The dashing rocks your sea-sick weary bark.
>
> (v. iii. 117)

So, too, earlier, he has presentiment of tragedy and dreams of 'untimely death'; and concludes:

> But He, that hath the steerage of my course,
> Direct my sail!
>
> (I. iv. 112)

Sorrow is often a wreck:

> Eighty odd years of sorrow have I seen,
> And each hour's joy wreck'd with a week of teen.
>
> (*Richard III*, IV. i. 96)

This is typical:

> .. I, in such a desperate bay of death
> Like a poor bark, of sails and tackling reft,
> Rush all to pieces on thy rocky bosom.
>
> (*Richard III*, IV. iv. 232)

Richard III, before he is king, pretends, in mock humility, to refuse greatness as 'being a bark to brook no mighty sea' (III. vii. 162). Lucrece cries:

> O, this dread night, wouldst thou one hour come back,
> I could prevent this storm and shun thy wrack!
>
> (*Lucrece*, 965)

So also Mariana in *All's Well* talks of 'the wreck of maidenhood' (III. v. 24). Constance, cursing the hour of her grief, aptly condemns that day to lasting tragedy:

> But on this day let seamen fear no wreck.
>
> (*King John*, III. i. 92)

The individual may, at any moment, in good or evil

fortune, be compared to a ship. Warwick and King
Edward oppose each other:

> *Warwick.* I had rather chop this hand off at a blow,
>   And with the other fling it at thy face,
>   Than bear so low a sail, to strike to thee.
> *K. Edward.* Sail how thou canst, have wind and tide thy
>   friend . . .   (*3 Henry VI*, v. i. 50)

So also nobles 'strike sail to spirits of vile sort' at *2 Henry
IV*, v. ii. 18. Thus speaks the dying King John:

> The tackle of my heart is crack'd and burn'd,
> And all the shrouds wherewith my life should sail
> Are turned to one thread, one little hair.
>   (*King John*, v. vii. 52)

Mortal favour is untrustworthy, unsafe as the swaying
mast of a ship:

> O, momentary grace of mortal men,
> Which we more hunt for than the grace of God!
> Who builds his hopes in air of your good looks,
> Lives like a drunken sailor on a mast,
> Ready, with every nod, to tumble down
> Into the fatal bowels of the deep.
>   (*Richard III*, iii. iv. 98)

Which reminds us of Wolsey in *Henry VIII*. All mortal
insecurity is a matter of tempests; so the agonized unrest
of kingship is in a noble passage contrasted with the less
tempestuous rocking of the ocean waves. Henry IV
addresses the sleep that he has 'frighted' from his couch:

> Wilt thou, upon the high and giddy mast
> Seal up the ship boy's eyes and rock his brains
> In cradle of the rude imperious surge,
> And in the visitation of the winds,
> Who take the ruffian billows by the top,
> Curling their monstrous heads and hanging them
> With deafening clamour in the slippery clouds,
> That with the hurly, death itself awakes?
> Can'st thou, O partial sleep, give thy repose
> To the wet sea-boy in an hour so rude,

And in the calmest and most deadest night,
With all appliances and means to boot
Deny it to a king? Then, happy low, lie down;
Uneasy lies the head that wears a crown.
                              (*2 Henry IV*, iii. i. 18)

Observe the words 'monstrous', 'curling', and 'tops'; and
the tempest-death association. Such sea tempests and
ships are often visual projections of the soul's unrest.
And this tempest of unrest is contrasted with music
(iii. i. 14). Juliet in her tears is compared to a bark
tossed on the seas of her grief:

                    In one little body
Thou counterfeit'st a bark, a sea, a wind;
For still thy eyes, which I may call the sea,
Do ebb and flow with tears; the bark thy body is,
Sailing in this salt flood; the winds thy sighs;
Who raging with thy tears, and they with them,
Without a sudden calm, will overset
Thy tempest-tossed body. (*Romeo and Juliet*, iii. v. 131)

Which shows how powerful and exact may be this tempest and bark imagery as applied to the soul's distress.

And yet sea and ship images need not suggest tragedy.
They may point the exact opposite. The sea often represents pure 'fortune'; and fortune may be favourable, its
sea calm. For example:

Now am I like that proud insulting ship
Which Caesar and his fortune bare at once.
                              (*1 Henry VI*, i. ii. 138)

To Romeo Juliet's bed is the 'high top-gallant' of his joy
(*Romeo and Juliet*, ii. iv. 202). Now in *Henry V* fortune is
kind. Thus the King can boast:

But tell the Dauphin I will keep my state,
Be like a king and show my sail of greatness
When I do rouse me in my throne of France.
                              (i. ii. 273)

Hence we have a fine description of the English fleet
leaving for France. Remembering our more usual tragic-

colourings we may be receptive to the extreme significance of this more happy and fortune-blessed adventure:

> *Chorus.* Thus with imagined wing our swift scene flies
>   In motion of no less celerity
>   Than that of thought. Suppose that you have seen
>   The well-appointed king at Hampton pier
>   Embark his royalty; and his brave fleet
>   With silken streamers the young Phoebus fanning:
>   Play with your fancies, and in them behold
>   Upon the hempen tackle ship-boys climbing;
>   Hear the shrill whistle which doth order give
>   To sounds confused: behold the threaden sails,
>   Borne with the invisible and creeping wind
>   Draw the huge bottoms through the furrow'd sea,
>   Breasting the lofty surge: O, do but think
>   You stand upon the rivage and behold
>   A city on the inconstant billows dancing;
>   For so appears this fleet majestical,
>   Holding due course to Harfleur. Follow, follow:
>   Grapple your minds to sternage of this navy . . .
>   (III. Pro. 1)

Notice how here the 'whistle' imposes 'order' on 'things confused'. Here the imagery of 'silken streamers', 'Phoebus', 'fanning', 'tackle' and 'boys', the 'invisible and creeping wind', all recall the description of Cleopatra in the barge at Cydnus. Nor is this strange. In both plays we have an optimistic vision; both visions correspondingly present happy sea and ship imagery. In both man is superior to fortune; in both his civilization is glorified; and this is suggested by his ability to make 'cities' on the sea. 'A city on the inconstant billows dancing.' We should compare Antony's

>   I that with my sword
>   Quarter'd the world, and o'er green Neptune's back
>   With ships made cities . . .
>   (*Antony and Cleopatra*, IV. xii. 57)

A passage I shall notice later. So the sea is aptly shown to honour King Henry when he returns victorious:

> Now we bear the king
> Toward Calais: grant him there; there seen,
> Heave him away upon your winged thoughts
> Athwart the sea. Behold, the English beach
> Pales in the flood with men, with wives and boys,
> Whose shouts and claps out-voice the deep-mouth'd sea,
> Which like a mighty whiffler 'fore the king
> Seems to prepare his way: so let him land,
> And solemnly see him set on to London.   (v. Pro. 6)

The ocean of his glory buoys him up, his subjects' applause shouts louder than the sea, the sea itself does homage to him. But even this happy king knows the ocean of world-glory to hold a tragic unrest:

> No, thou proud dream,
> That play'st so subtly with a king's repose;
> I am a king that find thee, and I know
> 'Tis not the balm, the sceptre and the ball,
> The sword, the mace, the crown imperial,
> The intertissued robe of gold and pearl,
> The farced title running 'fore the king,
> The throne he sits on, nor the tide of pomp,
> That beats upon the high shore of this world,
> Not, not all these, thrice gorgeous ceremony,
> Not all these, laid in bed majestical,
> Can sleep so soundly as the wretched slave,
> Who, with a body fill'd and vacant mind,
> Gets him to bed, cramm'd with distressful bread. . . .
>   (iv. i. 274)

The 'tide of pomp'. Which suggests another use of this sea-imagery, which I shall next shortly observe.

V

The ocean suggests vastness and majesty. Hence our phrase 'the tide of pomp'. There is such a suggestion, too, in Constance's words:

> What hath this day deserved? What hath it done
> That it in golden letters should be set
> Among the high tides in the calendar?
>   (*King John*, iii. i. 84)

A tide may have widely varied applications, but it often suggests glory:

> The tide of blood in me
> Hath proudly flow'd in vanity till now:
> Now doth it turn and ebb back to the sea,
> Where it shall mingle with the state of floods
> And flow henceforth in formal majesty.
>   (*2 Henry IV*, v. ii. 129)

The smaller tide gives its selfish pride to 'mingle' with the greater. A similar thought is found in *The Merchant of Venice* where a 'substitute's' glory is like an 'inland brook' which empties itself into the 'main' of royalty on meeting a king (v. i. 96). In something of the same way Bertram, in *All's Well*, 'in his proper stream o'erflows himself' (iv. iii. 25–30): that is, he is like a river overflowing its banks and so disturbing its own essential nature which is to flow to the sea. This image serves to link our present glory-tide associations with the flood-disorder set already observed. In the same way, in a passage already quoted from *King John*, rebels will, like a 'bated and retired flood' stoop again 'within those bounds' they have overflowed and run on in obedience 'even to our ocean, to our great King John' (v. iv. 53–8). Thus kingly glory is often compared to the ocean. So a man may rashly bear 'the title of a king, as if a channel should be call'd the sea' (*3 Henry VI*, ii. ii. 141). So, too, speaks King Edward:

> You are the fount that makes small brooks to flow:
> Now stops thy spring; my sea shall suck them dry,
> And swell so much the higher by their ebb.
>   (*3 Henry VI*, iv. viii. 54)

Kingly 'fortune' is a flood in *1 Henry IV*:

> But in short space
> It rain'd down fortune showering on your head;
> And such a flood of greatness fell on you . . . . (v. i. 46)

Again in *Lucrece*:

> 'Thou art', quoth she, 'a sea, a sovereign king;
> And, lo, there falls into thy boundless flood

Black lust, dishonour, shame, misgoverning,
Who seek to stain the ocean of thy blood.
If all these petty ills shall change thy good,
  Thy sea within a puddle's womb is hearsed,
  And not the puddle in thy sea dispersed.'   (652)

We can next relate this type of sea-image to our former sea-tragedy imagery. This great ocean of kingly glory, Henry V's 'tide of pomp', we saw to hold a vast unrest, responsibility; and thus it blends with the turbulent sea whereby, in a similar speech (both are 'sleep' speeches) to Henry V's, Henry IV, as we have seen, compares the insecurity and misery of kingship to a 'ship-boy' on a mast in a tempest. Kingship thus means a vast responsibility in world affairs; no less than the control of an ocean of glory, an ocean of responsibility, and so a good king, ultimately, must be master of fickle 'fortune' itself. Hence the sea-fortune association (fortune and tragedy are clearly directly related) is equivalent to the sea-glory association. Only one king, Henry V, is shown as mastering the seas of fate: and even he feels an inward dread of his task. Kingship is thus fraught with infinite care, infinite burdens. Which 'infinity' suggestion may lead us further. The sea is, too, an infinity symbol. It often suggests the infinity of passion, or any emotional quality whatever, compared with the limiting and finite reason. Hence our former passages wherein floods overflow to suggest passion breaking across and over the impediments of rational control in the 'state of man'. The king has to control a national sea of passions, just as the individual has to master a personal one.

    Now this 'infinity' metaphor is exceedingly various. 'A little water in a spoon' will be as the 'ocean' to drown a man whose guilt is 'infinite' (*King John*, IV. iii. 117, 130–134). This is typical:

    Alas, poor duke! the task he undertakes
    Is numbering sands and drinking oceans dry.
            (*Richard II*, II. ii. 145)

With which we might compare Helena's speech on
miracles:

> So holy writ in babes hath judgement shown,
> When judges have been babes; great floods have flown
> From simple sources, and great seas have dried
> When miracles have by the greatest been denied.
>
> (*All's Well*, ii. i. 141)

Vast sorrow may be given an ocean-metaphor, so that a
human heart is 'as full of sorrow as the sea of sands' (*Two
Gentlemen*, iv. iii. 33). We have an 'ocean of salt tears':

> Fain would I go to chafe his paly lips
> With twenty thousand kisses and to drain
> Upon his face an ocean of salt tears . . .
>
> (*2 Henry VI*, iii. ii. 141)

Again, we have 'seas of tears' in *3 Henry VI*, ii. v. 105.
All emotional quality, of good or evil suggestion, may be
'infinite': thus the 'wide sea' cannot wash off the stain of
Hero's disgrace (*Much Ado*, iv. i. 142), nor 'all the waters
of the rough rude sea' remove the sacred balm from
Richard's anointed head (*Richard II*, iii. ii. 54). So it is
clear that the infinite value of kingship—kingship being
a powerful Shakespearian value—is well bodied into the
infinity-metaphor of the 'sea'. But, as Henry V knows,
the infinity of world glory is, at the last, a cheat: it
cannot give the infinitely craving soul peace. Only love
can give the perfect rest. Love is the only true infinity.
Love's tears witness an infinite emotion:

> Tear for tear, and loving kiss for kiss,
> Thy brother Marcus tenders on thy lips:
> O, were the sum of these that I should pay
> Countless and infinite, yet would I pay them!
>
> (*Titus Andronicus*, v. iii. 156)

Again, with sea-imagery:

> A thousand oaths, an ocean of his tears,
> And instances of infinite of love,
> Warrant me welcome to my Proteus.
>
> (*Two Gentlemen*, ii. vii. 69)

A still finer example, with no tragic unrest, is Juliet's:

> My bounty is as boundless as the sea,
> My love as deep; the more I give to thee,
> The more I have, for both are infinite.
>
> *(Romeo and Juliet*, II. ii. 133)

So in *Twelfth Night*, as I shall observe, love 'receiveth as the sea' and is 'all as hungry as the sea'. Thus the sea may be charged with varied significance. It may register indecision:

> 'Tis with my mind
> As with the tide swell'd up unto his height
> That makes a still-stand, running neither way.
>
> *(2 Henry IV*, II. iii. 62)

An image we meet again in *Antony and Cleopatra*, and elsewhere. Generally tempestuous, it is a symbol of death, disorder; but calm, it may be, correspondingly, the stage set for prosperity, success, and love. Thus an 'hour' may 'o'erflow with joy' so that 'pleasure' may 'drown the brim' (*All's Well*, II. iv. 47). Finally, the sea is that infinite continuum of psychic experience within which all human desires, tragedies, and joys have their being. It may be vastly tumultuous, or a vast peace. Only a clear recognition of the power beating in Shakespeare's sea-imagery will give a clear understanding of the wondrous delight imaged in those scenes, where we see Cleopatra on her barge at Cydnus and Pericles on his ship in the harbour of Mytilene: in both, still waters blend with music, and the theme of both is love.

We have worked through a mass of tempest-imagery to the theme of love. I will now develop that relation, drawing still primarily on the Histories, Poems, and early Tragedies; first making some general remarks on disorder and some more elaborate statements on Shakespeare's use of music.

VI

Tempests are things of disorder, unrest, severance.
They are constantly interwoven with other disorder-symbolism, events of unnatural portentousness in the stellar
or mundane worlds. The connexion is clear from a line
in Sonnet xxxv:

> Clouds and eclipses stain both moon and sun.

Tempests are, indeed, part of the wider universal and
natural symbolism recurrent in Shakespeare. Such universal disorder-symbols may register disorder in the state,
as in *Richard II*:

> 'Tis thought the king is dead; we will not stay.
> The bay-trees in our country are all wither'd,
> And meteors fright the fixed stars of heaven;
> The pale-faced moon looks bloody on the earth
> And lean-look'd prophets whisper fearful change;
> Rich men look sad and ruffians dance and leap,
> The one in fear to lose what they enjoy,
> The other to enjoy by rage and war:
> These signs forerun the death or fall of kings. (II. iv 7)

Or in *King John*:

> *Hubert.* My lord, they say five moons were seen to-night;
> Four fixed, and the fifth did whirl about
> The other four in wondrous motion.
> *K. John.* Five moons!
> *Hubert.* Old men and beldams in the streets
> Do prophesy upon it dangerously . . .   (IV. ii. 182)

So, earlier in this play, our already quoted phrase 'no
common wind, no customed event' is associated with 'no
natural exhalation in the sky', and both with 'meteors,
prodigies, and signs, abortives, presages, and tongues of
heaven' (III. iv. 153–8). This is a usual symbolism. It
recurs in *Julius Caesar* powerfully. It may also, like
tempests, apply to the individual:

> Look'd he or red or pale, or sad or merrily?
> What observation madest thou in this case
> Of his heart's meteors tilting in his face?
> > (*Comedy of Errors*, IV. ii. 4)

This is, however, rare. Now the opposite of tempests and such portentous phenomena are, in Shakespeare, images of sun, moon, or star in natural splendour; still airs and waters; sweet flowers; and music. Sonnet xxi might be set against the disorder-symbolism I have noted to suggest its direct opposite:

> So is it not with me as with that Muse
> Stirr'd by a painted beauty to his verse,
> Who heaven itself for ornament doth use
> And every fair with his fair doth rehearse;
> Making a couplement of proud compare,
> With sun and moon, with earth and sea's rich gems,
> With April's first-born flowers, and all things rare
> That heaven's air in this huge rondure hems.
> O, let me, true in love, but truly write,
> And then believe me, my love is as fair
> As any mother's child, though not so bright
> As those gold candles fix'd in heaven's air:
> > Let them say more that like of hearsay well:
> > I will not praise that purpose not to sell.

Here we should observe the 'heaven' imagery, the word recurring twice; the sun, moon, and stars—'gold candles', 'rich gems' of earth and sea; 'air', thrice-mentioned, its softness suggested rather than any sort of turbulence; and April's 'flowers'. All this is characteristic. And all this is blurred, stained, hidden, or distorted by the murk and violence of tempests or any disorder-portents. We may remember *Macbeth*. Whereas this sonnet is exactly relevant to the *Antony and Cleopatra* vision: and such happy universal imagery is typical of Shakespeare's love-poetry. Henry V tells Katharine that a good heart is 'the sun and the moon, or rather the sun and not the moon, since the moon changes' (*Henry V*, v. ii. 170). The moon's changes are often so observed; and thus the moon is set a little below the sun as a symbol of glory. So we have disorder and conflict against concord and love; tempests against the universal music they blot out; and in Shakespeare music themes especially run parallel to, or inter-threading, tempests. Shortly—not exhaustively—I shall note some early passages where the music-concord association is explicit.

Music and tempests of discord are ever to be contrasted:

> The winds grow high; so do your stomachs, lords.
> How irksome is this music to my heart!
> When such strings jar, what hope of harmony?
> I pray, my lords, let me compound this strife.
>
> *(2 Henry VI*, II. i. 54)

In *1 Henry VI* 'the jarring discord of nobility' is an important phrase: it is here associated with 'raging broils', 'dissension'—the word occurring frequently—'division' and 'confusion' (*1 Henry VI*, IV. i. 185–94, 116, 139). All these are most important words. A quarrel is ever a 'discord' (*1 Henry VI*, IV. IV. 22). But men embrace to 'music':

> By that music let us all embrace.
>
> *(1 Henry IV*, v. ii. 99)

This is typical. The tempest-music contrast vitalizes a paradox in *Henry V*:

> List his discourse of war, and you shall hear
> A fearful battle render'd you in music.   (I. i. 43)

An exact statement concerning the political implications of music occurs in *Henry V*:

> For government, though high and low and lower,
> Put into parts, doth keep in one consent,
> Congreeing in a full and natural close
> Like music.   (I. ii. 180)

'Natural': ever in Shakespeare all disorder and conflict is considered unnatural. Hence our disorder portents. It is in the sense implied by this *Henry V* passage that, in *The Merchant of Venice*:

> The man that hath no music in himself
> Nor is not mov'd with concord of sweet sounds,
> Is fit for treasons, stratagems, and spoils:

The motions of his spirit are dull as night,
And his affections dark as Erebus:
Let no such man be trusted.   (v. i. 83)

'Stratagems' and 'treasons' are to be opposed to the
'music' of state, and, consequently, to be associated with
fierce beasts, as when 'Minotaurs' are coupled with 'ugly
treasons' in *1 Henry VI*, v. iii. 189. So in the History
Plays music may mark moments of peace and love amid
the turbulences of civil war. There is the magic music
charmed by Glendower in *1 Henry IV*, and the Welsh
song sung by Lady Mortimer (III. i). Here music and
family love is to be contrasted with the stress and turmoil
of civil war: a contrast clearly pointed by both Lady Percy
and Lady Mortimer in the play. An exactly analogous use
of music occurs in *2 Henry IV*, where the love of Doll
Tearsheet for Falstaff rises to a lyric beauty before his
departure for the wars (II. iv. 245). There is, too, the
music asked for by the King at *2 Henry IV*, IV. v. 3, at a
moment of that stillness and peace that so often in Shakespeare preludes the final tragedy. Music, too, occurs with
similar power in *Richard II*. The incident is important and
its understanding involves more attention than I can give
it here. Richard is in prison. He meditates on his, and all
human, tragedy, passing to a resigned stoicism. Then
music sounds, a lovely finish to his thoughts. We watch a
progress from mental perplexity and spiritual division to
a consummation in music. The speech reflects the Shakespearian progress from tragedy to myth to be written later;
which thought I have developed elsewhere. Now the music
must be considered to continue for a while; next, it irritates
Richard, and he compares it to the music of state in which
he himself has so lamentably failed. First:

Music do I hear?

Here we may imagine a pause. Then:

Ha, ha! keep time: how sour sweet music is,
When time is broke and no proportion kept!
So is it in the music of men's lives.

And here have I the daintiness of ear
To check time broke in a disorder'd string;
But for the concord of my state and time
Had not an ear to hear my true time broke.

(v. v. 41)

Here music is directly associated with the 'concord' of
'state'. A favouring king 'tunes his bounty to sing happiness' to a subject (*All's Well*, iv. iii. 12). But the drum of
an enemy sings 'heavy music' to a 'timorous soul'
(*1 Henry VI*, iv. ii. 40).

Now, as our *Henry IV* incidents suggest, music may
often be associated with purely personal love. Our tempest-music contrast may thus also correspond to any
angry passions or madness contrasted with happy love.
Music, says Richard, has been known to 'help madmen to
their wits' (v. v. 62); thus is it opposed to the tempests of
mental agony in *Hamlet* and *Lear*, where madness is considered, in both, as discordant music. I note the passages
later. In another passage I return to later, from *The Two
Gentlemen of Verona*, Julia compares herself to a stream,
which, hindered 'impatiently doth rage', but would otherwise give 'a gentle kiss' to every sedge, and 'make sweet
music with the enamell'd stones': therefore she prays that
her course of love be not hindered, but that she may find
her 'Elysium' as the stream does the 'ocean' (ii. vii. 25–38).
Again,

> Thy eye Jove's lightning bears, thy voice his dreadful thunder,
> Which, not to anger bent, is music and sweet fire.

(Love's Labour's Lost, iv. ii. 119;
The Passionate Pilgrim, v. 67)

'Fire' and 'air' may suggest pure love, being finer elements
than 'earth' and 'water'. Which elemental suggestion is
powerful in *Antony and Cleopatra*: and, indeed, this couplet
is close to Cleopatra's description of her dream-Antony,
whose voice in love was 'as the tuned spheres' but became
'rattling thunder' in ire. Fire, especially sunlight, is often
close to music. In *Richard II*, 'the tongues of dying men
enforce attention like deep harmony', and 'music at the

close' is like a setting sun (II. i. 5–12). The human voice in itself may be music and the 'tongue' of death 'a stringless instrument' (*Richard II*, II. i. 149). The image occurs again in *Richard II*:

> And now my tongue's use is to me no more
> Than an unstringed viol or a harp,
> Or like a cunning instrument cased up,
> Or, being open, put into his hands
> That knows no touch to tune the harmony.
>
> (I. iii. 161)

Good news in Shakespeare is as music, but ill news is delivered by a 'care-tun'd tongue' (*Richard II*, III. ii. 92). Lucrece's tongue in grief is hoarse and 'untuned' (*Lucrece*, 1214). Music, however, occurs most often in direct relation to love's voice. A lover's voice is often considered as music:

> Music to hear, why hear'st thou music sadly?
> Sweets with sweets war not, joy delights in joy.
> Why lovest thou that which thou receivest not gladly,
> Or else receivest with pleasure thine annoy?
> If the true concord of well tuned sounds,
> By unions married, do offend thine ear,
> They do but sweetly chide thee, who confounds
> In singleness the parts that thou shouldst bear.
> Mark how one string, sweet husband to another,
> Strikes each in each by mutual ordering;
> Resembling sire and child and happy mother,
> Who, all in one, one pleasing note do sing:
> > Whose speechless song, being many, seeming one,
> > Sings this to thee: 'Thou single wilt prove none.'
>
> (Sonnet VIII)

Notice the word 'concord', important in Shakespeare, the close music-love comparison, string husband to string. Here the loved one is reproached for not joining in the universal song of marriage. And observe the lovely image of 'sire and child and happy mother' singing one note of love. This sonnet inevitably suggests the triple family reunions and music that characterize the Final Plays.

The voice of love is as 'ditties highly penn'd' sung by a queen 'with ravishing division to her lute' (*1 Henry IV*, III. i. 209). But again, the lover may be jealous of music, and wish his love would play on him rather than the virginal she fingers:

> How oft, when thou, my music, music play'st,
> Upon that blessed wood whose motion sounds
> With thy sweet fingers, when thou gently sway'st
> The wiry concord that mine ear confounds,
> Do I envy those jacks that nimble leap
> To kiss the tender inward of thy hand,
> Whilst my poor lips, which should that harvest reap,
> At the wood's boldness by thee blushing stand!
> To be so tickled, they would change their state
> And situation with those dancing chips,
> O'er whom thy fingers walk with gentle gait,
> Making dead wood more blest than living lips.
> > Since saucy jacks so happy are in this,
> > Give them thy fingers, me thy lips to kiss.

(Sonnet CXXVIII)

Again the loved one is music: 'my music'. And we again have 'concord'. Adonis's 'mermaid's voice' in anger is 'deep-sweet music' and 'melodious discord' to Venus (*Venus and Adonis*, 429–32). One might also quote Sonnet CII. Here the 'wild music' is not real music but the nightingale's song; which, however, is, by common consent and poetic tradition, a kind of music. The nightingale in Shakespeare is a 'musician' (*The Merchant of Venice*, v. i. 106) and birds, bird-song, and music all blend with each other in Shakespeare's love-imagery.[1] Bird-song, music, and prosperity are associated at *2 Henry IV*, v. v. 113–14. The lover serenades his love with 'musics of all sorts and songs' (*All's Well*, III. vii. 40). In *Love's Labour's Lost* we hear that Love is

> as sweet and musical
> As bright Apollo's lute, strung with his hair;
> And when Love speaks, the voice of all the gods

---

[1] See Appendix A, 'The Shakespearian Aviary'.

Make heaven drowsy with the harmony.
Never durst poet touch a pen to write
Until his ink were temper'd with Love's sighs;
O, then his lines would ravish savage ears
And plant in tyrants mild humility.   (IV. iii. 342)

Another comparison of love's voice to music; and a contrast of love-poetry with 'savage ears', which recalls the description of music, charming wild beasts, 'stones' and 'floods' and all things 'full of rage' in *The Merchant of Venice* (v. i. 71–82). So that we have a clear opposition of music on the one side, and our tempest-beast association on the other.

  Romeo and Juliet is rich in music-thought:

It is my soul that calls upon my name:
How silver-sweet sound lovers' tongues by night,
Like softest music to attending ears!   (II. ii. 165)

Juliet's voice is 'rich music's tongue' to enfold love's 'imagined happiness' at Romeo and Juliet's marriage (II. vi. 27); love's 'sweet news' is 'music' (II. v. 23). And there is the marriage music later prepared for Juliet's marriage with Paris, and the musicians' dialogue with Peter about 'silver music' (IV. v). It is observed how this music is ill timed: happy 'instruments' are changed to 'melancholy bells'; 'hymns' to 'dirges' (IV. v. 86–9); 'wedding cheer' to a 'burial feast'; 'bridal flowers' are used for a corpse. Such broken music is powerfully symbolical in a love-tragedy. This music is the music of the soul's desire which we find again in the Lorenzo and Jessica dialogue in *The Merchant of Venice*, where again it is associated with night: 'Soft stillness and the night become the touches of sweet harmony.' I return to that passage later. *Romeo and Juliet* is, indeed, necessarily rich in music-thought. H. Granville-Barker has finely noted the exquisite effect of the lovers' first encounter in the Ball scene—dances themselves continually blend with music to accompany love: 'they share the speaking of a sonnet together and it is a charming device'. If we remember the close associations of love's voice and music in Shakespeare we shall add to Mr.

Granville-Barker's comment the idea that the lovers blend
like two strings of music, one string the 'sweet husband'
to the other. Moreover, a sonnet is clearly a kind of music.
Music and poetry are close in Shakespeare:

> If music and sweet poetry agree,
> As they must needs, the sister and the brother,
> Then must the love be great 'twixt thee and me,
> Because thou lovest the one, and I the other.
> Dowland to thee is dear, whose heavenly touch
> Upon the lute doth ravish human sense;
> Spenser to me, whose deep conceit is such
> As, passing all conceit, needs no defence.
> Thou lovest, to hear the sweet melodious sound
> That Phoebus' lute, the queen of music, makes;
> And I in deep delight am chiefly drown'd
> Whenas himself to singing he betakes.
>> One god is god of both, as poets feign;
>> One knight loves both, and both in thee remain.
>
> *(The Passionate Pilgrim,* VIII)

To return to *Romeo.* Tragedy forces the lovers asunder.
They part in a lovely scene full of poetic melody and
associations of bird-music:

> *Juliet.* Wilt thou be gone? it is not yet near day:
> It was the nightingale, and not the lark,
> That pierced the fearful hollow of thine ear;
> Nightly she sings on yond pomegranate tree:
> Believe me, love, it was the nightingale.
> *Romeo.* It was the lark, the herald of the morn,
> No nightingale . . .   (III. V. 1)

But Romeo gives way to Juliet's love:

> Nor that is not the lark whose notes do beat
> The vaulty heaven so high above our heads. . . .
>   (III. V. 21)

Then Juliet, too, changes at once:

> It is the lark that sings so out of tune,
> Straining harsh discords and unpleasing sharps.
> Some say the lark makes sweet division;
> This doth not so, for she divideth us:

Some say the lark and loathed toad change eyes;
O, now I would they had changed voices too! (III. v. 27)

Observe how here separation and division take place to
bird-music and dawn—usually pure love-associations;
and how the poet is aware of the discrepancy and, by
pointing it, resolves it again into harmony. No study of
symbolism is adequate that does not recognize that
disaster may be equally effective if given a gloomy or an
ironically bright setting. The effect, say, of a realistic
novelist who effectively presents misery on a spring morning, though not directly Shakespearian—since Shakespeare more usually makes the simple association—may be
called Shakespearian in essence: nor is this only 'realism'
—it is as purely 'symbolic' as anything in Shakespeare.
Observe, too, in our *Romeo* passage, how the 'sweet
division', which is a harmony, of music is contrasted with
the discordant 'dividing' of the lovers; music usually
accompanying union, tempests being the natural accompaniment to dispersal and severance. So here the lark
is said to sing 'out of tune', 'straining harsh discords'.
This scene is most important for our understanding of the
tempest-music opposition. So, too, Mercutio, quarrel-
ling with Tybalt, asks if Tybalt takes him and Benvolio for
'musicians': 'Look to hear nothing but discords', he continues (*Romeo and Juliet*, III. i. 51–5). Quarrels are continually discord, love is continually music.

Music indeed suggests in Shakespeare all that is most
divine and ethereal. Consider the Dauphin's praise of his
horse:

> . . . Ça, ha! he bounds from the earth, as if his entrails were
> hairs; le cheval volant, the Pegasus, chez les narines de feu!
> When I bestride him, I soar, I am a hawk: he trots the air; the
> earth sings when he touches it; the basest horn of his hoof is
> more musical than the pipe of Hermes. . . . It is a beast for
> Perseus: he is pure air and fire; and the dull elements of earth
> and water never appear in him, but only in patient stillness
> while his rider mounts him: he is indeed a horse; and all other
> jades you may call beasts.   (*Henry V*, III. vii. 13–26)

The horse is continually idealized in Shakespeare and to be contrasted with the 'beasts'. Observe here the usual associations of the *Antony and Cleopatra* sort: ethereal and aspiring life (the hawk), 'he trots the air', the earth singing, as in *Antony and Cleopatra* where there is music in 'the earth'; the idea of the horse's very hoof being 'musical', 'air' and 'fire' contrasted with 'earth' and 'water'. A very important speech.

Now all these varied instances that I have quoted may be said to establish a close love-music association; and some of them have shown, too, a music-tempest contrast in relation to love. For my immediate purpose, love may be taken in a wide sense, suggesting both political concord and the individual's romantic joy. Sometimes we may feel both at once; as when the battling of England and France in *Henry V* gives place to Henry's wooing, and Katharine's voice is to the warrior king as 'music' (v. ii. 263). I shall next observe love and 'tempests' in opposition.

VII

Tempests are love's antagonists. 'Time's ruin, beauty's wreck, and grim care's reign' is a natural association (*Lucrece*, 1451). Again, in *Venus and Adonis*:

> Love comforteth like sunshine after rain,
> But Lust's effect is tempest after sun.   (799)

Which 'sunshine' thought is to be related to our universal images: 'tempests' shut out the universe. Venus will be a 'park' to her Adonis, and 'within the circuit of this ivory pale' of her arms she will shelter him, her 'deer', from 'tempest' and 'rain' (*Venus and Adonis*, 230–8). But the scornful ruby of Adonis' love-refusing lips are:

> Like a red morn, that ever yet betoken'd
> Wreck to the seaman, tempest to the field.   (453)

This is a presage as when the wind 'is hushed before it raineth' (458). Love is 'an ever-fixed mark' looking on

'tempests' but 'never shaken'; it is 'a star to every wandering bark' (Sonnet cxvi). Love is like the sun, one moment
splendid,

> Gilding pale streams with heavenly alchemy,

but next the 'basest clouds' ride

> With ugly wrack on his celestial face. . . .

So the 'region cloud' masks the loved one from his lover
(Sonnet xxxiii). Then,

> Why didst thou promise such a beauteous day
> And make me travel forth without my cloak,
> To let base clouds o'ertake me in my way,
> Hiding thy bravery in their rotten smoke?
> 'Tis not enough that through the cloud thou break,
> To dry the rain on my storm-beaten face. . . .
>
>   (Sonnet xxxiv)

This comparison of love with a bright sun or moon is
usual, and is, of course, as in Sonnet xxi quoted above, an
instance of universal imagery in its peaceful aspect, the
obverse of the usual disorder-symbolism. So Lucrece's
eyes in grief are as 'two suns' 'cloud-eclipsed' (*Lucrece*,
1224). In just this way *Antony and Cleopatra*, as I have
observed, presents a contrast to *Macbeth*.

Love in Shakespeare is very often found compared to
a jewel, or any precious stone:

>   Where, alack,
> Shall Time's best jewel from Time's chest lie hid?
>
>   (Sonnet lxv)

The association is simple and so multitudinous that quotation is unnecessary. This love-jewel is sometimes cast
into the sea. When Adonis leaves her, Venus is

> amazed, as one that unaware
> Hath dropp'd a precious jewel in the flood.
>
>   (*Venus and Adonis*, 824)

The loved one is here significantly imaged as a jewel
thrown in water. So, too, to lose one's honour ('the immediate jewel' of the soul, *Othello*, iii. iii. 156) is to 'sink'

it (*All's Well*, v. iii. 181). In *A Lover's Complaint*, we
have:

> A thousand favours from a maund she drew
> Of amber, crystal, and of beaded jet,
> Which one by one she in a river threw,
> Upon whose weeping margent she was set. . . .   (36)

The lovers Queen Margaret and Suffolk part:

Queen.   . . . let me hear from thee;
> For wheresoe'er thou art in this world's globe,
> I'll have an Iris that shall find thee out.
Suffolk. I go.
Queen.   And take my heart with thee.
Suffolk. A jewel, lock'd into the wofull'st cask
> That ever did contain a thing of worth.
> Even as a splitted bark, so sunder we:
> This way fall I to death.   (*2 Henry VI*, iii. ii. 405)

Notice the bark-death association. Later he fulfils the
prophecy which said he should die 'by water' (iv. i. 35).
The scene of his death is of great importance. The stage
direction is vivid:

> *Alarum. Fight at sea. Ordnance goes off. Enter a Captain, a
> Master, a Master's-mate, Walter Whitmore, and others; with
> them Suffolk, and others, prisoners.*

Pirates are significant throughout Shakespeare. Here their
actions are powerfully imagined. We have, too, a typical
association in 'loud-howling wolves' (iv. i. 3). Suffolk
wishes he was 'a god to shoot forth thunder' on these
pirates he despises (iv. i. 104). He continues:

>   this villain here
> Being captain of a pinnace, threatens more
> Than Bargulus the strong Illyrian pirate.   (iv. i. 106)

Which recalls the pirate-theme in *Twelfth Night*.
    But to return to jewels. Seas are hostile to love's delicate
jewel and the bark of love. They keep the glories they
have swallowed through ages of tempestuous rage: they
are rich with treasures. Scotland is

as rich with praise

As is the ooze and bottom of the sea
With sunken wreck and sumless treasuries.

(Henry V, I. ii. 163)

Clarence, in *Richard III*, recounts the dream wherein,
guilt-tormented, he thinks himself drowning, struck by
Gloucester into the sea:

Clarence.   As we paced along
   Upon the giddy footing of·the hatches,
   Methought that Gloucester stumbled; and, in falling,
   Struck me, that thought to stay him, overboard,
   Into the tumbling billows of the main.
   Lord, Lord! methought, what pain it was to drown!
   What dreadful noise of waters in mine ears!
   What ugly sights of death within mine eyes!
   Methought I saw a thousand fearful wrecks;
   Ten thousand men that fishes gnaw'd upon;
   Wedges of gold, great anchors, heaps of pearl,
   Inestimable stones, unvalued jewels,
   All scattered in the bottom of the sea:
   Some lay in dead men's skulls; and in those holes
   Where eyes did once inhabit, there were crept,
   As 'twere in scorn of eyes, reflecting gems,
   Which woo'd the slimy bottom of the deep,
   And mock'd the dead bones that lay scattered by.
Brakenbury. Had you such leisure in the time of death
   To gaze upon the secrets of the deep?
Clarence. Methought I had; and often did I strive
   To yield the ghost: but still the envious flood
   Kept in my soul, and would not let it forth
   To seek the empty, vast, and wandering air;
   But smothered it within my panting bulk,
   Which almost burst to belch it in the sea.
Brakenbury. Awaked you not with this sore agony?
Clarence. O no, my dream was lengthened after life;
   O, then began the tempest to my soul,
   Who pass'd, methought, the melancholy flood,
   With that grim ferryman which poets write of,
   Unto the kingdom of perpetual night. . . .   (I. iv. 16)

A fine passage with various characteristic elements.

Notice the 'tempest to my soul' suggesting the torments of guilt; and the vivid description of drowning, the most vivid in Shakespeare. Notice, too, the strong sea-death association; 'ugly sights of death', and the ironic thought of gems 'wooing' the slime in place of men's 'eyes'; eyes being ever the ambassadors of love in Shakespeare. Thus again we have a jewel-love contrast and association. But when love is prosperous, this glorious jewel imagery itself transfigures the sea and its rocks, as when Valentine, in a passage I quote later, says that he is as 'rich' in having such a 'jewel' as Silvia as 'twenty seas' with sands of 'pearl', water of 'nectar' and rocks of 'gold' (*Two Gentlemen of Verona*, ii. iv. 169). The sea-jewel or sea-riches association is important; the most usual thought being that of vast riches buried in the ocean. In this sense the ocean is rich, infinitely rich; rich as death itself crammed with all the treasures of love it has won from life throughout the ages. Hence the power of our image by which a jewel is thrown into the sea: it is as love itself lost in the seas of adverse fortune or death.

A sea-crossing, tempest, and love's jewel are all finely interwoven in a long speech by that tempestuous lady, Queen Margaret:

> Was I for this nigh wreck'd upon the sea
> And twice by awkward wind from England's bank
> Drove back again unto my native clime?
> What boded this, but well forewarning wind
> Did seem to say 'Seek not a scorpion's nest,
> Nor set no footing on this unkind shore'?
> What did I then, but cursed the gentle gusts
> And he that loosed them forth their brazen caves;
> And bid them blow toward's England's blessed shore,
> Or turn our stern upon a dreadful rock?
> Yet Æolus would not be a murderer,
> But left that hateful office unto thee:
> The pretty-vaulting sea refused to drown me,
> Knowing that thou wouldst have me drown'd on shore,
> With tears as salt as sea, through thy unkindness:
> The splitting rocks cower'd in the sinking sands

And would not dash me with their ragged sides,
Because thy flinty heart, more hard than they,
Might in thy palace perish Margaret.
As far as I could ken thy chalky cliffs,
When from thy shore the tempest beat us back,
I stood upon the hatches in the storm,
And when the dusky sky began to rob
My earnest-gaping sight of thy land's view,
I took a costly jewel from my neck,
A heart it was, bound in with diamonds,
And threw it towards thy land: the sea received it,
And so I wish'd thy body might my heart:
And even with this I lost fair England's view
And-bid my eyes be packing with my heart,
And call'd them blind and dusky spectacles,
For losing ken of Albion's wished coast.
How often have I tempted Suffolk's tongue,
The agent of thy foul inconstancy,
To sit and witch me, as Ascanius did
When he to madding Dido would unfold
His father's acts commenced in burning Troy!
Am I not witch'd like her? or thou not false like him?
Ay me, I can no more! die, Margaret!
For Henry weeps that thou dost live so long.
                              (2 *Henry VI*, iii. ii. 82)

A speech to read, and read again and again, if we are to
understand, both emotionally and rationally, the pulsing
life that beats in Shakespeare's tempest-imagery. Here,
especially, we should notice with care the jewel, love,
grief, and tempest associations. 'Splitting rocks', 'flinty
heart', 'jewel' and 'diamonds'; all are characteristic. So is
the comparison of tears with the salt sea.

Thus tempests oppose love. Rough seas sever man from
his soul's desire. Richard II comes to his England, after his
'late tossing' on the 'breaking seas' to greet it 'as a long-
parted mother with her child' (iii. ii. 2–8). The mother is
imaged as weeping and smiling at once: a thought we
find often, notably in *Lear*, when Kent describes Cordelia's
tears. The poet thinks of his love as separated from him

by 'sea and land' in Sonnet XLIV; and, though thought can swiftly traverse such distance, yet he himself, cut off by 'so much earth and water', must give way to 'heavy tears'. Love draws man across seas, actual or imagined. Turbulent seas separate man from love. Another passage concerning Henry VI and Margaret is valuable. The King speaks:

> Your wondrous rare description, noble earl,
> Of beauteous Margaret hath astonish'd me:
> Her virtues graced with external gifts
> Do breed love's settled passions in my heart:
> And like as rigour of tempestuous gusts
> Provokes the mightiest hulk against the tide,
> So am I driven by breath of her renown
> Either to suffer shipwreck or arrive
> Where I may have fruition of her love.
>
> (*1 Henry VI*, v. v. 1)

Venus watches her love depart:

> as one on shore
> Gazing upon a late-embarked friend,
> Till the wild waves will have him seen no more,
> Whose ridges with the melting clouds contend. . . .
>
> (*Venus and Adonis*, 817)

So waters separate the lover from his, or her, love. In the same way, Gloucester sees the crown, his only love, set beyond seas of difficulty, luring him to ambition's attainment across all impediments:

> Why, then, I do but dream on sovereignty;
> Like one that stands upon a promontory,
> And spies a far-off shore where he would tread,
> Wishing his foot were equal with his eye,
> And chides the sea that sunders him from thence,
> Saying, he'll lade it dry to have his way;
> So do I wish the crown, being so far off;
> And so I chide the means that keeps me from it;
> And so I say, I'll cut the causes off,
> Flattering me with impossibilities.
>
> (*3 Henry VI*, III. ii. 134)

The image is in the usual tradition, since 'crowns' of kingship and love's loyalty are often associated or contrasted. Dangerous seas prevent man from happiness. It is as the old thought of sirens or mermaids. Thus Tamora is

> This siren that will charm Rome's Saturnine,
> And see his shipwreck and his commonweal's.
> *(Titus Andronicus,* II. i. 23)

So Gloucester, continuing his speech, determines to do the drowning himself, to spread death and tragedy:

> I'll drown more sailors than the mermaid shall.
> *(3 Henry VI,* III. ii. 186)

It reminds us of the tale of Hero and Leander, mentioned by Shakespeare at *Much Ado,* v. ii. 30–1 and *As You Like It,* IV. i. 101–7. Love is usually a matter of sea journeys. The infinite worth of the loved one may be as the calm sea buoying up all boats, great and small, on its breast:

> O, how I faint when I of you do write,
> Knowing a better spirit doth use your name,
> And in the praise thereof spends all his might,
> To make me tongue-tied, speaking of your fame!
> But since your worth, wide as the ocean is,
> The humble as the proudest sail doth bear,
> My saucy bark, inferior far to his,
> On your broad main doth wilfully appear.
> Your shallowest help will hold me up afloat,
> Whilst he upon your soundless deep doth ride;
> Or, being wreck'd, I am a worthless boat,
> He of tall building and of goodly pride:
>   Then if he thrive and I be cast away,
>   The worst was this; my love was my decay.
> (Sonnet LXXX)

Here the sea-infinity suggestion blends with shipwrecks to suggest the great spiritual safety and yet the equally great uncertainty of love. Again, the unfaithful lover 'hoists sail' to winds that drive him from

his love. The poet suggests his love may thus accuse
him:

> That I have frequent been with unknown minds,
> And given to time your own dear-purchased right;
> That I have hoisted sail to all the winds
> Which should transport me farthest from your sight.
>
> (Sonnet cxvii)

Here the purchase-metaphor suggests merchandise, and
love is almost as often equated with merchandise as it
is with jewels. The one is the prize of merchant-ships
on dangerous coasts, the other often, as I have observed,
thrown into tempestuous seas. In both we see the love-
tempest contrast. So the lover is pilot or merchant.
Tarquin cries:

> Desire my pilot is, beauty my prize;
> Then who fears sinking where such treasure lies?
>
> (*Lucrece*, 279)

Again,

> Huge rocks, high winds, strong pirates, shelves and sands,
> The merchant fears, ere rich at home he lands.
>
> (*Lucrece*, 335)

And after Lucrece's shame, her husband is 'the hopeless
merchant of this loss' (*Lucrece*, 1660). The image is repeated in *Romeo and Juliet*:

> *Juliet*. By whose direction found you out this place?
> *Romeo*. By love, who first did prompt me to inquire;
> He lent me counsel, and I lent him eyes.
> I am no pilot; yet, wert thou as far
> As that vast shore wash'd with the farthest sea,
> I would adventure for such merchandise.   (ii. ii. 79)

Again,

> Was it the proud full sail of his great verse
> Bound for the prize of all too precious you. . . .
>
> (Sonnet lxxxvi)

The universal content of the merchant and merchandise
idea can be seen from a passage in *Henry V*. The King
speaks:

So, if a son that is by his father sent about merchandise do
sinfully miscarry upon the sea, the imputation of his wickedness, by your rule, should be imposed upon his father that
sent him.   (IV. i. 157)

The merchant enterprise here is associated with the King's
national adventure, the King the merchant, the common
soldier, the son. Nor does the passage become coherent
unless we recognize the close association of 'sea wrecks'
and moral failure: 'wickedness' being as a wreck in life's
voyage.
   The Shakespearian 'merchant' sends his ventures far
and in various directions, but the most insistent thought
is that of love's merchandise. The spiritual treasure is
often set eastward, in lands of mystery and romantic suggestion. The rich glamour of the East is apt to the rich
glamour of love. India, Ethiopia, Egypt: all are usual
suggestions. So Juliet is 'like a rich jewel in an Ethiope's
ear' (*Romeo and Juliet*, I. v. 48). Most often the fairyland
of love is India, or the 'Indies', East or West. Love is
associated with India in *Love's Labour's Lost*:

>   Who sees the heavenly Rosaline,
>   That, like a rude and savage man of Ind,
>   At the first opening of the gorgeous east,
>   Bows not his vassal head and strucken blind
>   Kisses the base ground with obedient breast?
>   What peremptory eagle-sighted eye
>   Dares look upon the heaven of her brow,
>   That is not blinded by her majesty?
>
>   (IV. iii. 221)

Love is thus associated with the East; either eastern lands
or the upblazing rise of day. The sun is variously used
in Shakespeare's love imagery; often in the Sonnets, as I
have noted, in contrast with clouds and tempests. For
tempests as I have observed, are but part of a wider universal symbolism. 'Majesty' is noteworthy, too. Love's
royalty and earthly kingship are often compared: which
comparison is most important. The same sun and

majesty comparisons occur in a love passage from
1 Henry VI:

> O stay! I have no power to let her pass;
> My hand would free her, but my heart says no.
> As plays the sun upon the glassy streams,
> Twinkling another counterfeited beam,
> So seems this gorgeous beauty to mine eyes.

And:

> Ay, beauty's princely majesty is such,
> Confounds the tongue and makes the senses rough.
>
> (*1 Henry VI*, v. iii, 60–71)

Helena, too, in *All's Well*, uses similar imagery:

> . . . thus, Indian-like,
> Religious in mine error, I adore
> The sun, that looks upon his worshipper,
> But knows of him no more.   (I. iii. 210)

The love-India-jewel association is perfect in *As You
Like It*:

> From the East to Western Ind
> No jewel is like Rosalind.   (III. ii. 93)

Love beckons to a sea-shore fairyland, to imperial delight,[1]
to dances and song-music on the level sands:

> Bid me discourse, I will enchant thine ear,
> Or, like a fairy, trip upon the green,
> Or, like a nymph, with long dishevell'd hair,
> Dance on the sands and yet no footing seen.
>
> (*Venus and Adonis*, 145)

Such are the Siren voices which break through the Shakespearian tempests: rich stones, unvalued merchandise,
thoughts of orient fire and imperial splendour on mysterious and Indian shores, safe fairylands of love and music
by the sands of the endangering sea.

---

[1] The Shakespearian imagery of love's paradisal delight in terms of both
sea-shore dances and imperial splendour is exactly reflected in Wordsworth's 'Immortality' ode. There the dances of children on the shore
towards the end suggest the paradise which is earlier imaged as an 'imperial
palace'.

III

THE ROMANTIC COMEDIES

I

I PASS to the Romantic Comedies, whose patterns will help us to understand tempests or whose tempests will simplify our understanding of their patterns. We have, in my last section, seen an abundance of pure tempests. I shall therefore vary the monotony by noticing first plays where no actual tempests occur powerfully, observing in them, however, the kindred effects of sun, nature, spring and winter, and, wherever it occurs, music. Clearly in our Romances music and other optimistic impressions will preponderate over tempests; just as in our Histories tempests preponderate over music. Merchandise will be, also, very important. I shall notice these plays, therefore, in order of convenience rather than composition. From *All's Well That Ends Well* I have already quoted and shall quote again. My first group, where actual and vigorous tempests are not exceedingly powerful, will include *Love's Labour's Lost*, and *As You Like It*, plays notable for a summer-winter opposition; and *Much Ado*, where we find especially, 'birds' and 'dances'. Thereafter we have plays where the sea, in calm or tempest, is important in imagery or action: *The Two Gentlemen of Verona*, *The Merry Wives of Windsor*, *The Taming of the Shrew*, *The Comedy of Errors*, *Twelfth Night*, and *The Merchant of Venice*. Finally, I offer a more comprehensive analysis of *A Midsummer Night's Dream*.

In *Love's Labour's Lost*, love is often imaged as a sun or moon, and this continual association is important. It recurs throughout Shakespeare, especially powerful in the Sonnets. Also it is indirectly helpful to our understanding of tempests, since tempests of sky or human passion obscure the lights of heaven, the sun, the moon, or

again, the eyes of love. Now in this play 'learning' is
clearly a rival to 'love': and it is natural that 'truth' also
should be imaged as a 'sun'. The same process occurs in
Much Ado where wit gives place to love just as learning
does here. In that play both wit and love blend with the
bird-imagery of the play; and similarly in *Antony and
Cleopatra* both the empire theme and its victor, the love
theme, are equally to be related to the fine effects of imperial splendour. Biron speaks at length using the sun
image, contrasting the sun of truth with the sun of love.
(I. i. 72–93.) Usually, however, the sun is a pure love
symbol:

> So sweet a kiss the golden sun gives not
>   To those fresh morning drops upon the rose,
> As thy eye-beams, when their fresh rays have smote
>   The night of dew that on my cheeks down flows:
> Nor shines the silver moon one half so bright
>   Through the transparent bosom of the deep,
> As doth thy face through tears of mine give light;
>   Thou shinest in every tear that I do weep.
>   (IV. iii. 26)

Sun, moon, and the pictured idea of still, 'transparent',
water: all these are typical of the Shakespearian love
poetry. So Biron, mocking at Dumain's infatuation, caps
his words about his lady, 'as fair as day', with 'Ay, as some
days; but then no sun must shine' (IV. iii. 90–1). I have
already in my last chapter quoted a glorious speech where
Biron compares his Rosaline to the rising sun, at 'the first
opening of the gorgeous east', before which the Indian
worshipper bows his 'vassal head' (IV. iii. 221–8). The
King's answer is typical:

> What zeal, what fury, hath inspired thee now?
> My love, her mistress, is a gracious moon;
> She an attending star, scarce seen a light.
>   (IV. iii. 229)

Biron answers with more praises of his lady, concluding:

> A wither'd hermit, five-score winters worn,
>   Might shake off fifty, looking in her eye:

Beauty doth varnish age, as if new-born,
   And gives the crutch the cradle's infancy:
O, 'tis the sun that maketh all things shine.

(IV. iii. 242)

The thought of age, the 'wither'd hermit', associated with
'winter' is important: and both are contrasted with 'beauty'
and the 'sun'. Thus women's eyes 'sparkle still the right
Promethean fire' (IV. iii. 351). In the mask, the ladies are
asked to behold the show with their 'sun-beamed eyes'
(v. ii. 168). Again, Biron repeats his former imagery:

Vouchsafe to show the sunshine of your face,
   That we, like savages, may worship it.   (v. ii. 201)

Then:

Rosaline. My face is but a moon, and clouded too.
King. Blessed are clouds, to do as such clouds do!
   Vouchsafe, bright moon, and these thy stars, to shine,
   Those clouds removed, upon our watery eyne.

(v. ii. 203)

But Rosaline is only variably kind: 'Thus change I like
the moon' (v. ii. 212). Again, from a love-speech of Biron:

   . . . when we greet,
With eyes best seeing, heaven's fiery eye,
By light we lose light. . . .   (v. ii. 374)

The image is scattered over the play. And it is important
throughout Shakespeare, such lights blending with soft
airs, flowers, music, and love.

Another speech here may be quoted to illustrate the
use of gentle air and spring imagery:

On a day—alack the day!—
Love, whose month is ever May,
Spied a blossom passing fair
Playing in the wanton air:
Through the velvet leaves the wind,
All unseen, can passage find;
That the lover, sick to death,
Wish himself the heaven's breath.
Air, quoth he, thy cheeks may blow;
Air, would I might triumph so!

But, alack, my hand is sworn
Ne'er to pluck thee from thy thorn;
Vow, alack, for youth unmeet,
Youth so apt to pluck a sweet! (iv. iii. 101)

Spring, flowers, the 'wanton air' of May, 'heaven's breath'—we may recall Banquo's use of the phrase—'love' and springtime delight: all this is typical, and to be set against tempests. The play riots in luxuriant imagery not only of love, sun, fire, but of flowers, air, and all springtime happiness:

King. Biron is like an envious sneaping frost
That bites the first-born infants of the spring.
Biron. Well, say I am; why should proud summer boast
Before the birds have any cause to sing?
Why should I joy in any abortive birth?
At Christmas I no more desire a rose
Than wish a snow in May's new-fangled mirth;
But like of each thing that in season grows. (i. i. 100)

And there is music. Music is often the voice of love in Shakespeare. Here in Armado it is the voice of self-love:

A man in all the world's new fashion planted,
That hath a mint of phrases in his brain;
One whom the music of his own vain tongue
Doth ravish like enchanting harmony. (i. i. 165)

There is the scene between Armado and Moth:

Armado. Warble, child; make passionate my sense of hearing.
Moth. Concolinel. [*Singing*
Armado. Sweet air! Go, tenderness of years; take this key, give enlargement to the swain, bring him festinately hither: I must employ him in a letter to my love. (iii. i. 1)

Love and music are continually thus associated. Moth emphasizes the intimate connexion between songs and love:

. . . to jig off a tune at the tongue's end, canary to it with your feet, humour it with turning up your eyelids, sigh a note and sing a note, sometime through the throat, as if you swallowed love with singing love, sometime through the nose, as if you snuffed up love by smelling love. . . . (iii. i. 11)

There is the music which accompanies the lovers in their disguise:

> *Enter Blackamoors with music; Moth; the King, Biron, Longa-*
> *ville, and Dumain, in Russian habits, and masked.*
>
> (v. ii. 158)

During this scene the 'music plays' (v. ii. 211). The play is thus full of love's delight, love's imagery, and music. Some of the finest love-music lines in Shakespeare occur here. I have quoted them already. Love is

> as sweet and musical
> As bright Apollo's lute, strung with his hair;
> And when Love speaks, the voice of all the gods
> Make heaven drowsy with the harmony.   (iv. iii. 342)

So when a poet's pen is inspired by love his lines

> would ravish savage ears
> And plant in tyrants mild humility.   (iv. iii. 348)

A good instant of the beast-music opposition. The romance and adventurous fire of love 'still climbing trees in the Hesperides' (iv. iii. 341) is finely imaged in this speech of Biron's. The play is full of love's brilliance, its rich glamour and delight. But there is a darker side. The ending of this play is most significant for our future understanding of tempests.

Love's Labour's Lost shows a peculiar rhythm. First we have the three heroes light-heartedly renouncing all joys for study. Their intent is quickly conquered by love: this love thus showing their original purpose to be superficial. Now Biron clearly vindicates the right of love to exert sovereignty over study:

> For when would you, my liege, or you, or you,
> In leaden contemplation have found out
> Such fiery numbers as the prompting eyes
> Of beauty's tutors have enriched you with? (iv. iii. 320)

It is a fine and profound speech. Beauty is the only origin

of understanding, the true impulsive force behind all
learning:

> From women's eyes this doctrine I derive:
> They sparkle still the right Promethean fire;
> They are the books, the arts, the academes,
> That show, contain, and nourish all the world.
>
> (IV. iii. 350)

The poet in this speech well expresses love's imperial
power over all human life. The romantic vision is its only
prize and purpose, it would seem. So, learning put aside,
the lovers gaily prepare for all typical Shakespearian
amatory delights:

> For revels, dances, masks, and merry hours
> Forerun fair Love, strewing her way with flowers.
>
> (IV. iii. 379)

But love is not so easily won. This play of golden merriment may not so readily be allowed the crown of a happy
consummation.

The ladies reject their lovers, telling them that they
must not expect the consummation of love till they have
advanced beyond their scatter-brained and shallow merriment. They must first serve an apprenticeship in grief
and suffering. The King must

> ... go with speed
> To some forlorn and naked hermitage,
> Remote from all the pleasures of the world;
> There stay until the twelve celestial signs
> Have brought about the annual reckoning.
> If this austere insociable life
> Change not your offer made in heat of blood;
> If frosts and fasts, hard lodging and thin weeds
> Nip not the gaudy blossoms of your love,
> But that it bear this trial and last love;
> Then, at the expiration of the year,
> Come challenge me, challenge me by these deserts,
> And, by this virgin palm now kissing thine,
> I will be thine. (V. ii. 804)

Notice with care the poetic impressions here: the lonely

bleakness suggested, far from pleasures and society; the
wintry pain of it and the hunger; and the close relation of
this winter frost of exile to the 'gaudy blossoms' of love.
All this is important: it is an extension of our usual
'tempest' thoughts, which must ever be considered to
blend with all wintry and bleak natural effects. So the
King must, before he enjoys love, first show himself able
to endure this lonely, freezing, and tragic pain. Biron,
whose volatile wit so largely fills the play, has an even
sterner task:

> You shall this twelvemonth term from day to day
> Visit the speechless sick and still converse
> With groaning wretches; and your task shall be,
> With all the fierce endeavour of your wit
> To enforce the pained impotent to smile.

And this clearly shows how close to nature's tempests
and winter sorrow is the other thought of human tragedy
in Shakespeare. The two are never really distinct. Biron
answers:

> To move wild laughter in the throat of death?
> It cannot be; it is impossible:
> Mirth cannot move a soul in agony.
> *Rosalind.* Why, that's the way to choke a gibing spirit,
> Whose influence is begot of that loose grace
> Which shallow laughing hearers give to fools.

She tells him that

> if sickly ears,
> Deaf'd with the clamours of their own dear groans,
> Will hear your idle scorns, continue then,
> And I will have you and that fault withal;
> But if they will not, throw away that spirit. . . .
> (v. ii. 860–77)

'Deaf'd' and 'clamours' are tempest words. Here, too,
we have 'tempest' suggestion. There is deep meaning
here, a meaning which clarifies tempest-themes in the
other comedies: tempests are the condition of romance.
Thoughtless love may well be victor over 'learning'. It

meets a sterner antagonist in knowledge of human suffering. Henceforth romance is ever to be related to tragedy.
No Shakespearian comedy sports in such golden fun at the
start: none ends so sadly. This rhythm is in future reversed: tempests first, then the happy conclusion. *Love's
Labour's Lost* is profound; too profound to find a happy
ending.

The final song is important. First, we have Spring,
and all its delights painted, with yet a suggestion of man's
married infelicity:

> *Spring.* When daisies pied, and violets blue,
>   And lady-smocks all silver-white,
> And cuckoo-buds of yellow hue,
>   Do paint the meadows with delight,
> The cuckoo then, on every tree,
> Mocks married men; for thus sings he,
>   Cuckoo;
> Cuckoo, cuckoo,—O word of fear!
> Unpleasing to a married ear.
>
> When shepherds pipe on oaten straws,
>   And merry larks are ploughmen's clocks,
> When turtles tread, and rooks, and daws,
>   And maidens bleach their summer smocks,
> The cuckoo then, on every tree,
> Mocks married men; for thus sings he,
>   Cuckoo;
> Cuckoo, cuckoo,—O word of fear!
> Unpleasing to a married ear.

Then Winter, freezing and cruel:

> *Winter.* When icicles hang by the wall,
>   And Dick the shepherd blows his nail,
> And Tom bears logs into the hall,
>   And milk comes frozen home in pail,
> When blood is nipp'd, and ways be foul,
> Then nightly sings the staring owl,
>   To-who;
> To-whit, to-who, a merry note,
> While greasy Joan doth keel the pot.

When all aloud the wind doth blow,
   And coughing drowns the parson's saw,
And birds sit brooding in the snow,
   And Marian's nose looks red and raw,
When roasted crabs hiss in the bowl,
Then nightly sings the staring owl,
               To-who;
To-whit, to-who, a merry note,
While greasy Joan doth keel the pot.   (v. ii. 904)

The order is most significant: spring, winter. And yet
the song is, nevertheless, music. The pain is dissolved in
music. So our final statement is:

    The words of Mercury are harsh after the songs of Apollo.

For words would only develop the same thought now,
intuition of romance and bitter grief entwined. The poet's
mood will not shirk the tragic realities which condition all
human joy. And we shall see that in Shakespeare happy
romance must always endure first its tempest.

In *As You Like It*—a much later play, which I notice
here mainly because it has few 'sea' effects and shows a
summer-winter opposition like *Love's Labour's Lost*—we
have a contrast between nature's rough unkindness, or
kindness, and man's more tempestuous cruelty. Our protagonists buy their happiness by suffering, driven out into
the rough winds of wild nature, like Valentine, Lear,
Timon, and Bellarius, expelled from civilization. We
must ever be prepared to relate rough, and especially
cold, nature to 'tempests'. Yet these winds are throughout, explicitly or implicitly, contrasted with the bitterer
cruelties endured through man's ingratitude. At the
start there is discord, division; then human tragedy
blends with nature's rough tempestuous unkindness,
yet less unkind than man; finally all is united to music.
Rosalind and the 'weaker vessel' (II. iv. 6), Celia, thus
brave the storms of exile and leave all comfort and
the 'pride' of civilization, pride 'hugely' flowing 'as the
sea' (II. vii. 72), for the rough Arcadian solitudes of

Arden, its lyric peace and shepherd love. There the Duke welcomes

> the icy fang,
> And churlish chiding of the winter's wind,
> Which, when it bites and blows upon my body,
> Even till I shrink with cold, I smile and say
> 'This is no flattery. . . .'   (II. i. 6)

This winter suggestion is an extension of tempests: clearly, since tempests are but a part of Shakespeare's wider and varied weather-imagery. This life is an Elysium, holding the 'precious jewel' (II. i. 14) of soul-content:

> Under the greenwood tree
> Who loves to lie with me,
> And turn his merry note
> Unto the sweet bird's throat,
> Come hither, come hither, come hither:
> Here shall he see
> No enemy
> But winter and rough weather.   (II. v. 1)

So melody of birds, happy woodland, and human song, are blended. Or, if nature be harsh:

> Blow, blow, thou winter wind,
> Thou art not so unkind
>   As man's ingratitude;
> Thy tooth is not so keen,
> Because thou art not seen,
>   Although thy breath be rude.

And, again:

> Freeze, freeze, thou bitter sky,
> That dost not bite so nigh
>   As benefits forgot:
> Though thou the waters warp,
> Thy sting is not so sharp
>   As friend remember'd not.   (II. vii. 174–90)

We have, too, the brighter spring-song towards the end of the play, a song brimming with the season's happiness:

> It was a lover and his lass,
>   With a hey, and a ho, and a hey nonino,
> That o'er the green corn-field did pass
>   In the spring-time, the only pretty ring-time,
> When birds do sing, hey ding a ding ding:
> Sweet lovers love the spring. (v. iii. 17)

Observe the close association of spring, corn-fields, bird-music, and love. But the first songs struck a more sombre note. Yet in them music itself makes concord with nature's tempests to point the more tempestuous cruelty and iniquity of man: which casts our thoughts forward to *Lear*, *Timon*, and *Cymbeline*.

Here the thought of life's uncertainty, nature's bleak winds, and music are woven for a pattern wherein a land of love and humour blend with tempests to contrast with a background of tragic human ingratitude and discord. But at the end all is joy and harmony. Not only is there our spring-song of delight: at the close Hymen, goddess of marriage, brings together the varied threads of our plot. Hymen joins the lovers' hands, all is recognized and reconciled, and union succeeds our original discords and confusion. There is 'still music'. Hymen speaks:

> Then is there mirth in heaven,
> When earthly things made even
>   Atone together. (v. iv. 114)

Observe the clear suggestion that the romantic consummation is a matter rather of heaven than earth: all happy-ending romances are, fundamentally, transcendental. Again Hymen speaks:

> Peace, ho! I bar confusion:
> 'Tis I must make conclusion
>   Of these most strange events. (v. iv. 131)

A conquest of 'confusion': the Shakespearian imagination ever works in terms of discord and harmony. The visionary quality of these 'comedies' is often ignored. They are all profound. They give us dream-pictures of romantic fulfilment blended with, or set beyond, the tempests which toss mortality. Here our end is music, union, and love. There is a song in honour of Hymen:

> Wedding is great Juno's crown:
> O blessed bond of board and bed!
> 'Tis Hymen peoples every town;
>   High wedlock then be honoured:
> Honour, high honour and renown,
> To Hymen, god of every town.   (v. iv. 147)

There is more music at the end. 'Play, music!' (v. iv. 184). Through all our romances we must see clear tragic relations. As *Love's Labour's Lost* clearly suggests, the poet's integrity will not let him write even fanciful romances without relating their happy conclusions to more sombre themes. There he started light-heartedly; and so finished sadly. Elsewhere he can imagine the tragedies of discord and severance somehow fancifully conquered by union and harmony. But he will not, or cannot, make a single play wherein tragedy is ignored. Thus tempests and music are found in close juxtaposition throughout Shakespeare.

As You Like It has also a few minor images, to be observed. As usual, love or any human adventure is a 'voyage'. Celia is a 'weaker vessel' (II. iv. 6), a phrase, however, of ambiguous suggestion. Love is compared to a 'south sea of discovery' (III. ii. 207). The cynical Jaques thus bids farewell to Touchstone and Audrey:

> And you to wrangling; for thy loving voyage
> Is but for two months victuall'd.   (v. iv. 197)

Love is ever a sea adventure, a 'voyage'. Even Hymen told them that they were 'sure together, as the winter to foul weather' (v. iv. 141). 'Weather' and 'season' imagery is, as usual, significant here:

> . . . No, no, Orlando; men are April when they woo, December when they wed: maids are May when they are maids, but the sky changes when they are wives.
>   (IV. i. 152)

Silvius in **distressful** passion follows Phoebe 'like foggy

South puffing with wind and rain' (III. v. 50). To him any kindness from Phoebe is a 'harvest'.

> I shall think it a most plenteous crop
> To glean the broken ears after the man
> That the main harvest reaps: loose now and then
> A scatter'd smile, and that I'll live upon.   (III. v. 101)

Jaques' wit must have as 'large a charter as the wind' to blow on whom he pleases (II. vii. 48). Adam's old age is 'as a lusty winter, frosty, but kindly' (II. iii. 52). Finally we might observe the close association of the 'hungry' lioness and an oak 'whose boughs were moss'd with age, and high top bald with dry antiquity' (IV. iii. 101–27). The 'tops' of trees, and fierce beasts are often found with tempests: here the 'oak'—a usual tempest-tree—is closely associated with a usual tempest-beast.

Much Ado about Nothing presents a somewhat similar beginning to *As You Like It*. Again, we find two brothers opposed: there has been a war, and now the division is healed. During the action, however, Don John, a first-class villain, puts his evil intents into practice and nearly precipitates tragedy. There is not any powerful tempest imagery: but Don John is himself a tempest force, and we clearly have tempest equivalents in the discord and division which all but undermines the surface fun and merriment.

Much of the play is given over to light-hearted wit. But Benedick and Beatrice are more than jesters: their wit is often merry, sometimes bitter, but never scatter-brained. When the action becomes tragic, they know how to act. And though they scoff at love, when love overtakes them, they know how to love. Now this play of wit and love is accompanied with bird-imagery, dances, and music.[1] First, I observe some bird references:

Benedick. Well, you are a rare parrot-teacher.
Beatrice. A bird of my tongue is better than a beast of yours.
                                          (I. i. 145)

---

[1] For an acknowledgement of a debt here to Miss Spurgeon I refer the reader to my Preface.

Don John, in his sulks, refuses to 'sing' in his 'cage' (I. iii. 35). He calls Hero 'a very forward March-chick' (I. iii. 58). When Benedick is melancholy, there is 'a partridge wing saved' at supper (II. i. 155). Claudio is jealous—therefore:

> Alas, poor hurt fowl! Now will he creep into sedges.
>
> (II. i. 209)

Benedick thinks Don Pedro has forestalled Claudio in love, like a boy stealing a bird's-nest shown him by a friend. Don Pedro answers:

> I will but teach them how to sing, and restore them to the owner.   (II. i. 239)

When Benedick, in the 'orchard' (II. iii. 3), is being trapped into love, Claudio thinks of him as a bird being stalked:

> O, ay: stalk on, stalk on; the fowl sits.   (II. iii. 102)

Again, fishing is suggested: 'Bait the hook well: this fish will bite' (II. iii. 121). Water-life and air-life are both usual in Shakespeare's love imagery, as in *Antony and Cleopatra*. Again, we have the 'oyster' in Benedick's soliloquy (II. iii. 26). Elsewhere we find the crow (I. i. 134), the hawk (III. iv. 55), the capon (v. i. 156), the woodcock (v. i. 158). A bird image is curiously used by Beatrice:

> *Benedick.* You take pleasure then in the message?
> *Beatrice.* Yea, just so much as you may take upon a knife's point
> and choke a daw withal.   (II. iii. 275)

But the best examples of such bird-imagery are found in the scene where Beatrice is tricked. The poetry here strikes a delightful lyric note which contrasts with the prose elsewhere, harmonizing beautifully with the rising love. Hero tells Margaret to let Beatrice know she and Ursula are in the 'orchard' talking of her:

> And bid her steal into the pleached bower,
> Where honeysuckles, ripen'd by the sun,
> Forbid the sun to enter . . .   (III. i. 7)

Again:

> *Hero.*   Now begin.
>   For look where Beatrice, like a lapwing, runs
>   Close by the ground, to hear our conference.
> *Ursula.* The pleasant'st angling is to see the fish
>   Cut with her golden oars the silver stream,
>   And greedily devour the treacherous bait:
>   So angle we for Beatrice; who even now
>   Is couched in the woodbine coverture.   (III. i. 24)

Notice again the lyric river-imagery, the gold and silver suggestion, the water-life. In their talk they compare Beatrice to an untamed falcon:

> No, truly, Ursula, she is too disdainful;
> I know her spirits are as coy and wild
> As haggerds of the rock.   (III. i. 34)

At the end of the scene Beatrice uses the same sort of imagery. This is our loveliest bird-reference of all:

> And, Benedick, love on; I will requite thee,
> Taming my wild heart to thy loving hand.   (III. i. 111)

All this imagery of sweet nature, sun, bird, fish, and translucent stream is continually close bound in Shakespeare with love, fun, happiness. But the reverse is tempest, cloud, ugly or fierce beasts, gloom. Thus all these nature images are here set against 'bears' and 'apes'. The ape is associated with the wit Benedick discards for love (v. i. 209) and the state of maidenhood discarded by Beatrice:

> ... therefore I will even take sixpence in earnest of the bear-
> ward and lead his apes into hell.   (II. i. 42)

'Bear-ward': bears, too, are to be contrasted with our lyric love images. Beatrice and Benedick in their wit combats are as 'two bears' (III. ii. 80). The bear is one of Shakespeare's favourite—or rather most hated—animals. But though this wit may have one aspect bear-like in comparison with the love they reach at the end, it is also an airy volatile essence blending with the bird suggestion throughout. Hence the many references to arrows and

shooting. Benedick 'challenged Cupid at the flight' and
a fool, says Beatrice, answered by challenging Benedick
'at the bird-bolt' (I. i. 40–2). Benedick carries on the
image, suggesting that if he ever falls in love, Pedro may
hang him 'in a bottle like a cat' and shoot at him (I. i. 267).
This volatile imagery blends with the volatility of swift
wit or swift love (both are often 'swift' in Shakespeare[1]):
hence 'quips' and 'sentences' are 'paper bullets of the
brain' (II. iii. 260). And all this suggestion of swift wit,
only less ethereal and birdlike than the love that van-
quishes it, is to be set against the dull wits of Dogberry,
who, in aspiring to intelligence, is to be 'writ down an
ass'. In which opposition of the ethereal and asinine we
clearly have a parallel to Bottom and Titania. Indeed,
Dogberry and Verges are respectively very similar to
Bottom and Quince.

We may contrast also with our general love-imagery
such lines as these:

> Why, what's the matter,
> That you have such a February face,
> So full of frost, of storm and cloudiness?   (v. iv. 40)

Set against our two Orchard scenes of comedy and
romance we have the gloomy one where Don John's
drunkard villain Borachio tells Conrade of his master's
iniquitous plot. The weather is appropriate for villainy:

> Stand thee close, then, under this pent-house, for it drizzles
> rain; and I will, like a true drunkard, deliver all to thee.
>
> (III. iii. 110)

Shakespeare imagines most things in terms of weather.
Conrade, addressing Don John, uses characteristic
weather-imagery:

> You have of late stood out against your brother, and he hath
> ta'en you newly into his grace; where it is impossible you should
> take true root but by the fair weather that you make yourself:
> it is needful that you frame the season for your own harvest.
>
> (I. iii. 22)

---

[1] For further thoughts on this strain of imagery see Appendix A, 'The
Shakespearian Aviary'.

A typical speech. So Beatrice tells Benedick he is 'duller than a great thaw' (II. i. 251), and Benedick says that Beatrice exceeds Hero in beauty as much as 'the first of May doth the last of December' (I. i. 201): a characteristic use of seasons.

But except for Don John, himself a tempest, the negative forces are not strong here. I have noticed the spring or summery suggestions, the birds and fishes. Miss Spurgeon has also observed 'riding' metaphors. There are very many. And we continually find the 'horse' and 'riding' closely associated with other happy effects in Shakespeare, though speed-imagery, with 'riding' suggestion, may be satanic, as in *Macbeth*. It remains now to notice music. Music is often suggested. This is typical: 'Come, in what key shall a man take you, to go in the song?' (I. i. 194). In the masked ball Pedro's hidden face is compared to a 'lute', his visor to its 'case' (II. i. 98); and, again, when Benedick is in love his 'jesting spirit' is 'crept into a lute-string and is now governed by stops' (III. ii. 60). In the same way Claudio, relinquishing 'war' for 'love', gives over 'the drum and the fife' for 'the tabor and the pipe' (II. iii. 13–14). Beatrice in distress, love's melancholy, is 'out of tune':

> *Hero.* Why, how now? do you speak in the sick tune?
> *Beatrice.* I am out of all other tune, methinks.
> *Margaret.* Clap's into 'Light o' love', that goes without a burden: do you sing it, and I'll dance it.   (III. iv. 41)

'Dance'. There is much dancing here. 'There was a star danc'd' and under it was Beatrice born (II. i. 349). There is the elaborate masked ball with music in Act II, and the dance talk therein. Characteristically, the company of gliding dancers is imaged as a 'fleet':

> I am sure he is in the fleet: I would he had boarded me.
>   (II. i. 148)

Sea and music thought often blend thus. The play ends with a dance, and its last words are, 'Strike up, pipers'.

The play is full of music, dance, and wit. Beatrice compares the fortunes of marriage to dances:

> For, hear me, Hero: wooing, wedding, and repenting, is as a Scotch jig, a measure, and a cinque pace: the first suit is hot and hasty, like a Scotch jig, and full as fantastical; the wedding, mannerly modest, as a measure, full of state and ancientry; and then comes repentance and, with his bad legs, falls into the cinque pace faster and faster, till he sink into his grave.
>
> (II. i. 75)

All effects of music and dance are clearly closely associated with love. And there is song-music. Before the trapping of Benedick there is music and a song:

> *Don Pedro.* Come, shall we hear this music?
> *Claudio.* Yea, my good lord. How still the evening is,
>   As hush'd on purpose to grace harmony!   (II. iii. 39)

The love-music association is ever close: here music sets the note and prepares the atmosphere for love. It is verbally entwined, too, with love ideas. Balthasar at first is reluctant to 'slander music' with his voice, and Pedro says: 'I pray thee, sing, and let me woo no more'. Balthasar answers:

> Because you talk of wooing, I will sing;
> Since many a wooer doth commence his suit
> To her he thinks not worthy. Yet he wooes,
> Yet will he swear he loves.   (II. iii. 51)

He speaks 'crochets'. Benedick listens to the music. Critic of love, he aptly criticizes music, too:

> Now, divine air! now is his soul ravished! Is it not strange that sheeps' guts should hale souls out of men's bodies?
>
> (II. iii. 60)

Then there is the song with a typical sea-image:

> Sigh no more, ladies, sigh no more,
>   Men were deceivers ever,
> One foot in sea and one on shore,
>   To one thing constant never.   (II. iii. 64)

Toward the close of *Much Ado* there is a Chapel scene, where Claudio repents his rash cruelty to Hero:

> Now, music, sound, and sing your solemn hymn.
> (v. iii. 11)

There follows the song:

> Pardon, goddess of the night,
> Those that slew thy virgin knight;
> For the which, with songs of woe,
> Round about her tomb they go.
>   Midnight, assist our moan;
>   Help us to sigh and groan,
>   Heavily, heavily:
>   Graves, yawn and yield your dead,
>   Till death be uttered,
>   Heavily, heavily.   (v. iii. 12)

Song-music in Shakespeare continually accompanies love's tragedy. Notice here the suggestion of resurrection at the close of the song. And, indeed, Hero is restored. The Final Plays are forecast. So, too, Hymen in *As You Like It* reminds us of those plays. Shakespeare's early comedies are not different in texture from his latest work: in both discord, death, and tempest are set against unity, love, and music. In these earlier plays, the final visions are often vaguely foreshadowed. At the close of this scene we have some interesting lines on dawn:

> Good morrow, masters; put your torches out:
>   The wolves have prey'd; and look, the gentle day,
> Before the wheels of Phoebus, round about
>   Dapples the drowsy east with spots of grey.
> (v. iii. 24)

In this passage, as in *Macbeth*, the wolf is associated with the dark hours. 'Wolves'. The wolf is a tempest beast, to be contrasted with pretty song-birds, especially the nightingale or lark. Here we have no lark, but the dawn practically implies the lark to Shakespeare. Darkness and light are always important in Shakespeare's imagery: and the dawn-effects in Shakespeare always particularly beautiful.

II

I have observed three romances. In *Love's Labour's Lost* we noticed primarily a sun-winter opposition; in *As You Like It*, human treachery more cruel than nature's bitter winds, giving place to nature's kindness, song, music, and love; in *Much Ado*, birds, music, and dance, opposed to drizzling rain, treachery, and discord. The tempest-music opposition is at the root of all these. I pass now to romances where the sea plays an important part, in imagery, plot, or both.

First I shall observe the varied sea suggestions in *The Two Gentlemen of Verona*. They are particularly fine and often presented with an amazing lyrical and happy beauty. The sea in Shakespeare is not necessarily tempestuous: imaged as calm, it may often blend with music. Here Julia and Proteus love each other. Julia receives a love-letter from Proteus, and tears it to pieces, pretending anger. After, she pieces it together, reproaching herself the while:

> Be calm, good wind, blow not a word away
> Till I have found each letter in the letter,
> Except mine own name: that some whirlwind bear
> Unto a ragged fearful-hanging rock
> And throw it thence into the raging sea!   (I. ii. 118)

'Raging' again. Now in this play the sea is powerful. It separates Proteus and Julia just as their love begins. Seas in Shakespeare continually separate lovers. Proteus is sent abroad, as is customary for young men—like Lucentio in *The Taming of the Shrew*—to widen their experience:

> Some to the wars, to try their fortune there;
> Some to discover islands far away.   (I. iii. 8)

To Proteus it is a tragedy:

> Thus have I shunn'd the fire for fear of burning,
> And drench'd me in the sea, where I am drown'd.
> I fear'd to show my father Julia's letter,

Lest he should take exceptions to my love;
And with the vantage of mine own excuse
Hath he excepted most against my love.
O, how this spring of love resembleth
   The uncertain glory of an April day,
Which now shows all the beauty of the sun,
   And by and by a cloud takes all away!   (I. iii. 78)

Here both sea and weather imagery are used to suggest
the tragedy of young love. Observe the sun-obscuring
qualities of the cloud. So Proteus leaves with Launce.
Launce describes the grief of parting:

> I think Crab my dog be the sourest-natured dog that lives: my
> mother weeping, my father wailing, my sister crying, our maid
> howling, our cat wringing her hands, and all our house in a
> great perplexity, yet did not this cruel-hearted cur shed one
> tear.   (II. iii. 5)

Thus sea journeys tend to be things of grief. Next
Panthino enters:

> . . . What's the matter? Why weepest thou, man? Away,
> ass! you'll lose the tide, if you tarry any longer.
>   (II. iii. 38)

There is punning on the word 'tied' and 'tide'. Panthino
continues:

> Tut, man, I mean thou'lt lose the flood, and, in losing the
> flood, lose thy voyage, and, in losing thy voyage, lose thy
> master. . . .   (II. iii. 46)

Finally, with typical 'wind' and 'sigh' association:

> *Launce.* Lose the tide, and the voyage, and the master, and the
> service, and the tied! Why, man, if the river were dry, I am
> able to fill it with my tears; if the wind were down, I could
> drive the boat with my sighs.   (II. iii. 56)

The tide-tears association is usual in Shakespeare; Proteus
used it earlier:

> The tide is now: nay, not thy tide of tears:
> That tide will stay me longer than I should.
>   (II. ii. 14)

The parting of lovers by sea is a usual idea. Here we have
an actual sea journey as part of the plot.

The sea is often love's enemy, the barrier of love's rich merchandise, and the 'jewel' of love, as I have noted, is often lost in tempestuous seas. But happy love may transform the ocean and its rocks themselves to riches:

> *Valentine.*   . . . Why, man, she is mine own,
>   And I as rich in having such a jewel
>   As twenty seas, if all their sand were pearl,
>   The water nectar and the rocks pure gold.   (II. iv. 168)

Notice the peculiar brilliance of our sea-imagery. The sea is associated with gold, pearls, jewels. Another passage has some lovely sea and tear imagery:

> Ay, ay; and she hath offer'd to the doom—
> Which, unreversed, stands in effectual force—
> A sea of melting pearl, which some call tears:
>
>   .   .   .   .   .
>
> But neither bended knees, pure hands held up,
> Sad sighs, deep groans, nor silver-shedding tears,
> Could penetrate her uncompassionate sire;
> But Valentine, if he be ta'en, must die.
> Besides, her intercession chafed him so. .
>
>   (III. i. 222)

'Chafed' again. And in our next quotation we have a fine river-image. Julia's fiery love is fierce as a torrent:

> The more thou damm'st it up, the more it burns,
> The current that with gentle murmur glides,
> Thou know'st, being stopp'd, impatiently doth rage;
> But when his fair course is not hindered,
> He makes sweet music with the enamell'd stones,
> Giving a gentle kiss to every sedge
> He overtaketh in his pilgrimage,
> And so by many winding nooks he strays
> With willing sport to the wild ocean.
> Then let me go and hinder not my course:
> I'll be as patient as a gentle stream
> And make a pastime of each weary step,
> Till the last step have brought me to my love;
> And there I'll rest, as after much turmoil
> A blessed soul doth in Elysium.   (II. vii. 24)

Here we have a powerful torrent-music contrast.
Notice how the gentle stream 'makes music' and 'kisses'
the sedge. Music and love are ever close. Notice, too, the
word 'pilgrimage', a religious colouring often given to
love. But thwarted passion is like a 'raging' stream—the
usual epithet: a torrent may often thus take the place of
tempestuous seas. The sea here is 'wild'. Notice the conclusion: the consummation of love is like 'Elysium' to the
'blessed soul'. Throughout Shakespeare we must be prepared to regard the love interest of his plots with a mystical
sympathy responding to the poet's imagination.

Music is important here, related, as usual, to love:

> Except I be by Silvia in the night,
> There is no music in the nightingale;
> Unless I look on Silvia in the day,
> There is no day for me to look upon. . . .   (III. i. 178)

The nightingale's music is continually associated with
love. And we have a fine love-poetry speech:

> *Duke.* Ay.
>   Much is the force of heaven-bred poesy.
> *Proteus.* Say that upon the altar of her beauty
>   You sacrifice your tears, your sighs, your heart:
>   Write till your ink be dry, and with your tears
>   Moist it again, and frame some feeling line
>   That may discover such integrity:
>   For Orpheus' lute was strung with poets' sinews,
>   Whose golden touch could soften steel and stones,
>   Make tigers tame and huge leviathans
>   Forsake unsounded deeps to dance on sands.
>   After your dire-lamenting elegies,
>   Visit by night your lady's chamber-window
>   With some sweet concert; to their instruments
>   Tune a deploring dump: the night's dead silence
>   Will well become such sweet-complaining grievance.
>   This, or else nothing, will inherit her.   (III. ii. 71)

The reference to Orpheus is important: it occurs again.
And notice that Orpheus' music touches not only 'steel'
and 'stones' but can tame the 'tiger', an animal in our

tempest-group, and also the 'huge leviathans', monsters
of the deep. We may recall the similar speeches in *Love's
Labour's Lost*, *The Merchant of Venice*, and *The Tempest*.
Observe, too, that these beasts are made to 'dance on
sands': the usual image of the soul's Elysian happiness in
Shakespeare, pointing our thoughts to *Venus and Adonis*,
A Midsummer Night's Dream, and *The Tempest*. Finally,
this music of poetry is to be the voice of love, the only
language with which to serenade the loved one. So, we
have the music of Act IV and the song 'Who is Silvia?'
After it, there is a conversation between Julia and the Host
in which Julia plays on the thought of the false music of
Proteus's love:

> *Host.* How now! are you sadder than you were before? How
> do you, man? the music likes you not.
> *Julia.* You mistake; the musician likes me not.
> *Host.* Why my pretty youth?
> *Julia.* He plays false, father.

Again:

> *Host.* You would have them always play but one thing?
> *Julia.* I would always have one play but one thing.
>
> (IV. ii. 54–72)

In this play the sea is beautiful, its rocks imaged as transformed into gold, itself as 'melting pearl'. Its 'sands' are
often mentioned. Silvia's heart is 'as full of sorrows as the
sea of sands' (IV. iii. 33). The sea is more beautiful than
usual, more calm, a still translucent depth. And music is
here, in our last passage, sad. Sad music and brilliant sea
blend with each other, a process forecasting the Final
Plays. So also Valentine, in exile, sorrowfully enjoys the
sad music of the nightingale:

> How use doth breed a habit in a man!
> This shadowy desert, unfrequented woods,
> I better brook than flourishing peopled towns:
> Here can I sit alone, unseen of any,
> And to the nightingale's complaining notes
> Tune my distresses and record my woes.   (V. iv. 1)

A fine blending of love-sorrow, the nightingale's music,

and a town-nature contrast. This early play here forecasts
As You Like It as surely as its plot elsewhere forecasts *Twelfth Night*. It is throughout rich in typical
imagery, especially sea-imagery used in relation to love:

> A thousand oaths, an ocean of his tears
> And instances of infinite of love
> Warrant me welcome to my Proteus.   (II. vii. 69)

In no early play does the poet write of the sea with such
jewelled delight, so rich and strange an extravagance.
Here our main opposition, or association, is the sea, thus
rapturously imagined, and music.

The *Merry Wives of Windsor* has some notable imagery.
There is a fine description of Sackerson, the bear, at the
beginning of the play. And before passing to sea-imagery
we might observe Fenton's comparison of love with
'gold':

> Albeit I will confess thy father's wealth
> Was the first motive that I woo'd thee, Anne:
> Yet, wooing thee, I found thee of more value
> Than stamps in gold or sums in sealed bags;
> And 'tis the very riches of thyself
> That now I aim at.   (III. iv. 13)

A very typical speech. Now Falstaff embarks on a love
adventure. The imagery is in the usual tradition. Mistress
Page is compared by him to rich Indian merchandise:

> . . . she bears the purse too; she is a region in Guiana, all gold
> and bounty. I will be cheater to them both, and they shall be
> exchequers to me; they shall be my East and West Indies, and
> I will trade to them both.   (I. iii. 76)

He uses Robin as his messenger:

> Hold, sirrah, bear you these letters tightly;
> Sail like my pinnace to these golden shores.   (I. iii. 88)

And Pistol cries:

> This punk is one of Cupid's carriers:
> Clap on more sails; pursue; up with your fights:
> Give fire: she is my prize, or ocean whelm them all!
>   (II. ii. 141)

Mistress Ford carries on the idea, with modifications:

> What tempest, I trow, threw this whale, with so many tuns
> of oil in his belly, ashore at Windsor?   (II. i. 64)

A most important comparison for our understanding of
this play. We may remember the Leviathan of the *Two
Gentlemen*. Then the image is changed. Mistress Page
uses the phrase 'boarded me':

> *Mistress Ford.* 'Boarding' call you it? I'll be sure to keep him
> above deck.
> *Mistress Page.* So will I: if he come under my hatches, I'll
> never to sea again.   (II. i. 94)

'Boarding' is a very usual Shakespearian metaphor. Here,
perhaps, the ladies are rich ships and Falstaff a pirate.
Page, too, thinks Falstaff's suit a 'voyage':

> If he should intend this voyage towards my wife, I would
> turn her loose to him.   (II. i. 188)

Love's quest is ever a 'voyage' in Shakespeare; though
here, it is nearer 'lust' than 'love'.

In actual fact, too, we may observe that Falstaff is all
but drowned in pursuit of his love:

> The rogues slighted me into the river . . . and you may know
> by my size that I have a kind of alacrity in sinking; if the
> bottom were as deep as hell, I should down. I had been
> drowned, but that the shore was shelvy and shallow,—a death
> that I abhor.   (III. v. 9)

We should observe that in braving 'Ford' Falstaff falls
foul of 'Brook'. The names are significant. The text suggests as much:

> Mistress Ford! I have had ford enough; I was thrown into
> the ford; I have my belly full of ford.   (III. v. 36)

Falstaff's punishment is important. There is poetic justice
in it. He is not only lustful: his whole being is an adver-
tisement for foul bodily indulgence generally. And his
fleshly desires are punished with appropriate ignominy.
He is pushed into a buck-basket:

. . . rammed me in with foul shirts and smocks, socks, foul
stockings, greasy napkins; that, Master Brook, there was the
rankest compound of villanous smell that ever offended
nostril.   (III. v. 90)

He is packed in 'with stinking clothes that fretted in their
own grease' (III. v. 117) and thrown into 'the muddy ditch
close by the Thames side' (III. iii. 16). He is 'half-stewed
in grease' (III. v. 123). The language here continually
emphasizes, broadly, the fatness of Falstaff: metaphors
from 'cheese', 'butter' and 'oil' occur in this connexion.
Falstaff is here 'a whale', bodily grossness personified;
and both his experience in the basket and his particularly
ignominious drowning or semi-drowning are appropriate.
Such ducking is elsewhere imaged as a punishment, particularly undignified, for that most undignified of Shakespeare's persons, Parolles in *All's Well*. Here it is purely
metaphorical, yet equally important. After his shaming,
Parolles, down in fortune, speaks thus of himself:

> I have ere now, sir, been better known to you, when I have
> held familiarity with better clothes; but I am now, sir,
> muddied in fortune's mood, and smell somewhat strong of her
> strong displeasure.

The Clown replies:

> Truly, fortune's displeasure is but sluttish, if it smell so
> strongly as thou speakest of: I will henceforth eat no fish of
> fortune's buttering.

Notice how fishes may suggest foulness as well as pretti-
ness. There is more talk of foul smells. Then:

> Here is a purr of fortune's, sir, or of fortune's cat—but not a
> musk-cat—that has fallen into the unclean fish-pond of her
> displeasure, and, as he says, is muddied withal; pray you, sir,
> use the carp as you may; for he looks like a poor, decayed, in-
> genious, foolish, rascally knave. (*All's Well*, v. ii. 1–25)

'Fishpond', and 'carp'. We are reminded of Caliban and
Trinculo's remark, 'a very ancient and fish-like smell'
(*The Tempest*, II. ii. 27). And, indeed, this matter of

Parolles and Falstaff clearly forecast the punishment of
Caliban, Trinculo, and Stephano in the 'filthy-mantled
pool' (*The Tempest*, IV. i. 182). There essential coarseness
is punished by being thrown into a stinking pool; next,
they are chased and tormented by Prospero's 'spirits'.
Exactly what happens to Falstaff. Excessive fleshiness is
eventually punished by 'spirits' or 'fairies', that spiritual
element that has been outraged by lust or any excessive
bodily indulgence.

So Falstaff, though all but drowned, runs on his fate.
He keeps his appointment at 'Herne's Oak'. He thinks
at last to have accomplished his 'voyage', braved his 'tempest', and come safely into his haven of love in Windsor
Forest:

> . . . Let the sky rain potatoes; let it thunder to the tune of
> Green Sleeves, hail kissing-comfits and snow eringoes; let
> there come a tempest of provocation, I will shelter me here.
>
> (v. v. 20)

But the mock-fairies punish him. Evans 'smells' a 'man
of middle-earth':

Mistress Quickly. With trial-fire touch me his finger-end:
    If he be chaste, the flame will back descend
    And turn him to no pain; but if he start,
    It is the flesh of a corrupted heart.
Pistol. A trial, come.
Evans.   Come, will this wood take fire?
                    [*They burn him with their tapers*
Falstaff. Oh, oh, oh!
Mistress Quickly. Corrupt, corrupt, and tainted in desire!
    About him, fairies; sing a scornful rhyme;
    And, as you trip, still pinch him to your time.

Song.
        Fie on sinful fantasy!
        Fie on lust and luxury!
        Lust is but a bloody fire,
        Kindled with unchaste desire,
        Fed in heart, whose flames aspire
        As thoughts do blow them, higher and higher.

> Pinch him, fairies, mutually;
> Pinch him for his villany;
> Pinch him and burn him and turn him about,
> Till candles and starlight and moonshine be out.
>
> (v. v. 88)

Here music and fairies succeed the rough and tumble of farce: and they are set against the earthy whale-like corpulence of Falstaff, his 'voyages' of lust, his muddy mock-drowning. Exactly the same muddy punishment is suffered by those guilty of gluttony in Dante's *Inferno*. Essential earthiness and its tempestuous desires are punished first by a corresponding indignity—'and away went I for foul clothes' (III. v. 108)—and next by fairies and music: these latter suggesting the antithesis of lust, uncleanness, and all earthiness of instinct.

Petruchio's story in *The Taming of the Shrew* may also be told in terms of tempests and music. First, however, I would observe the Induction, beginning with a passage where some typical Shakespearian images suggesting Elysian delight cluster close together:

> Look how thy servants do attend on thee,
> Each in his office ready at thy beck.
> Wilt thou have music? hark! Apollo plays   [*Music*
> And twenty caged nightingales do sing:
> Or wilt thou sleep? We'll have thee to a couch
> Softer and sweeter than the lustful bed
> On purpose trimm'd up for Semiramis.
> Say thou wilt walk; we will bestrew the ground:
> Or wilt thou ride? thy horses shall be trapp'd,
> Their harness studded all with gold and pearl.
> Dost thou love hawking? thou hast hawks will soar
> Above the morning lark: or wilt thou hunt?
> Thy hounds shall make the welkin answer them
> And fetch shrill echoes from the hollow earth.
>
> (Ind. ii. 35)

First we have 'music', then the 'nightingale', then the 'soft' and 'sweet' bed, with thoughts of love. All these are *Antony and Cleopatra* images: a play suggested also by the feminine vowel-sounds in 'Semiramis'. Next we have flowers, implied by the word 'bestrew', and thoughts of 'horses'. 'Horses' are usually idealized in Shakespeare: as in *Venus and Adonis, Henry V, Timon,* and *Antony and Cleopatra.* The word 'trapp'd' recalls *Timon:* 'milk-white horses trapped in silver' (*Timon,* i. ii. 189). These impressions, indeed, correspond closely to those in the early acts of *Timon:* there also we hear of hounds and hunting. 'Flowers' and the word 'strew' also recall *Antony and Cleopatra:* so does the riches-imagery of 'gold' and 'pearl'. Next we have more birds: the 'lark' and 'hawk'. Birds continually accompany Shakespeare's love-poetry, especially powerful in *Much Ado* and *Antony and Cleopatra.* Finally, the 'hounds' are also suggestive of a passage in *A Midsummer Night's Dream* to be observed later. All these are important anti-tempest impressions. Here they build a fine atmosphere of aesthetic pleasure. They are, continued:

> *First Servant.* Say thou wilt course; thy greyhounds are as swift
>   As breathed stags, ay, fleeter than the roe.
> *Second Servant.* Dost thou love pictures? we will fetch thee straight
>   Adonis painted by a running brook
>   And Cytherea all in sedges hid,
>   Which seem to move and wanton with her breath,
>   Even as the waving sedges play with wind. (Ind. ii. 49)

'Greyhounds' are pleasant animals in Shakespeare. Timon is presented with 'greyhounds' as well as 'milk-white horses'. The 'pictures' here recall the painter and his picture in *Timon.* The 'running-stream', playful 'wind', Adonis and Cytherea: all suggest a rich aesthetic delight.

Now all these lovely *Timon* images are curiously thrown at Christopher Sly. Why does the poet lavish such lyrical beauty on this queer theme? The Induction does, however, illustrate very closely the main thread we have just traced in *The Merry Wives:* the opposition between the earthy and spiritual in man. Sly is a drunken 'tinker'. He is found dead-drunk.

Lord. What's here? one dead, or drunk? See, doth he breathe?
Second Hunter. He breathes, my lord. Were he not warm'd with ale,
   This were a bed but cold to sleep so soundly.
Lord. O monstrous beast! how like a swine he lies!
   Grim death, how foul and loathsome is thine image!

(Ind. i. 31)

'Monstrous beast', 'swine', 'foul', 'loathsome'. Imaginatively, this touches many other Shakespearian persons: Falstaff in *The Merry Wives*, Bottom (in so far as his animality is contrasted with Titania), Parolles (in reference to the 'fish-pond' passage recently quoted), and Caliban. The tempest-music opposition may always, indirectly, be related to the conflicts endured by man in the present dispensation due to the co-existence in his nature of two elements, the bestial and spiritual: what Melville in *Clarel* called 'the running conflict of the star and clod'. This conflict is implicit, as I show in *The Wheel of Fire*, in *Lear*. There it is given on a grand scale. In *The Merry Wives* and here it is rather comic. The animal is the 'swine' rather than the 'wolf' or 'bear'. We may remember, however, that the 'boar' is a powerful tragedy force, and that Richard III is compared to a 'hog'. In this sense the swine too is a tempest–beast. And in these comic visions the beast-spirit opposition is particularly forceful. Now here the Lord is struck with the idea of surrounding this drunken sot with the finest aesthetic pleasures:

Second Hunter. It would seem strange unto him when he waked.
Lord. Even as a flattering dream or worthless fancy.
   Then take him up and manage well the jest:
   Carry him gently to my fairest chamber
   And hang it round with all my wanton pictures:
   Balm his foul head in warm distilled waters
   And burn sweet wood to make the lodging sweet:
   Procure me music ready when he wakes,
   To make a dulcet and a heavenly sound;
   And if he chance to speak, be ready straight
   And with a low submissive reverence

Say, 'What is it your honour will command?'
Let one attend him with a silver basin
Full of rose-water and bestrew'd with flowers;
Another bear the ewer, the third a diaper,
And say, 'Will't please your lordship cool your hands?'

(Ind. i. 43)

Notice again the clustering images of fine sensuous delight: 'wanton pictures', 'warm distilled waters', the scent
of 'sweet woods' burning, 'dulcet' and 'heavenly' music, a
'silver basin' with rose-water, and 'bestrew'd with flowers'.
All this is again exactly correspondent to the early acts of
Timon—especially the 'silver basin'. Observe, too, how all
this will seem to the bestial Sly as a 'flattering dream'; and
compare the closely similar speech of Caliban, where there
is music, 'sweet airs' that lure him to sleep, where the
heavens open in dream to disclose riches, so that on
waking he cries 'to sleep again'. In this Induction we have
clearly an exact little dramatic pattern setting exquisite
aesthetic delights against bestiality; and this tug of the
spiritual, wrenching animality from its inertia, is a constant theme in Shakespeare. It vitalizes the *Lear* vision.
This opposition is at the root of the Shakespearian
Tempest: hence the many recurrent tempest-beasts,
especially the wolf and bear. We are not surprised to
find Christopher Sly (may we even see a spiritual-roguery
opposition in his paradoxical name?) has been a 'bear-
herd' (Ind. ii. 21). He may be related to Shakespeare's
tempest-beasts in general, what I have called the 'hate-
theme' in the sombre plays, to Caliban, Falstaff, Dogberry,
and Bottom. Like Bottom, he is fond of 'beef' (Ind. ii. 8).
Indeed, his replies when offered rich food exactly recall
Bottom's answers to the Fairies in a similar situation.

Now the Shakespearian tempest is often, and perhaps
always if we look deep enough, the conflict of the beast
and the angel in man. And here we have clearly a contrast
of these two. One person only in the Induction may be
imagined as enduring a sense of tension, or pain and joy
commingled, owing to these two conflicting incompatibles

in one person: Sly's supposed wife. In her, therefore, we
may expect our tempest. Twice we have it suggested:

> Bid him shed tears, as being overjoy'd
> To see her noble lord restored to health,
> Who for this seven years hath esteemed him
> No better than a poor and loathsome beggar:
> And if the boy have not a woman's gift
> To rain a shower of commanded tears,
> An onion will do well for such a shift. . . .
>
> (Ind. i. 120)

'To rain a shower'. Later Sly is told of his sorrowing
spouse:

> And till the tears that she hath shed for thee
> Like envious floods o'er-run her lovely face,
> She was the fairest creature in the world. . . . (Ind. ii. 66)

The bestial on one side; the spiritual (especially 'music')
on the other; and, resultant from this conflict, a 'shower'
and 'envious floods'. Curiously, this Induction is a perfect
signpost to our understanding of *Lear* and, indeed,
Shakespeare's work as a whole. In it we see the Caliban-
Ariel opposition.

I pass to the story of Petruchio and Katharina. Petruchio's story may be told in terms of tempests. He is a
strong man who boasts:

> Have I not in my time heard lions roar?
> Have I not heard the sea puff'd up with winds
> Rage like an angry boar chafed with sweat?
> Have I not heard great ordnance in the field,
> And heaven's artillery thunder in the skies?
>
> (I. ii. 201)

Notice the beasts: 'lions', the 'angry boar', and the usual
word 'chafed'. Elsewhere a man 'rages' like 'a chafed
bull' and threatens 'death' (3 *Henry VI*, II. v. 126–7).
Notice especially here the close tempest-boar association. We may remember how in *Venus and Adonis* love's
tragedy is brought about by 'an angry-chafing boar'
(*Venus and Adonis*, 662). Now Petruchio's fight is

pre-eminently a fight with a tempest. Katharina is a
'wild-cat'—another tempest-beast: 'Will you woo this
wild-cat?' (I. ii. 197) asks Gremio. Again,

> For I am he am born to tame you, Kate,
> And bring you from a wild Kate to a Kate
> Conformable as other household Kates. (II. i. 270)

Here again, as in the Induction, we are pointed to a contrast between the bestial and the spiritual in humanity.
Katharina is also like a tempest:

> . . . Mark'd you not how her sister
> Began to scold and raise up such a storm
> That mortal ears might hardly endure the din?
> (I. i. 176)

But Petruchio will woo her though she be as 'rough'

> As are the swelling Adriatic seas. (I. ii. 73)

Again, when Hortensio says he 'would not wed her for a
mine of gold', Petruchio replies:

> Hortensio, peace! thou know'st not gold's effect:
> Tell me her father's name and 'tis enough;
> For I will board her, though she chide as loud
> As thunder when the clouds in autumn crack.
> (I. ii. 93)

'Board' is a usual Shakespearian metaphor for any human
encounter. He will meet her 'fire' like a blast of wind
whose 'extreme gusts' will blow it out, for he is as
'peremptory as she proud-minded' (II. i. 132). 'Peremptory' we have met before. So he goes to her armed

> as mountains are for winds,
> That shake not though they blow perpetually.
> (II. i. 141)

Mountains, with their 'pines', are elsewhere found in
tempest passages, resisting 'winds'. Katharina's temper
is indeed tempestuous. It is like 'frosts' or 'whirlwinds'
spoiling beauty's flower, stirring up her crystal beauty like
a muddy stream. These 'frosts' and 'whirlwinds' suggest

the close relation of all wintry effects to tempests. Her temper

> ... blots thy beauty as frosts do bite the meads,
> Confounds thy fame as whirlwinds shake fair buds,
> And in no sense is meet or amiable.
> A woman moved is like a fountain troubled,
> Muddy, ill-seeming, thick, bereft of beauty;
> And while it is so, none so dry or thirsty,
> Will deign to sip or touch one drop of it.   (v. ii. 139)

So speaks Katharina at the end. But first she has to be conquered.

Throughout Petruchio behaves with shipman's manners. At the moment of his first victory at the church, having married her, he aptly celebrates his central success like a sailor after a tempest:

> 'A health!' quoth he, as if
> He had been aboard, carousing to his mates
> After a storm.   (iii. ii. 172)

Such an image at so especially crucial a point—it is the same in *Timon*—seems to suggest that the poet, even when actual tempests are not present, yet is all the time, as it were, seeing his story as a sea-adventure. And this tempest-victory is naturally accompanied by music:

> Such a mad marriage never was before:
> Hark, hark! I hear the minstrels play.   [*Music*
>   (iii. ii. 184)

So, at the close, Katharina recognizes the strong masculine power that, being made to fight the tempests of existence, gives man the right and prerogative of tempestuous behaviour. A husband is

> one that cares for thee,
> And for thy maintenance commits his body
> To painful labour both by sea and land,
> To watch the night in storms, the day in cold,
> Whilst thou liest warm at home, secure and safe.
>   (v. ii. 147)

Another cold-storm association: all bleak effects blend with tempests.

But these themes of tempest and wild-beast rage are everywhere woven with themes of music, maiden docility, costly dowries, merchants, and ships. Bianca is to be contrasted with Katharina. Her sweetness is given lovely sea-imagery:

> *Lucentio.* O yes, I saw sweet beauty in her face,
>   Such as the daughter of Agenor had,
>   That made great Jove to humble him to her hand,
>   When with his knees he kiss'd the Cretan strand.
>
> (I. i. 172)

Again 'strand'. She has 'coral lips' (I. i. 179). Set between these two pieces of love-imagery is a description—already quoted—of Katharina's 'storms'. The contrast is vivid. Hortensio woos Bianca in guise of a music-master: 'a fine musician, to instruct our mistress' (I. ii. 174). Music, we are here told, refreshes 'the mind of man' (III. i. 11). His music-lesson is really a love-lesson. So he cannot tolerate a third presence:

> You may go walk, and give me leave a while;
> My lessons make no music in three parts.
>
> (III. i. 59)

A clear music-love association. In this scene there is much talk of music, and of Hortensio's tuning of his instrument. Finally, he gives his lesson in terms of love. Bianca reads it:

> 'Gamut' I am, the ground of all accord,
>   'A re' to plead Hortensio's passion;
> 'B mi', Bianca, take him for thy lord,
>   'C fa ut', that loves with all affection:
> 'D sol re', one clef, two notes have I:
>   'E la mi', show pity, or I die.   (III. i. 73)

Finally Bianca weds Lucentio:

> *Biondello.* I have seen them in the church together: God send
>   'em good shipping!   (V. i. 42)

Marriage is a sea-voyage. Music and Bianca are thus to be contrasted with tempests and Katharina. Hence

Katharina and music do not agree: they are clearly opposites. Thus in his sarcasm Petruchio says:

> Say that she rail; why then I'll tell her plain
> She sings as sweetly as the nightingale:
> Say that she frown; I'll say she looks as clear
> As morning roses newly wash'd with dew.   (II. i. 171)

I have already referred to the nightingale's music: it is frequent in Shakespeare's love-passages. Also 'dew' and 'roses' are typical examples of tempests inverted. Now Katharina naturally opposes a music-master:

> *Baptista.* What, will my daughter prove a good musician?
> *Hortensio.* I think she'll sooner prove a soldier:
> Iron may hold with her but never lutes.
> *Baptista.* Why, then thou canst not break her to the lute?
> *Hortensio.* Why, no; for she hath broke the lute to me.
> I did but tell her she mistook her frets,
> And bow'd her hand to teach her fingering;
> When, with a most impatient devilish spirit,
> 'Frets, call you these?' quoth she; 'I'll fume with them':
> And with that word, she struck me on the head,
> And through the instrument my pate made way;
> And there I stood amazed for a while,
> As on a pillory, looking through the lute;
> While she did call me rascal fiddler
> And twangling Jack.   (II. i. 145)

A very vivid tempest-music contrast. At the moment of Petruchio's tempest-victory, when he returns married from church, just after the description of him as a 'mate' on shipboard 'after a storm', there is, as I have observed, the sound of 'minstrels' and music.

The play is, also, full of other typical imagery. Lucentio has come from Pisa to Padua

> as he that leaves
> A shallow plash to plunge him in the deep
> And with satiety seeks to quench his thirst.   (I. i. 22)

Friends meet with a characteristic phrase:

> And tell me now, sweet friend, what happy gale
> Blows you to Padua here from old Verona?   (I. ii. 47)

Moreover, love is here very clearly a matter of merchandise. Petruchio admittedly braves his 'tempest' primarily for the rich merchandise of Katharina's fortune. Baptista regards it as a merchant transaction, too:

> *Gremio.* Was ever match clapp'd up so suddenly?
> *Baptista.* Faith, Gentlemen, now I play a merchant's part,
>   And venture madly on a desperate mart.
> *Tranio.* 'Twas a commodity lay fretting by you
>   'Twill bring you gain or perish on the seas. (II. i. 319)

Wherein Katharina's matrimonial future is imaged as a voyage. After this dialogue Gremio and Tranio bargain for Bianca. Gremio outlines his riches: plate, gold, basins, ewers, 'Tyrian tapestry', ivory coffers full of crowns, cypress chests, arras counterpoints, costly apparel, tents, canopies, linen, 'Turkey cushions boss'd with pearl', valance of Venice gold in needlework' (II. i. 340–8). It sounds like 'merchandise'. And indeed the two suitors later vie with each other in boast of their ships:

> *Gremio.*   . . . besides an argosy
>   That now is lying in Marseilles' road.
>   What, have I choked you with an argosy?
> *Tranio.* Gremio, 'tis known my father hath no less
>   Than three great argosies; besides two galliasses,
>   And twelve tight galleys: these I will assure her,
>   And twice as much, whate'er thou offer'st next.
>
>   (II. i. 368)

Vincentio is 'a merchant of incomparable wealth' (IV. ii. 97). The play is full of typical themes: tempests, beasts, discord; music, merchandise, riches, and final concord. The final banquet scene is important: banquets, as in *Macbeth* and *Timon*, continually suggesting love and joy. This one Lucentio introduces with a fine phrase:

> At last, though long, our jarring notes agree:
> And time it is, when raging war is done,
> To smile at scapes, and perils overblown.   (V. ii. 1)

'Raging', 'overblown'. An instructive music-tempest contrast.

III

I pass to plays where tempests are even more powerful, where they are actualized as part of the plot. In *The Comedy of Errors* a tempest is important. We are brought to a world of gold and fun where the tragic work of a tempest is finally remedied by reunions. The sea-tempest is here an actual event, the tragic background to a romantic comedy. Aegeon describes, at length, the original tragedy, his words heavy with grief and the turbulence of his misfortunes:

Aegeon. A league from Epidamnum had we sail'd,
Before the always wind-obeying deep
Gave any tragic instance of our harm:
But longer did we not retain much hope;
For what obscured light the heavens did grant
Did but convey unto our fearful minds
A doubtful warrant of immediate death;
Which though myself would gladly have embrac'd,
Yet the incessant weepings of my wife,
Weeping before for what she saw must come,
And piteous plainings of the pretty babes,
That mourned for fashion, ignorant what to fear,
Forced me to seek delays for them and me.
And this it was, for other means was none:
The sailors sought for safety by our boat,
And left the ship, then sinking-ripe, to us:
My wife, more careful for the latter-born,
Had fasten'd him unto a small spare mast,
Such as sea-faring men provide for storms;
To him one of the other twins was bound,
Whilst I had been like heedful of the other.
The children thus dispos'd, my wife and I,
Fixing our eyes on whom our care was fix'd,
Fasten'd ourselves at either end the mast;
And floating straight, obedient to the stream,
Were carried towards Corinth, as we thought.
At length the sun, gazing upon the earth,
Dispersed those vapours that offended us;
And, by the benefit of his wished light,
The seas wax'd calm, and we discovered

Two ships from far making amain to us,
Of Corinth that, of Epidaurus this:
But ere they came,—O, let me say no more!
Gather the sequel by that went before.

Duke. Nay, forward, old man; do not break off so;
For we may pity, though not pardon thee.

Aegeon. O, had the gods done so, I had not now
Worthily term'd them merciless to us!
For, ere the ships could meet by twice five leagues,
We were encounter'd by a mighty rock;
Which being violently borne upon,
Our helpful ship was splitted in the midst;
So that, in this unjust divorce of us,
Fortune had left to both of us alike
What to delight in, what to sorrow for.
Her part, poor soul! seeming as burdened
With lesser weight, but not with lesser woe,
Was carried with more speed before the wind;
And in our sight they three were taken up
By fishermen of Corinth, as we thought.
At length, another ship had seiz'd on us;
And, knowing whom it was their hap to save,
Gave healthful welcome to their shipwreck'd guests;
And would have reft the fishes of their prey,
Had not their bark been very slow of sail,
And therefore homeward did they bend their course.
Thus have you heard me sever'd from my bliss,
That by misfortunes was my life prolong'd,
To tell sad stories of my own mishaps.   (I. i. 63)

Notice here the words 'tragic' and 'disperse', the latter
showing an inversion of the usual use, the 'sun' here
dispersing the tempest as tempests so often 'disperse'
lovers or communities. Observe also the association of the
'sun' with calm seas, and the word 'wax' applied to the sea
as in *Titus Andronicus*. The words 'splitted' and 'fortune'
are important. 'Divorce', too, is powerfully significant, so
is 'sever'd', a usual word. The 'fishermen' recall *Pericles*.
Such a tempest is peculiarly Shakespearian. We meet it
again and again. Tempests always, as here, tragic, tend
to 'disperse', the resulting play to reunite, the people

scattered in the tempest. Antipholus of Syracuse thus
compares himself to a drop of water seeking for another
drop, his mother and brother, in the world's ocean, and so
he 'confounds' and loses himself in the 'quest': he is thus
without 'content' (I. ii. 33–40). These are typical thoughts.
The ocean is the enemy to love's desire, seeking to engulf
the searcher; and 'content', throughout Shakespeare, is
an important word.

So in this play a family is first dispersed by a tempest.
Next, the action shows a remarkable series of mistakes in
a magic land of merchants and riches, with a final consummation in union and happiness. The play is full of
riches-imagery especially. There is the 'thousand marks
in gold' (III. i. 8) that causes so much irritation; the 'two-
hundred ducats' (IV. iv. 137) owed by Angelo; a 'bag of
gold' (IV. iv. 99); 'angels' (IV. iii. 40), a 'diamond' (V. i.
391), 'rings, jewels' (V. i. 144). This is typical:

> Give her this key, and tell her, in the desk
> That's cover'd o'er with Turkish tapestry
> There is a purse of ducats.   (IV. i. 103)

There is the Syracusan Dromio's description of the
kitchen wench in terms of geography including a fine
riches-India association blended with 'caracks'[1]:

Antipholus S. Where America, the Indies?
Dromio S. Oh, sir, upon her nose, all o'er embellished with
rubies, carbuncles, sapphires, declining their rich aspect to the
hot breath of Spain; who sent whole armadoes of caracks to
be ballast at her nose.   (III. ii. 136)

The central action turns on a 'chain of gold', made by the
'goldsmith', Angelo, for the Ephesian Antipholus:

Angelo. Saving your merry humour, here's the note
How much your chain weighs to the utmost carat,
The fineness of the gold and chargeful fashion,
Which doth amount to three odd ducats more
Than I stand debted to this gentleman:
I pray you see him presently discharged,
For he is bound to sea and stays but for it.   (IV. i. 27)

[1] A 'carack' is a merchant vessel.

Angelo owes money to a 'merchant' who is in direct need of it:

> . . I am bound
> To Persia and want guilders for my voyage.   (IV. i. 3)

He is in a hurry: 'both wind and tide' stays for him (IV. i. 46). This chain of gold and all the violent troubles it gives rise to constitute much of the play's later action. 'Gold' is emphasized strongly throughout. Consider this speech:

> When I desired him to come home to dinner,
> He ask'd me for a thousand marks in gold:
> ''Tis dinner time', quoth I; 'My gold!' quoth he:
> 'Your meat doth burn', quoth I; 'My gold!' quoth he:
> 'Will you come home?' quoth I; 'My gold!' quoth he,
> 'Where is the thousand marks I gave thee, villain?'
> 'The pig', quoth I, 'is burn'd'; 'My gold!' quoth he. . . .
> (II. i. 60)

Consider also the jealous Adriana's curious speech:

> I see the jewel best enamelled
> Will lose his beauty; yet the gold bides still,
> That others touch, and often touching will
> Wear gold: and no man that hath a name
> By falsehood and corruption doth it shame.
> (II. i. 109)

The play is full of gold and other riches, of merchants, and sea-voyages. There is continual suggestion both of the 'mart' and of the sea.

The sea is always in the background, especially in the Syracusan Antipholus' constant intention of sailing away:

> Go hie thee presently, post to the road:
> An if the wind blow any way from shore,
> I will not harbour in this town to-night:
> If any bark put forth, come to the mart,
> Where I will walk till thou return to me.
> (III. ii. 152)

Later news is brought (to his brother, however) that there is a 'bark of Epidamnum', a ship 'in her trim', with a 'merry wind' blowing 'fair from land' (IV. i. 85). So here love, as in the *Two Gentlemen*, may be expressed in luxuriantly coloured sea-imagery:

> O, train me not, sweet mermaid, with thy note,
>> To drown me in thy sister's flood of tears:
> Sing, siren, for thyself, and I will dote:
>> Spread o'er the silver waves thy golden hairs,
> And as a bed I'll take them and there lie,
>> And in that glorious supposition think
> He gains by death that hath such means to die:
>> Let Love, being light, be drowned if she sink!
>>>> (III. ii. 45)

Elsewhere in Shakespeare such lovely sea-pictures are word-painted to suggest love immortal; continually they are juxtaposed with song or music. Of such, *The Tempest* itself is built: sirens, music, dances on the yellow sand, and still waters. This is the Shakespearian haven, and heaven, to storm-tossed mortality. But there are tragic essences in this play, too. And it is natural that in this atmosphere of riches, merchants, and tempests, human rage and unrest generally should be directly related to sea-loss:

> *Adriana.* This week he hath been heavy, sour, sad,
>> And much different from the man he was;
>> But till this afternoon his passion
>> Ne'er brake into extremity of rage.
> *Abbess.* Hath he not lost much wealth by wreck of sea?
>> Buried some dear friend? . . .   (v. i. 45)

Notice how the 'wreck' is followed by thought of the death 'of some dear friend'. It suggests *The Merchant of Venice*. The whole is typically Shakespearian.

In *The Comedy of Errors* there is both tragedy and comedy interwoven. Our last quotation may lead us to consider the matter of Adriana's jealousy. She is a trying woman who troubles her husband, and in her much of the later thought of *The Taming of the Shrew* is personified. She, too, is 'shrewish' (III. i. 2). Luciana tries to persuade her that women should be subject to their husbands' wills:

> Why, headstrong liberty is lash'd with woe.
> There's nothing situate under heaven's eye

> But hath his bound, in earth, in sea, in sky:
> The beasts, the fishes, and the winged fowls
> Are their males' subjects and at their controls:
> Men, more divine, the masters of all these,
> Lords of the wide world and wild watery seas,
> Indued with intellectual sense and souls,
> Of more pre-eminence than fish and fowls,
> Are masters to their females, and their lords:
> Then let your will attend on their accords.   (II. i. 15)

Notice the comparison of human family order with vast symbols of order, natural and universal. Notice, too, how closely this elevation of man as lord of the 'wild watery seas' resembles a passage I have quoted from *The Taming of the Shrew* when Katharina admits the supremacy of man who commits his body to labour 'by sea, and land' and gives himself 'to watch the night in storms' for his wife's sake. Now Adriana is a tempest force here. The Abbess clearly emphasizes the terrors of domestic hostility:

> The venom clamours of a jealous woman
> Poisons more deadly than a mad dog's tooth.   (v. i. 69)

This leads to the 'raging fire' of 'fever', and so to 'madness', and all 'pale distemperatures and foes to life':

> In food, in sport, and life-preserving rest
> To be disturb'd, would mad or man or beast. . . .
>   (v. i. 83)

Which close association of typical Shakespearian life forces may help our understanding of both *Macbeth* and *Antony and Cleopatra*.

Besides Adriana, there are, too, the numerous other mistakes, dissensions, and difficulties that bring the action near to disaster. And we must remember the first grim scene where Aegeon is condemned to death:

> Merchant of Syracusa, plead no more.   (I. i. 3)

'Merchant'. Every one here seems to be a merchant. The word occurs continually: 'merchant' and 'mart'. So

Aegeon describes his tempest-grief, the loss and dispersal of his family. And in this description, quoted at the
start of my essay, we may observe that Aegeon's tragedy
'was wrought by nature, not by vile offence' (I. i. 35).
Such are our tempests often: they suggest the inscrutable
enginry of fate that drives human barks on to their
wreckage. Shakespeare does not only present tragedy in
terms of weak 'character'. And we should here observe
clearly how the tempest is closely associated with themes
of birth—'a joyful mother of two goodly sons' (I. i. 51).
This happy family, this life-joy of father, mother, and their
new-born children, is smashed, severed, 'dispersed' by
'tempest'. So the 'tempest' here is clearly opposed to life,
a death force, 'tragic' (I. i. 65). And throughout the action
Aegeon's first organ dirge of sea sorrow lingers in our
minds, together with the knowledge of his sentence to
death. This play is dark with tragedy.

And yet, set against all this, is our gold-imagery, our
passages of lyric beauty, our sense of rippling comedy. It is
a glorious little play. And, at the close, all is united again,
the end is peace, reunion, and pardon, outside the Abbey
where Aemilia, Aegeon's wife, has long taken refuge.
Aegeon finds one of his twin sons, who does not recognize
him:

> *Aegeon.* Not know my voice! O time's extremity,
>   Hast thou so crack'd and splitted my poor tongue
>   In seven short years, that here my only son
>   Knows not my feeble key of untuned cares?
>   Though now this grained face of mine be hid
>   In sap-consuming winter's drizzled snow
>   And all the conduits of my blood froze up,
>   Yet hath my night of life some memory,
>   My wasting lamps some fading glimmer left,
>   My dull deaf ears a little use to hear. . . .   (v. i. 307)

Observe how the wearing of old age is thus a 'tempest',
implied by the tempest words 'crack'd' and 'splitted';
and how cares are therefore tuneless, or 'untuned'; so
that again tempests and music are contrasted. Next,

10

Aegeon compares himself to a tree 'grained' and its 'sap'
—probably the oak—hidden by winter's drizzling snow,
so that his blood is frozen; which shows how close is the
thought of winter with tempests, and again brings in
the 'tree' symbol so usual in tempest passages. And
finally, observe how our dualism takes a third closely
related form of light as against darkness. Aegeon is
indeed a tragic figure. But all is quickly now resolved:

> *Aegeon.* If I dream not, thou art Aemilia:
>   If thou art she, tell me where is that son
>   That floated with thee on the fatal raft?   (v. i. 346)

So this 'wreck at sea' (v. i. 359) is at last remedied. This
play concludes in joy, its reunions peculiarly forecasting
Pericles. As in *Pericles* Thaisa takes refuge in Diana's
temple, so here Aemilia is an Abbess. We may aptly compare the 'rude fishermen' who rescue Aegeon (v. i. 351)
with the similar fishermen who rescue Pericles. Both plays
show us a story starting with birth, with next the dispersal
of a family in tempest, and then a final reunion. There
is there a more intense religious and mythical suggestion. But here, too, it is more than once recognized that
this Ephesus is a land of supernatural mystery:

> Sure, these are but imaginary wiles
> And Lapland sorcerers inhabit here.   (iv. iii. 10)

In this land of gold, merchants, and mystery, all odds
are made even, all sea sorrow finally dissolved in joy
and love. This play, like *The Taming of the Shrew*, ends
with a feast.

Finally we may note a curious number of house-names
here—either private houses or hotels: the 'Centaur', 'Por-
pentine', 'Phoenix', and 'Tiger'. They are not closely
relevant to my present purpose, save to show that we
cannot be too definite in relating the ship's name *Tiger*
in *Macbeth* and *Twelfth Night* to the tiger as a tempest
beast. In *Twelfth Night* we have two ships, the *Tiger* and
the *Phoenix*, as well as an hotel, the 'Elephant'. Therefore
two of our present house-names are ship-names in *Twelfth*

Night. And possibly we may here best approach a curious speech in *All's Well*. Helena declares how in her heart there is for Bertram a wide stage of love wherein he and his fortunes or disasters play out their act as in another reflected world. It is a lovely speech:

> Not my virginity yet.
> There shall your master have a thousand loves,
> A mother and a mistress and a friend,
> A phoenix, captain, and an enemy,
> A guide, a goddess, and a sovereign,
> A counsellor, a traitress, and a dear;
> His humble ambition, proud humility,
> His jarring concord, and his discord dulcet,
> His faith, his sweet disaster; with a world
> Of pretty, fond, adoptious christendoms,
> That blinking Cupid gossips. Now shall he—
> I know not what he shall.   (*All's Well*, i. i. 179)

Perhaps no lines in Shakespeare more perfectly sum up the delicate mystery of love. Notice how Helena breaks off suddenly as Cleopatra does on a similar occasion where the intuition of love outreaches words. Here I would point especially to the fourth and eighth lines. The one clearly seems to refer to a ship called the *Phoenix*; and it is quite in the usual tradition that such a ship image should take a place among these other wide suggestions of life's fortunes and failures. The other sweetly imagines the loved one's life and human fate as a blending of 'dulcet' concord and 'jarring' discord: which is exactly the final impression and statement of the tempest-music opposition throughout the whole of Shakespeare.

Twelfth Night is an exquisite blending of *The Comedy of Errors* and *The Merchant of Venice*: the plot of the one charged with the imaginative richness and deep emotions of the other. Again the tempest-music opposition is exquisitely developed. Wrecked and divided, the twins, Viola and Sebastian, find themselves in Illyria, land of music and romance. Music is here stronger than in any other of these romantic comedies, and the pattern of romantic love more exquisitely therewith entwined. The tempest which prologues the action is described for us:

> *Viola.* And what should I do in Illyria?
> My brother he is in Elysium.
> Perchance he is not drown'd: what think you, sailors?
> *Captain.* It is perchance that you yourself were saved.
> *Viola.* O my poor brother! and so perchance may he be.
> *Captain.* True, madam: and, to comfort you with chance,
> Assure yourself, after our ship did split,
> When you and those poor number saved with you
> Hung on our driving boat, I saw your brother,
> Most provident in peril, bind himself,
> Courage and hope both teaching him the practice,
> To a strong mast that lived upon the sea;
> Where, like Arion on the dolphin's back,
> I saw him hold acquaintance with the waves
> So long as I could see.   (I. ii. 3)

The association of the sea and 'chance' is important. The thought is often embedded in this tempest-imagery: waves are fickle as fortune, the sea suggests all the chances of mortality. This description of Sebastian in the waters is close to a similar passage on Ferdinand in *The Tempest.* Now Sebastian, too, recalls the wreck. He is with Antonio, bereft of his loved sister, derelict and purposeless: 'my determinate voyage is mere extravagancy' (II. i. 11): here all human adventure is a 'voyage' and nearly every one employs the metaphor. Sebastian tells Antonio of his father, and twin sister; then,

> ... some hour before you took me from the breach of the sea
> was my sister drowned.   (II. i. 23)

There follows a characteristic image:

> ... She is drowned already, sir, with salt water, though I seem
> to drown her remembrance again with more. (II. i. 32)

It is the same as Laertes' thought about the drowned Ophelia:

> Too much of water hast thou, poor Ophelia,
> And therefore I forbid my tears.
> (*Hamlet*, IV. vii. 186)

Antonio later recalls how he rescued Sebastian

> From the rude sea's enraged and foamy mouth.
>
> (v. i. 81)

'Enraged' again. 'A wreck past hope he was', says Antonio. So a tempest here disperses and divides, setting the stage for reunion and joy.

Twelfth Night takes us to a world of music:

> If music be the food of love, play on;
> Give me excess of it, that, surfeiting,
> The appetite may sicken and so die.
> That strain again! it had a dying fall:
> O, it came o'er my ear like the sweet sound,
> That breathes upon a bank of violets,
> Stealing and giving odour.   (i. i. 1)

'Violets'. The name Viola suggests both flowers and music, music of the 'viol', mentioned in *Pericles*. Music and soft zephyrs: we shall find them again in the person of Imogen. Viola can speak 'in many sorts of music' (i. ii. 58). This is a natural phrase. Personal qualities tend to reflect poetic associations. Thus love-heroines are continually gifted with love-associations: Portia has riches, Viola, Desdemona, Marina and many others are musical, Perdita and Ophelia carry flowers, Imogen is 'a piece of tender air'. But in this play music is more important than any other love-suggestion:

> *Duke.* Give me some music. Now, good morrow, friends.
> Now, good Cesario, but that piece of song,
> That old and antique song we heard last night:
> Methought it did relieve my passion much,
> More than light airs and recollected terms
> Of these most brisk and giddy-paced times:
> Come, but one verse.   (ii. iv. 1)

Orsino reminds us of Cleopatra: 'music, moody food of us that trade in love' (where, by the way, we may observe the typical merchandise metaphor 'trade'). Music plays.

> *Orsino.*   . . . How dost thou like this tune?
> *Viola.* It gives a very echo to the seat
> Where Love is throned.   (ii. iv. 20)

Here is another fine love-music comparison:

> *Olivia.* But, would you undertake another suit,
>   I had rather hear you to solicit that
>   Than music from the spheres.   (III. i. 119)

Feste sings a song which 'dallies with the innocence of love' (II. iv. 48). Feste embodies the play's essence. Humour and music are blent in his person. And in his earlier song, too, singing and love are close-twined:

> O mistress mine, where are you roaming?
> O stay and hear; your true love's coming,
>   That can sing both high and low.   (II. iii. 40)

And there are some fine phrases spoken in Viola's embassy of love to Olivia. First she tells how her master loves

> With adorations, fertile tears,
> With groans that thunder love, with sighs of fire.
>   (I. v. 274)

A curious passage where love, to suit Viola's purpose, itself becomes imaginatively a thing of terrible, god-like power to which mortality must submit. Next, she tells how she, in her master's place, would sing her love:

> *Olivia.*   Why, what would you?
> *Viola.* Make me a willow cabin at your gate,
>   And call upon my soul within the house;
>   Write loyal cantons of contemned love
>   And sing them loud, even in the dead of night;
>   Holla your name to the reverberate hills,
>   And make the babbling gossip of the air
>   Cry out 'Olivia!' O you should not rest
>   Between the elements of air and earth
>   But you should pity me!   (I. v. 286)

Throughout, however, sea-thought and voyages are inwoven in our world of music. Sebastian's sudden love-joy at the end is a 'flood of fortune' (IV. iii. 11). Orsino's love, 'receiveth as the sea' and is 'all as hungry as the sea', infinite as the ocean itself (I. i. 11; II. iv. 103). And, like the ocean, he is changeable, uncertain. Says Feste:

... I would have men of such constancy put to sea, that their business might be every thing and their intent every where; for that's it that always makes a good voyage of nothing.

(II. iv. 77)

'I am for all waters', he says later (IV. ii. 68). Sir Toby is 'drowned' in drink (I. v. 140), just as the mind is often imaged as 'drowned' by any mastering emotion. Malvolio says of Cesario: "'tis with him in standing water, between boy and man' (I. v. 168), a queer image such as we find in *Antony and Cleopatra*. Viola is love's ambassador and therefore, as happens elsewhere in *The Merry Wives of Windsor*, and *Troilus*, imaged as a ship:

> *Maria.* Will you hoist sail, sir? here lies your way.
> *Viola.* No, good swabber; I am to hull here a little longer.
>
> (I. v. 215)

Again:

> *Sir Toby.* Will you encounter the house? my niece is desirous you should enter, if your trade be to her.
> *Viola.* I am bound to your niece, sir; I mean, she is the list of my voyage.   (III. i. 82)

'Board' is used in relation to love in Sir Toby's 'Board her, woo her, assail her' (I. iii. 60). There is rich jewel imagery, too. Rings and pearls are associated with love, and Orsino makes a fine 'jewel' comparison:

> But 'tis that miracle and queen of gems
> That nature pranks her in, attracts my soul.   (II. iv. 88)

Maria, whom Sir Toby eventually marries, is his 'metal of India' (II. v. 17). Such Eastern imagery variously accompanies Shakespearian love. So Orsino compares himself to an angry lover of legend: 'the Egyptian thief' (v. i. 121), and a lover's smile is compared to a map of the 'Indies' (III. ii. 86). But tragic sea-adventures are in our background. Antonio is throughout a tragic figure, associated with sea-fights and stern events:

> Once, in a sea-fight, 'gainst the count his galleys
> I did some service.   (III. iii. 26)

Orsino describes the action:

> That face of his I do remember well;
> Yet, when I saw it last, it was besmear'd
> As black as Vulcan in the smoke of war:
> A bawbling vessel was he captain of,
> For shallow draught and bulk unprizable,
> With which such scathful grapple did he make
> With the most noble bottom of our fleet,
> That very envy and the tongue of loss
> Cried fame and honour on him.   (v. i. 54)

He is a 'notable pirate' and 'salt-water thief' (v. i. 72),
according to Orsino. His passionate love of Sebastian
causes him to make a metaphorical 'voyage' in following
him (iii. iii. 7). His love is tragically passionate, a more
dangerous reality than our other love-themes: he is a forecast of Othello. But tragedy is not given much freedom
here. Terror is often humorous, as in the duel scene.
There a 'bear' is mentioned as an image of terror (iii. iv.
323). Malvolio was originally annoyed about a bear, too
(ii. v. 10). All, however, if we except Malvolio, is blended
in a final joy. At the moment of reunion the amazed
Sebastian cries:

> I had a sister,
> Whom the blind waves and surges have devour'd. . . .
>   (v. i. 235)

Sebastian, too, has risen from 'his watery tomb' (v. i. 241).
Both find that 'tempests are kind and salt waves fresh in
love' (iii. iv. 419).

Here, then, we find a pattern of music, love, and
precious stones, threaded by the sombre strands of a sea
tempest and a sea-fight. Finally there is love, reunion, and
joy. Even Orsino has a share ' in this most happy wreck'
(v. i. 273). 'Journeys end in lovers meeting', sings Feste
(ii. iii. 44): they are sea-journeys, the storm-tossed life of
man voyaging to love's Illyrian coasts. Like Christopher
Sly's strange experience, this golden romance is all like a
sweet dream come true, or a bad dream gone:

What relish is in this? How runs the stream?
Or I am mad, or else this is a dream:
Let fancy still my sense in Lethe steep;
If it be thus to dream, still let me sleep!   (IV. i. 64)

Continually the Shakespearian imagination plays on this
thought of dream; and his romances are dreamland
actualized. But never was the whole world of sweet
dream so perfectly and harmoniously bodied into a purely
human plot as here. And even Malvolio only falls by
aspiring to the fine and rich delight of an impossible love.
All tragic and tempestuous things are finally blended in
the music of Feste's final song, with its refrain,

With hey, ho, the wind and the rain . . . .
and
The rain it raineth every day.

Which song presents a microcosm of the play: tempests
dissolved in music. Perhaps this is the most harmonious
of Shakespeare's human romances.

The merchant-theme is developed further in *The Merchant of Venice*. In no play of this period is there so clear
and significant a contrast between the tempests of tragedy
and the music of romance. The play opens with a fine
description of Antonio's argosies:

Salarino. Your mind is tossing on the ocean,
There, where your argosies with portly sail,
Like signiors and rich burghers on the flood,
Or, as it were, the pageants of the sea,
Do overpeer the petty traffickers,
That curtsy to them, do them reverence,
As they fly by them with their woven wings.
Salanio. Believe me, sir, had I such venture forth,
The better part of my affections would
Be with my hopes abroad. I should be still
Plucking the grass, to know where sits the wind,
Peering in maps for ports, and piers, and roads;
And every object that might make me fear
Misfortune to my ventures, out of doubt
Would make me sad.

Salarino.   My wind cooling my broth
      Would blow me to an ague, when I thought
      What harm a wind too great at sea might do.
      I should not see the sandy hour-glass run,
      But I should think of shallows and of flats,
      And see my wealthy Andrew dock'd in sand,
      Vailing her high top lower than her ribs
      To kiss her burial. Should I go to church,
      And see the holy edifice of stone,
      And not bethink me straight of dangerous rocks,
      Which, touching but my gentle vessel's side,
      Would scatter all her spices on the stream,
      Enrobe the roaring waters with my silks,
      And, in a word, but even now worth this,
      And now worth nothing? Shall I have the thought
      To think on this; and shall I lack the thought,
      That such a thing bechanc'd would make me sad?
      But tell not me; I know, Antonio
      Is sad to think upon his merchandise.   (i. i. 8)

Notice how the sea is impregnated with melancholy suggestion. So is it in another passage, referring to human
enthusiasm and its all-too-quick extinction:

      How like a younker or a prodigal
      The scarfed bark puts from her native bay,
      Hugg'd and embraced by the strumpet wind!
      How like the prodigal doth she return,
      With over-weather'd ribs and ragged sails,
      Lean, rent, and beggar'd by the strumpet wind!
                                          (ii. vi. 14)

Such is a true Shakespearian image of life's voyages. We
see how universal is the content of our 'bark' and 'tempest'
passages.

      Throughout this play we must observe the opposition
of sea-tragedy and romance, which opposition is more
powerfully and exactly significant here than in any other
of these plays. The tempest-music opposition is indeed
more essentially dramatic here than in our former plays:
the two impressions oppose each other almost like dramatic
persons. From Venice and Antonio's melancholy we are

taken eastward over seas to Love's magic land, Belmont.
Bassanio tells Antonio of the rich Portia—we may remember that love itself is a kind of 'riches'—and her home
across the sea:

> Nor is the wide world ignorant of her worth,
> For the four winds blow in from every coast
> Renowned suitors, and her sunny locks
> Hang on her temples like a Golden Fleece;
> Which makes her seat of Belmont Colchos' strond,
> And many Jasons come in quest of her.   (I. i. 167)

Bassanio's quest is a 'sea' adventure. But we may also
note that Bassanio's journey separates him from his lover,
Antonio. The farewell is described (II. viii). We may,
too, observe a Venice-Belmont contrast. Venice is, of all
towns, most closely associated with the sea, even interwoven with it; and Belmont suggests a more airy height,
a finer element. Venice is the scene of tragedy, Belmont
of love. The one is overcast with gloom—we may note
that even the masque never actually comes off; the other
is a land of music, love, and 'holy crosses'. Morocco later
repeats the idea expressed by Bassanio in his 'Jason'
speech:

> The Hyrcanian deserts and the vasty wilds
> Of wide Arabia are as throughfares now
> For princes to come view fair Portia:
> The watery kingdom, whose ambitious head
> Spits in the face of heaven, is no bar
> To stop the foreign spirits, but they come,
> As o'er a brook, to see fair Portia.   (II. vii. 41)

Another good example of sea-crossing in the quest of
love. There are a few points to observe here. First, the
tempest-desert association is valuable, helping us to feel
tempest suggestion in thoughts of nature's uncivilization
in many contexts; next, the Hyrcanian-tempest association recalls Macbeth's 'rugged Russian bear', the 'arm'd
rhinoceros' and 'Hyrcan tiger', which I shall observe
later in its relation to the very important tempest-beast
association. And, finally, we may notice the metaphoric

anthropomorphism whereby the sea spits in the face of heaven: which, if visualized in human terms, illustrates the anti-love impregnation of the tempest-image. Such anthropomorphism is usual and may be observed elsewhere, as when, in *Lear*, the winds are told to blow till they 'crack' their 'cheeks'. Conversely, as in a *Titus Andronicus* quotation observed above, human beings in grief may be imaged as sea and sky tempestuous; or, in love, as moon and sea peacefully contemplating each other, an image I have noted in *Love's Labour's Lost* and shall note in the Final Plays.

To return to *The Merchant of Venice*. Antonio undertakes the venture for love's merchandise. He loves Bassanio, and his risk is wholly a merchant's venture for the sake of love; his love for Bassanio, Bassanio's for Portia. The gold of love is finely associated and yet strongly contrasted with love's gold in the Casket scene. Morocco's, Arragon's, and Bassanio's speeches on the gold, silver, and lead caskets are most significant. This play is full of 'riches' imagery. Such ornament

> is but the guiled shore
> To a most dangerous sea; the beauteous scarf
> Veiling an Indian beauty. (III. ii. 97)

Again the Siren idea, here given in terms of an 'Indian beauty'. Though this may at first suggest 'Indian' to have a wholly derogatory sense, we may compare the lover who 'sees Helen's beauty in a brow of Egypt' (*A Midsummer Night's Dream*, v. i. 11). And we remember Cleopatra. Such passages suggest, partly at least, the mystery and glamour of the East, the dangerous Indian shores of fairyland, that fairyland's too often untrustworthy and cheating lure. So merchandise, gold and silver caskets, Portia's ring, all the usual associations interthread our texture. But here they are unusually powerful, both actualized and dramatically active. Imagery is becoming the very plot itself. Twenty merchants (III. ii. 282) have attempted to placate Shylock. Antonio is 'a royal merchant' (III. ii. 242); Portia's boundless wealth is emphasized again and again; riches are scattered over the play. Shylock himself loses both his loved daughter and vast riches, 'ducats', jewels, his 'turquoise'. Love and riches are ever close. The play is full of ducats and wealth. Shylock rates his ducats and jewels above his daughter, strongly as he loves her; but Bassanio's and Portia's love is finely shown as being of an integrity that sees through the superficial brilliance of gold to the true worth within: hence Bassanio's choice of the leaden casket. These caskets are intensely symbolical. As in *Timon*, the spiritual gold of true love is contrasted with the outward gilding which decorates the false.

And there is music. Belmont is the home of love and music:

> Let music sound while he doth make his choice;
> Then, if he lose, he makes a swan-like end,
> Fading in music: that the comparison
> May stand more proper, my eye shall be the stream
> And watery death-bed for him. He may win;
> And what is music then? Then music is
> Even as the flourish when true subjects bow
> To a new-crowned monarch: such it is
> As are those dulcet sounds in break of day
> That creep into the dreaming bridegroom's ear
> And summon him to marriage.   (III. ii. 43)

A lovely speech, rich in typical suggestion. We should note the death and music association, the eye-stream comparison, and the 'watery death-bed': death by water made sweet in music, like Ophelia's death or like the music in which the tragedy of *Othello* dissolves in beauty. And, after the 'death' thought, the victory of love: love 'crowned' like a king, the music that awakes the sleeper, bidding him take his happiness. So Hermione 'awakes' to music in *The Winter's Tale*. The purely imaginative order reflects the progress later developed from the Tragedies to the Final Plays. So here there is a song, 'Tell me, where is fancy bred?', and music, and Bassanio

wins his joy. He is like Hercules rescuing his lady from
'the sea-monster' (III. ii. 55–8); and if we remember that
both the sea and all fierce beasts are equally symbols of
mortal terror in Shakespeare we may understand the
terrific significance of sea-monsters here and elsewhere,
notably in *Lear*.

But Bassanio's joy is short-lived. Throughout we fear
the sinister forces of tempest on which the action depends. We know, like Shylock, that the sea is dangerous:

> . . . he hath an argosy bound to Tripolis, another to the
> Indies; I understand, moreover, upon the Rialto, he hath a
> third at Mexico, a fourth for England, and other ventures he
> hath, squandered abroad. But ships are but boards, sailors but
> men: there be land-rats and water-rats, water-thieves and
> land-thieves, I mean pirates, and then there is the peril of
> waters, winds, and rocks. . . . .   (I. iii. 18)

Fears are justified:

> I reason'd with a Frenchman yesterday,
> Who told me, in the narrow seas that part
> The French and English, there miscarried
> A vessel of our country richly fraught.   (II. viii. 27)

Again,

> *Salanio.* Now, what news on the Rialto?
> *Salarino.* Why, yet it lives there unchecked that Antonio hath a
> ship of rich lading wrecked on the narrow seas; the Goodwins,
> I think they call the place; a very dangerous flat and fatal,
> where the carcases of many a tall ship lie buried. . . .
>   (III. i. 1)

Tubal, who 'spoke with some of the sailors that escaped
the wreck' (III. i. 109), tells Shylock that Antonio 'hath an
argosy cast away, coming from Tripolis' (III. i. 105). All
Antonio's ships have failed:

> But is it true, Salerio?
> Have all his ventures fail'd? What, not one hit?
> From Tripolis, from Mexico, and England,
> From Lisbon, Barbary, and India?
> And not one vessel 'scape the dreadful touch
> Of merchant-marring rocks?   (III. ii. 269)

'Twenty merchants' (III. ii. 282) sue on Antonio's behalf. But Shylock is firm. Tempests have leagued with Shylock, both equally forces of tragedy to be set against love, music, and Portia.

It is significant that Shylock hates festive music:

> Lock up my doors: and when you hear the drum
> And the vile squealing of the wry-neck'd fife,
> Clamber not you up to the casements then,
> Nor thrust your head into the public street
> To gaze on Christian fools with varnished faces,
> But stop my house's ears, I mean my casements;
> Let not the sound of shallow foppery enter
> My sober house.   (II. v. 29)

He 'has no mind of feasting forth'. He is to be contrasted with music and feasting. His 'music' phrases are naturally hostile: witness his other words about when the 'bagpipe sings i' the nose' (IV. i. 49) and its unpleasant effects. Now Shylock himself is like a 'tempest'. He is the tragedy-force in the play. 'The very tyranny and rage' of his 'spirit' (IV. i. 13) is a typical tempest-impression recalling the music in *Love's Labour's Lost* that could 'ravish savage ears and plant in tyrants mild humility' (*Love's Labour's Lost*, IV. iii. 348). The 'current' of his cruelty is 'unfeeling' (IV. i. 63–4). Again,

> I pray you, think you question with the Jew:
> You may as well go stand upon the beach
> And bid the main flood bate his usual height;
> You may as well use question with the wolf
> Why he hath made the ewe bleat for the lamb;
> You may as well forbid the mountain pines
> To wag their high tops and to make no noise,
> When they are fretted with the gusts of heaven;
> You may as well do any thing most hard,
> As seek to soften that—than which what's harder?—
> His Jewish heart.   (IV. i. 70)

'Tops' is a usual word in tempest-passages, applied both to waves and mountain-trees. 'Pines' are important in such passages. Here we should observe also (i) the sea,

(ii) the wolf, and (iii) the winds: all associated with human cruelty, and the forces of tragedy. Here the wolf, thus enclosed by the other two, stresses the association. Elsewhere Shylock is powerfully compared to a wolf in a speech which vividly outlines the Shakespearian intuition of the beast in man:

> O, be thou damn'd, inexecrable dog!
> And for thy life let justice be accused.
> Thou almost makest me waver in my faith
> To hold opinion with Pythagoras,
> That souls of animals infuse themselves
> Into the trunks of men: thy currish spirit
> Govern'd a wolf, who, hang'd for human slaughter,
> Even from the gallows did his fell soul fleet,
> And, whilst thou lay'st in thy unhallow'd dam
> Infused itself in thee; for thy desires
> Are wolvish, bloody, starved and ravenous.
>
> (IV. i. 128)

This play as certainly as, and more tragically than, the Induction to *The Taming of the Shrew*, sets the beast in man against love and music. The tempest-beast association is always important. And here both are clearly to be related to Shylock and tragedy.

Tragedy in the form of merchant-marring tempests breaks into the music of Bassanio's joy at the moment of his love-success at Belmont. But Portia, love's queen, descends from the fairyland of music and love, Belmont, into the turmoil and dust of human conflict and cruelty at Venice. She is as a being from a different world. We may observe that she, like Shakespeare's other heroines, is often associated directly with thoughts of divinity. Here, we have Portia's lovely Mercy speech, and her pretended pilgrimage, reminding us of Helena in *All's Well*. So she takes arms against the tragic forces of tempest and wins.

We are finally brought back to Belmont, where again we find romance and music. Jessica and Lorenzo make love by moonlight:

The moon shines bright; in such a night as this
When the sweet wind did gently kiss the trees
And they did make no noise, in such a night
Troilus methinks mounted the Troyan walls
And sigh'd his soul toward the Grecian tents,
Where Cressid lay that night.   (v. i. 1)

Soft airs and love: a usual association, most notable of all
in *Antony and Cleopatra* and *Cymbeline*. Themselves happy,
these lovers yet image love's tragedies: Troilus sighing
his soul out to the gentle sigh of the wind, Thisbe who
'saw the lion's shadow' and 'ran dismay'd away' (v. i. 8),
and finally, Dido, parted by cruel waters from her lover:

          In such a night
Stood Dido with a willow in her hand
Upon the wild sea-banks, and waft her love
To come again to Carthage.   (v. i. 9)

A typical thought of love parted by water; and an inverse
of our other sea-shore and love image, wherein love
beckons across dangerous seas. The triple imagery is
again important: (i) 'wind' and 'sighs', (ii) the 'lion', and
(iii) the 'sea'—an almost exact repetition of our sea-beast-
wind association just observed. Here it is less tempestuous,
the beast nobler. Twice the 'beast' is thus sandwiched
between 'sea' and 'wind', which, being the main elements
of our 'tempest' symbol, here point clearly to the close
beast-tempest association. Lorenzo calls for music to
be brought forth 'into the air'. Then,

Lorenzo. How sweet the moonlight sleeps upon this bank!
     Here will we sit and let the sounds of music
     Creep in our ears: soft stillness and the night
     Become the touches of sweet harmony.
     Sit, Jessica: look, how the floor of heaven
     Is thick inlaid with patines of bright gold:
     There's not the smallest orb which thou behold'st,
     But in his motion like an angel sings,
     Still quiring to the young-ey'd cherubins:
     Such harmony is in immortal souls;
     But, whilst this muddy vesture of decay
     Doth grossly close it in, we cannot hear it.

Enter Musicians.

Come, ho! and wake Diana with a hymn:
With sweetest touches pierce your mistress' ear,
And draw her home with music.

[*Music*

Jessica. I am never merry when I hear sweet music.
Lorenzo. The reason is, your spirits are attentive:
For do but note a wild and wanton herd,
Or race of youthful and unhandled colts,
Fetching mad bounds, bellowing, and neighing loud,
Which is the hot condition of their blood:
If they but hear perchance a trumpet sound,
Or any air of music touch their ears,
You shall perceive them make a mutual stand,
Their savage eyes turn'd to a modest gaze
By the sweet power of music: therefore the poet
Did feign that Orpheus drew trees, stones, and floods;
Since nought so stockish, hard, and full of rage,
But music for the time doth change his nature.
The man that hath no music in himself,
Nor is not mov'd with concord of sweet sounds,
Is fit for treasons, stratagems, and spoils;
The motions of his spirit are dull as night,
And his affections dark as Erebus:
Let no such man be trusted.—Mark the music.

(v. i. 54)

Here we should observe the association of music, stillness, the moon, and love: all are elsewhere important. Stars, too, are a development of the moon idea and blend with jewel and gold imagery: 'patines of bright gold'. We remember the 'gold candles' of Sonnet XXI, quoted already. See, too, how the 'music of the spheres' mentioned also in *Twelfth Night* and *Pericles*, there, too, with love-suggestion, is here quaintly and beautifully taken from its Ptolemaic context and given a Copernican significance. This spheral music is heard only by 'immortal souls'—we may thus note its aptness in the paradisal vision of *Pericles*—but the universal harmony is blurred to mortal understanding. Here Portia, love's queen, is to be drawn home 'with music'. But Jessica is made sad by the too-great sweetness of music: we might compare Sonnet VIII, quoted already. Music thus charms the wildness of animals, a music-beast opposition; and music, similarly, can draw 'trees, stones, and floods'. Notice the tree-tempest association: it is often important. And a man who has not 'music' in him is apt to disintegrate states: since music is equally suggestive of personal love or political concord. His soul is 'dull as night' and 'dark as Erebus': hence the 'darkness' in connexion with conspiracy or murder in *Julius Caesar* and *Macbeth*. Music, stars, moonlight, and love are thus set against tempests, wild beasts, and dark conspiracy. We must ever observe the universal imagery of star, moon, and sun which blends with love and music.

So Portia returns. And in this final scene of love's victory over tragedy we should not be surprised that the melancholy Antonio, too, finds his way to Belmont, and that victorious love in Portia's person brings news of his ships' miraculous survival:

> Antonio, you are welcome;
> And I have better news in store for you
> Than you expect: unseal this letter soon;
> There you shall find three of your argosies
> Are richly come to harbour suddenly:
> You shall not know by what strange accident
> I chanced on this letter.   (V. i. 273)

Antonio risked all material merchandise, even the rich merchandise of his own life, for Bassanio, for love. Love's prize, in turn, gives him back his ships. It is the conquest of romance over tragedy, music and love's gold over tempests. No play more perfectly illustrates the Shakespearian feeling for merchants, riches, gold, tempests, and music entwined and interactive. These elements are here most concretely embodied in the plot, in the action. Imaginative forces conflict, and the plot is made to suit them. The play is thus highly charged with poetic power from start to finish.

In these romances I have noticed certain outstanding themes which blend either with tempests or music. But it must not be thought that these special veins of suggestion, variously powerful in different plays, are not to be found elsewhere. For example, I have observed the birds in *Much Ado*. But we may find a closely similar suggestion in a love-context elsewhere. Thus in *The Comedy of Errors* we have Adriana's:

> Far from her nest the lapwing cries away:
> My heart prays for him, though my tongue do curse.
>
> (IV. ii. 27)

After the music-speech of Lorenzo in *The Merchant of Venice* Portia, love's queen victorious, is drawn home to the sounds of music. She also talks of birds:

> The crow doth sing as sweetly as the lark
> When neither is attended, and I think
> The nightingale, if she should sing by day,
> When every goose is cackling, would be thought
> No better a musician than the wren.
>
> (*The Merchant of Venice*, v. i. 102)

Bird-music blends here with moonlight—'Peace, ho! the moon sleeps with Endymion . . .' (v. i. 109)—music, and romance generally. These are the usual associations. But in *Much Ado* bird-imagery blends with other volatile suggestion, often mechanical, of 'arrows', 'bolts', and 'bullets': these suggest wit, itself lifeless and mechanical compared with love. And exactly such a suggestion occurs also in *Love's Labour's Lost*:

> The tongues of mocking wenches are as keen
>   As is the razor's edge invisible,
> Cutting a smaller hair than may be seen,
>   Above the sense of sense; so sensible
> Seemeth their conference; their conceits have wings
> Fleeter than arrows, bullets, wind, thought, swifter things.
>
> (v. ii. 256)

Similarly, sun, moon, and star references are frequently used in relation to love. *Love's Labour's Lost*, with its numerous sun-love associations, is merely an extreme example. In *Twelfth Night*, as the gold of romantic joy matures towards the end, we have Sebastian's:

> This is the air; that is the glorious sun;
> This pearl she gave me, I do feel't and see't.
>
> (IV. iii. 1)

Or again, in *The Two Gentlemen of Verona*, Proteus uses the same association:

> At first I did adore a twinkling star,
> But now I worship a celestial sun.   (II. vi. 9)

We have a powerful spring-winter opposition in the songs of *Love's Labour's Lost*, and *As You Like It*; and this is frequent, directly expressed or indirectly suggested, throughout Shakespeare. The rich sea-imagery of *The Two Gentlemen of Verona* recurs in a passage I have quoted from *The Comedy of Errors*. And gold, so powerful in that play, is found often elsewhere, blending on the one side with merchandise and riches generally, on the other with pearls and jewels: which latter are so ubiquitously associated with love in Shakespeare that quotation is unnecessary. Pearls and rings are also continually used as love-gifts. Merchants are scattered throughout these plays, and are found often in Shakespeare's love-poetry. Perhaps one of the most important ideas that emerges from our attention to these plays—apart from the tempest-music opposition itself—is the very frequent suggestion of beasts. They may be rough and fierce, as the 'bears' in *Much Ado*, or may suggest grossness generally, as the 'swine' in the Induction to *The Taming of the Shrew* and the 'whale' in *The Merry Wives*; block-headed stupidity, as with Dogberry, 'writ down an ass'; or savage ferocity, as with Katharina, the 'wild-cat'. All these beasts in human form are clearly the cause of tempests, and to be set against the more spiritual essences: hence the whale-fairy contrast in *The Merry Wives*. Much of Shakespeare's comedy plays on this contrast of the flesh and spirit. We find it especially strong in Christopher Sly

and Falstaff; and a somewhat similar suggestion vitalizes
the comedy of Malvolio's aspiration towards marriage
with his lady. He is thus 'an affectioned ass' (II. iii. 160;
184–5) on the one side. But, in his love aspirations he is
compared to birds: he is a 'turkey-cock' and 'jets under
his advanced plumes' (II. v. 36); a 'woodcock near the gin'
(II. v. 92), a 'staniel' checking at a 'dish o' poison' (II. v.
124–7), a 'gull' (II. v. 205).

IV

Now the romances, full of varied strains of poetic
colour, yet illustrate continually the tempest-music
opposition, or at least a very similar contrast. Naturally,
they, unlike the histories, emphasize music more than
tempests. They almost all have their powerful music,
but not all possess an actual tempest. It is, however, very
necessary to observe that they all possess clear tragic
relations. There is always a discord to be harmonized, a
dispersal to be unified, or a beast to be tamed or purified.
Some are more sombre than others. *Much Ado* and *The
Comedy of Errors* have some really black tragic effects; but
Twelfth Night never leads our thoughts far from its central
golden fun and romance, and what tragic essences appear
—the original tempest, Antonio's passionate jealousy,
and Malvolio's downfall—are not allowed to usurp too
great an interest. All is dissolved in music and romantic
joy.

The last play we analysed, *The Merchant of Venice*,
presents all our varied elements in a more exact and comprehensive pattern than any of the others. In it very
clearly there is a black threat of tragedy powerfully entwined with tempests and beasts; opposed by the riches
of love, its divine strength, its music. Venice is a tragic
world; Belmont a dream-world. And the dream wins.
Here especially we may see how very skilfully the Shakespearian poetic suggestions are made into active, dramatic
forces. The worth and riches of love are often emphasized.
Here we have Portia, actually an heiress, saying:

Pay him six thousand, and deface the bond;
Double six thousand, and then treble that. . . .

(III. ii. 302)

I have noticed the symbolic effects of the Caskets. Love in Shakespeare is often both contrasted and associated with gold. Tempests are also here very dramatic. The whole plot turns on the failure of Antonio's shipping. The play is called *The Merchant of Venice*. Tempests here exactly league with the beast, the wolf-hearted Shylock. When we are at Belmont we get music; at Venice, Antonio's melancholy and Shylock's tragedy. Two views of life, tragic and romantic, are opposed. Their emissaries meet in the Trial scene. Portia opposes Shylock; and in the shock of that meeting two worlds contest together. The music of Belmont wins against the tempests of Venice.

Having thus prepared the way, I shall now attempt to do some scant justice to Shakespeare's most wonderful romantic comedy. This play I notice in more detail; partly because here the interplay of imagery and symbolism is especially complex and beautiful; partly so that for once we may see with greater exactitude how tempests and music blend with other effects; and partly, perhaps, because I like the play more than most.

In *A Midsummer Night's Dream* all the best of Shakespeare's earlier poetry is woven into so comprehensive and exquisite a design that it is hard not to feel that this play alone is worth all the other romances. We have observed plays where 'ill-dispersing' tempests are associated or contrasted with magic lands of fun, reunion, and final happiness. The happier elements of these plays are most perfectly embodied in Feste, song and comedy entwined, and perhaps this is why *Twelfth Night* appears so exquisite a flowering of humour and romance. Tempests and merchants, gold, jewels, and music are recurrent. But, whether love's setting be Arden, Ephesus, Belmont, or Illyria, we know that it is in reality a land of purely fanciful delight, a fairyland of successful, tempest-vanquishing romance. 'Illyria' is, indeed, more truly 'Elysium'. Yet such must be clearly related to those other images where, in the Histories and Early Tragedies, amid more realistic and tragic stress, the poet makes fleeting suggestion of the soul's desire set beyond rough seas of disaster and disorder, fairy riches on far-off Indian strands of the soul. Here we are actually introduced to this Indian fairyland; or, rather, the fairies have come from their Indian home to the 'wood near Athens' which is our scene. In this play fairyland interpenetrates the world of human action. And that world is varied, ranging from the rough simplicity of the clowns, through the solid common sense and kind worldly wisdom of Theseus, to the frenzied fantasies of the lovers: which in their turn shade into fairyland itself. The play thus encloses remarkably a whole scale of intuitions. Nor in any other early romance is the interplay of imagery more exquisitely varied. The night is a-glimmer with moon and star, yet it is dark and fearsome; there are gentle birds and gruesome beasts. There is a gnomish, fearsome, *Macbeth*-like quality about the atmosphere, just touching nightmare: yet these fairies are the actualization of Shakespeare's Indian dream. The total result resembles those dreams, of substance unhappy to the memorizing intellect, which yet, on waking, we find ourselves strangely regretting, loath to part from that magic even when it leaves nothing to the memory but incidents which should be painful. Such are the fairies here. They are neither good nor bad. They are wayward spirits which cause trouble to men, yet also woo human love and favour: as when Oberon and Titania quarrel for their Indian boy or wrangle in jealousy of Theseus or Hippolyta. The whole vision sums and expresses, as does no other work, the magic and the mystery of sleep, the dewy sweetness of a midsummer dream, dawn-memoried with sparkling grass and wreathing mists; a morning slope falling from a glade where late the moonbeams glimmered their fairy light on shadowed mossy boles and fearsome dells, and the vast woodland silence.

The action depends largely on Oberon's quarrel with

Titania. Dissension has entered fairyland itself, due to these spirits' desire for human love, just as later human beings are caused trouble by their contact with the fairies:

> Why art thou here,
> Come from the farthest steppe of India?
> But that, forsooth, the bouncing Amazon,
> Your buskin'd mistress and your warrior love,
> To Theseus must be wedded, and you come
> To give their bed joy and prosperity.   (II. i. 68)

Oberon parries Titania's speech with reciprocal jealousy. Now this dissension makes 'tempests' in nature, untuning the melodic procession of the seasons:

> *Titania.* These are the forgeries of jealousy:
> And never, since the middle summer's spring,
> Met we on hill, in dale, forest, or mead,
> By paved fountain, or by rushy brook,
> Or in the beached margent of the sea,
> To dance our ringlets to the whistling wind,
> But with thy brawls thou hast disturb'd our sport.
> Therefore the winds, piping to us in vain,
> As in revenge, have suck'd up from the sea
> Contagious fogs; which, falling in the land,
> Have every pelting river made so proud
> That they have overborne their continents:
> The ox hath therefore stretch'd his yoke in vain,
> The ploughman lost his sweat; and the green corn
> Hath rotted ere his youth attain'd a beard;
> The fold stands empty in the drowned field,
> And crows are fatted with the murrion flock;
> The nine-men's morris is fill'd up with mud;
> And the quaint mazes in the wanton green
> For lack of tread are undistinguishable:
> The human mortals want their winter here;
> No night is now with hymn or carol blest:
> Therefore the moon, the governess of floods,
> Pale in her anger, washes all the air,
> That rheumatic diseases do abound:
> And thorough this distemperature we see
> The seasons alter: hoary-headed frosts
> Fall in the fresh lap of the crimson rose,

> And on old Hiems' thin and icy crown
> An odorous chaplet of sweet summer buds
> Is, as in mockery, set: the spring, the summer,
> The childing autumn, angry winter, change
> Their wonted liveries: and the 'mazed world,
> By their increase, now knows not which is which:
> And this same progeny of evil comes
> From our debate, from our dissension;
> We are their parents and original.   (II. i. 81–117)

Unruly floods, disorder in the seasons, storm and mud and all natural confusion result from this dissension in fairyland. And this tempest is at the heart of the play, sending ripples outward through the plot, vitalizing the whole middle action. Hence our dissensions and mistakes, our comedy; in fact, our drama: most of the action is related to the Oberon-Titania quarrel.

Fairyland is set against mortality. Close to her tempest speech Titania has a lovely passage on the fairies' Indian home:

> *Titania.*   Set your heart at rest:
> The fairy land buys not the child of me.
> His mother was a votaress of my order:
> And, in the spiced Indian air, by night,
> Full often hath she gossip'd by my side,
> And sat with me on Neptune's yellow sands,
> Marking the embarked traders on the flood,
> When we have laugh'd to see the sails conceive
> And grow big-bellied with the wanton wind;
> Which she, with pretty and with swimming gait
> Following,—her womb then rich with my young squire,—
> Would imitate, and sail upon the land,
> To fetch me trifles, and return again,
> As from a voyage, rich with merchandise. . . .
>   (II. i. 121)

Notice the 'spiced air' and also the 'yellow sands', reminding us of Venus's promise to dance, like a nymph, on the sands, 'and yet no footing seen'; and also the ship and 'merchandise' imagery; and the thought of Titania and her Indian 'votaress' amused at 'the traders on the flood'.

India, we must remember, is fairyland itself; and the
Indian votaress all but an immortal. Therefore, as we
watch Titania and her loved friend laughing at the
'traders on the flood', imitating their 'voyage' on the
waters of life, we see fairyland laughing at storm-tossed
mortality. We must not forget the universal suggestion
with which voyages are impregnated in Shakespeare.
This is, indeed, an exquisite prologue to the middle action,
where Puck befools poor mortals:

> Shall we their fond pageant see?
> Lord, what fools these mortals be!
>
> (III. ii. 114)

Titania's merchandise speech beautifully reflects this
essential spirit, as a prologue to our middle scenes.

For humanity here indeed suffers some cruelly comic
distresses. In the first scene we find tragic tempests:

> *Lysander.* How now, my love! why is your cheek so pale?
> How chance the roses there do fade so fast?
> *Hermia.* Belike for want of rain, which I could well
> Beteem them from the tempest of my eyes.   (I. i. 128)

In this play passionate love gives vent to 'showers of
oaths' (I. i. 245), and Bottom by the power of his acting
will 'move storms' (I. ii. 29); while in the midnight wood
the troubles of Hermia and Helena are increased. These
scenes are dark; dark with distress of lovers, dark with the
shadowed and gnomish fearsomeness that reigns through
a woodland night. Lysander and Hermia have lost their
way in the forest (II. ii. 36); Hermia is 'faint' with wandering (II. ii. 35). Helena follows Demetrius, imploring pity,
receiving curses from the love-tormented and distracted
youth. She is 'out of breath' with her fond chase (II. ii. 88).
Then she finds Lysander, sleeping:

> But who is here? Lysander! on the ground!
> Dead? or asleep? I see no blood, no wound.
> Lysander, if you live, good sir, awake.
>
> (II. ii. 100)

'Dead', 'blood': this play is full of fears, and such satanic
suggestions are frequent. Again,

> If thou hast slain Lysander in his sleep,
> Being o'er shoes in blood, plunge in the deep,
> And kill me too.   (III. ii. 47)

This recalls *Macbeth*. Again,

> It cannot be but thou hast murder'd him;
> So should a murderer look, so dead, so grim.
>
>   (III. ii. 56)

The play continually suggests a nightmare terror. It is
dark and fearsome. The nights here are 'grim-look'd'
(v. i. 171). And yet this atmosphere of gloom and dread
is the playground for the purest comedy. Romance and
fun interthread our tragedies here. So, too, a pale light
falls from moon and star into the darkened glades, carving
the trees into deeper darkness, black voiceless giants; yet
silvering the mossy slopes; lighting the grass with misty
sparkles of flame; setting green fire to the glimmering eyes
of prowling beasts; dissolving Oberon and Puck invisible
in their magic beams.

The play is full of moonlight.[1] The opening lines are a
fine introduction:

> *Theseus.* Now, fair Hippolyta, our nuptial hour
>   Draws on apace; four happy days bring in
>   Another moon: but, O, methinks how slow
>   The old moon wanes! She lingers my desires
>   Like to a step-dame or a dowager
>   Long withering out a young man's revenue.
> *Hippolyta.* Four days will quickly steep themselves in night;
>   Four nights will quickly dream away the time;
>   And then the moon, like to a silver bow
>   New bent in heaven, shall behold the night
>   Of our solemnities.   (I. i. 1)

Egeus accuses Lysander of singing love verses 'by moonlight' to Hermia (I. i. 30); and Theseus images nuns as

---

[1] For acknowledgement of a debt here to Mgr. Kolbe I refer the reader
to my Preface

'chanting faint hymns to the cold fruitless moon' (I. i. 73);
both these associating moonlight with music. Hermia is
to reach her decision 'by the next new moon' (I. i. 83).
Then Lysander plots his and her escape, and tells Helena,
using a lovely 'moon' image:

> To-morrow night, when Phoebe doth behold
> Her silver visage in the watery glass,
> Decking with liquid pearl the bladed grass . . .
>
> (I. i. 209)

A fine association of the moon, smooth waters, and
jewel-imagery. Titania's fairy wanders 'swifter than the
moon's sphere' (II. i. 7). In Titania's tempest-speech, no
night is 'with hymn or carol blest' and therefore the moon,
'governess of floods', is 'pale' with anger, and washes
the air with rheumatic dampness (II. i. 102). Another
association of the moon with votive song. Oberon tells
how he saw Cupid flying 'between the cold moon and the
earth' (II. i. 156), and how his arrow was 'quench'd in the
chaste beams of the watery moon' (II. i. 162). Titania
would have her elves 'fan the moonbeams' from Bottom's
'sleeping eyes' (III. i. 176), and shortly after speaks these
lines:

> The moon, methinks, looks with a watery eye;
> And, when she weeps, weeps every little flower,
> Lamenting some enforced chastity.   (III. i. 203)

Again, from Hermia:

> I'll believe as soon
> This whole earth may be bored and that the moon
> May through the centre creep and so displease
> Her brother's noontide with the Antipodes.
>
> (III. ii. 52)

Having healed the breach of their dissension, Oberon and
Titania prepare for flight:

> We the globe can compass soon,
> Swifter than the wandering moon.   (IV. i. 101)

Then there is the Moon of the Pyramus and Thisbe

interlude. First, there is an elaborate discussion during a
rehearsal as to how a moon can be brought in:

> *Snout.* Doth the moon shine that night we play our play?
>   (III. i. 52)

There is more argument about 'moonshine', but eventually
the moon is properly impersonated:

> This man with lanthorn, dog, and bush of thorn,
> Presenteth Moonshine . . . .   (v. i. 136).

Again, there are Pyramus' lines:

> Sweet Moon, I thank thee for thy sunny beams;
>   I thank thee, Moon, for shining now so bright;
> For, by thy gracious, golden, glittering gleams,
>   I trust to take of truest Thisbe sight.   (v. i. 276)

The spectators continually pass remarks on 'moonshine';
and finally observe that 'Moonshine and Lion are left to
bury the dead' (v. i. 355). When all is still and 'fairy
time' again possesses the darkness, we have Puck's

> Now the hungry lion roars,
> And the wolf behowls the moon.   (v. ii. 1)

We may remember the wolf in Macbeth's Tarquin
speech that howls at night when 'o'er the one half world
nature seems dead'. There are many sombre *Macbeth*
effects in *A Midsummer Night's Dream*. The 'moon' here
does, in fact, have wide suggestions: moonlight is usually
romantic, as in *The Merchant of Venice* and *Romeo and Juliet*,
and, indeed, all these lights are generally to be opposed to
cloud and tempest. But the moon also is clearly to be
associated directly with darkness, too. It occurs in the
'Hecate' scenes of *Macbeth*. And in this play the satanic
and romantic attributes of a moonlit woodland are blended.
    The play has stars, too. The nights here are 'glimmer-
ing'. 'Didst thou not lead him through the glimmering
night?' asks Oberon (II. i. 77), and again:

> Through the house give glimmering light . . .
>   (v. ii. 21)

Titania has a fine love-speech continuing this 'glimmer' effect:

> The honey bags steal from the humble-bees,
> And for night tapers crop their waxen thighs
> And light them at the fiery glow-worm's eyes,
> To have my love to bed and to arise.   (III. i. 171)

Often stars or planets are compared to love's eyes:

> What wicked and dissembling glass of mine
> Made me compare with Hermia's sphery eyne?
> (II. ii. 98)

Again, Oberon speaks enchantment over Demetrius:

> When his love he doth espy
> Let her shine as gloriously
> As the Venus of the sky.   (III. ii. 105)

And, to Lysander, Helena

> more engilds the night
> Than all yon fiery oes and eyes of light.
> (III. ii. 187)

Hermia's eyes are 'lode-stars' (I. i. 183). These love-star suggestions cluster through the middle scenes. Love's brilliance is, paradoxically, murderous:

> Yet you, the murderer, look as bright and clear
> As yonder Venus in her glimmering sphere.
> (III. ii. 60)

A clear blending of sombre and light effects; and, again, the word 'glimmering'. Or again, love's eyes may be as still water, or 'crystal':

> To what, my love, shall I compare thine eyne?
> Crystal is muddy.   (III. ii. 138)

Anything bright or transparent may be a love image. 'Transparent Helena!' (II. ii. 104) cries Lysander. These star and water images are close: hence they may be associated directly together:

> And now they never meet in grove or green,
> By fountain clear, or spangled starlight sheen,
> But they do square . . .   (II. i. 28)

Throughout the middle scenes we have thus a glimmering world; and the poor distraught lovers long for daylight to break on their troubled dreams.

All these glimmering lights shine on a world which yet
endures fears, mistakes, darkness. Once they are grimly
blanketed as by a *Macbeth* murk:

> Thou see'st these lovers seek a place to fight:
> Hie therefore, Robin, overcast the night:
> The starry welkin cover thou anon
> With drooping fog as black as Acheron. . . .
>
> (III. ii. 354)

In this pitch darkness the 'testy rivals' are to be led
'astray',

> Till o'er their brows death-counterfeiting sleep
> With leaden legs and batty wings doth creep.
>
> (III. ii. 364)

Notice the sombre suggestion there, again recalling *Macbeth*, where the guests at Inverness are told to 'shake off'
the 'downy sleep, death's counterfeit' and to look on
'death itself'. 'Batty', too, enforces a *Macbeth* impression.
Sleep, as in *Macbeth*, may here be nightmare. Hermia
wakes with a start:

> Help me, Lysander, help me! do thy best
> To pluck this crawling serpent from my breast!
>
> (II. ii. 145)

Many of the persons sleep: all the lovers, once at least,
some twice. Titania is enchanted in her sleep so that she
endures a nightmare madness in love. Our world is one
of dim fears and sleep-consciousness; gnomish, fearsome,
haunted:

> What night-rule now about this haunted grove?
>
> (III. ii. 5)

The vast night-poetry of *Hamlet* and *Macbeth* is struck
here with a similar grandeur:

> The iron tongue of midnight hath told twelve.
>
> (V. i. 370)

Darkness and fear permeate this play. It is a darkness spangled, or shot, with light. So Lysander outlines the tragedies in store for true love:

> Or, if there were a sympathy in choice,
> War, death, or sickness did lay siege to it,
> Making it momentany as a sound,
> Swift as a shadow, short as any dream,
> Brief as the lightning in the collied night,
> That, in a spleen, unfolds both heaven and earth,
> And ere a man hath power to say, 'Behold!'
> The jaws of darkness do devour it up:
> So quick bright things come to confusion.   (I. i. 141)

'Confusion': a pure *Macbeth* idea. And we may observe how a tempest effect, 'lightning', here suggests a positive essence for once, as in the almost exactly similar speech in *Romeo and Juliet*, II. ii. 116–20; but, indeed, wherever we have lightning emphasized, there is a certain vivid, electric suggestion corresponding to the concept 'spirit'. Continually this play suggests *Macbeth*; elves and gnomes take the place of witches and ghosts, and here our dark strands are inwoven with brighter ones, and the total effect is, as I have observed, that of a dream whose fairyland is sweet even though it be troubled. I have observed, so far, tempests, lights, and the *Macbeth* dark. Next, I shall notice some of our typical tempest-beasts.

This play has many tempest-beasts: beasts fearsome, ravenous, and grim. So Demetrius threatens to run from Helena and leave her 'to the mercy of wild beasts' (II. i. 228); but she answers that his scorn shows him to have a heart more cruel than the wildest, thus contrasting love with fierce beasts. It is significant, too, that to Oberon the leviathan comes as a natural image:

> Fetch me this herb and be thou here again
> Ere the leviathan can swim a league.   (II. i. 174)

The bear, the most usual tempest-beast, is frequent. Helena cries:

> No, no, I am as ugly as a bear,
> For beasts that meet me run away for fear. (II. ii. 94)

She is a 'monster' (II. ii. 97). The bear is found in other passages where there are significant groups suggesting fearsome animal-life. Oberon wishes that Titania may love a 'monster' (III. ii. 377):

> The next thing then she waking looks upon,
> Be it on lion, bear, or wolf, or bull,
> On meddling monkey or on busy ape,
> She shall pursue it with the soul of love.
>
> (II. i. 179)

The second line clearly contains the usual tempest-beasts; as for the third, we may remember the part played by apes in *Othello* and *Timon*. Oberon varies his animals a little when he speaks the actual charm:

> Be it ounce, or cat, or bear,
> Pard, or boar with bristled hair,
> In thy eye that shall appear
> When thou wakest, it is thy dear.   (II. ii. 30)

The ounce and pard are new, but clearly in the usual tradition; the cat recalls the 'wild-cat' to which Katharina, the Shrew, is compared; the boar and bear are old friends—or enemies. The bear especially hardly ever fails to put in an appearance on these occasions. Such are the nightmare beasts Oberon's tempestuous jealousy would introduce to a Fairy Queen's love. And all these suggestions build an atmosphere of fearsomeness in our play. So, too, Puck is a terror to the Athenian clowns, assuming animal-shapes to frighten them from their wits:

> I'll follow you, I'll lead you about a round,
> Through bog, through bush, through brake, through brier:
> Sometime a horse I'll be, sometime a hound,
> A hog, a headless bear, sometime a fire;
> And neigh, and bark, and grunt, and roar, and burn,
> Like horse, hound, hog, bear, fire, at every turn.
>
> (III. i. 109)

The 'bush' is frequent in this play—and we may remember the 'bush of thorn' held by moonshine in the Interlude. Indeed, the 'bush' may suggest the waking daylight reality

that takes the place of our midnight terrors, as in *Lucrece*,
973. Theseus wisely comments on the lovers' stories:

> Or in the night, imagining some fear,
> How easy is a bush supposed a bear!   (v. i. 21)

In this speech Theseus aptly analyses the swift phantasms
of imagination that are so vividly sovereign here: phantasms of poetry, love, and madness. So 'the lunatic, the
lover and the poet' are grouped together. Nor is it a
strange association. Shakespeare's thought ever suggests
the kinship of madness, the *Macbeth* nightmare frenzy, the
super-consciousness of love, and poetry. And scarcely in
any play do we find all together so finely and freely
imagined and interwoven, as here: Theseus's speech is
indeed appropriate. For this play is more than a merry
romance. It is thick with clustering and profound imaginations, sweet and sombre.

Towards the close of the play Puck utters another truly
Macbeth-like speech, which yet blends exquisitely with
thoughts of holiness:

> Now the hungry lion roars,
>   And the wolf behowls the moon;
> Whilst the heavy plowman snores,
>   All with weary task fordone.
> Now the wasted brands do glow,
>   Whilst the screech owl, screeching loud,
> Puts the wretch that lies in woe
>   In remembrance of a shroud.
> Now it is the time of night
>   That the graves, all gaping wide,
> Every one lets forth his sprite
>   In the church-way paths to glide:
> And we fairies that do run
>   By the triple Hecate's team,
> From the presence of the sun,
>   Following darkness like a dream,
> Now are frolic: not a mouse
> Shall disturb this hallow'd house:
> I am sent with broom before,
> To sweep the dust behind the door.   (v. ii. 1)

Notice the 'hungry lion', the 'wolf', the 'screech owl'; the death thoughts, especially the idea of ghosts; then, the description of the fairies, associated with Hecate, spirits of darkness and dream; yet also frolicsome, and here bent on expelling all beasts—even the 'mouse'—from the bridal chambers of happy love; fairies of darkness, yet with power to 'hallow' the house in which their gossamer footsteps tread. The play is thus full of fierce beasts. There is the lion who, like the boar in *Venus and Adonis*, opposes happy love in the Pyramus and Thisbe interlude:

> You ladies, you, whose gentle hearts do fear
> The smallest monstrous mouse that creeps on floor,
> May now perchance both quake and tremble here,
> When lion rough in wildest rage doth roar.
>
> (v. i. 222)

We may remember Bottom's desire to take this part, and the numerous arguments about the lion throughout rehearsal and during the performance. Bottom is, indeed, himself one of our 'beasts'.

Oberon charms Titania to 'wake when some vile thing is near': he expects a tempest-beast, but instead she wakes to love Bottom, ass-headed. Throughout we must see an exquisite contrast between these two, Bottom and Titania. The one is 'the shallowest thick-skin of that barren sort' (III. ii. 13); the other, all queenly, feminine, and fairy grace. Bottom's name is probably significant, like Dogberry's, Ford's, Katharina's, Viola's. So recalling his dream of an ass's head, he says he will call it Bottom's Dream 'because it hath no bottom' (IV. i. 221). We may recall Pompey Bum in *Measure for Measure*, where the two names make a paradox after the fashion of 'Christopher Sly'. Thus our Bottom-Titania contrast is at root similar to those oppositions of the bestial and spiritual I have observed in *The Merry Wives*, the Induction and play of *The Taming of the Shrew*, and *The Merchant of Venice*. The two extremes of our very varied dramatic persons are here brought together in the Bottom-Titania union: and in this incident a certain beauty shines through the comedy. It is a symbolic union: symbolic of the whole play where opposites are so exquisitely blended in unity.

This is a union of the material and the spiritual; or the bestial and the birdlike. Birds in Shakespeare suggest spiritual essences: both through their ethereality and their song-music. They are thus to be contrasted with rough beasts. And the bird-beast opposition is vivid here:

> The dove pursues the griffin; the mild hind
> Makes speed to catch the tiger.   (II. i. 232)

Bottom's heavy wit or blundering ignorance gives us other examples. Here is one:

> . . . I will roar you as gently as any sucking dove; I will roar you an 'twere any nightingale.   (I. ii. 84)

Again:

> . . . to bring in—God shield us!—a lion among ladies, is a most dreadful thing; for there is not a more fearful wild-fowl than your lion living. . . .   (III. i. 31)

The humour in these clearly depends on the bird-beast contrast. Rough beasts are ever to be contrasted with ladies. Now much of our paradoxical comedy turns on the beast-bird opposition, if we remember always to regard Bottom himself as a beast. We often hear of his voice. 'He is a very paramour for a sweet voice' (IV. ii. 12). He will 'sing' the tale of his dream before the Duke (IV. i. 224). He clearly prides himself on his voice. And when he finds himself deserted by his companions he passes off an embarrassing situation by singing, and all about birds too:

> I will walk up and down here, and I will sing, that they shall hear I am not afraid.   (III. i. 126)

So he sings two stanzas of the 'ousel cock', 'the throstle with his note so true', the 'wren', the 'finch', 'sparrow' and 'lark', and the 'plain-song cuckoo'. They are all song birds.[1] And this music enraptures Titania:

> I pray thee, gentle mortal, sing again:
> Mine ear is much enamour'd of thy note.
>
> (III. i. 140)

Ass-headed Bottom, song-birds, and Titania: the union of these is profoundly comic, depending for our full understanding on full awareness of the bird-beast opposition. For Titania, also, must clearly be directly associated with birds and contrasted with evil beasts. Consider the lovely song invoking 'Philomel' to sing 'with melody' in the 'sweet lullaby' of the Fairy Queen (II. ii. 9–24). 'Snakes', 'hedgehogs', the 'newt', and 'blindworm', 'spiders', 'beetles', the 'worm' and 'snail'—these are to be charmed away: they are evil, reptilian, of *Macbeth* suggestion again. Instead, the nightingale's music. And all this is a contrast between the gross and ethereal; which contrast is exquisitely imagined in the love of Titania for Bottom:

> I'll give thee fairies to attend on thee,
> And they shall fetch thee jewels from the deep,
> And sing while thou on pressed flowers dost sleep:
> And I will purge thy mortal grossness so
> That thou shalt like an airy spirit go.   (III. i. 160)

'Mortal grossness'—so also the clowns' interlude is 'this palpable gross play' (v. i. 374). And 'an airy spirit'. It is the Caliban-Ariel contrast; and we have already met it in the story of Falstaff and the fairies, or of Christopher Sly, who endures a very similar experience to that of Bottom as he wakes from swinish drunkenness to miraculous aesthetic delights.

There is much 'bird' and 'flower' reference. Most of the birds I have had occasion to notice. We might add the 'clamorous owl' that 'hoots and wonders' at the fairies (II. ii. 6): a sombre bird mentioned again in a speech of

---

[1] I take the 'sparrow' to be the hedge-sparrow. I think I have been told this, but can give no authority.

Puck already quoted. And love is often given delicate bird-imagery in Shakespeare:

> Begin these wood-birds but to couple now?
>
> (IV. i. 144)

There is a fine 'dispersal' speech, describing the confusion Puck strikes into the Athenian villagers:

> When they him spy,
> As wild geese that the creeping fowler eye,
> Or russet-pated choughs, many in sort,
> Rising and cawing at the gun's report,
> Sever themselves and madly sweep the sky,
> So at his sight, away his fellows fly. . . .   (III. ii. 19)

Birds are variably used. But volatile suggestion most often occurs in relation to swift apprehension, ethereal emotions, spiritual intuitions. Spirits are bird-like in their arrow-flight:

> I go, I go; look how I go,
> Swifter than arrow from the Tartar's bow.
>
> (III. ii. 100)

So, too, in their 'flight' (IV. i. 103) Titania and Oberon can compass the globe 'swifter than the wandering moon' (IV. i. 102). Cupid has wings. And winged Cupid's arrows of love fly birdlike, swift and sure:

> That very time I saw, but thou could'st not,
> Flying between the cold moon and the earth
> Cupid all armed: a certain aim he took
> At a fair vestal throned by the west,
> And loosed his love-shaft smartly from his bow,
> As it should pierce a hundred thousand hearts;
> But I might see young Cupid's fiery shaft,
> Quench'd in the chaste beams of the watery moon
> And the imperial votaress passed on
> In maiden meditation, fancy-free.   (II. i. 155)

Again, birds are musical. We have already met the nightingale, the song invocation to Philomel to blend his melody with the Fairy Queen's lullaby. We also have Helena's:

>   . . . and your tongue's sweet air
> More tuneable than lark to shepherd's ear,
> When wheat is green, when hawthorn buds appear.
>
> (I. i. 183)

Here bird-music is associated with love. Which passage leads on to other nature suggestion. There is much else, more than I can notice here.

Much already has been quoted. There are many flowers—the 'little western flower, before mik-white, now purple with love's wound' (II. i. 167); the 'rose' of maidenhood distilled in marriage (I. i. 76); Oberon's lovely and detailed description of flowery delight—'I know a bank where the wild thyme blows' (II. i. 249); all the varied nature speeches of Titania, her tempest speech; the 'pressed flowers' on which Bottom is to be lulled to sleep with fairy song (III. i. 162); the fairies Pease-blossom, Moth, Cobweb, and Mustardseed; the grapes and figs and mulberries and humble-bees. Nature is here rich with midsummer increase, beauty, and bounty. And often this nature poetry is beautifully blended with jewel imagery, as the moonbeams light the sparkling dew that carpets the forest. Phoebe is thus imaged as

> Decking with liquid pearl the bladed grass.
>
> (I. i. 211)

Titania's fairy tells us:

> And I serve the fairy queen,
> To dew her orbs upon the green.
> The cowslips tall her pensioners be:
> In their gold coats spots you see;
> Those be rubies, fairy favours,
> In those freckles live their savours:
> I must go seek some dew-drops here
> And hang a pearl in every cowslip's ear.   (II. i. 8)

'Rubies', 'pearl': jewel-imagery blends beautifully with nature images. Again:

> For she his hairy temples then had rounded
> With coronet of fresh and fragrant flowers;
> And that same dew, which some time on the buds
> Was wont to swell like round and orient pearls,
> Stood now within the pretty flowerets' eyes
> Like tears that did their own disgrace bewail.
>
> (IV. i. 54)

'Orient pearls'—a typical Shakespearian thought. And all this jewel imagery is also part of Shakespeare's usual love-jewel association. At the start we hear Lysander has bewitched Hermia

> With bracelets of thy hair, rings, gawds, conceits.
>
> (I. i. 33)

And after the middle scenes, Helena, half dreaming still, dazedly wonders:

> And I have found Demetrius like a jewel,
> Mine own, and not mine own.   (IV. i. 195)

Between these, we are in a dream-world, where a magic wood sparkles with dew-jewelled flowers, glimmering in the moonbeams; which dream is yet a love-dream, tossed though it be by unrest and frenzy. As the darkness pales, the moon gives place to sunrise, jewels of grass and dew to a happy dawn of love and human life.

The waking from our dream is delicately imagined. The middle scenes show us a dream-world; but the magic of dream is nowhere more mysterious than in that dawn consciousness where two worlds meet. Then all our mistakes and frenzies shall be as a sleep-vision, half-forgotten:

> When they next wake, all this derision
> Shall seem a dream and fruitless vision. . . .
>
> (III. ii. 370)

So our dream-tossed mortals

> May all to Athens back again repair
> And think no more of this night's accidents
> But as the fierce vexation of a dream.   (IV. i. 70)

'Fierce vexation'. It is no easy dream, albeit one of

sweetest fancy and happy remembrance. In their night
distress the lovers long for dawn:

> O weary night, O long and tedious night,
> Abate thy hours! shine comforts from the east. . . .
>
> (III. ii. 431)

The fairies hasten to remedy the distresses of their moonlit
dream-world to prepare for the other world of dawn and
daylight: yet they do not altogether fear that brighter sun,
and Oberon boasts of his power to face its brilliance:

> *Puck.* My fairy lord, this must be done with haste,
> For night's swift dragons cut the clouds full fast,
> And yonder shines Aurora's harbinger;
> At whose approach, ghosts, wandering here and there,
> Troop home to churchyards: damned spirits all,
> That in crossways and floods have burial,
> Already to their wormy beds are gone;
> For fear lest day should look their shames upon,
> They wilfully themselves exile from light
> And must for aye consort with black-brow'd night.
> *Oberon.* But we are spirits of another sort:
> I with the morning's love have oft made sport,
> And, like a forester, the groves may tread,
> Even till the eastern gate, all fiery red,
> Opening on Neptune with fair blessed beams,
> Turns into yellow gold his salt green streams.
> But, notwithstanding, haste; make no delay:
> We may effect this business yet ere day. (III. ii. 378)

Notice the *Hamlet* and *Macbeth* impressions in Puck's
speech. And next, the up-blazing dawn, gilding a smooth
sea; sun and sea together creating a gold splendour that
mates the elements of air and water; the sudden grandeur
of day after the mystic glimmerings and gossamer fears
that weave the fairyland of sleep. In this dawn the lovers
wake to Theseus's hunting horns, the daily trumpet of
life dispelling death, recalling that other 'trumpet', there
'hideous', that shatters the 'downy sleep' in *Macbeth*.
Theseus enters on our night of fears and fairyland as a
rising sun. Throughout he is, in his wisdom and gold-

hearted charity, a richly human force, more potent than
fairies, wiser than dream-tossed lovers. Christ-like,[1] he
rises on the tormenting imaginations of fairyland, the pagan
terrors of the midnight wood. In Theseus fairyland and
mortality hold no nightmare contest. For in him the
furthest potentialities of Oberon and Bottom are blended.
So his horns sound a clarion challenge to all fantastic fears.
The lovers wake, their vision still half in fairyland; they
reply 'half sleep, half waking' (IV. i. 151). Even when left
alone, they are not sure of themselves:

> Are you sure
> That we are awake? It seems to me
> That yet we sleep, we dream.   (IV. i. 196)

The dream is quickly dissolving, farther and farther, lost in
the distance, the infinite distance severing sleep from daylight life. But on first waking, reality too is vague, distant:

> These things seem small and undistinguishable,
> Like far-off mountains turned into clouds.   (IV. i. 191)

So they all return to Athens, and happy love.

Finally, all is love, harmony, music. Starting with
tempests and dissension, I have traced the moon and
darkness suggestion; the atmosphere of Macbeth-like
nightmare, the mistakes and tragic passions, the fearsome
beasts; again, the birds with which these are contrasted, a
contrast perfectly and beautifully symbolized in the
Bottom-Titania union; the sparkling jewel-imagery applied to grass and flowers; finally, the dawn-poetry, the
waking back to human life. I have yet to observe the music
which inter-threads our pattern.

First, I will note references to music; next, actual music.
Early we hear that Lysander has 'sung' verses to his love
(I. i. 30) by moonlight; and with this we may remember
the image of nuns 'chanting faint hymns' to the moon
(I. i. 73); and Titania's other association of the moon with

---

[1] I cannot defend the analogy here; but I may some day write further
on Theseus. Observe his words to Hippolyta before the Interlude.

votive hymns and carols. Titania accuses Oberon of
'playing on pipes of corn and versing love to amorous
Phillida' (II. i. 67). There are the numerous references to
bird-song already observed, many contrasting humorously
with Bottom. Especially we may remember Titania's line
on being waked by Bottom's singing:

> What angel wakes me from my flowery bed?
>
> (III. i. 132)

Her ear is 'enamour'd' of his 'note' (III. i. 141), and her
fairies shall 'sing' to him while he rests on 'pressed
flowers' (III. i. 162). The quarrels of the lovers are, however, a 'jangling' (III. ii. 353): music ever accompanies
love or peace of any kind, but all quarrels are a discord.
Titania is always offering her ass-headed love music:

> *Titania.* What, wilt thou hear some music, my sweet love?
> *Bottom.* I have a reasonable good ear in music. Let's have the
>   tongs and the bones.   (IV. i. 28)

Bottom, here and elsewhere, considers himself musical.
And our sense of comedy depends largely on this incon-
gruity. The bridal revels bring us to more music suggestion. Theseus asks Philostrate what masques or music he
has ready (v. i. 40). The programme offers him

> The riot of the tipsy Bacchanals,
> Tearing the Thracian singer in their rage.   (v. i. 48)

A rage-music opposition. Again, we have

> The thrice three Muses mourning for the death
> Of Learning, late deceased in beggary.   (v. i. 52)

Music-language is frequent in this scene:

> How shall we find the concord of this discord?
>
> (v. i. 60)

And,

> Indeed he hath played on his prologue like a child on a
> recorder; a sound, but not in government.
>
> (v. i. 123)

There are also two other especially fine music-passages.
The first is Oberon's:

> My gentle Puck, come hither. Thou rememberest
> Since once I sat upon a promontory,
> And heard a mermaid on a dolphin's back
> Uttering such dulcet and harmonious breath
> That the rude sea grew civil at her song
> And certain stars shot madly from their spheres,
> To hear the sea-maid's music.   (II. i. 148)

This is a typical Shakespearian speech. 'Promontory' we
meet again in fine and important passages in *Antony and
Cleopatra* and *The Tempest*. The mermaid, dolphin—
the dolphin recurs in *Antony and Cleopatra*—and music all
contrast with the 'rude sea' which yet is by them charmed
to civility. Notice, too, the 'star' thought: how the stars,
elsewhere associated with music, here charge headlong
from their stations to blend themselves with the mermaid's
siren song. Such is the 'sea-maid's music'. Our next
passage is spoken by Theseus and Hippolyta:

> *Theseus.* Go, one of you, find out the forester;
>   For now our observation is perform'd;
>   And since we have the vaward of the day,
>   My love shall hear the music of my hounds.
>   Uncouple in the western valley; let them go:
>   Dispatch, I say, and find the forester.
>   We will, fair queen, up to the mountain's top
>   And mark the musical confusion
>   Of hounds and echo in conjunction.
> *Hippolyta.* I was with Hercules and Cadmus once,
>   When in a wood of Crete they bay'd the bear
>   With hounds of Sparta: never did I hear
>   Such gallant chiding; for, besides the groves,
>   The skies, the fountains, every region near
>   Seem'd all one mutual cry: I never heard
>   So musical a discord, such sweet thunder.
> *Theseus.* My hounds are bred out of the Spartan kind,
>   So flew'd, so sanded, and their heads are hung
>   With ears that sweep away the morning dew;
>   Crook-knee'd, and dew-lapp'd like Thessalian bulls;

Slow in pursuit, but match'd in mouth like bells,
Each under each. A cry more tuneable
Was never holla'd to, nor cheer'd with horn,
In Crete, in Sparta, nor in Thessaly:
Judge when you hear. But, soft! what nymphs are these?
                                                    (IV. i. 107)

The music thought here is most interesting, especially in
its blending of diversity—which gives tempests—with
unity, which is music. We have a 'musical confusion',
'so musical a discord', and 'such sweet thunder': clearly
this is another variation being played on our tempest-
music opposition, and one which reflects the final impression of the whole of Shakespeare's work: tempests
dissolved in a sublime unity of music. Observe here, too,
how our most eminent tempest-beast, the bear, is aptly
attacked by these more musical beasts of Theseus. The
'bells' are also important, since 'jangling' is a recurrent
word for human discords—thus Hamlet's madness is
as 'sweet bells jangled'. Also we may observe, what
is characteristic of Shakespeare always, that though
this speech is universally and typically Shakespearian,
it is yet woven in a fabric peculiar to its own play.
Notice the forester, groves, fountains, morning-dew—all,
especially if we remember the varied nature-images of
Titania's tempest speech, are particular to this vision.
Finally, note especially how these lovely speeches of discords resolved in music are blended with dawn, 'the
vaward of the day', and exquisitely prelude the awakening
of the lovers whose long night of 'jangling' (III. ii. 353) is
to be now harmonized in the music of love: 'But, soft!
what nymphs are these?' And all these effects here are the
finer if we remember that they are spoken by Theseus.

But there is actual music, too. Oberon and Titania
suffer a dissension, and we have Titania's lengthy 'tempest' speech. Next, in solitary pride, Titania would enjoy
peace and music, and we have the lullaby sung by her
fairies and the invocation to Philomel. Here there is song,
but no actual direction for music. But Oberon breaks into

her peaceful sleep with his charm, and all its hideous
beasts. This song, then, is similar to the music in Act III
of *Othello*: it suggests the peace which is shortly to be
disturbed. It is to be contrasted with the tempest-beasts
of Oberon's charm. True, when she awakes to love
Bottom, she does not feel distress; rather she truly loves
him, and offers him, too, music. But, from Oberon's
view, and hers later, she endures a temporary disaster; and
she finally loses her Indian boy. When, however, she and
Oberon are reconciled. we may observe our only effect of
pure and actual symbolic music, which clearly contrasts
powerfully with the tempest-poetry of their original quarrel:

Oberon. Silence awhile. Robin, take off this head.
  Titania, music call; and strike more dead
  Than common sleep of all these five the sense.
Titania. Music, ho! music, such as charmeth sleep!
                                              [*Music, still.*
Puck. Now, when thou wakest, with thine own fool's eyes peep.
Oberon. Sound, music! Come, my queen, take hands with me,
  And rock the ground whereon these sleepers be
  Now thou and I are new in amity
  And will to-morrow midnight solemnly
  Dance in Duke Theseus' house triumphantly
  And bless it to all fair prosperity:
  There shall the pairs of faithful lovers be
  Wedded, with Theseus, all in jollity.   (IV. i. 83)

Reunion and music replace tempest and dissension.

Here, too, there is dance. Throughout the play there
are references to fairy revels and fairy dance. Oberon,
says Puck, 'doth keep his revels here to-night' (II. i. 18).
Titania and her fairies love to 'dance' their 'ringlets' to
the 'whistling wind' (II. i. 86)—a suggestion that these
are spirits of tempest as well as music, as, indeed, they
are, creatures of unrestful and delightful fancy; she asks
if Oberon will 'dance in our round' (II. i. 140); she has 'a
roundel and a fairy song' before sleeping (II. ii. 1), for it
is her custom to sleep in flowers first 'lull'd' by 'dances and
delight' (II. i. 254). So at the end, after the Interlude has

been concluded by the players' Bergomask (v. i. 361), when human lovers have gone to happy rest, dismissing all woodland fairies from their thoughts as they enter the other fairyland of love, Oberon and Titania and Puck return, to tread silently, light as 'bird from brier', across the deserted hall, the fire-brands fading cold and pale, pale as the moon whose beams steal silently through the casement; and there they bless the bridal night with their fairy dance:

> *Oberon.* Through the house give glimmering light,
>   By the dead and drowsy fire:
> Every elf and fairy sprite
>   Hop as light as bird from brier;
> And this ditty after me,
> Sing, and dance it trippingly.
> *Titania.* First, rehearse your song by rote,
>   To each word a warbling note:
> Hand in hand, with fairy grace,
> Will we sing and bless this place.   (v. ii. 21)

There is a 'song and dance'. The fairies go to consecrate each chamber with 'field-dew'; and Oberon and Titania, no longer jealous, to bless the 'best bride-bed' (v. ii. 33) of their loves, Theseus and Hippolyta. Theseus wooed Hippolyta with his sword (i. i. 16) but has wedded her 'in another key' (i. i. 18) with revelling and feast; the lovers and old Egeus are in harmony; and fairyland and mortality are at peace once more.

Three persons here have especial autonomy, existing, as it were, in their own right: Theseus, Oberon, and Bottom. Each is sovereign in his sphere, king over his companions, and demands our respect. Nor can we, who watch, say with confidence that one is more real than the others. And the remarks I am to make on Theseus and the fairies must not be taken to mean that those fairies are purely unreal. Rash fancies may be dangerous, inexpedient to man: it does not follow that they are untrue. Now at the start we have a discord, among men and fairies, and in each world the discord may be said to derive from the other. The

Athenian lovers and Egeus find their imaginations and desires conflicting with actualities; that is, their fairy dreams of happiness will not materialize. And in the wood Oberon and Titania quarrel, and their dissension is due wholly to their contact with humanity—rivalry for the Indian boy, jealousy respectively of Theseus and Hippolyta. Oberon accuses Titania of leading Theseus 'through the glimmering night' and making him break faith with Perigenia, Aegle, Ariadne, and Antiopa—is she then a personification, from a mortal's view, of the unrestful fancy and love-longing which torments mankind? And Titania also accuses Oberon of disguising himself as Corin and piping love to 'amorous Phillida' (ii. i. 61–80). Oberon cures Titania of her violent love for the boy by making her love the ass-headed Bottom: after that, she suffers a revulsion from excessive mortal desire. Dissension thus enters fairyland through the fairies' love of mortals; there is dissension at Athens through mortals aspiring to the fairyland of their love. The lovers then violently pursue their love into the magic wood, and find themselves in confusion. Thus the action shows us first the clash, then the reharmonizing of fairyland and human life. So the original tempest gives place finally to music, revelry, and feast.

But of all our persons Theseus is the calmest and wisest. Whatever old unrest he has endured is now over; and he will not believe in the lovers' story. Why? He shows an exquisite and wide love and deep human knowledge; witness his remarks to Hippolyta before the play. But he groups the lunatic, the frenzied lover, and the poet together as untrustworthy and fantastic story-tellers. He is a greater than they. For such deal in pure fancies: whereas Theseus himself blends all such imaginations with life. Poetry is to him thus purely fanciful:

> The best in this kind are but shadows; and the worst are no worse if imagination amend them.   (v. i. 214)

Set midway between the two kings Bottom and Oberon, himself a mightier king than they, he is master of all that

13

is best in either.[1] Living, then, the life of inward music,
Theseus himself makes no division between fairyland
and actuality: therefore pure fairyland is, to him, non-
existent, and he can smile at the extravagances of un-
disciplined fancy. And yet it is Theseus who gently
introduces the fairies at the end:

> Lovers, to bed; 'tis almost fairy time   (v. i. 371)

And it is right that the words should be his.

For, on the bridal night if never else, the lovers all
enjoy this harmony natural to Theseus, this peace, this
blending of spirit-dreams with their own lives; and this
it is that is symbolized by the fairies' final entry, song,
and dance, to honour, without wrangling, their loved ones
on earth. These wayward spirits and mankind here blend
in one harmony, and the two worlds, fact and fairyland,
which have been divided in tempest, now embrace to
music.

[1] The Bottom-Oberon contrast repeats that of Falstaff and the fairies
in *The Merry Wives of Windsor*. Theseus holds the balance exact of
earthliness and spirituality, Caliban and Ariel.

IV

THE TRAGEDIES

I

FROM the tempestuous welter of Shakespeare's earlier work in history or tragedy we find born from time to time the vague image of the soul's Siren delight. The romantic Comedies are set in another world than the Histories: they are dreamland itself. In them the poet, taking his dreamland as actuality, yet silhouettes his theme against the tempests of discord and division. Tempests are active between fairyland and actuality: which relation is vivid in *A Midsummer Night's Dream*. But in the latter half of Shakespeare's work a change occurs. Tempests begin to assume a new and powerful significance. They are vividly present, at the very core of the play's action. In the Histories tempests are powerfully related to the turbulences of actual life, but they are for the most part confined to imagery. In the Romances they are, in relation to the several plots, often actualized; but those plots themselves are less close-twined with realism, and the tempests, actual though they be, remain in the background. In the great Tragedies, however, the tempest becomes often the very heart of the organism. The poet makes his recurrent intuition of discord the centre of his action: exactly, minutely, he now penetrates into the metaphysic of disorder, expressing in a series of tragedies different facets of this one theme. We begin to see clearly how this tempest is a tragedy–symbol: it is often so perfectly embodied in a human plot that its significance is crystal clear. And, opposed to tempests, we have music, suggesting love and concord. Next I shall therefore glance shortly at the plays of this period, grouping them rather in order of convenience than composition, and noting first the two problem plays, *Troilus*, and *Measure for Measure*; and next *Hamlet*. In these plays tempests are not so exactly used at the heart of the action as in the plays of my second section.

Tempests are important in *Troilus and Cressida.* Here the poet very carefully and deliberately analyses his tempests and love-themes, giving that analysis clear and careful expression. Agamemnon and Nestor argue with Ulysses on tempests, stressing the essential nobility of man's tragic struggle. Agamemnon observes that all men alike show well 'in fortune's love':

> But, in the wind and tempest of her frown,
> Distinction, with a broad and powerful fan,
> Puffing at all, winnows the light away;
> And what hath mass and matter, by itself
> Lies rich in virtue and unmingled.   (I. iii. 26)

Nestor continues:

>   In the reproof of chance
> Lies the true proof of men: the sea being smooth,
> How many shallow bauble boats dare sail
> Upon her patient breast, making their way
> With those of nobler bulk!
> But let the ruffian Boreas once enrage
> The gentle Thetis, and anon behold
> The strong-ribb'd bark through liquid mountains cut,
> Bounding between the two moist elements,
> Like Perseus' horse: where 's then the saucy boat
> Whose weak untimber'd sides but even now
> Co-rivall'd greatness? Either to harbour fled,
> Or made a toast for Neptune. Even so
> Doth valour's show and valour's worth divide
> In storms of fortune; for in her ray and brightness
> The herd hath more annoyance by the breese
> Than by the tiger; but when the splitting wind
> Makes flexible the knees of knotted oaks,
> And flies fled under shade, why, then the thing of courage
> As roused with rage with rage doth sympathize,
> And with an accent tuned in selfsame key
> Retorts to chiding fortune.   (I. iii. 33)

Observe the tiger-tempest association: and the usual word 'fortune'. Notice, too, the 'splitting' wind, and

the 'oak'. Oaks, pines, and cedars often occur, like
fierce beasts, in these tempest-passages. Also the word
'rage' is emphasized here. Ulysses answers that such a
sublimation of tragic conflict as an ideal is unsound: it
is an apotheosis of disorder. He speaks at length on
disorder, using the usual Shakespearian phraseology
of sun, planets, air, sea, and earth. The wind and sea
references bear close resemblance to others that I have
quoted:

> . . . but when the planets
> In evil mixture to disorder wander,
> What plagues and what portents! what mutiny!
> What raging of the sea! shaking of earth!
> Commotion in the winds!   (I. iii. 94)

Again,

> Take but degree away, untune that string,
> And, hark, what discord follows! each thing meets
> In mere oppugnancy: the bounded waters
> Should lift their bosoms higher than the shores
> And make a sop of all this solid globe. . . .   (I. iii. 109)

Observe, again, the association whereby order is music:
'untune that string'. And notice the fine hyperbole in our
usual flood-disorder tradition. The whole of Ulysses'
speech is most important for any understanding of Shakespeare's disorder-thought such as occurs in Timon's
curses, or in the symbolism of *Macbeth* and *Julius Caesar*.
Order is one of the profoundest and most widespread
thoughts in Shakespeare.

   In *Troilus* the Trojans are idealists, and their world one
of love, honour, and romance generally; whereas the
Greek party are intellectuals and cynics, and shown almost
as disorder-forces, though Ulysses knows the necessity for
order and both Agamemnon and Nestor touch the gentle
idealism of the Trojans. The music noted in the stage
direction of Act III, scene i, and associated with Paris and
Helen, is thus significant, blending with its romantic
setting. Throughout the play tempest-images occur. A

'smile' buries a 'sigh' as the 'sun' lights a 'storm' (i. i. 37).
Agamemnon talks of how better men than Achilles

> watch
> His pettish lunes, his ebbs, his flows, as if
> The passage and whole carriage of this action
> Rode on his tide. (ii. iii. 138)

Again, we have 'the stream of his dispose' (ii. iii. 174).
Wisdom is a 'shore' confining other qualities (ii. iii.
260). Lovers vow to 'weep seas' and 'tame tigers' (iii. ii.
84), a clear example of our tempest-beast association.
Water is 'false' (iii. ii. 198). Tears are as 'rain' to lay
the 'wind' of grief (iv. iv. 55). Rage is finely bodied into
a tempest-simile:

> . . . not the dreadful spout
> Which shipmen do the hurricano call,
> Constringed in mass by the almighty sun,
> Shall dizzy with more clamour Neptune's ear
> In his descent than shall my prompted sword
> Falling on Diomed. (v. ii. 171)

Achilles uses a characteristic image:

> My mind is troubled, like a fountain stirr'd;
> And I myself see not the bottom of it. (iii. iii. 311)

Here, too, love is three times imaged as set beyond the
sea. Early in the play Troilus speaks a few lines which
most perfectly in all Shakespeare clarify for us this particular image:

> Tell me, Apollo, for thy Daphne's love,
> What Cressid is, what Pandar, and what we?
> Her bed is India; there she lies, a pearl:
> Between our Ilium and where she resides,
> Let it be call'd the wild and wandering flood,
> Ourself the merchant, and this sailing Pandar
> Our doubtful hope, our convoy, and our bark.
> (i. i. 101)

'India', the 'pearl', the 'merchant', and 'bark'. Again,

> I stalk about her door,
> Like a strange soul upon the Stygian banks
> Staying for waftage. O, be thou my Charon,
> And give me swift transportance to those fields
> Where I may wallow in the lily-beds
> Proposed for the deserver! O gentle Pandarus,
> From Cupid's shoulder pluck his painted wings,
> And fly with me to Cressid!   (III. ii. 9)

Here we have first a boat-suggestion, then 'flying': a water and air association which is relevant to the water and air imagery of *Antony and Cleopatra*. Always these love-journeys are to be understood as suggesting metaphorically the richness of a finer consciousness, the difficult love-vision, both immediately present and infinitely far: thus Cressid, who in one sense lives next door, in another has to be placed in India. In another of Troilus's speeches 'eyes and ears' are as 'traded pilots 'twixt the dangerous shores of will and judgement', so unifying man's divided being to create the incandescent intuition of love (II. ii. 64–5). Troilus is here defending the cause of love. Helen must be guarded by Troy:

> We turn not back the silks upon the merchant,
> When we have soiled them. . . .

Paris sought her across the seas:

> Your breath of full consent bellied his sails;
> The seas and winds, old wranglers, took a truce
> And did him service. . . .

He won a prize of infinite worth:

> Is she worth keeping? why, she is a pearl,
> Whose price hath launch'd above a thousand ships,
> And turn'd crown'd kings to merchants.

Her 'estimation' is 'prized richer than sea and land'. This long speech (II. ii. 61–96) is crammed with love-imagery in the usual tradition: rough seas, the pilot, ships, merchants, silks, pearls. Music, as I have noted, accompanies the entrance of Helen, Queen of Love (III. i); and the voice of Cressida is 'sweet music' (III. ii. 142) to Troilus.

There is comparatively little to observe in *Measure for Measure*. There are, however, some interesting 'pirate' ideas. Pirates are quite important in Shakespeare. There is the very powerfully written episode of Suffolk's death in *2 Henry VI* which I have already observed; and in *Twelfth Night* the deepest tragic notes are related to tempests and the accusation of piracy, probably undeserved, against Antonio. Pirates occur also in *Hamlet* and *Pericles*; and are mentioned in *The Merchant of Venice*. In *Measure for Measure* we have early the amusing dialogue about the 'sanctimonious Pirate' and the ten commandments: the point depending wholly on our sense of piratical villainy. The pirate in Shakespeare is, like sea monsters, doubly villainous; he is a thief and murderer by trade and also has all the additional terrors associated with the deep added to his human iniquity:

> *Lucio.* Thou concludest like the sanctimonious pirate, that went to sea with the Ten Commandments, but scraped one out of the table.
> *Second Gentleman.* 'Thou shalt not steal'?
> *Lucio.* Ay, that he razed.
> *First Gentleman.* Why, 'twas a commandment to command the Captain and all the rest from their functions: they put forth to steal.   (I. ii. 7)

The dialogue serves well to strike the note of religion and ethical argument blended with wit and penetrative analysis which characterizes this play. Indeed, this is a microcosm of the whole. *Measure for Measure* shows us that no ethic can be rigid; sexual purity, pursued as an absolute, becomes hideous. So the main problem is neatly expressed here in the problem of the pirate who, to be a good and successful pirate, must needs erase at least one commandment. Or again, we may see in his comic sanctimoniousness a parody of Angelo's: he, like Angelo, has undertaken more than his nature will let him accomplish. But pirates are usually sombre and evil forces in

Shakespeare rather than humorous. And we may note another curious pirate-reference here. The Duke decides that Barnardine must not be executed: indeed, if we ever saw the Duke condemn or punish any one during the action, our idea of him as a prophet of forgiveness would be seriously modified. But a head must be produced to satisfy Angelo. The poet characteristically overcomes the difficulty with a pirate:

> *Provost.*   Here in the prison, father,
> There died this morning of a cruel fever
> One Ragozine, a most notorious pirate,
> A man of Claudio's years; his beard and head
> Just of his colour.   (IV iii. 73)

If some one has to die, let it be a pirate. The Shakespearian trend of thought is curiously patent here. Another typical Shakespearian mechanism occurs elsewhere. Mariana's marriage to Angelo was tragically thwarted by a sea-disaster:

> She should this Angelo have married; was affianced to her by
> oath, and the nuptial appointed: between which time of the
> contract and limit of the solemnity, her brother Frederick was
> wrecked at sea, having in that perished vessel the dowry of his
> sister.   (III. i. 221)

Again, we have sea-tempests opposing love.

Two other tempest-passages in the play are important. Isabella speaks some fine lines on man's paltry authority, how if great men could thunder they would usurp and misuse the ire of God:

> Could great men thunder
> As Jove himself does, Jove would ne'er be quiet,
> For every pelting, petty officer
> Would use his heaven for thunder;
> Nothing but thunder! Merciful Heaven,
> Thou rather with thy sharp and sulphurous bolt
> Split'st the unwedgeable and gnarled oak
> Than the soft myrtle. . . .   (II. ii. 110)

Notice here the tempest-oak association; and the recurrent word 'split'. Thunder is, as elsewhere, notably in

Lear and *Cymbeline*—where the 'bolt' is actually thrown—
the symbol of divine wrath. So, often, is tempest. And
so Claudio's idea of hell is

> To be imprison'd in the viewless winds,
> And blown with restless violence round about
> The pendent world.   (III. i. 124)

Other suggestions relative to this essay occur at III. ii.
51–3, where the 'tune' of Pompey's amatory profession is
drowned in the 'rain' of his punishment; at III. ii. 150,
where life is as a 'stream'; and at III. ii. 273, where the
Provost's excessive trouble to alter an official decree is like
a sea-journey to the 'extremest shore' of modesty. Finally,
the song-music of Mariana (IV. i) is most important: song
and music are continually the language of love's distress
amid the tempests of tragedy. Here even music is criti-
cized by the Duke: it can both 'make bad good' and 'good
provoke to harm' (IV. i. 15): which is natural in an ethical
play which so closely criticizes and analyses all ideals.

Tempests suggest tragic fate and man's passionate
response. They are things of conflict and violence.
Where there is little tragedy, as in *Antony and Cleopatra*,
or little passion, as in *Hamlet*, tempests will be less
powerful. In *Hamlet* there are, however, many minor
images to observe. Melancholy is like 'clouds' (I. ii. 66);
the breath of grief is 'windy' (I. ii. 79), tears a 'fruitful
river' (I. ii. 80), perfect love protects its object from 'the
winds of heaven' (I. ii. 141)—a love-tempest contrast such
as we have noted elsewhere; 'airs from heaven' are set
against 'blasts from hell' (I. iv. 41)—an *Antony and Cleo-
patra-Macbeth* contrast; deceptive love may 'wreck' Ophelia
(II. i. 113); the soul in anguish is as 'a sea of troubles' (III.
i. 59); Laertes' rebellion is like an 'ocean' rising above its
limits and overspreading 'the flats' (IV. v. 99). Hamlet once
draws a very clear comparison of 'tempests' to tragic art:

> . . . for in the very torrent, tempest, and, as I may say, the
> whirlwind of passion, you must acquire and beget a temperance
> that may give it smoothness.   (III. ii. 6)

Hamlet's madness is like tempest:

> Mad as the sea and wind, when both contend
> Which is the mightier.   (IV. i. 6)

But, in contrast, we may remember Hamlet's assurance:

>   Ecstasy!
> My pulse, as yours, doth temperately keep time,
> And makes as healthful music.   (III. iv. 139)

The music of sanity, of mental health and harmony. So, too, Ophelia uses a music metaphor:

> And I, of ladies most deject and wretched,
> That suck'd the honey of his music vows,
> Now see that noble and most sovereign reason
> Like sweet bells jangled, out of tune and harsh;
> That unmatch'd form and feature of blown youth
> Blasted with ecstasy.   (III. i. 163)

We might add another. Laertes' youthful exploits abroad are, in contrast to Hamlet's destiny, clearly things of happy life, in tune with life just as Hamlet is out of tune with it: 'Let him ply his music' (II. i. 73), says Polonius. So, too, the entry of the pleasure-loving and lively King is accompanied by a 'Danish March' (III. ii). But for much of the action Hamlet cannot feel either harmoniously or tempestuously, and is, as it were, numbed with pain. Probably the most powerful piece of tempest-poetry thus occurs in that passionate speech of the player which rouses Hamlet's envy:

> But, as we often see, against some storm,
> A silence in the heavens, the rack stand still,
> The bold winds speechless and the orb below
> As hush as death, anon the dreadful thunder
> Doth rend the region. . .   (II. ii. 513)

It is significant that in a moment of exultation, when he has recaptured his sense of purpose directly after the play, and makes harmonious though hostile contact with the reality of his world, Hamlet first sings and then calls for music:

Ah, ha! Come, some music! come, the recorders!
(III. ii. 302)

But usually Hamlet is out of tune with his world: it can 'fret' him but not 'play upon' him (III. ii. 395). The whole incident of the recorders and their 'eloquent music' is most important. So Hamlet will not 'discourse' music to Rosencrantz and Guildenstern. Love's distress again finds expression in song, Ophelia's plaintive tunes. In her, as Laertes observes, all discordant elements of madness become beautiful. Also the Gravedigger's songs herald a scene in which Hamlet is at peace with death and speaks a serene lyric acceptance of mortal destiny. These songs may seem scarcely music. Yet they contribute somewhat to the melody of this scene: there is a sense of peace, a backwater in the turbulent stream of tragedy. Finally, we should note the beautiful description of Ophelia's drowning:

> There is a willow grows aslant a brook,
> That shows his hoar leaves in the glassy stream;
> There with fantastic garlands did she come
> Of crow-flowers, nettles, daisies, and long purples,
> That liberal shepherds give a grosser name,
> But our cold maids do dead men's fingers call them:
> There, on the pendent boughs her coronet weeds
> Clambering to hang, an envious sliver broke;
> When down her weedy trophies and herself
> Fell in the weeping brook. Her clothes spread wide;
> And, mermaid-like, awhile they bore her up;
> Which time she chanted snatches of old tunes;
> As one incapable of her own distress,
> Or like a creature native and indued
> Unto that element: but long it could not be,
> Till that her garments, heavy with their drink,
> Pull'd the poor wretch from her melodious lay
> To muddy death.   (IV. vii. 167)

Notice the 'flowers', the 'weeping brook', the 'mermaid' thought. And there is music. Watery death is here sweet. Ophelia is to be contrasted ever with the sombre essences of the play. Here still waters and music blend, contrasting with tempests elsewhere: this speech reflects a reality comparable with the vision of *Antony and Cleopatra*. The fourth act of *Hamlet* is full of melody.

There is, too, in a different kind, Horatio's fine description of Hamlet's danger in the Ghost scene:

> What if it tempt you toward the flood, my lord,
> Or to the dreadful summit of the cliff
> That beetles o'er his base into the sea. . . .   (I. iv. 69)

—a warning certainly justified, if we remember the full value of the image, in terms of spiritual rather than physical danger. For this sea is fierce. As you look down you hear it 'roar beneath'. It is a raging sea, a deadly sea. And Hamlet lives a life of death henceforth. His sea voyage and pirate adventure, perhaps, may be allowed to hold a corresponding spiritual significance. It is a lonely voyage on the seas of death. But death, in shape of pirates, will not yet have him. He is 'to do a good turn' for them (IV. vi. 22). He returns to do it. The whole description of the sea-fight, and Hamlet's account of his altering ot the sealed orders on shipboard, is vivid and important. All must be related to the death-atmosphere of this play. This death theme attains a solemn beauty of its own in the dead march played at the end. In death there is no disharmony. So the 'soldiers' music' speaks for Hamlet at the last.

II

I pass now to four plays where tempests are particularly finely welded into the dramatic pattern.

Othello has numerous minor images. Iago complains that he has been 'be-lee'd and calm'd' (I. i. 30); human excellence is a matter of 'fathom' (I. i. 153); human power a matter of 'cable' (I. ii. 17); love is richer than 'the sea's worth' (I. ii. 28). Thus speaks Iago of Othello's marriage:

> 'Faith, he to-night hath boarded a land-carack:
> If it prove lawful prize, he's made for ever.   (I. ii. 50)

Grief is of 'a flood-gate and o'erbearing nature' (I. iii. 56); Othello's life of adventure has known 'moving accidents by flood and field' (I. iii. 135); Desdemona's sudden and reckless marriage is a 'downright violence and storm of fortunes' (I. iii. 250); friendship a matter of 'cables' (I. iii. 343). As Iago's plot takes form, his 'boat sails freely both with wind and stream' (II. iii. 65); hearts are 'brimful of fear' (II. iii. 214); worry 'puddles' the clear spirit of man (III. iv. 143). Love to Othello is

> The fountain from the which my current runs,
> Or else dries up. . .   (IV ii. 59)

Desdemona is 'false as water' (v. ii. 134). At the end, Othello speaks of his tragedy in terms of navigation:

> Here is my journey's end, here is my butt,
> And very sea-mark of my utmost sail.   (v. ii. 267)

We may compare the journeys which end in lovers meeting of Feste's song. Tragedy and romance alike in Shakespeare are usually to be imaged as sea-journeys; and all these images are, in their own way, in the tradition of those separate kinds I observe at the beginning of my essay. There is, too, Othello's fine description of his passion which will move

> Like to the Pontic sea,
> Whose icy current and compulsive course
> Ne'er feels retiring ebb, but keeps due on
> To the Propontic and the Hellespont. . . . (III. iii. 453)

Music, too, is set against tragedy. Actual music preludes the tragic movement of Act III. Its harmony suggests the love concord shortly to give place to chaos. Desdemona's 'willow' song accompanies her love-distress; Emilia 'plays the swan' and 'dies in music' (v. ii. 247). Desdemona is, indeed, a skilled musician:

> . . . an admirable musician: O! she will sing the savageness
> out of a bear. . . .   (IV. i. 199)

Bears and tigers are, as I have observed, both continually used as symbols of ferocity in contexts suggestive of tempests. Here there is a neat music-bear opposition.

But there is more than tempest-imagery. We hear much of the Turks' warlike navigation in Act I; and a tempest is powerful in Act II as a tragedy-symbol. Othello and Desdemona cross to Cyprus and their voyage is tempestuous. The tempest is vividly described. Montano and the various 'gentlemen' vie with each other in painting its unprecedented terror:

> *Montano.* Methinks the wind hath spoke aloud at land;
>   A fuller blast ne'er shook our battlements:
>   If it hath ruffian'd so upon the sea,
>   What ribs of oak, when mountains melt on them,
>   Can hold the mortise? What shall we hear of this?
> *Second Gent.* A segregation of the Turkish fleet:
>   For do but stand upon the foaming shore,
>   The chidden billow seems to pelt the clouds;
>   The wind-shaked surge, with high and monstrous mane,
>   Seems to cast water on the burning bear,
>   And quench the guards of the ever-fixed pole:
>   I never did like molestation view
>   On the enchafed flood.   (II. i. 5)

Observe the human association in 'ruffian'd'; the 'oak' suggestion, and 'mountains'. Note, too, the passionate suggestion in 'chidden'. And, especially, the 'burning bear' opposed to the sea's 'monstrous mane'. Here is another tempest-bear association. Sea and sky face each other not as raging men but raging beasts: the bear and lion, both tempest-animals. We have 'enchafed' again. The tempest, however, although 'segregating' or dispersing the Turks, for once respects love's divinity:

> Tempests themselves, high seas and howling winds,
> The gutter'd rocks and congregated sands—
> Traitors ensteep'd to clog the guiltless keel,—
> As having sense of beauty, do omit
> Their mortal natures, letting go safely by
> The divine Desdemona.   (II. i. 68)

Observe the tragic significance in 'guiltless'. Tempests are ever brimful of significance, things of universal import. Again,

> Great Jove, Othello guard,
> And swell his sail with thine own powerful breath,
> That he may bless this bay with his tall ship,
> Make love's quick pants in Desdemona's arms,
> Give renew'd fire to our extinct spirits,
> And bring all Cyprus comfort! (II. i. 77)

The tempest thus supports, buoys up, and inflates the happiness and fortune of love. Its turbulence lends glory to the love it cannot, or will not, wreck. But it is in the same order of image or symbol as our other tempests wherein love is lost or frustrated. Desdemona is 'the riches of the ship' (II. i. 83). Here physical tempests are to be contrasted and compared with spiritual ones. Hence Othello's:

> It gives me wonder great as my content
> To see you here before me. O my soul's joy!
> If after every tempest come such calms,
> May the winds blow till they have waken'd death!
> And let the labouring bark climb hills of seas
> Olympus high and duck again as low
> As hell's from heaven! If it were now to die,
> 'Twere now to be most happy; for, I fear,
> My soul hath her content so absolute
> That not another comfort like to this
> Succeeds in unknown fate. (II. i. 185)

Notice here the 'hills of seas', and the reiterated word 'content', Shakespeare's word for spiritual peace; also the ideas of hell and heaven. The idea of awakening death we have met already in a passage from *2 Henry IV*; the tempest-death association is always important. The symbolic relevance of this tempest to the later tragedy is clear. The Turks are drowned. Desdemona and Othello conquer the tempest together and embrace, doubly victorious. But Iago, himself (V. ii. 362) 'more fell than hunger, anguish, or the sea' ('hunger' suggesting the bears or 'empty tigers' elsewhere compared with tempests), watches and remarks:

> O, you are well tun'd now!
> But I'll set down the pegs that make this music,
> As honest as I am.   (II. i. 201)

This play vividly shows tempests and music in opposition. We have the music of married love clearly emphasized; the tempests of jealousy; the plaintive music of Desdemona's distress, the music of love, its swan-song in tempest; and the final tragedy, itself so beautiful that passion's tempests themselves become a noble music.

The recurrent love-jewel association is also used to fine effect:

> Nay, had she been true,
> If heaven would make me such another world
> Of one entire and perfect chrysolite,
> I'd not have sold her for it.   (v. ii. 143)

Othello is one who

> Like the base Indian, threw a pearl away
> Richer than all his tribe.   (v. ii. 347)

'Indian', 'pearl'—usual love-images. Throughout Othello's romantic glamour expresses itself in oriental allusions: the Egyptian sibyl, Arabian trees, Aleppo.

I pass now to three plays, *Julius Caesar*, *Macbeth*, and *Lear*, where the texture is more intricate, the poetry and poetic symbols more metaphysical, than in those so far observed. Here tempests are closely and beautifully woven into the story. They mark the perfection of Shakespeare's use of tempests as symbols of tragic disorder.

Julius Caesar has a few noteworthy minor images. The citizens are imaged as filling the Tiber with their tears (I. i. 63–5); mutiny is a 'flood' (III. ii. 214); Brutus is a 'vessel full of grief' which 'runs over even at his eyes' (v. v. 13). A characteristic speech occurs:

> There is a tide in the affairs of men,
> Which, taken at the flood, leads on to fortune;
> Omitted, all the voyage of their life

Is bound in shallows and in miseries.
On such a full sea are we now afloat;
And we must take the current when it serves,
Or lose our ventures.   (IV. iii. 218)

Or again:

Why, now, blow wind, swell billow and swim bark!
The storm is up and all is on the hazard.   (V. i. 67)

Human adventure is often a sea-voyage, the soul of man,
or his enterprise, a bark. There is also a well-known
speech, spoken by Cassius, which gains added point and
purpose if we remember the dynamic poetic meanings of
all rough waters and all flood-adventures. I refer to
Cassius's swimming contest with Caesar. Cassius thus
narrates the incident:

I was born free as Caesar; so were you:
We both have fed as well, and we can both
Endure the winter's cold as well as he:
For once, upon a raw and gusty day,
The troubled Tiber chafing with her shores,
Caesar said to me 'Darest thou, Cassius, now
Leap in with me into this angry flood,
And swim to yonder point?' Upon the word,
Accoutred as I was, I plunged in
And bade him follow; so indeed he did.
The torrent roar'd, and we did buffet it
With lusty sinews, throwing it aside
And stemming it with hearts of controversy;
But ere we could arrive the point proposed,
Caesar cried, 'Help me, Cassius, or I sink!'
I, as Aeneas our great ancestor,
Did from the flames of Troy upon his shoulder
The old Anchises bear, so from the waves of Tiber
Did I the tired Caesar   (I. ii. 97)

This is an important speech. Notice the 'winter' reference
at the start, winter reference being often entwined with
tempests; the 'wind' suggestion, the 'raw and gusty day';
the usual word 'chafing'; the personification of the river,
which is imaged as 'troubled', 'angry', 'roaring', and so
thought of as 'buffeted' by the swimmers. It is a speech

in the usual tradition: and, remembering this, we find it to hold a new interest. The chafing and angry Tiber becomes almost a symbol of life itself and life's tempestuous struggles. As such Cassius uses it, to assert his own strength and Caesar's weakness. Cassius is ever strong in adversity, and twice in this play he is shown pictorially as undaunted by tempests: this is one instance, and the other we shall meet shortly.

Julius Caesar has an actual tempest at its heart and centre. There is first concord and peace close-knit in the harmony of Caesar's rule. Caesar's entrance is thus accompanied by music:

> *Caesar.* Who is it in the press that calls on me?
>   I hear a tongue, shriller than all the music,
>   Cry 'Caesar!' Speak; Caesar is turn'd to hear. (I. ii. 15)

The Soothsayer's voice interrupts the music, prophesying disaster and disorder. Next we see the powers of conspiracy and discord loosed, the tempests of disorder liberated in Rome. This tempest is a thing not only of human action: it is a vivid actuality, a fiery tempest shaking earth and heaven, releasing fires and gliding ghosts to range the streets and skies of Rome. The act to be is a rough dislocation of concord: like the violent antagonism of sea and sky raging in tempestuous strife. There is 'thunder and lightning'. Casca describes our tempest as a thing of hitherto unimagined violence, like that in *Othello*:

> Are you not moved, when all the sway of earth
> Shakes like a thing unfirm? O Cicero,
> I have seen tempests, when the scolding winds
> Have rived the knotty oaks, and I have seen
> The ambitious ocean swell and rage and foam,
> To be exalted with the threatening clouds:
> But never till to-night, never till now,
> Did I go through a tempest dropping fire.
> Either there is a civil strife in heaven,
> Or else the world, too saucy with the gods,
> Incenses them to send destruction.   (I. iii. 3)

As usual, the land-tempest is an excuse for sea-imagery. Notice the typical words 'swell' and 'rage'; the human suggestion of 'threatening' and 'scolding'; the recurrent 'knotty oaks', as in *Troilus*, and the word 'ambitious', also in *Troilus* (I refer to Nestor's speech quoted above). Finally observe how tempests are equated with 'civil strife'. But Cassius, brave in the troubled waters of Tiber, is equally brave before the tempests of heaven. 'Whoever saw the heavens menace so?' asks Casca, and he answers:

> For my part, I have walk'd about the streets,
> Submitting me unto the perilous night,
> And, thus unbraced, Casca, as you see,
> Have bared my bosom to the thunder-stone;
> And when the cross blue lightning seem'd to open
> The breast of heaven, I did present myself
> Even in the aim and very flash of it.   (I. iii. 46)

Spiritually, Cassius is secure amid all the turbulences of existence, the very 'thunder-stones' of adversity. So the tempest continues, 'thunder still'. It is a thing of fire and blood, blending with the fire and blood of the whole vision:

> Fierce fiery warriors fought upon the clouds,
> In ranks and squadrons and right form of war,
> Which drizzled blood upon the Capitol. (II. ii. 19)

This tempest is accompanied by fierce beasts, especially the lion. A lion stalks the Capitol (I. iii. 20); 'a lioness hath whelped in the streets' (II. ii. 17); and Caesar and Danger itself oppose each other as 'two lions litter'd in one day' (II. ii. 46). The close connexion of the tempest and the lion is clear in Cassius's words:

> Now could I, Casca, name to thee a man
> Most like this dreadful night,
> That thunders, lightens, opens graves, and roars
> As doth the lion in the Capitol,
> A man no mightier than thyself or me
> In personal action, yet prodigious grown
> And fearful, as these strange eruptions are.   (I. iii. 72)

The heart of the play is anarchy, division, tempest. All this must be closely related to the conflict and tempest in Brutus's soul, itself suffering 'the nature of an insurrection'.

Toward the end of the play Brutus, who has refused love for honour, yet still finds that honour has not brought him peace. We should observe how the disorder-force of the conspiracy is itself on the point of further self-disintegration in the Quarrel scene. In so far as it creates disorder it suffers it too. But Cassius's love saves it, intact. And after the temporary division of this tempestuous quarrel, Brutus in a solitary hour would solace himself with love and music. He asks Lucius, whom he loves dearly, to play to him:

> Canst thou hold up thy heavy eyes awhile,
> And touch thy instrument a strain or two?
> (IV. iii. 256)

This music in the falling action is generally a broken music, disjointed or interrupted. There is first the music of Caesar's peaceful rule, corresponding to the music played in Act III of *Othello* suggesting Desdemona's and Othello's love ('I'll set down the pegs that make this music', says Iago earlier); then tempests of conflict; finally, before the end, a music-in-sadness, like Desdemona's willow song, here the music of Lucius:

> I will not hold thee long: if I do live,
> I will be good to thee.   [*Music and a song.*
> This is a sleepy tune. O murderous slumber,
> Lay'st thou thy leaden mace upon my boy,
> That plays thee music?   (IV. iii. 265)

Music, love, a sad, yet sweet, gentleness. But the evil of Brutus's own divided soul, the ghost of Caesar, shatters this momentary peace. A monstrous apparition intrudes to strike a nightmare fear into the house of love. The 'tempest' is not to be stilled till Brutus's death.

The form of *Macbeth* is close to that of *Julius Caesar*. It, too, has its tempests. Here they are especially violent. In this play we see chaos, disintegration, and death embattled against degree and order—we may recall Ulysses' speech—hospitality, love, and life. Here especially our effects often suggest the concept 'chaos'. A tempest-metaphor aptly describes the early rebellion reported by the Sergeant:

> As whence the sun 'gins his reflection
> Shipwrecking storms and direful thunders break,
> So from that spring whence comfort seem'd to come
> Discomfort swells. (I. ii. 25)

Observe the typical word 'swells'. We also have a metaphor from swimming, which recalls Cassius's speech, to point the nature of this battle:

> Doubtful it stood,
> As two spent swimmers that do cling together
> And choke their art. (I. ii. 7)

Now in this play the Weird Sisters are personified forces of disorder, disintegration, and conflict; hence, also, of tempests. They meet 'in thunder, lightning, or in rain' (I. i. 2), and 'hover through the fog and filthy air' (I. i. 12). Aptly, they specialize in sea-disasters. One of them will torment a sailor, gone eastward to Aleppo,[1] 'master of the Tiger'. Here, and in *Twelfth Night* (v. i. 65), a ship is named *The Tiger*: which is apt, if we remember our tempest beasts of which the tiger is one. The ship is thus endued with a ferocity and power comparable with the strength of tempests. So she will follow him sailing in a sieve. The others promise to give her winds:

> *Second Witch.* I'll give thee a wind.
> *First Witch.* Thou'rt kind.
> *Third Witch.* And I another.
> *First Witch.* I myself have all the other,
>   And the very ports they blow,
>   All the quarters that they know
>   I' the shipman's card.
>   I will drain him dry as hay:
>   Sleep shall neither night nor day

---

[1] I have heard it stated that Aleppo was in Elizabethan times the port for India.

Hang upon his pent-house lid;
He shall live a man forbid:
Weary se'nnights nine times nine
Shall he dwindle, peak and pine:
Though his bark cannot be lost,
Yet it shall be tempest-tost.
Look what I have.
Second Witch. Show me, show me.
First Witch. Here I have a pilot's thumb,
Wreck'd as homeward he did come.[1]   (i. iii. 11)

She will torment him with sleeplessness, Macbeth's very punishment. Clearly the two victims are all but identical. This incident is thus a microcosm of the whole play. Moreover, the spiritual agony, the wreckage of the soul, is here so closely twined with the thought of tempests and stormy sea-voyage, that we cannot fail to recognize their exact relation in the poet's mind.

The Weird Sisters are thus forces of tragedy and tempest, and their aim is to wreck the 'state of man' (*Julius Caesar*, ii. i. 67; *Macbeth*, i. iii. 140)—or nation. We here endure a hell more violent than elsewhere. The first stage direction is 'thunder and lightning'. Yet we are told, as if to reassure us, that though the bark be 'tempest-toss'd' it cannot finally be lost. As Macbeth puts it:

Time and the hour runs through the roughest day.
(i. iii. 147)

He endures and survives. But the play's tempest is hideous. Violent forces are loosed. It is like Claudio's hell. Pity strides 'the blast', heaven's angels are horsed 'upon the sightless couriers of the air', they

Shall blow the horrid deed in every eye
That tears shall drown the wind.   (i. vii. 21–5)

[1] A former pupil of mine at Dean Close School, Mr. F. J. Berry, pointed out to me that this speech has a very exact significance. Macbeth is to be wrecked just as he is entering the haven of success. He comes 'homeward', safe and victorious after tempestuous battles: and yet this is the moment of his disaster.

Macbeth's crime is so hideous that the vast sea's infinity
cannot cleanse the guilt on his hand:

> Will all great Neptune's ocean wash this blood
> Clean from my hand? No, this my hand will rather
> The multitudinous seas incarnadine,
> Making the green one red.   (II. ii. 60)

The night of the murder, where Life itself is shaken at its
foundation, is tempestuous:

> *Lennox.* The night has been unruly: where we lay,
> Our chimneys were blown down; and, as they say,
> Lamentings heard i' the air; strange screams of death,
> And prophesying with accents terrible
> Of dire combustion and confused events
> New hatch'd to the woeful time: the obscure bird
> Clamour'd the livelong night: some say, the earth
> Was feverous and did shake.
> *Macbeth.*   'Twas a rough night.
> *Lennox.* My young remembrance cannot parallel
> A fellow to it.   (II. iii. 59)

That final remark is typical of these greater plays. The
tempest is always described as a thing of unique violence.
Again, 'this sore night hath trifled former knowings'
(II. iv. 3). Here the tempest is black, murky, hideous.
It blots out the sun, eclipses the universe. We may feel
a clear tempest-universe opposition. Tempests are, at
the extreme, things of darkness, obscuring all light. The
tempest here is part of the wider disorder-symbolism in
animal, earth, air, and sun. The fearsomeness of this
vision is bodied, too, into varied animal-symbolism. Fierce
beasts are here: the 'wolf' is murder's 'sentinel' (II. i. 53);
accusing conscience strikes more deadly terror than 'the
rugged Russian bear, the arm'd rhinoceros or the Hyrcan
tiger' (III. iv. 100); Macbeth at bay is like a bear at the
stake (v. vii. 1). These are all of the tempest kind of
beast. Throughout the play there is a violent, chaotic
turbulence. All is chaos:

> But cruel are the times, when we are traitors
> And do not know ourselves, when we hold rumour

From what we fear, yet know not what we fear,
But float upon a wild and violent sea
Each way and move.   (IV. ii. 18)

Such agony on earth strikes heaven itself so that its
thunder resounds 'as if it felt with Scotland' (IV. iii. 7),
reverberating human woe. There is music, too. As usual,
the peace which is to be shattered is accompanied by music,
as in *Othello*, *Julius Caesar*, and *Timon*. Duncan is to be
feasted at Macbeth's castle:

> *Hautboys and torches. Enter a server, and divers servants with*
> *dishes and service, and pass over the stage.*   (I. vii)

This is the hospitality which Macbeth desecrates, thereby
exposing himself to a truly poetic justice in the Banquet
scene. It is an exact replica of Brutus's story. Brutus
desecrates the music of harmonious government and
national concord: the ghost of Caesar will not let him enjoy
the peace induced by love and music. Macbeth desecrates
hospitality, here associated with music, and so the ghost
of one of his victims forbids his own peaceful feasting with
his lords.

In the Cauldron scene we have some extremely important effects, and a clear tempest-music opposition.
Here I omit the Hecate incidents and other passages
generally considered non-Shakespearian; but, since they
contain three music references, I investigate the matter
separately.[1]

Macbeth decides to visit the Weird Sisters, determined
on pursuing his evil course irrespective of all things but
his own safety:

>   For mine own good,
> All causes shall give way: I am in blood
> Stepp'd in so far that, should I wade no more,
> Returning were as tedious as go o'er.   (III. iv. 135)

A vast sea of blood and crime. So, addressing the
mysterious sisters of evil in their cavern, he asks to be

---

[1] See Appendix B: The 'Hecate' Scenes in *Macbeth*.

satisfied though the whole world be torn asunder by riot-
ing forces, till turbulence become utter chaos:

> Though you untie the winds and let them fight
> Against the churches; though the yesty waves
> Confound and swallow navigation up;
> Though bladed corn be lodged and trees blown down. . . .
>
> (IV. i. 52)

So violent, so chaotic, are the tempest-forces here. Macbeth would let them rage 'even till destruction sicken', so
he be satisfied. So the Weird Sisters satisfy him by raising
tempestuous spirits from their cauldron, whose ingredients
hold, among other evils, parts of tempest-beasts, of the
tiger and 'ravin'd salt-sea shark'. These three central
apparitions, in order, present a miniature of our whole
drama, which turns on the conflict of destruction and
creation, or death and life. Here is our death-symbol:

> *Thunder. First Apparition: an armed Head.*

An armed head. Destruction, iron force of destruction,
arming a head severed from its body. So hideously unnatural, futile, death-doomed, is this death-dealing thing.
What use to arm a head that has lost its body? So Macbeth is arming himself continually, without knowing that
his first crime severed him for ever, king though he be,
from the body of Scotland, of humanity, of life. So, too,
will his own head finally be severed from the physical body
of his life. Armed destruction is raging in Scotland. But
in blood and agony a creative force is preparing to wrench
back life into safety. From blood and death is yet born
the bloody child of Life's revenging force:

> *Thunder. Second Apparition: a bloody Child.*

This Child is a symbol of Life-born-out-of-Death. This
is the birth of that creation which in travailing agony produces life even from the blood-weltering evil, the chaos,
the destruction. From death its own antagonist, life, is
born. Then we have the third act of our little drama:

> *Thunder. Third Apparition: A Child crowned, with a tree in
> his hand.*

Here is the symbol of Life victorious, its 'baby-brow' imperially crowned with the golden circlet of Nature's innocence, its little hand sceptred with the Tree of Life. So Life, in this Child apparition, confronts the phantasmal deathly royalty of Macbeth. The three Apparitions exquisitely suggest the drama of Destruction pitted against Creation, Death against Life. This is one of the most profound conflicts in Shakespeare; and, the whole miniature drama suggesting a conflict, each apparition comes with thunder. Such is the thunderous shock of Life and Death opposed. Now all these Apparitions, suggesting as a whole conflict, arise from the cauldron. Macbeth derives hope from their words, remaining blind, however, to themselves. But he is not satisfied; wants to know if Banquo's descendants shall be kings; whether Life's integrity will eventually displace the evil and destruction in which he himself is now a living Death. The Death Sisters urge him not to press further—'Seek to know no more' (IV. i. 103). They are themselves loath to expose the royalty of that creation which they are powerless to impede. Macbeth is insistent:

> I will be satisfied: deny me this,
> And an eternal curse fall on you! Let me know.
> Why sinks that cauldron? and what noise is this?
>
> [*Hautboys.*

Even the apparitions were the Weird Sisters' masters (IV. i. 63). The vision of Banquo's line of kings does not appear from the cauldron. The cauldron vanishes. There is next music, the music of Creation. And to that music the creative process itself, in crowned glory, marches before Macbeth:

> *A show of Eight Kings, the last with a glass in his hand; Banquo's ghost following.*

This glittering line of royalty, this vision of Creation in all its splendour and eternal sanction, this music of Life itself, maddens Macbeth who has done his little best to shatter that music into discord, to disintegrate that life in death. So exquisitely is here set down for us the thunderous and tempestuous conflict of life and death, which is yet but a ripple on the wide sea of the eternal, a single instrument within the orchestral music of creation.

Our tempests may be used very clearly as pure symbols carefully woven into the plot for a poetic purpose. Sea-tempests especially may be used almost independently of other naturalistic effects. But in some plays the tempest is also very clearly part of the play's nature-setting. In *As You Like It* nature's roughness is an integral theme: what tempest-thought there is, is there part of this general naturalism. But in *Twelfth Night* and *Othello*, for example, the tempest is less characteristic of the whole: a sudden, vivid, powerful nature-effect is used to suggest tragic fortune. Now in *Lear* the naturalism recalls *The Two Gentlemen* and *As You Like It*: in all three nature's roughness is contrasted with the more cruel unkindness of civilization. And in *Lear* we have a very powerful tempest. Indeed, all bleak and wintry effects of nature are ever to be related to tempests; all summery delight, flowers, and gentle airs or waters, the sun and moon, to music. In *Lear* the one great tempest is thus both finely symbolical and finely realistic, more naturally blended with the plot than the tempest of *Othello*, perhaps even more widely powerful as a single overbrooding reality throughout the play than the more varied tempest-effects in *Julius Caesar* and *Macbeth*.

We hear the storm rising, 'Let us withdraw; 'twill be a storm', says Cornwall (II. iv. 290); and Gloucester:

> Alack, the night comes on, and the bleak winds
> Do sorely ruffle; for many miles about
> There's scarce a bush.   (II. iv. 303)

And again, from Cornwall:

> Shut up your doors, my lord; 'tis a wild night:
> My Regan counsels well: come out o' the storm.
>   (II. iv. 311)

The bleak surrounding heath is vivid to our imaginations.

We are prepared gradually for the climax. We hear of Lear

> Contending with the fretful element;
> Bids the wind blow the earth into the sea,
> Or swell the curled waters 'bove the main,
> That things might change or cease; tears his white hair,
> Which the impetuous blasts, with eyeless rage,
> Catch in their fury, and make nothing of;
> Strives in his little world of man to out-scorn
> The to-and-fro conflicting wind and rain.
> This night, wherein the cub-drawn bear would couch,
> The lion and the belly-pinched wolf
> Keep their fur dry, unbonneted he runs,
> And bids what will take all.   (III. i. 4)

Observe Lear's 'ambitious' retort to tempests, recalling Nestor's speech; the words, 'swell', 'rage', 'fury'; the inhuman cruelty suggested by 'eyeless'; the 'little world of man' contrasted with the raging world of storm; 'contending' and 'conflicting'; 'curled', a word met before; and finally, the ever-recurring lion, bear, and wolf. So starts our third act. We may observe, too, how sea imagery is twined with land-tempests; and how here the tempest is part of nature's universal roughness and cruelty, yet less cruel than man. Hence:

> *Lear.* Blow, winds, and crack your cheeks! rage! blow!
> Your cataracts, and hurricanoes, spout
> Till you have drench'd our steeples, drown'd the cocks!
> You sulphurous and thought-executing fires,
> Vaunt-couriers to oak-cleaving thunderbolts,
> Singe my white head! And thou, all-shaking thunder,
> Smite flat the thick rotundity o' the world!
> Crack nature's moulds, all germens spill at once,
> That make ingrateful man!
> *Fool.* O nuncle, court holy-water in a dry house, is better than
> this rain-water out o' door. Good nuncle, in, and ask thy
> daughters' blessing: here's a night pities neither wise man nor
> fool.
> *Lear.* Rumble thy bellyful! Spit, fire! spout, rain!
> Nor rain, wind, thunder, fire, are my daughters:

> I tax not you, you elements, with unkindness ;
> I never gave you kingdom, call'd you children,
> You owe me no subscription: then, let fall
> Your horrible pleasure; here I stand, your slave,
> A poor, infirm, weak, and despis'd old man:
> But yet I call you servile ministers,
> That have with two pernicious daughters join'd
> Your high engender'd battles 'gainst a head
> So old and white as this. O! O! 'tis foul!
>
> *Fool.* He that has a house to put 's head in, has a good head-
>   piece.   (III. ii. 1)

Notice the violent anthropomorphism of 'crack your cheeks', 'bellyful', 'spit', and the usual oak-tempest association in relation to thunderbolts. Also the 'battle' metaphor and the thought that the tempest is leagued with Lear's daughters. The tempest here both points the tempest in Lear's mind and, more realistically, shows Lear as braving the cruelty of nature as an anodyne to human unkindness. As usual, the tempest is a thing of unique fury:

> ... since I was man,
> Such sheets of fire, such bursts of horrid thunder,
> Such groans of roaring wind and rain, I never
> Remember to have heard: man's nature cannot carry
> The affliction nor the fear.   (III. ii. 45)

The storm is an instrument of divine judgement:

> Let the great gods
> That keep this dreadful pother o'er our heads,
> Find out their enemies now.   (III. ii. 49)

Let such cry 'these dreadful summoners grace' (III. ii. 59). *Lear* is a play which continually emphasizes 'justice'; and here the thunder, the tempest, the conflicting wrath of winds and rain, all are as divine summoners calling man to a dreaded acknowledgement of crime. Thunder in Shakespeare is often thus an instrument of divine wrath. So, earlier, Lear expressed a similar thought:

> I do not bid the thunder-bearer shoot,
> Nor tell tales of thee to high-judging Jove.
>
>   (II. iv 230)

A thought throwing back to *Measure for Measure* and forward to *Cymbeline*. The fury of this storm is, indeed, tyrannical:

> *Kent.* Here is the place, my lord; good my lord, enter:
> The tyranny of the open night's too rough
> For nature to endure.   [*Storm still.*
>   (III. iv. 1)

Lear's answer is significant:

> Thou think'st 'tis much that this contentious storm
> Invades us to the skin: so 'tis to thee;
> But where the greater malady is fix'd,
> The lesser is scarce felt. Thou'ldst shun a bear;
> But if thy flight lay toward the raging sea
> Thou'ldst meet the bear i' the mouth. When the mind's free,
> The body's delicate: the tempest in my mind
> Doth from my senses take all feeling else
> Save what beats there.   (III. iv. 6)

Notice, again, the sea; the recurrent bear; the clear reference of the physical to the spiritual, 'the tempest in my mind'; and the word 'raging'. Then, again, we are pointed to a stern realism. The tempest will not give Lear leave to ponder on his own more agonizing mental pain (III. iv. 24). Then again the cruel storm draws noble charity from Lear, replacing his ire:

> Poor naked wretches, wheresoe'er you are,
> That bide the pelting of this pitiless storm,
> How shall your houseless heads and unfed sides,
> Your loop'd and window'd raggedness, defend you
> From seasons such as these? O, I have ta'en
> Too little care of this! Take physic, pomp;
> Expose thyself to feel what wretches feel,
> That thou mayst shake the superflux to them,
> And show the heavens more just.   (III. iv. 28)

All the sufferings of mortality, their pain and their redemption; all the enigmatic purposes of God, His justice, His mercy, and His wrath; all are concentrated in this titanic tempest. What reverberations of meaning echo in Lear's question to mad Tom o' Bedlam: 'What is the

cause of thunder?' (III. iv. 160). Such is Lear's tempestuous purgatory. The storm is often remembered,
even after it has been stilled. Says Gloucester later:

> The sea, with such a storm as his bare head
> In hell-black night endured, would have buoy'd up,
> And quench'd the stelled fires:
> Yet, poor old heart, he holp the heavens to rain.
>
> (III. vii. 59)

The 'stelled fires' recall the *Othello* tempest: but indeed
all these tempests are one tempest, toned variously for the
play in which they appear. And Cordelia mentions it, too:

> Was this a face
> To be opposed against the warring winds?
> To stand against the deep dread-bolted thunder?
> In the most terrible and nimble stroke
> Of quick, cross lightning? to watch—poor perdu!—
> With this thin helm? Mine enemy's dog,
> Though he had bit me, should have stood that night
> Against my fire; and wast thou fain, poor father,
> To hovel thee with swine, and rogues forlorn,
> In short and musty straw? (IV. vii. 31)

More 'thunderbolt' suggestion. Throughout *Lear* we
find the thought of man's relation to the powers divine
that overstand his drama: in tragedy, where such powers
are wrathful, that wrath is often a thing of thunder and
thunderbolts.

These lines of Cordelia occur in the scene where
Lear awakes to love, awakes to self-knowledge and re-
deeming love:

> *A tent in the French camp. Lear on a bed asleep, soft music
> playing. . . .*

Music and love; replacing for awhile tempest and
mental agony, the music of a daughter's love to heal the
harsh unmusic of madness.

> O you kind gods,
> Cure this great breach in his abused nature!
> The untuned and jarring senses, O, wind up
> Of this child-changed father! (IV. vii. 14)

Sleep, music, nature's simples and Cordelia's love are the
Doctor's medicines. Now the Doctor would have him
wake: 'Louder the music there!' (IV. vii. 25). Cordelia
kisses him, speaks those lines we have just quoted
recalling the tempest, so that recollection of that tempest
is now divinely enclosed in music. Lear wakes, and
is redeemed into sanity, love, peace. Again in *Lear*
we have a powerful tempest-music opposition. Consider
the Shakespearian sonnet where child and father and
happy mother sing one note of family concord. That
harmony is broken here in the first act; the 'tempest' of
division, anguish, and madness ensues; then restoration
is born for awhile on Cordelia's lips, and Lear wakes, as a
mortal man to immortality, wakes into music and love.

Throughout the play we have much animal-imagery.
Very often the beasts are fierce in the tempest-tradition.
Some of these I have noticed already; but a few more may
be observed. There are Lear's words:

> Ingratitude, thou marble-hearted fiend,
> More hideous when thou show'st thee in a child
> Than the sea-monster! (I. iv. 281)

Sea-monsters occur elsewhere. They are, clearly, like
pirates, doubly charged with sombre suggestion, with
all the terrors of beasts and the sea too. Albany is dis-
gusted at Goneril's cruelty, and compares her to a series
of fierce beasts.

> Tigers, not daughters, what have you perform'd?
> A father, and a gracious aged man,
> Whose reverence even the head-lugg'd bear would lick,
> Most barbarous, most degenerate! have you madded.
> (IV. ii. 40)

'Tigers', and the 'bear': the usual tempest-beasts. Albany
continues:

> If that the heavens do not their visible spirits
> Send quickly down to tame these vile offences,
> It will come,
> Humanity must perforce prey on itself,
> Like monsters of the deep. (IV. ii. 46)

15

Other fierce beasts are scattered throughout the imagery. And many minor tempest-passages occur. Edgar, like Lear, determines to 'out-face the winds and persecutions of the sky' (II. iii. 11); and in his mock lunacy he mutters, or sings, part of an old rhyme: 'Still through the hawthorn blows the cold wind' (III. iv. 102). Often he mutters 'Tom's a-cold', continually contributing to our sense of the bleak, wintry effects, which so powerfully impregnate the middle scenes. So does the Fool, with his rhyme 'with hey, ho, the wind and the rain' (III. ii. 75) recalling Feste's song; or his plaintive witticisms, 'This cold night will turn us all to fools and madmen' (III. iv. 80); or, 'Prithee, nuncle, be contented; 'tis a naughty night to swim in' (III. iv. 115). The early action of the play is dominated by the tempest: it drenches everything, saturating the phraseology. Here is another example, from the early acts:

> That sir which serves and seeks for gain,
>   And follows but for form,
> Will pack when it begins to rain,
>   And leave thee in the storm.   (II. iv. 79)

Here 'storm' is emblematic of human fortune generally. Kent uses it in the same sense, when, inveighing against 'smiling rogues' such as Oswald he notes how they

> Renege, affirm, and turn their halcyon beaks
> With every gale and vary of their masters. . . .
>   (II. ii. 84)

Lear imprecates 'lightnings' on Goneril (II. iv. 167) at the beginning of the play; and, towards the end, uses a characteristic rain-tears association:

> Why this would make a man a man of salt,
> To use his eyes for garden water-pots,
> Ay, and laying autumn's dust.   (IV. vi. 199)

We should note, too, Edgar's vivid description of the sea from Dover cliff (IV. vi. 11–24), which recalls the similar lines spoken by Horatio to Hamlet: in these speeches there is strong suggestion of death or danger. In this sombre, storm-furious, and wintry-bleak play, however, we must not forget the one transcendently beautiful theme of love's music. So also is Cordelia's sorrow for her father's suffering a thing of beauty:

> You have seen
> Sunshine and rain at once: her smiles and tears
> Were like a better May. (IV. iii. 19)

Or perhaps we should read 'day'. At the end, where Cordelia's love rules for awhile, the bleak and wintry atmosphere gives place, as Mr. Edmund Blunden has observed, to effects of summery delight. We must always be prepared to relate the tempest-music opposition to that of winter and summer, and all wider natural suggestion. This is very necessary in dealing with our next play.

III

In our last three tragedies tempests are variously employed. *Timon of Athens* repeats the themes of *As You Like It* and *Lear* in that it contrasts powerfully nature's roughness with civilization's more bitter and keen-piercing cruelty. There is no actual tempest in the plot, such as we have observed in *Othello*, *Julius Caesar*, *Macbeth*, and *Lear*, partly because there is no conflict within Timon himself: he swerves swiftly from boundless love to boundless hate. But the disorder-thought in his curses is important, set against the music of the early scenes; the atmosphere of nature's bleakness is most powerful in the later acts; sun and moon imagery is vivid; and the sea is powerfully used to suggest chaos. There are also minor images in the usual tradition.

The play is in two contrasted halves: first, we see Timon's love, and his setting of sense-pleasures and all life-joys, feasting, entertainment, music:

> *A banqueting-room in Timon's house. Hautboys playing loud music. A great banquet served in.* (I. ii)

Again:

> *Music: Re-enter Cupid, with a mask of Ladies as Amazons,*
> *with lutes in their hands, dancing and playing.*
>
> (I. ii. 136)

And,

> *. . . all dance, men with women, a lofty strain or two to the haut-*
> *boys. . . .*   (I. ii. 150)

Music, feasting, love: the usual grouping in Shakespeare,
as in *Macbeth* and *Antony and Cleopatra*. The only discordant voice is Apemantus's: and so he is told to 'come
with better music' than railing on society (I. ii. 250-2).

But all this gives place to Timon's hate. With his love
are thus contrasted both the wholesale disintegration he
imprecates on mankind and society, and the bleak hermit-
age in the woods to which he retires:

> Timon will to the woods; where he shall find
> The unkindest beast more kinder than mankind.
>
> (IV. i. 35)

The 'beast' again. Timon's hate is in the tempest
tradition. As for society, he would wish all piety, fear,
religion, peace, justice, truth, all domesticity and friendli-
ness, all manners, trades, degree, customs, and laws, to
'decline' to their 'confounding contraries', and so, 'let
confusion live' (IV. i. 15-21). All physical or moral
health or harmony he would have poisoned, since men
have proved themselves but 'wolves' (IV. i. 2). So Timon
abhors 'all feasts, societies, and throngs of men' (IV. iii. 21).
For them gold has power to gild the sickliest horror to the
'April day again' (IV. iii. 41). Gold is the only springtime
in their barren souls. Soldiers he would have to slay the
aged man, the matron, virgin, babe (IV. iii. 111-22); and
again, mothers, maids, babes, and priests (IV. iii. 124-6):
they are to 'make large confusion' (IV. iii. 127). All this is
an almost exact replica of Ulysses' 'order' speech, which, as
we have seen, was related closely to tempests. Besides, all
these images of conflict and confusion are clearly tempest

thoughts. So Timon prays to the common mother, the earth, to produce only tempest-beasts:

> Ensear thy fertile and conceptious womb,
> Let it no more bring out ingrateful man!
> Go great with tigers, dragons, wolves, and bears;
> Teem with new monsters, whom thy upward face
> Hath to the marbled mansion all above
> Never presented!   (IV. iii. 187)

Tigers, wolves, bears: the usual animals. So the music of the early acts here gives place to the tempest fury of Timon's hate. But throughout gold is important both in association and contrast with the rich worth of love. This gold-symbolism is to be directly related to Shakespeare's usual love-jewel association.

There are sea-images, too. Passionate poetry—such as that of Timon's curses—is described with a fine torrent metaphor:

> . . . our gentle flame
> Provokes itself and like the current flies
> Each bound it chafes.   (I. i. 23)

Notice the usual word 'chafes'. 'He keeps his tides well' (I. ii. 56), says Apemantus of a lord. Timon's estate suffers 'ebb', his debts come as a 'great flow' (II. ii. 150). Ill fortune is as 'a cloud of winter showers' (II. ii. 180). Here we must be ready to see a winter-tempest equivalence: it is important elsewhere. At the turning-point of the play, at the sudden inrush of tragedy and the wreckage of Timon's household, Timon's servants characteristically compare themselves to seamen suffering disaster:

> . . . leak'd is our bark,
> And we, poor mates, stand on the dying deck,
> Hearing the surges threat: we must all part
> Into this sea of air.   (IV. ii. 19)

Timon of Athens is the universal tragedy: man would build a paradise of love, and embrace Fortune on earth. This dream is quickly shattered. Timon experiences uttermost tragedy. Then he would have all mankind plunge quickly into the deeps of death, and give over their unhappy voyage once and for all:

> Commend me to them,
> And tell them that, to ease them of their griefs,
> Their fears of hostile strokes, their aches, losses,
> Their pangs of love, with other incident throes
> That nature's fragile vessel doth sustain
> In life's uncertain voyage, I will some kindness do them. . . .
> (v. i. 200)

The kindness of death.

Timon has withdrawn from Athens to the woods, 'by the sea-shore'. But nature does not redeem him like Lear. It, too, is only cruel, senseless:

> What, think'st
> That the bleak air, thy boisterous chamberlain,
> Will put thy shirt on warm? will these moss'd trees,
> That have outliv'd the eagle, page thy heels,
> And skip where thou point'st out? will the cold brook,
> Candied with ice, caudle thy morning taste,
> To cure thy o'ernight's surfeit? Call the creatures
> Whose naked natures live in all the spite
> Of wreakful heaven, whose bare unhoused trunks,
> To the conflicting elements exposed
> Answer mere nature; bid them flatter thee. . . .
> (iv. iii. 221)

Observe the words 'bleak', 'ice', the 'cold brook'; the aged trees; all are important. Notice, too, the tempest-suggestion in 'conflicting'. Timon, naked in the woods, is alone in his utter severance from man, and compares himself to an oak stripped of its leaves. Friends

> That numberless upon me stuck as leaves
> Do on the oak, have with one winter's brush
> Fell from their boughs and left me open, bare
> For every storm that blows.   (iv. iii. 263)

A characteristic and important image: the oak is often a symbol of tragic endurance or destruction. So Timon will have none of man, of nature. Nor among the beasts can he find a home. He knows this, repudiating all beasts, the lion, the wolf, the bear and others (IV. iii. 330–49). To be a beast after the confusion of men would bring him no peace (IV. iii. 327). Nor Man nor Nature holds peace for him. Nor may the infinite lights of sun and moon assuage his pain. Sun and moon are ever the accompaniment in Shakespeare of love fulfilled on earth: Timon's love on earth, perplexed, banished its home, seeks fulfilment in the wide spaces of infinity. Unsatiated, it passes on to death's dark sea.

He has long lived by the sea, by that infinite death:

> Then, Timon, presently prepare thy grave;
> Lie where the light foam of the sea may beat
> Thy grave-stone daily. (IV. iii. 378)

The infinity of the soul's passion, the infinity of death; the peaceful rhythms of death. Sea-tempests are the surges of man's passionate soul, his death by the sea the sinking back within that soul's eternity which encompasses 'the bank and shoal of time' (*Macbeth*, I. vii. 6). Timon then steps from that ridge into the waters of death. Why keep his bark afloat when miserly greed is the only navigation of life? Gold, gold, gold:

> 'Tis thou that rigg'st the bark and plough'st the foam. . . .
> (V. i. 53)

Therefore:

> Come not to me again; but say to Athens
> Timon hath made his everlasting mansion
> Upon the beached verge of the salt flood;
> Who once a day with his embossed froth
> The turbulent surge shall cover. (V. i. 217)

He is dead, 'entomb'd upon the very hem o' the sea' (V. iv. 66). So

> rich conceit
> Taught thee to make vast Neptune weep for aye
> On thy low grave, on faults forgiven. Dead
> Is noble Timon. (V. iv. 77)

If we remember the wide significance of the sea-symbol— its infinity, its wealth, and its surging death, we will understand why Timon's end is, indeed, a 'rich conceit'. Here the sea has truly a wide meaning: all the varied Shakespearian significances are powerful in it. Timon retraces backward the process of creation from chaos to man's civilization; and this sea is chaos, the weltering chaos of the absolute negation to which he returns. And yet it is 'vast': a weltering 'nothing', yet infinity. And its undying requiem is sweet, the 'light foam' gently lapping the grave, wavelets softly whispering a deathless sympathy; but, again, it is as a solemn monotone of death, unending, sobbing above the 'everlasting mansion' of eternity; and, again, the grand passion-heart of Timon has here no final Mass for his soul but one as grandly turbulent as man's passionate aspiration: 'the turbulent surge'. Finally, the vast sea's infinity, the grief itself of ocean which overfloods the greater part of earth, shall 'weep for aye' on the breast of Timon, prince-hearted, love-crucified.

Coriolanus has no direct tempest-symbolism. But there are some intensely interesting tempest-ideas rooted in the play. Most of the play shows us a world of flinty-hard suggestion, metallic imagery well suiting the loveless theme. So to trust in the plebeians is to 'swim with fins of lead' (I. i. 184). But the most important point to notice here is the frequent comparison of Coriolanus with Jove and thunder. He makes his enemies shake 'as if the world were feverous and did tremble' (I. iv. 59). A figure of darkness and death, he is aptly honoured on his return to Rome by a doubtful welcome:

> . . . the nobles bended,
> As to Jove's statue, and the commons made
> A shower and thunder with their caps and shouts.
>
> (II. i. 281)

This is a minatory, grim suggestion; just as when he is spoken of as heralded by 'noise'. Notice the Jove-thunder association, continual in Shakespeare. Trumpets sound:

These are the ushers of Marcius: before him he carries
noise, and behind him he leaves tears. (II. i. 174)

This is his grim music. Or again, 'the thunder-like per-
cussion of thy sounds' (I. iv. 59). Volumnia encourages
his absurd, godlike proudness. She herself laments 'in
anger Juno-like' (IV. ii. 53). Both are stern, proud, inhuman. But Coriolanus is strong, appallingly strong, too
Jove-like to submit to human fate:

He would not flatter Neptune for his trident,
Or Jove for 's power to thunder. (III. i. 256)

Neptune and Jove clearly present aspects of our tempest
imagery. Coriolanus is ever a thing of thunder, assuming
divine prerogative. He is a superman. Throughout the
play he is god-like in power of warriorship, god-like in
pride:

Thou hast affected the fine strains of honour,
To imitate the graces of the gods;
To tear with thunder the wide cheeks o' the air,
And yet to charge thy sulphur with a bolt
That should but rive an oak. (v. iii. 149)

Again the 'oak'. We may here recall Isabella's speech on
such pride as his, pride that would usurp divine thunder.
Coriolanus thus 'wants nothing of a god but eternity and
a heaven to throne in' (v. iv. 26). He is thus grown 'from
man to dragon' (v. iv. 14): so we have again a tempest-
beast comparison. There is as much mercy in him as
'milk in a male tiger' (v. iv. 31). He is like a 'bear', the
plebeians like 'wolves' (II. i. 8–14). Or again he is a vast
ship, unbending to the seas of lesser men:

. . . as weeds before
A vessel under sail, so men obey'd
And fell below his stem. (II. ii. 109)

So he goes on, a mighty galleon unshaken by storms. He
is, as a Volscian says later on, 'the rock, the oak not to be
wind-shaken' (v. ii. 118). Again, the 'oak'. Coriolanus is
'brow-bound with the oak' (II. ii. 102); he comes 'the

third time home with the oaken garland' (II. i. 138). So
he would wish his son to

> Stick i' the wars
> Like a great sea-mark, standing every flaw,
> And saving those that eye thee!   (v. iii. 73)

The rage of the plebeians is like 'interrupted waters' (III.
i. 249). But tragedy overtakes him. He parts with his
mother and wife:

> Come, leave your tears: a brief farewell: the beast
> With many heads butts me away. Nay, mother,
> Where is your ancient courage? you were used
> To say extremity was the trier of spirits;
> That common chances common men could bear;
> That when the sea was calm all boats alike
> Show'd mastership in floating; fortune's blows,
> When most struck home, being gentle wounded, craves
> A noble cunning: you were used to load me
> With precepts that would make invincible
> The heart that conn'd them.   (IV. i. 1)

Notice the clear equation of sea-tempests with the vicissi-
tudes of human fate or fortune; notice, too, the association of a beast with tempests. So also Coriolanus's
tempestuous wars are earlier as a lion hunt: Aufidius being
a 'lion' he is 'proud to hunt' (I. i. 239).

And all this tempestuous pride and jarring rivalry, this
thunder of godhead ridiculously emanating from a man,
all this is to be contrasted with music:

> The shepherd knows not thunder from a tabor
> More than I know the sound of Marcius' tongue
> From every meaner man.   (I. vi. 25)

A most important contrast. Coriolanus usurps the tempestuous thunder of a god. So he leaves Rome. As a
figure of ill-omen he interrupts the music (IV. v) and
festivity of the Volscians. A thing of thunder he interrupts
music, conviviality, spreading discord. Therefore:

> *Aufidius.*   What is thy name?
> *Coriolanus.* A name unmusical to the Volscians' ears,
>   And harsh in sound to thine.

Aufidius.   Say, what's thy name?
   Thou hast a grim appearance, and thy face
   Bears a command in't; though thy tackle's torn,
   Thou show'st a noble vessel. . . .   (IV. v. 63)

They arrange to attack Rome 'pouring war' in like 'a bold
flood' (IV. v. 135–7). But at the last Coriolanus, strong in
all human strength to resist the tempests of circumstance,
finds the tempest of his god-like pride and wrath all too
weak to batter down the more stalwart dignity of love:

                       What is this?
   Your knees to me? to your corrected son?
   Then let the pebbles on the hungry beach
   Fillip the stars; then let the mutinous winds
   Strike the proud cedars 'gainst the fiery sun;
   Murdering impossibility, to make
   What cannot be, slight work.   (v. iii. 56)

Notice how the beach and winds are opposed to the
sun; and the insignificance of passionate pride, that is
tempests, compared with the universal majesty of love.
Observe also the cedar, often, with pines and oaks,
found in tempest-passages. Throughout this flint-and-
iron play there is continually the shimmer of sweet natural
imagery. Never is it allowed too much power to disturb
the prevailing atmosphere of city life, war, pride, pro-
vincialism; but it interthreads the drama, harvest
thoughts, love-imagery, tentative suggestion of sun and
moon—all are thin bright threads occasionally visible in
our dark cloth. Now suddenly the cloth is turned to the
light, we see the whole shot with a myriad silks of gold
answering the golden fires of love. As love breaks through
the leaden clouds of pride and hate, we know that love has
in truth ruled this world from the start, as Coriolanus
learns now love to be his only truth, and so music on
earth mingles with heaven's sun in joy:

   The trumpets, sackbuts, psalteries and fifes,
   Tabors and cymbals and the shouting Romans
   Make the sun dance.   (v. iv. 52)

Music, and more music. The universe opens at last on this stony, iron-plated scene. 'Music still with shouts' (v. iv. 60). Love's music is contrasted with the pride which has been a force of discord, of thunder, of tempest. Coriolanus's voice was as 'thunder' to a 'tabor'. Now in this music the reverberations of thunder are but an element of that tabor's notes. At the last, Coriolanus, like Hamlet, death-shadowed, is therefore given the muffled music of a dead march. The whole play thus turns throughout on a thunder-music opposition.

The peculiar quality of *Antony and Cleopatra* is well shown by the absence here of tempests. For once in a human tragedy tempests are stilled and music sounds clear over the tranquil waters of existence. Cleopatra's passions are, indeed, once called tempests:

> . . . her passions are made of nothing but the finest part of pure love: we cannot call her winds and waters sighs and tears; they are greater storms and tempests than almanacks can report: this cannot be cunning in her; if it be, she makes a shower as well as Jove.   (I. ii. 156)

There are tempestuous passions: but they are subdued to a new and gentler music. Cleopatra contrasts a strange storm of hail with her own love and love's fruitfulness:

Antony. Cold-hearted towards me?
Cleopatra.   Ah, dear, if I be so,
From my cold heart let heaven engender hail,
And poison it in the source; and the first stone
Drop in my neck: as it determines, so
Dissolve my life! The next Caesarion smite!
Till by degrees the memory of my womb,
Together with my brave Egyptians all,
By the discandying of this pelleted storm,
Lie graveless, till the flies and gnats of Nile
Have buried them for prey!   (III. xi. 158)

An important instance of the love-tempest opposition. But in this play of love nature's sweetness is necessarily more often noticed. Even this storm is curiously picturesque.

The airs here are generally still. 'The least wind i' the world' (II. vii. 2) is a natural image.

But no play has more thought of sea, rivers, and ships. I can only suggest a few prominent examples here. Occasionally the rivers are imaged as engulfing land (I. i. 33; I. ii. 50; II. v. 78). Even so, as I observe elsewhere, it is a melting or dissolving process; there is no turbulence. This blends with the constant thought of element dissolving in element, man with woman mingling in love:

> My mistress loved thee, and her fortunes mingled
> With thine entirely.   (IV. xii. 24)

Much of the action is concerned with ships and nautical terms are scattered widely: we hear of 'rigging' a 'great navy' (III. v. 20), a harbour (III. ix. 11), a rudder (III. ix. 57), ships' flags (III. xi. 11), a port (IV. iv. 23), galleys (IV. x. 12), swallows building nests in Cleopatra's sails (IV. x. 16). Those are a few: there are more, many more. The sea here is scarcely impregnated with tragic significance, since the play as a whole has not a tragic significance at all. The tragedy, such as it is, is shown clearly as a human conflict played on a stage of gentle and peaceful nature; nature thus harmonizing with the love-theme, not the conflict. Thus a sea-fight is tragic, but not the sea. It is emphasized again and again that Antony's failure in Act III is a sea-failure: which repeated emphasis is important. But so is the calmness of the sea. We hear of a navy quickly 'cutting' the Ionian Sea (III. vii. 23); an image suggesting a calm sea disturbed, if at all, only by man's activity; exactly our vision here, which presents the calmness and beauty of human love and nature generally, ruffled slightly by the discordant warrings of mankind. The thought is even clearer elsewhere:

> And that is it
> Hath made me rig my navy; at whose burthen
> The anger'd ocean foams.   (II. vi. 19)

Nature's placidity is angered by man's unloving actions.
The sea here moves with a soft undulation:

> And the ebb'd man, ne'er loved till ne'er worth love,
> Comes dear'd by being lack'd. This common body,
> Like to a vagabond flag upon the stream,
> Goes to and back, lackeying the varying tide,
> To rot itself with motion. (I. iv. 43)

Or again,

> . . . the swan's down-feather,
> That stands upon the swell at full of tide,
> And neither way inclines. (III. ii. 48)

This sea may sometimes in its placidity seem to resent
human action; or it may be an element of his imperial
power. Vast images of sea occur:

> Thou art, if thou darest be, the earthly Jove;
> Whate'er the ocean pales, or sky inclips,
> Is thine, if thou wilt ha't. (II. vii. 73)

Or again:

> I, that with my sword
> Quarter'd the world, and o'er green Neptune's back
> With ships made cities. . . . (IV. xii. 57)

Cities: recalling another play, *Henry V*, where the sea
and human success league to make a single glory. In these
two plays tempests are stilled, and so man can build his
cities on 'the inconstant billows' (*Henry V*, Pro. III. 15).
In both plays man conquers fate: in *Henry V* through
worldly success; here, through being able to say, 'I am
conqueror of myself' (IV. xii. 62). Here 'Neptune's back'
is kind. 'Green' suggests his calmness, unstirred by tempest. Man feasts and sings and plays music on Neptune. There is the scene laid on Pompey's galley, with
riotous joy and music, recalling *Timon*, with Antony's
description of the rich Nile basin:

> . . . the higher Nilus swells
> The more it promises. (II. vii. 23)

There is music:

> All take hands.
> Make battery to our ears with the loud music. . . .
>
> (II. vii. 114)

They join hands to music. Music, dance, conviviality, and friendship are blended. Notice the word 'battery' applied to music: it recurs in *Pericles*. So the revelry continues on the still waters:

> *Enobarbus.* Menas, I'll not on shore.
> *Menas.*   No, to my cabin.
> These drums! these trumpets, flutes! what!
> Let Neptune hear we bid a loud farewell
> To these great fellows. . . .   (II. vii. 137)

Description of harvesting, music, dance, song, and feasting on the sea: a significant association in terms of Shakespearian symbolism.

However, within the still harmonies of this vision we have occasional remembrances of tragic sea-imagery. But it is not tempestuous. Ships may sink, they are not 'tempest-tossed'. When Cleopatra deserts him Antony is 'leaky' and must be left to his 'sinking' (III. xi. 63–4); fortune is 'out of breath' and 'sinks' (III. viii. 34): Lepidus is warned to keep off 'quicksands' lest he 'sink' (II. vii. 65). Notice the placidity of these suggestions. A leader of men is a navigator: 'a rarer spirit never did steer humanity' (v. i. 31). Dissolving cloud is as the weeping of the gods (v. ii. 302). We hear of 'Jove that thunders' (III. xi. 85), at a moment of tragic passion, though such moments are ever dissolved in a strange optimism. Also at II. v. 77 we have, 'some innocents 'scape not the thunderbolt'. We do not lose sight of mortality or the changing flux of time on 'the varying shore of the world' (IV. xiii. 11); but we are never lost in tragic contemplation. Nature is fertile, fruitful, picturesque. The Nile overflows to fertilize its basin (I. ii. 49; II. vii. 23); the 'morn-dew' is on 'the myrtle-leaf' (III. x. 9); Caesar's lips 'rain'd kisses' on Cleopatra's hand (III. xi. 85); and Cleopatra will set the messenger

'in a shower of gold' and 'hail rich pearls' on him if he
brings good news of her love (II. v. 45). Gold and pearls.
So vividly is our storm-imagery transformed in this love
vision. Antony's description of the melting cloud forma-
tions of the evening sky (IV. xii) presents a peacefulness of
air corresponding to the peacefulness of ocean; and there
he sees images of trees, a bear, and lion, a dragon; unreal, bodies of vapour, fading. Images of tragedy, insubstantial. All is here rich in life and love. Natural imagery
continually suggests picturesque sea-life and air-life. We
have mermaids, the dolphin, fishes, the mallard, duck,
'Arabian bird' and many others. Cleopatra is 'my nightingale' to Antony. Translucent sea and soft air, and the life
they breed. All here is rich in natural sweetness. Gold and
jewels accompany the conviviality and love as in *Timon*.
I have noticed one instance. Also there is the 'ship laden
with gold' (III. ix. 4) which Antony promises to his followers. Antony is a 'jewel' (IV. xiii. 78) to Cleopatra. He
sends her an 'orient pearl' (I. v. 41) as a gift of love.

And there is music throughout. There is the music at
the feast on Pompey's galley (II. vii). And with Cleopatra
at Alexandria:

> Give me some music: music, moody food
> Of us that trade in love.   (II. v. 1)

'Trade' referring to the love-merchandise association.
News of Antony's marriage, is 'merchandise' too 'dear'
for Cleopatra (II. v. 104). Again,

> Give me mine angle; we'll to the river: there,
> My music playing far off, I will betray
> Tawny-finn'd fishes. . . .   (II. v. 10)

A fine river-music image. This love-fishing association
may be compared with *Much Ado*, III. i. 26-9. There is
the music of Antony's triumph:

>   Trumpeters,
> With brazen din blast you the city's ear;
> Make mingle with our rattling tambourines;
> That heaven and earth may strike their sounds together,
> Applauding our approach.   (IV. viii. 35)

Above all, we should observe the mysterious symbolic music that accompanies Antony's failure as a soldier and his dying into love.

Hautboys sound 'as under the stage'.

Then:

First Soldier. Music i' the air.
Third Soldier. Under the earth.

(IV. iii. 13)

There is, too, a fine thunder-music contrast—such as occurs throughout *Coriolanus*—in Cleopatra's dream of Antony:

... his voice was propertied
As all the tuned spheres, and that to friends;
But when he meant to quail and shake the orb,
He was as rattling thunder. (v. ii. 83)

Here love's voice, as often elsewhere, is compared with the spheral music of the universe. In this speech, too, Antony is imaged as enjoying a sportive life in the element of water:

... his delights
Were dolphin-like; they show'd his back above
The element they lived in. (v. ii. 88)

A change from our other sea-images. This love vision has also fine imagery of sun and moon: a contrast to *Macbeth*.

Perhaps of all our most vivid contrast to set against tempests is the description of Cleopatra in her barge at Cydnus:

Enobarbus. I will tell you.
The barge she sat in, like a burnish'd throne,
Burn'd on the water: the poop was beaten gold;
Purple the sails, and so perfumed, that
The winds were love-sick with them; the oars were silver,
Which to the tune of flutes kept stroke, and made
The water which they beat to follow faster,
As amorous of their strokes. For her own person,
It beggar'd all description: she did lie
In her pavilion—cloth-of-gold of tissue—
O'er-picturing that Venus where we see
The fancy out-work nature: on each side her
Stood pretty dimpled boys, like smiling Cupids,

16

   With divers-colour'd fans, whose wind did seem
   To glow the delicate cheeks which they did cool,
   And what they undid, did.
Agrippa.   O, rare for Antony!
Enobarbus. Her gentlewomen, like the Nereides,
   So many mermaids, tended her i' the eyes,
   And made their bends adornings: at the helm
   A seeming mermaid steers: the silken tackle
   Swell with the touches of those flower-soft hands,
   That yarely frame the office. From the barge
   A strange invisible perfume hits the sense
   Of the adjacent wharfs. The city cast
   Her people out upon her; and Antony,
   Enthron'd i' the market-place, did sit alone,
   Whistling to the air; which, but for vacancy,
   Had gone to gaze on Cleopatra too,
   And made a gap in nature.   (II. ii. 195)

Stillness; gold, silver, flowers, soft airs, and smooth
waters. The 'old wranglers', the winds, are 'love-sick'.
And music. Herein the tempests of tragedy are stilled
by the potency of love's queen, Cleopatra. We remember
our earlier images of love's Eastern voyage: we may
finally note the exquisite Shakespearian theme of Antony,
hero of Western power, drawn across the seas to Cleopatra
at Alexandria, Cleopatra, Orient Star of Love.
   The tempests which are so thickly scattered in earlier
plays become thus of even greater importance in the
tragedies of Shakespeare's maturity. What was first a
poetic image is now minutely woven into the action; indeed, we should say rather that the action itself is ever
but a new variation and embodiment of the tempest.
The tempest is central.   And, wherever we find tempests of tragedy, that is conflict and turbulence and disorder, we find also set against them the music of concord,
peace, and love. The most usual form is this: music of
concord early in the play; conflict and tempest at the
heart of it, breaking into that music; music again of pathos
and distress about the fourth act; then the tragic culmina-
tion, sometimes with a sterner music at the end, as when

drums are beaten at the close of *Timon*, or a dead march sounded in *Hamlet* and *Coriolanus*. The greater tragedies all revolve on the tempest-music opposition, with the exceptions of *Hamlet* where tempests are not violent, and *Antony and Cleopatra*. In *Antony and Cleopatra* the turbulence of mortality's warring is ever subdued to a new and strange harmony, and tempests are now enclosed in music, so that there is no direct tempest-symbolism, but instead the single fine supernatural effect of unearthly music. These greater tempests are all a blending of the metaphoric tempests in the Histories with the actualized tempests that make fanciful adventures throughout the early Romances; so that the tempest is at the last the dominant symbol in the metaphysic of tragedy. This is a usual process in Shakespeare. Metaphors and fancies of one period become expanded to plots, the very stuff of intellectual and poetical vision, in another. Thus birth or creation in Shakespeare is often imaged as the union of the divine and earthly; in death and destruction, correspondingly, these elements are harshly severed. Such thought is found first in metaphor, then in the destruction visions of *Julius Caesar* and *Macbeth*, wherein the violent severance of spirit-forms from actuality shows us the essence of evil. Similarly the early 'gold' metaphors of love give us the gold-symbolism of *Timon*; the 'flint' metaphors of hard-heartedness the metallic world of *Coriolanus*. Shakespeare's work shows an ever-increasing understanding, control, and exploitation of his own poetic imagination. This process is carried still further in his final period.

THE FINAL PLAYS

I

THE last group of plays shows again a development.
We have seen tempests become wedded to the plot,
closely entwined therewith, and expanding their significance
symbolically throughout the drama. Now the poetic image
tends not only to blend with, but actually to become the
plot. In *Pericles*, *The Winter's Tale*, and *Cymbeline* we shall
find old imagery curiously and, in *Pericles* especially, most
beautifully actualized. The poet draws now on the purest
elixir of his spontaneous imagination. Sometimes the
result is, dramatically, a little dangerous: often a wonder
and delight. The poetic inspiration has outrun the reason
of drama and the logic of life.

To analyse the tempests in *Pericles* would be to
analyse the whole play.[1] Here, therefore, I can do no more
than suggest the numerous tempest themes, and, also,
the music and jewel references scattered throughout.
There are numerous tempests. To avoid a conspiracy
against his life, Pericles flees from Tyre by ship. He

> puts himself unto the shipman's toil,
> With whom each minute threatens life or death.
>
> (i. iii. 24)

Thaliard, charged to slay him, characteristically regards
this as sufficient excuse for reporting Pericles' death:

> He 'scaped the land, to perish at the sea. (i. iii. 29)

Pericles, however, arrives safe at Tarsus:

> A portly sail of ships make hitherward. (i. iv. 61)

---

[1] I have no space to enter here the question of authorship. That the
play was rejected from the Folio indicates that it is not completely by
Shakespeare; and that this was done although so much of it was of Shakespeare's best, and the play itself so popular, shows us how scrupulous were
the Folio editors.

Returning to Tyre, he suffers wreck:

> He, doing so, put forth to seas,
> Where when men been, there 's seldom ease;
> For now the wind begins to blow;
> Thunder above and deeps below
> Make such unquiet, that the ship
> Should house him safe is wreck'd and split;
> And he, good prince, having all lost,
> By waves from coast to coast is tost.   (II. Pro. 27)

He is cast up at Pentapolis. 'Enter Pericles, wet':

> *Pericles.* Yet cease your ire, you angry stars of heaven!
> Wind, rain, and thunder, remember, earthly man
> Is but a substance that must yield to you;
> And I, as fits my nature, do obey you:
> Alas, the sea hath cast me on the rocks,
> Wash'd me from shore to shore, and left me breath
> Nothing to think on but ensuing death:
> Let it suffice the greatness of your powers
> To have bereft a prince of all his fortunes;
> And having thrown him from your watery grave,
> Here to have death in peace is all he'll crave.   (II. i. 1)

Notice the association of the tempest with stars, death, fortune. Tempests here, as usual, clearly suggest the tragedies of mortal destiny in a wide sense. Next three fishermen enter. They describe the wreck:

> Alas, poor souls, it grieved my heart to hear what pitiful cries
> they made to us to help them, when, well-a-day, we could
> scarce help ourselves.   (II. i. 21)

Never before has the 'wreck' come so close to us in Shakespeare. The fishermen 'marvel how the fishes live in the sea' (II. i. 29). There follows a queer humanity-monster association and music-sea contrast. Whales are like 'misers' swallowing the parish whole, including 'church, steeple, bells and all'. The Third Fisherman suggests that if he had been the sexton,

> . . . I would have kept such a jangling of the bells, that he
> should never have left, till he cast bells, steeple, church, and
> parish, up again.   (II. i. 45)

A microcosm of the play: music conquering the cruelty of
the sea. So the fishermen compare their 'watery empire' to
human affairs (ii. i. 54). Pericles introduces himself:

> A man whom both the waters and the wind,
> In that vast tennis-court, have made the ball
> For them to play upon, entreats you pity him.
> He asks of you that never used to beg.   (ii. i. 63)

They are kind. And Pericles' choice armour, handed
down by his father, is washed up to him:

> It kept where I kept, I so dearly loved it;
> Till the rough seas, that spare not any man,
> Took it in rage, though calm'd have given 't again:
> I thank thee for 't: my shipwreck now 's no ill.
>   (ii. i. 136)

'Rage', again. Now,

> By your furtherance I am clothed in steel;
> And, spite of all the rapture of the sea,
> This jewel holds his building on my arm.
>   (ii. i. 166)

And, with this armour, he wins a bride, Thaisa.
   He braves his tempest and gains the rich merchandise
of love. He tells Thaisa he is 'a gentleman of Tyre',

> Who, looking for adventures in the world,
> Was by the rough seas reft of ships and men,
> And after shipwreck driven upon this shore.
>   (ii. iii. 83)

Love and music succeed tempests. Pericles is a musician:

> *Simonides:*   I am beholding to you
> For your sweet music this last night: I do
> Protest my ears were never better fed
> With such delightful pleasing harmony.   (ii. v. 25)

He is 'music's master' (ii. v. 30). Next Pericles and his
bride leave Pentapolis. Thaisa is with child, but the cause
of their going—a matter of state and kingly responsibility—is urgent. Again, they run into another of
fortune's tempests:

>   Their vessel shakes
> On Neptune's billow; half the flood
> Hath their keel cut: but fortune's mood
> Varies again; the grisled north
> Disgorges such a tempest forth,
> That, as a duck for life that dives,
> So up and down the poor ship drives:
> The lady shrieks and well-a-near
> Does fall in travail with her fear:
> And what ensues in this fell storm
> Shall for itself itself perform.
> I nill relate, action may
> Conveniently the rest convey;
> Which might not what by me is told.
> In your imagination hold
> This stage the ship, upon whose deck
> The sea-tost Pericles appears to speak.

(III. Pro. 44)

So marriage and birth, like love so often, are also tossed in tempest. In mid-tempest the child is born. And now the 'bark', so long insistent in Shakespeare's tempest imagery, is now actually brought into the drama:

Enter Pericles on shipboard.

Pericles. Thou god of this great vast, rebuke these surges,
>   Which wash both heaven and hell; and thou, that hast
>   Upon the winds command, bind them in brass,
>   Having call'd them from the deep! O, still
>   Thy deafening, dreadful thunders; gently quench
>   Thy nimble, sulphurous flashes! O, how, Lychorida,
>   How does my queen? Thou stormest venomously;
>   Wilt thou spit all thyself? The seaman's whistle
>   Is as a whisper in the ears of death,
>   Unheard. Lychorida!—Lucina, O
>   Divinest patroness, and midwife gentle
>   To those that cry by night, convey thy deity
>   Aboard our dancing boat. . . .   (III. i. 1)

Notice the wide scope of our suggestion: heaven, hell, and the invocation of the great God himself; and the association, as in *Othello*, of the tempest and death.

Lychorida, the nurse, brings his child. His queen is reported dead:

> O you gods!
> Why do you make us love your goodly gifts,
> And snatch them straight away? (III. i. 22)

Next he speaks to his child:

> Now, mild may be thy life!
> For a more blusterous birth had never babe:
> Quiet and gentle thy conditions! for
> Thou art the rudeliest welcome to this world
> That ever was prince's child. Happy what follows!
> Thou hast as chiding a nativity
> As fire, air, water, earth, and heaven can make,
> To herald thee from the womb: even at the first
> Thy loss is more than can thy portage quit,
> With all thou canst find here. Now, the good gods
> Throw their best eyes upon 't. (III. i. 27)

So exactly does this birth and tempest suggest the entrance of life into the tempests of mortality. Ever in *Pericles* the tempests have the widest Shakespearian significance. Love, marriage, birth—all are here opposed by tempests, a whirl of sweet things rocked, lost, yet saved amid tempestuous adventure. So Pericles welcomes the new-born babe, 'this fresh-new sea-farer' (III. i. 41) on the waters of human life. But Thaisa is supposed dead. The sailors insist that she be cast into the raging sea:

> *Pericles.* A terrible childbed hast thou had, my dear;
> No light, no fire: the unfriendly elements
> Forgot thee utterly; nor have I time
> To give thee hallow'd to thy grave, but straight
> Must cast thee, scarcely coffin'd, in the ooze;
> Where, for a monument upon thy bones,
> And e'er-remaining lamps, the belching whale
> And humming water must o'erwhelm thy corpse,
> Lying with simple shells. (III. i. 57)

So Thaisa is thrown into the tempestuous sea. We remember the old love-imagery whereby a jewel is cast into rough waters: that image is now actualized, the jewel is

Thaisa herself. Thaisa is coffined with jewels (III. i. 67).
Nowhere do we find a purer essence of Shakespearian
poetry than here. No wonder, since the favourite love-
images—of sea-tempest, 'bark', and 'jewel', that is, Thaisa
—have become the very plot and drama itself. Soon we
shall see further how close is the Thaisa-jewel association.

Now at Ephesus Thaisa is cast ashore. Cerimon and
others discuss the tempest in the usual terms. It is such
a tempest as never has been known: this is the usual
phrase. The very earth seemed to quake, as in *Macbeth*.
There enter 'some persons who have been ship-wreck'd'
(III. ii). A servant says he has never 'endured' a night like
this. Again,

> Our lodgings, standing bleak upon the sea,
> Shook as the earth did quake;
> The very principals did seem to rend,
> And all-to topple. (III. ii. 14)

They open Thaisa's coffin, and the saintly Cerimon re-
stores her to life with music:

> The rough and woeful music that we have,
> Cause it to sound, beseech you.
> The viol once more: how thou stirr'st, thou block!
> The music there!—I pray you, give her air.
> Gentlemen,
> This queen will live: nature awakes; a warmth
> Breathes out of her: she hath not been entranced
> Above five hours: see how she gins to blow
> Into life's flower again! (III. ii. 88)

This death is a trance only. Notice how life is a 'flower'.
Now music revives the tempest-lost life:

> She is alive; behold,
> Her eyelids, cases to those heavenly jewels
> Which Pericles hath lost,
> Begin to part their fringes of bright gold;
> The diamonds of a most praised water
> Do appear, to make the world twice rich. (III. ii. 98)

So aptly does jewel-imagery honour this jewel of love,

Thaisa. And so finely does the pure image of poetry now flower at last into its full dramatic perfection.

But Pericles thinks his wife dead. Loss in tempest is the inevitable fate of mortality:

> *Pericles.*   We cannot but obey
> The powers above us. Could I rage and roar
> As doth the sea she lies in, yet the end
> Must be as 'tis. My gentle babe Marina, whom,
> For she was born at sea, I have named so, here
> I charge your charity withal . . .   (III. iii. 9)

Observe the words 'rage' and 'roar', the latter recalling our tempest-beasts. He leaves her at Tarsus, and departs in resigned tranquillity:

> *Cleon.* We'll bring your grace e'en to the edge o' the shore,
> Then give you up to the mask'd Neptune and
> The gentlest winds of heaven.   (III. iii. 35)

But tempests are not yet finally stilled. Thaisa is a priestess of Diana at Ephesus. Marina grows up, is taught music (IV. Pro. 8) at Tarsus. Lychorida, her nurse, dies:

>   Ay me! poor maid,
> Born in a tempest when my mother died,
> This world to me is like a lasting storm,
> Whirring me from my friends.   (IV. i. 18)

A vivid example of the tempest's dispersing quality, and its universal significance. Dionyza, her guardian, interrupts her in her grief, tells her harshly not to sorrow, takes her flowers from her:

>   Lord, how your favour 's changed
> With this unprofitable woe!
> Come, give me your flowers, ere the sea mar it.
>   (IV. i. 25)

The 'sea' is probably Marina's tears. Certainly this scene is 'an open place near the sea-shore'. But, in any case, the sea itself and grief are so close in the poet's imagination that there can be no exact distinction. Marina is left alone with Leonine, who is to murder her. She recalls the tempest of her birth:

Marina. Is this wind westerly that blows?
Leonine.   South-west.
Marina. When I was born, the wind was north.
Leonine.   Was't so?
Marina. My father, as nurse said, did never fear,
    But cried 'Good seamen!' to the sailors, galling
    His kingly hands, haling ropes;
    And, clasping to the mast, endured a sea
    That almost burst the deck.
Leonine. When was this?
Marina. When I was born:
    Never was waves nor wind more violent;
    And from the ladder-tackle washes off
    A canvas-climber. 'Ha!' says one, 'wilt out?'
    And with a dropping industry they skip
    From stem to stern: the boatswain whistles, and
    The master calls, and trebles their confusion.

                              (IV. i. 51)

Then he is about to slay her. His name, Leonine, is apt, the lion being a tempest-beast. At the crucial moment she is rescued by pirates, who regard her as a prize. Leonine reports her to be slain 'and thrown into the sea' (IV. i. 100), like Thaisa. Meanwhile, in happy expectancy, Pericles comes 'thwarting the wayward seas' (IV. iv. 10), his peace of mind reflected in his easy voyage, the 'well-sailing ships and bounteous winds' (IV. iv. 17).

               . . . think his pilot thought;
  So with his steerage shall your thoughts grow on. . . .
                              (IV. iv. 18)

which recalls the chorus in *Henry V.* Notice how his sea voyage is a matter of 'thought'. He finds his Marina reported dead. And now he takes another voyage of grief, again tempest-stricken:

    See how belief may suffer by foul show!
    This borrow'd passion stands for true old woe;
    And Pericles, in sorrow all devour'd,
    With sighs shot through, and biggest tears o'ershower'd,

> Leaves Tarsus and again embarks. He swears
> Never to wash his face, nor cut his hairs:
> He puts on sackcloth, and to sea. He bears
> A tempest, which his mortal vessel tears,
> And yet he rides it out. (IV. iv. 23)

Notice, again, how close—indeed inextricable—is the relation of the sea voyage to the tempest of the soul. So Pericles, in grief, leaves Tarsus thinking 'Thetis' birth-child' (IV. iv. 41) dead.

Meanwhile Marina endures her own tragedy: the characteristic Shakespearian one of a threat to her maidenly honour. Yet she survives her tempest. Her purity, suggests Lysimachus, prevents the house of evil, the brothel, from 'sinking' and 'overwhelming' its mistress (IV. vi. 128). And she finally wins by her ability to sing 'like one immortal' (v. Pro. 3) and the art of embroidery. Next we hear again of Pericles, 'on the sea', first in tempests, then at rest:

> We there him lost;
> Whence, driven before the winds, he is arrived
> Here where his daughter dwells; and on this coast
> Suppose him now at anchor. The city strived
> God Neptune's annual feast to keep; from whence
> Lysimachus our Tyrian ship espies,
> His banners sable, trimm'd with rich expense;
> And to him in his barge with fervour hies.
> In your supposing once more put your sight
> Of heavy Pericles; think this his bark. . . . (v. Pro. 13)

'Rich expense': this play is full of gold, silver, precious stones, and all things of 'rich expense'. So, in tranquillity, Lysimachus comes on a 'barge'—we remember Cleopatra's barge on Cydnus—Marina follows him and, at the feast of Neptune, the tempests are finally stilled. Pericles and Marina meet again at sea, but at peace. Malone's beautiful scene direction (v. i) is:

> *On board Pericles' ship, off Mytilene. A close pavilion on deck, with a curtain before it; Pericles within it, reclined on a couch. A barge lying beside the Tyrian vessel.*

A fine contrast with former scenes. This has a breathless
stillness, still as the harbour waters. Pericles is lost in
grief. Marina, the song-maiden, will restore him, as
Cordelia and music restored the 'untuned' senses of Lear:

> She questionless with her sweet harmony
> And other chosen attractions, would allure,
> And make a battery through his deafen'd parts,
> Which now are midway stopp'd. . . .   (v. i. 45)

'Battery' as in *Antony and Cleopatra*. She sings. Her
'music' (v. i. 81) first does not move him. They speak
together:

> *Pericles.*   What country-woman?
> Here of these shores?
> *Marina.*   No, nor of any shores. (v. i. 104)

She is like his jewel Thaisa:

> As silver-voiced; her eyes as jewel-like
> And cased as richly. . . .   (v. i. 111)

Another fine example of our love-jewel association, in
this play of all most powerful. Again Pericles speaks:

> I think thou said'st
> Thou hadst been toss'd from wrong to injury,
> And that thou thought'st thy griefs might equal mine,
> If both were open'd.   (v. i. 130)

Notice the close equation of tempest-metaphor with all
mortal griefs. At last the truth is clear to him. This scene
is very reminiscent of the Lear-Cordelia reunion:

> O, Helicanus, strike me, honour'd sir;
> Give me a gash, put me to present pain;
> Lest this great sea of joys rushing upon me
> O'erbear the shores of my mortality,
> And drown me with their sweetness. O, come hither,
> Thou that beget'st him that did thee beget;
> Thou that wast born at sea, buried at Tarsus,
> And found at sea again! O Helicanus,
> Down on thy knees, thank the holy gods as loud
> As thunder threatens us: this is Marina.   (v. i. 192)

Joy is now a 'great sea': for the great sea of Fortune is

now 'joy'. 'Tempests are kind', as in *Twelfth Night*, and restore their spoil. She is 'found at sea', on the 'feast of Neptune'. Neptune's hostility is over, and the 'holy gods' are to be thanked. Human thanks must be proportionate to the 'thunder' from which the gods have saved storm-tossed mortality. And now the final peace of tempest-conquering love breaks out in mysterious music:

> *Pericles.*   I embrace you.
>   Give me my robes. I am wild in my beholding.
>   O heavens bless my girl! But, hark, what music?
>   Tell Helicanus, my Marina, tell him
>   O'er, point by point, for yet he seems to doubt,
>   How sure you are my daughter. But, what music?
> *Helicanus.* My lord, I hear none.
> *Pericles.* None!
>   The music of the spheres! List, my Marina.
> *Lysimachus.* It is not good to cross him; give him way.
> *Pericles.* Rarest sounds! Do ye not hear?
> *Lysimachus.*   My lord, I hear.
>   [*Music.*
> *Pericles.* Most heavenly music!   (v. i. 223)

In no former play have we found so clear a mystic sense of a love reunion and victory consummating in music the long grief of misadventure in tempest.

Next, in obedience to Diana's command, Pericles and Marina pass to Ephesus. Winds are kind:

>   In feather'd briefness sails are fill'd,
>   And wishes fall out as they're will'd.   (v. ii. 15)

There Thaisa lives serving in Diana's 'silver livery' (v. iii. 7). Now the threads of this 'tempest' story are drawn together, the age-long sea-sorrow of birth and death and loss of love assuaged. Remembrance and reunion are sweet:

> *Thaisa.*   O, my lord,
>   Are you not Pericles? Like him you spake,
>   Like him you are: did you not name a tempest,
>   A birth, and death?
> *Pericles.*   The voice of dead Thaisa!
>   (v. iii. 31)

The mother finds her lord and child, her 'burden at the sea and called Marina' (v. iii. 47). So ends the sea-story of Pericles. I have shortly observed its tempests and music. Its imagery of riches I have only suggested: they are everywhere. Minor tempest-images embroider the action at I. i. 96; I. ii. 98, where a quarrel is a 'tempest': II. iv. 23–4; IV. Pro, 12; IV. ii. 20; IV. ii. 25; IV. ii. 159; IV. iv. 2; and elsewhere. In no play does Shakespeare's imagination move with a more careless and miraculous grace: exactly because he now writes from a centre where poetry is the only realism and so allows himself an un-hampered use of tempests and spheral music.

The Winter's Tale is a more studied work on the *Pericles* pattern. The wife and child themes are similar. Both Hermione and Perdita are supposed lost, and eventually restored. Hermione suffers the tempest of Leontes' jealousy, but no actual tempest occurs in this relation. There is one important tempest, however, which is curiously interesting. Antigonus has sailed to Bohemia— geography sacrificed to the imperative demands of tem-pests—and leaves his ship with Perdita who is to be exposed on the wild shore:

Antigonus. Thou art perfect then our ship hath touch'd upon
    The deserts of Bohemia?
Mariner.   Ay, my lord; and fear
    We have landed in ill time: the skies look grimly
    And threaten present blusters. In my conscience,
    The heavens with that we have in hand are angry
    And frown upon 's.
Antigonus. Their sacred wills be done! Go, get aboard;
    Look to thy bark: I'll not be long before
    I call upon thee.
Mariner. Make your best haste, and go not
    Too far i' the land: 'tis like to be loud weather;
    Besides, this place is famous for the creatures
    Of prey that keep upon 't.   (III. iii. 1)

Notice how, in these last plays, there is ever a sense of personal divine powers controlling tempests. Tempests

are thus here associated with 'creatures of prey': we remember our list of tempest beasts: the 'hungry lion',
'empty tigers', the bear, wolf, and boar.

Antigonus is alone with the child. The day 'frowns' on
him:

> *Antigonus.*   The storm begins: poor wretch
> That for thy mother's fault art thus exposèd
> To loss and what may follow! Weep I cannot,
> But my heart bleeds; and most accursed am I
> To be by oath enjoin'd to this. Farewell!
> The day frowns more and more: thou'rt like to have
> A lullaby too rough: I never saw
> The heavens so dim by day. A savage clamour!
> Well may I get aboard! This is the chase:
> I am gone for ever.   [*Exit, pursued by a bear.*
> (III. iii. 49)

This is another instance of the process I observed in
Pericles. A well-worn image becomes strangely alive before our eyes. The tempest-beast association is usual. I
have noted it continually in tempest-passages. The
most usual beast was a bear. Here the bear actually
appears, joining forces with our tempest. Just as the
'bark tempest-tossed' and the 'jewel-thrown-in-the-sea'
were actually presented in *Pericles*, here we have the
bear and tempest together. We hear more of them, the
association being closely pointed. The shepherd enters,
complaining of the 'weather'. Then to him comes the
Clown:

> *Clown.* I have seen two such sights, by sea and by land! but I am
> not to say it is a sea, for it is now the sky: betwixt the firmament
> and it you cannot thrust a bodkin's point.
> *Shepherd.* Why, boy, how is it?
> *Clown.* I would you did but see how it chafes, how it rages, how
> it takes up the shore! but that's not to the point. O, the most
> piteous cry of the poor souls! sometimes to see 'em, and not
> to see 'em; now the ship boring the moon with her main-mast,
> and anon swallowed with yest and froth, as you'ld thrust a
> cork into a hogshead. And then for the land-service, to see

how the bear tore out his shoulder-bone; how he cried to me
for help and said his name was Antigonus, a nobleman. But
to make an end of the ship, to see how the sea flap-dragoned
it: but, first, how the poor souls roared, and the sea mocked
them; and how the poor gentleman roared and the bear
mocked him, both roaring louder than the sea or weather.
Shepherd. Name of mercy, when was this, boy?
Clown. Now, now: I have not winked since I saw these sights:
the men are not yet cold under water, nor the bear half dined
on the gentleman: he's at it now.
Shepherd. Would I had been by, to have helped the old man!
Clown. I would you had been by the ship side, to have helped
her: there your charity would have lacked footing.

(III. iii. 84)

This dialogue reminds us of the fishermen discussing the
wreck in *Pericles*. Here, as with the tempest in *Pericles*,
the tempest and bear are important in their association
with death and birth. The shepherd points this birth-
death association. He shows the Clown the baby:

> . . . Now bless thyself: thou mettest with things dying, I with
> things new-born.   (III. iii. 116)

Such is the tempestuous heart of *The Winter's Tale*. But
here, too, the end is music. Perdita is found, and Hermione
restored to music:

> *Paulina.* Music, awake her; strike!   [*Music.*
> 'Tis time; descend; be stone no more; approach;
> Strike all that look upon with marvel. Come,
> I'll fill your grave up: stir, nay, come away,
> Bequeath to death your numbness, for from him
> Dear life redeems you.   (v. iii. 98)

So death awakes in music to life and love.

The music and tempest themes here are close to those
of *Pericles*. Beyond these, there are minor pieces of
imagery of the usual sort. Polixenes, long absent from his
own kingdom, fears 'sneaping winds at home' (i. ii. 13);
tears 'drown' (ii. i. 112); Leontes is 'a feather for each
wind that blows' (ii. iii. 154). There is a scene at 'a sea-port

in Sicilia' (III. i) wherein we have a powerful description
of the Delphic oracle:

> *Cleomenes.* The climate 's delicate, the air most sweet,
>   Fertile the isle, the temple much surpassing
>   The common praise it bears.
> *Dion.*   I shall report,
>   For most it caught me, the celestial habits,
>   Methinks I so should term them, and the reverence
>   Of the grave wearers. O, the sacrifice!
>   How ceremonious, solemn and unearthly
>   It was i' the offering!
> *Cleomenes.*   But of all, the burst
>   And the ear-deafening voice o' the oracle,
>   Kin to Jove's thunder, so surprised my sense,
>   That I was nothing.   (III. i. 1)

Observe this reference to 'Jove's thunder', a well-worn
Shakespearian thought; but notice also here its association
with an oracle. I shall have cause to return to it shortly.
To continue our list. Paulina describes an infinite penance
for Leontes in terms of 'storm perpetual' (III. ii. 214).
There are Perdita's flowers:

>   . . . daffodils
>   That come before the swallow dares, and take
>   The winds of March with beauty.   (IV. iii. 118)

A lovely flower-tempest contrast. In the love passages of
Florizel and the flower-maiden Perdita we have thoughts
of music, dance, and sun-glittering sea together:

>   . . . when you sing,
>   I'ld have you buy and sell so, so give alms,
>   Pray so; and for the ordering your affairs,
>   To sing them too: when you do dance, I wish you
>   A wave o' the sea, that you might ever do
>   Nothing but that.   (IV. iii. 137)

This scene, with its springtime festivity, music and dance,
is to be set against the wintry bitterness of the start. So,

>   He says he loves my daughter:
>   I think so too; for never gazed the moon
>   Upon the water as he'll stand and read
>   As 'twere my daughter's eyes.   (IV. iii. 171)

Which gaze of heaven's lamp on the calm breast of the
sea recalls Keats's *Bright Star* sonnet, wherein, to point a
human love, the star 'watches' the 'moving waters' and
'gazes' on the snow-masked moors. Love here, as elsewhere, finds an 'Ethiopian' image:

> I take thy hand, this hand,
> As soft as dove's down and as white as it,
> Or Ethiopian's tooth, or the fann'd snow that's bolted
> By the northern blasts twice o'er.   (iv. iii. 374)

But the 'blast' image, for once, is not directly relevant,
unless by inversion, to the love-tempest contrast.[1]
There is a reference to the riches which 'the profound
seas hide in unknown fathoms' (iv. iii. 503). Florizel
decides to put to sea with Perdita, going, he tells Camillo,
they know not where:

> . . . we profess
> Ourselves to be the slaves of chance and flies
> Of every wind that blows.   (iv. iii. 552)

Wherein 'chance' and 'wind' are clearly equated. There
is an interesting passage of Camillo's in reply in which
rash and purposeless sea-journeys are associated with
'miseries' and 'affliction' and shown to be the enemies of
love. He advises them to go to Sicily:

> A course more promising
> Than a wild dedication of yourselves
> To unpath'd waters, undream'd shores, most certain
> To miseries enough: no hope to help you,
> But as you shake off one to take another;
> Nothing so certain as your anchors, who
> Do their best office, if they can but stay you
> Where you'll be loath to be: besides you know
> Prosperity's the very bond of love,
> Whose fresh complexion and whose heart together
> Affliction alters.   (iv. iii. 578)

So they go happily with a 'prosperous south-wind' (v. i.

---

[1] I have already observed, in a note to my second chapter, how pure
snow is an optimistic impression in Shakespeare.

161) to Sicily, Camillo with them. Later Florizel thinks Camillo has betrayed him, Camillo

> Whose honour and whose honesty till now
> Endured all weathers. (v. i. 194)

At the end joy 'waded in tears' (v. ii. 52). And there is more talk about the original wreck off Bohemia (v. ii. 75–81). Here, as before, the synchronization of tempest, death, and the finding of the child is emphasized. Clearly, here and in *Pericles*, the tempest suggests the turbulent destinies of mortality. This play is in two contrasted parts. First, we have wintry bitterness, tempest, shipwreck and loss; and next, spring festivity, youth and love, reunion and music.

I turn to *Cymbeline*, noting first some minor images. We have the old idea of lovers parted by water:

> No, madam; for so long
> As he could make me with this eye or ear
> Distinguish him from others, he did keep
> The deck, with glove, or hat, or handkerchief,
> Still waving, as the fits and stirs of 's mind
> Could best express how slow his soul sail'd on,
> How swift his ship. (I. iii. 8)

The sea is mentioned in a piece of universal love-imagery recalling *Antony and Cleopatra*:

> What, are men mad? Hath nature given them eyes
> To see this vaulted arch, and the rich crop
> Of sea and land, which can distinguish 'twixt
> The fiery orbs above and the twinn'd stones
> Upon the number'd beach? and can we not
> Partition make with spectacles so precious
> 'Twixt fair and foul? (I. vi. 32)

We shall observe how often sea-imagery here is beautiful and music correspondingly solemn: the two make a strange and noble blending. Pitied by Imogen, Iachimo says:

> . . . what wreck discern you in me
> Deserves your pity? (I. vi. 84)

Music interthreads our tragic atmosphere. So Cloten

serenades his love with music (II. iii), and there is the song,
'Hark, hark! the lark at heaven's gate sings'—dawn and
bird-music. Sea-imagery is often here pleasant:

> The swiftest harts have posted you by land;
> And winds of all the corners kiss'd your sails,
> To make your vessel nimble.   (II. iv. 27)

Also we have Iachimo's description of Cleopatra at
Cydnus woven on a tapestry (II. iv. 66–76). The Queen
draws a fine picture of England

>   which stands
> As Neptune's park, ribbed and paled in
> With rocks unscaleable and roaring waters,
> With sands that will not bear your enemies' boats,
> But suck them up to the topmast.   (III. i. 18)

Which description recalls, as Mr. Percy Allen observes,[1]
Gaunt's speech in *Richard II*. So, at Caesar's invasion,

>   his shipping—
> Poor ignorant baubles!—on our terrible seas,
> Like egg-shells moved upon their surges, crack'd
> As easily 'gainst our rocks.   (III. i. 26)

Britain is 'a swan's nest' in 'a great pool' (III. iv. 142).
Another example of tranquil imagery. And towards the
close of the play, we have a fine peace-music association:

> The fingers of the powers above do tune
> The harmony of this peace.   (v. v. 466)

Guiderius and Arviragus, taken from civilization to a
life of simple nature by Belarius, endure an experience of
Nature's roughness such as we found in *As You Like It*,
Lear, and *Timon*:

>   What should we speak of
> When we are old as you? when we shall hear
> The rain and wind beat dark December, how,
> In this our pinching cave, shall we discourse
> The freezing hours away?   (III. iii. 35)

---

[1] In *The Oxford Shakespeare Case Corroborated*, pp. 273, 274. But I
fear I cannot follow Mr. Allen in his thesis that the one speech is a copy,
by a different writer, of the other.

Belarius gives his answer, again in terms of *Timon* imagery:

> Cymbeline loved me,
> And when a soldier was the theme, my name
> Was not far off: then was I as a tree
> Whose boughs did bend with fruit: but in one night,
> A storm or robbery, call it what you will,
> Shook down my mellow hangings, nay, my leaves,
> And left me bare to weather.   (III. iii. 58)

Again, the tree-image. Slander 'rides on the posting winds' (III. iv. 38). Imogen, creature of soft airs and music, will please Lucius 'if that his head have ear in music' (III. iv. 178). Often Shakespeare's sweetest heroines are all but personifications of music. Imogen is given a medicine to help her 'if you are sick at sea' (III. iv. 192). Characteristically, she eventually takes it for 'heart' sickness, which is, in Shakespeare, all but the same:

> Gods, what lies I have heard!
> Our courtiers say all 's savage but at court:
> Experience, O, thou disprovest report!
> The imperious seas breed monsters, for the dish
> Poor tributary rivers as sweet fish.
> I am sick still; heart-sick. Pisanio,
> I'll now taste of thy drug.   (IV. ii. 32)

An interesting contrast between 'sweet fish' of rivers (such as I have observed in *Antony and Cleopatra* and *Much Ado* in relation to love) and sea-monsters.

Guiderius and Arviragus love the supposed boy, Fidele. He sings 'angel-like' (IV. ii. 47). Arviragus describes him in a speech resembling the account of Cordelia's grief—'sunshine and rain at once'—a speech which vividly shows the grief-tempest identity:

> Nobly he yokes
> A smiling with a sigh, as if the sigh
> Was that it was, for not being such a smile;
> The smile mocking the sigh, that it would fly
> From so divine a temple, to commix
> With winds that sailors rail at.   (IV. ii. 51)

Guiderius kills Cloten and says he will give his head to the sea:

> I'll throw 't into the creek
> Behind our rock; and let it to the sea,
> And tell the fishes he 's the queen's son, Cloten:
> That 's all I reck.   (IV. ii. 151)

An interesting death-sea association. The temperaments of Guiderius and Arviragus are described in terms of weather:

> O thou goddess,
> Thou divine Nature, how thyself thou blazon'st
> In these two princely boys! They are as gentle
> As zephyrs blowing below the violet,
> Not wagging his sweet head; and yet as rough,
> Their royal blood enchafed, as the rudest wind,
> That by the top doth take the mountain pine,
> And make him stoop to the vale.   (IV. ii. 169)

A characteristic speech. The 'violet' and 'zephyrs' recall *Twelfth Night*. 'Chafe' is a very usual word in 'tempest' passages; so is the 'pine' or 'cedar'; and 'top' occurs often, too. Here there is both gentle and tempestuous weather imagery. That is true of *Cymbeline* as a whole. Tempests alternate with gentle airs and music. At Fidele's supposed death there is 'solemn music' (IV. ii. 186):

> *Belarius.*   My ingenious instrument!
> Hark, Polydore it sounds! But what occasion
> Hath Cadwal now to give it motion? Hark!
>   (IV. ii. 186)

Imogen, as though dead, is brought in:

> O melancholy!
> Who ever yet could sound thy bottom? find
> The ooze, to show what coast thy sluggish crare
> Might easiliest harbour in?   (IV. ii. 203)

Here 'melancholy' is a vast sea, a bottomless sorrow. Guiderius and Arviragus sing a dirge over the supposed dead boy (IV. ii. 258–81). In this, tempest—and other—imagery is associated with the trials of mortality: 'the

furious winter's rages', 'the lightning flash', 'the all
dreaded thunder-stone', all entwine with thoughts of the
'frown o' the great', 'slander', 'censure rash'; and in death
the boy shall be safe from 'ghosts' (cf. *Hamlet*) and 'witchcraft' (cf. *Macbeth*). Such is their prayer or song, bearing
close relevance to the tragedies of Shakespeare. But in
Cymbeline all unhappy things—and there are many—are
ever dissolved in melody. Next Imogen wakes and thinks
the headless body is Posthumus's:

> Damn'd Pisanio
> Hath with his forged letters,—damn'd Pisanio—
> From this most bravest vessel of the world
> Struck the main-top!   (IV. ii. 317)

So the Roman Captain later calls the body a 'sad wreck'
(IV. ii. 366). Navigation-imagery is strong in *Cymbeline*.
Cowards in battle are 'like fragments in hard voyages'
(V. iii. 44). But again, our imagery may be sweet:

> The benediction of these covering heavens
> Fall on their heads like dew.   (V. v. 350)

We may observe how large a part Milford Haven plays
in the suggestion of the play. Reunion and happiness is
the conclusion, tempests are conquered, and the boat is
safe in the haven of love:

> See,
> Posthumus anchors upon Imogen,
> And she, like harmless lightning, throws her eye
> On him, her brothers, me, her master, hitting
> Each object with a joy. . . .   (V. v. 392)

'Anchors', 'harmless lightning'. Airs are soft here at the
last, soft as zephyr and sweet music, Shakespearian companions to love. Imogen is a thing of melody and maiden
zephyr. The two thoughts are intrinsicate in Shakespeare's
mind: we may recall *Twelfth Night*, where music is 'like
the sweet south' breathing on 'a bank of violets' (I. i. 5).
Therefore she is, in the oracle, a 'piece of tender air'
(V. iv. 140; V. v. 438), or 'mollis aer' (V. v. 447), or again
'this most tender air' (V. v. 452). So also in the oracle

Posthumus Leonatus is the 'lion's whelp' and Cymbeline the 'stately cedar'. Both these images suggest noble strength, strength comparable with that of tempests. For the lion is not equivalent to the bear quite. Macbeth dies as a bear at the stake; Antony as an 'old lion'. A pointed contrast. Cedars, too, are 'stately' or 'proud' as in *Coriolanus*: they do not bend to tempests as do the pines.

The oracle itself is most important. At the heart of this play we have the vision of Jupiter (v. iv) and the oracular statement he leaves. Posthumus, like Pericles, sleeps; and a divine being appears. But first Posthumus's relations enter:

> *Solemn music. Enter, as in an apparition, Sicilius Leonatus, father to Posthumus, an old man, attired like a warrior; leading in his hand an ancient matron, his wife, and mother to Posthumus, with music before them: then, after other music, follow the two young Leonati, brothers to Posthumus, with wounds as they died in the wars. They circle Posthumus round, as he lies sleeping.*

Solemn music, as at Fidele's 'death'. The play is one of kind tempests, 'harmless lightning', gentle seas and airs, and solemn music; an exquisite blending. Now Posthumus's relations chant a dirge full of universal significance, repeating the 'birth' thought of *Pericles* and *The Winter's Tale*, and crying against Jupiter for the harshness of human destiny:

> No more, thou thunder-master, show
>   Thy spite on mortal-flies.   (v. iv. 30)

We recall Lear: 'as flies to wanton boys are we to the gods'. In *Lear*, too, thunder and tempest are the ire of the gods, there 'high-judging Jove' is the 'thunder-bearer'. The Jove-thunder thought is continual in Shakespeare. It is often found close to 'Neptune' imagery, as in a passage I have quoted from *Coriolanus* and elsewhere in *The Winter's Tale*. Here the ghosts cry to Jupiter, again and again. Then he appears:

> *Jupiter descends in thunder and lightning, sitting upon an eagle: he throws a thunderbolt. The ghosts fall on their knees.*

Again our old imagery is actualized. The process of *Pericles* and *The Winter's Tale* is repeated, with here a third type of image newly brought to life. Jupiter, symbol of Divine judgement, responsible for man's tragedy, yet ever just, is frequent in Shakespeare's imagery. In *The Winter's Tale*, moreover, the 'ear-deafening voice o' the oracle' was 'kin to Jove's thunder' (III. i. 9). Here Jove and his thunder appear and bring an oracular message exactly like that in *The Winter's Tale*, both referring to lost children and prophesying reunion. It is perhaps noteworthy that the rare word 'celestial' occurs in both scenes. (*Cymbeline*, v. iv. 114). We see how the 'Jove' suggestion has worked long in the poet's mind, was given a new and vivid description in *The Winter's Tale*, and becomes dramatically actual in *Cymbeline*. The poet made peace with Neptune in *Pericles*; now he makes his peace with Jupiter. So here, enclosed in the music of human love, is suddenly exposed the naked thunder-personification of the Deity. At his majesty the sorrowful tunes are stilled, and God—the tragic 'gods' of Lear—justified by His own authority. The importance of this scene has been, indeed, grossly misrepresented.[1] Tragic destiny is set against human love; thunder and lightning against music. Tempests are justified:

> No more, you petty spirits of region low,
>   Offend our hearing; hush! How dare you ghosts
> Accuse the thunderer, whose bolt, you know,
>   Sky-planted batters all rebelling coasts?   (v. iv. 93)

'Coasts': a suggestion recalling many others, of the battering of stormy waters against the rocks of existence. At the last, the 'thunder-master' is kind:

> Whom best I love I cross; to make my gift
> The more delay'd, delighted.—   (v. iv. 101)

So also in *Pericles*:

> This, this: no more, you gods! Your present kindness
> Makes my past miseries sports. . . .   (v. iii. 40).

[1] The vision is clearly authentic: I have written a detailed defence, which appears in *The Crown of Life*.

In *Cymbeline* we are brought to the solemn knowledge of divine guidance. So 'the powers above' are said to 'tune the harmony' of the final peace (v. v. 466).

Next, we will notice tempests in *Henry VIII*. The play probably succeeded *The Tempest*, but it is more convenient to notice it here. As in the other Final Plays, we have characteristic tempest-imagery; the recurrent child-theme; a sense of temporal insecurity; supernatural apparitions and a general atmosphere of religious ceremony and assurance; and also thoughts of riches and India. Tragedy is powerful. Buckingham, Queen Katharine, and Wolsey all meet with tragedy. But all live through it to a serene religious peace.

Tempest-imagery is frequent. Here it is contrasted with peace:

> *Norfolk.* Grievingly I think,
>   The peace between the French and us not values
>   The cost that did conclude it.
> *Buckingham.*   Every man,
>   After the hideous storm that follow'd, was
>   A thing inspired; and, not consulting, broke
>   Into a general prophecy: That this tempest,
>   Dashing the garment of this peace, aboded
>   The sudden breach on't.   (I. i. 87)

As tragedy overtakes him, Buckingham says:

> I am the shadow of poor Buckingham,
> Whose figure even this instant cloud puts on,
> By darkening my clear sun.   (I. i. 224)

Buckingham prays that his conscience may 'sink' him at his death if he 'be not faithful' (II. i. 60). He is conducted 'to the waterside' (II. i. 95) on his way to execution. A *Timon* thought recurs:

>   . . . for those you make friends
> And give your hearts to, when they once perceive
> The least rub in your fortunes, fall away
> Like water from ye, never found again
> But where they mean to sink ye.   (II. i. 127)

The King himself describes his conscience-agonies concerning the legitimacy of his marriage and his child's death:

> This respite shook
> The bosom of my conscience, enter'd me,
> Yea, with a splitting power, and made to tremble
> The region of my breast.   (II. iv. 181)

'Region' meaning 'sky' as in *Hamlet* (II. ii. 517), quoted above. 'Splitting' again. Again, he continues further on with:

> Thus hulling in
> The wild sea of my conscience, I did steer
> Toward this remedy.   (II. iv. 199)

A vivid instance of spiritual discord imaged as a turbulent sea.

Queen Katharine's tragedy is a major theme here. It is associated with both tempests and music. She would have music 'disperse' her forebodings:

> Take thy lute, wench: my soul grows sad with troubles;
> Sing, and disperse 'em, if thou canst.   (III. i. 1)

Observe the inverted use of 'disperse', as in *The Comedy of Errors*. We have a song (III. i. 3–14) which tells of Orpheus whose music won response from 'trees', and was like 'sun and showers' to make 'a lasting spring':

> Everything that heard him play,
> Even the billows of the sea,
>   Hung their heads, and then lay by.
> In sweet music is such art,
> Killing care and grief of heart
>   Fall asleep, or hearing, die.   (III. i. 9)

A clear sea-grief association; and a vivid music-tragedy contrast. Queen Katharine speaks to her ladies in typical tempest-imagery:

> Alas, poor wenches, where are now your fortunes!
> Shipwreck'd upon a kingdom, where no pity,
> No friends, no hope; no kindred weep for me;
> Almost no grave allow'd me: like the lily,
> That once was mistress of the field and flourish'd,
> I'll hang my head and perish.   (III. i. 148)

'Shipwreck'd upon a kingdom': a phrase suggesting numerous past plays.

Wolsey advises her against stubborn bearing and obvious distress:

> The hearts of princes kiss obedience,
> So much they love it; but to stubborn spirits
> They swell, and grow as terrible as storms.
>
> (III. i. 162)

'Kiss' and 'storms': a clear love-tempest contrast again. And the word 'swell'. Katharine's end is serenely beautiful:

> Good Griffith,
> Cause the musicians play me that sad note
> I named my knell, whilst I sit meditating
> On that celestial harmony I go to.   (IV. ii. 77)

There is 'sad and solemn music'. It all reminds us of Desdemona and her 'willow' song. 'Solemn' again; and, as in *The Winter's Tale* and *Cymbeline*, the word 'celestial'. Next:

> *The Vision. Enter, solemnly tripping one after another, six personages, clad in white robes, wearing on their heads garlands of bays, and golden vizards on their faces; branches of bays or palm in their hands. . . .*

The direction continues at length, in great detail and worded with exquisite care. Finally,

> *. . . and so in their dancing vanish, carrying the garland with them. The music continues.*

So the tragedy dissolves, as in our other later plays, in music.

With Wolsey we have another tragic theme. The King wonders at Wolsey's wealth. In this play gold and riches are throughout important ideas. The King has come across an inventory of

> The several parcels of his plate, his treasure,
> Rich stuffs, and ornaments of household.   (III. ii. 125)

Next he sounds Wolsey; tells him how favoured he has

been, how the power of royalty has 'rain'd honour' (III. ii. 185) on him. Wolsey speaks assurance of his loyalty:

> ... though perils did
> Abound, as thick as thought could make 'em, and
> Appear in forms more horrid,—yet my duty,
> As doth a rock against the chiding flood,
> Should the approach of this wild river break,
> And stand unshaken yours.   (III. ii. 194)

'Perils' are contrasted with a 'wild river' whose waters, like the sea so often, are imaged as beating against a 'rock'. 'Chiding'—a usual word. The King parts angrily from Wolsey:

> He parted frowning from me, as if ruin
> Leap'd from his eyes: so looks the chafed lion
> Upon the daring huntsman that has gall'd him;
> Then makes him nothing.   (III. ii. 205)

The moment of tragedy; and the characteristic tempest word 'chafed'. And really this strikes exactly the note of our tempest-passages: we remember the lions, 'empty tigers', and bears associated with the tempests of past plays. Wolsey recognizes the insubstantiability of temporal glory, the deep dangers of all mortal adventure:

> I have ventured,
> Like little wanton boys that swim on bladders,
> This many summers in a sea of glory,
> But far beyond my depth: my high-blown pride
> At length broke under me and now has left me,
> Weary and old with service, to the mercy
> Of a rude stream, that must for ever hide me.
> Vain pomp and glory of this world, I hate ye:
> I feel my heart new open'd.   (III. ii. 358)

Here a sea-image exactly expresses the insubstantial glories 'of this world'. We may recall Henry V's 'tide of pomp' that 'beats upon the high shore of this world'. Wolsey continues to compare the favour of princes with the distresses of wars and love: from which we can see the universal tragic suggestion of this passage. He has been overloaded with honour, but now feels a serene peace:

> I know myself now: and I feel within me
> A peace above all earthly dignities,
> A still and quiet conscience. The king has cured me,
> I humbly thank his grace; and from these shoulders,
> These ruin'd pillars, out of pity, taken
> A load would sink a navy, too much honour:
> O, 'tis a burden, Cromwell, 'tis a burden
> Too heavy for a man that hopes for heaven!
>   (III. ii. 378)

So he finally gives noble counsel to Cromwell:

> Say, Wolsey, that once trod the ways of glory,
> And sounded all the depths and shoals of honour,
> Found thee a way, out of his wreck, to rise in;
> A sure and safe one, though thy master miss'd it.
> Mark but my fall, and that that ruin'd me.
> Cromwell, I charge thee, fling away ambition:
> By that sin fell the angels; how can man then,
> The image of his maker, hope to win by it?
>   (III. ii. 435)

All the tragedies in this play dissolve in peace. Buckingham, Katharine, Wolsey, all meet their end more in heaven than on earth. The play is throughout charged with a thrilling solemnity.

Minor water or storm imagery occurs, sometimes peaceful as when 'proofs' are 'clear as founts in July when we see each grain of gravel' (I. i. 154). Malicious censurers are 'as ravenous fishes' who

> do a vessel follow
> That is new-trimm'd, but benefit no further
> Than vainly longing.   (I. ii. 79)

Expense 'seems to flow' from Wolsey (III. ii. 109). At Queen Anne's coronation the applause was a noise 'as the shrouds make at sea in a stiff tempest, as loud and to as many tunes' (IV. i. 72): a music-tempest association. There is, too, imagery of riches. I have noticed the matter of Wolsey's 'plate'. There is the fine description of the

Field of the Cloth of Gold, where the resplendent dresses
'made Britain India' (i. i. 21). A more interesting image
occurs elsewhere in close relevance to love:

> Sir, as I have a soul, she is an angel;
> Our king has all the Indies in his arms,
> And more and richer, when he strains that lady. . . .
>
> (iv. i. 45)

Love and music are associated in the dialogue about the
French fiddlers:

> . . . the sly whoresons
> Have got a speeding trick to lay down ladies;
> A French song and a fiddle has no fellow.   (i. iii. 39)

Music is frequent: it occurs elaborately in the Coronation
scene, and, as I have observed, in the Vision; also at the
King's entrance at Act I, Scene iv. Throughout *Henry VIII*
we may observe a blending of tempests and music.

This stately play ends on a note prophetic. As with all
these Final Plays, the tragedy is justified by a birth and the
final earthly hope is in the child,[1] here the infant Elizabeth:

> She shall be loved and fear'd: her own shall bless her;
> Her foes shake like a field of beaten corn,
> And hang their heads with sorrow.   (v. v. 31)

This 'corn' image has many Shakespearian parallels.
Then:

> So shall she leave her blessedness to one,
> When heaven shall call her from this cloud of darkness,
> Who from the sacred ashes of her honour
> Shall star-like rise, as great in fame as she was,
> And so stand fix'd.   (v. v. 44)

He
> shall flourish,
> And, like a mountain cedar, reach his branches
> To all the plains about him. . . .   (v. v. 53)

Though the image ends there, we are used to this 'cedar',
'oak', or 'pine', and may for once add the thought that it
is to stand firm amid all tempests.

---

[1] My understanding of the 'child' symbol here, with all its historical
association, is helped by the Rev. T. F. Royds' study of Virgil's Messianic
Eclogue: *Virgil and Isaiah*, Blackwell, 1918.

II

The Tempest is probably Shakespeare's last play but one. In it the poet presents a reflection of his whole work. Necessarily, now, tempests and music are of over-powering importance: indeed, the play is throughout compacted mainly of this tempest-music opposition. In addition, numerous other fleeting and delicate poetic suggestions that recur throughout Shakespeare are present now in dramatic personification or incident. The process of poetic actualization, so striking in the other Final Plays, is here the ruling principle throughout. Moreover, the human story, as I have shown elsewhere,[1] repeats, as it were, in miniature, the separate themes of Shakespeare's greater Plays. *The Tempest* is an amazing work. One of the shortest of the plays, it yet distils the poetic essence of the whole Shakespearian universe. Here I can only note shortly those themes which bear directly on my present purpose, without attempting anything like a final interpretation.

We start with a wreck, vividly and strikingly actualized:

On a Ship at Sea. A tempestuous noise of thunder and lightning heard.
Enter a Shipmaster and a Boatswain severally.

Master. Boatswain!

Boatswain. Here, master: what cheer?

Master. Good, speak to the mariners: fall to't yarely, or we run ourselves aground: bestir, bestir.   [*Exit.*

Enter Mariners.

Boatswain. Heigh, my hearts! cheerly, cheerly, my hearts! yare, yare! Take in the topsail. Tend to the master's whistle.— Blow, till thou burst thy wind, if room enough!

Enter Alonso, Sebastian, Antonio, Ferdinand, Gonzalo, and others.

Alonso. Good boatswain, have care. Where's the master? Play the men.

Boatswain. I pray now, keep below.

Antonio. Where is the master, boatswain?

Boatswain. Do you not hear him? You mar our labour: keep your cabins: you do assist the storm.   (I. i. I)

---

[1] In *Myth and Miracle.*

This wreck performs the usual task of dividing father and family, brother and brother:

> *A confused noise within*: 'Mercy on us!'—'we split, we split!'—
> 'Farewell, my wife and children!'—'Farewell, brother!—we
> split, we split, we split!'   (i. i. 65)

Miranda describes the tempest:

> If by your art, my dearest father, you have
> Put the wild waters in this roar, allay them.
> The sky, it seems, would pour down stinking pitch,
> But that the sea, mounting to the welkin's cheek,
> Dashes the fire out. O, I have suffer'd
> With those that I saw suffer: a brave vessel,
> Who had, no doubt, some noble creature in her,
> Dash'd all to pieces. O, the cry did knock
> Against my very heart. Poor souls, they perish'd.
> Had I been any god of power, I would
> Have sunk the sea within the earth, or ere
> It should the good ship so have swallow'd and
> The fraughting souls within her.   (i. ii. 1)

We are familiar with such descriptions. This direful tempest is, however, like the tempests in *Pericles* or the thunder of Jupiter in *Cymbeline*, but a provisional and temporary appearance of disaster:

>   Wipe thou thine eyes; have comfort.
> The direful spectacle of the wreck, which touch'd
> The very virtue of compassion in thee,
> I have with such provision in mine art
> So safely ordered that there is no soul—
> No, not so much perdition as an hair
> Betid to any creature in the vessel
> Which thou heard'st cry, which thou saw'st sink.
>   (i. ii. 25)

This tempest is, in part, a means of redressing an old wrong. Prospero describes the original treachery of his brother:

> In few, they hurried us aboard a bark,
> Bore us some leagues to sea; where they prepared
> A rotten carcass of a boat, not rigg'd,
> Nor tackle, sail, nor mast; the very rats

Instinctively have quit it: there they hoist us,
To cry to the sea that roar'd to us, to sigh
To the winds whose pity, sighing back again,
Did us but loving wrong.   (I. ii. 144)

A speech whose mournful rhythms of sea-tragedy echo
the long story of the Shakespearian tempest. Such was
Prospero's and Miranda's 'sea sorrow' (I. ii. 170). Then
we have the vivid narration by Ariel, how he has performed
Prospero's bidding and 'dispersed'—the word occurs
twice—the ship's crew:

Ariel. All hail, great master! grave sir, hail! I come
    To answer thy best pleasure; be't to fly,
    To swim, to dive into the fire, to ride
    On the curl'd clouds: to thy strong bidding task
    Ariel and all his quality.
Prospero.   Hast thou, spirit,
    Perform'd to point the tempest that I bade thee?
Ariel. To every article.
    I boarded the king's ship; now on the beak,
    Now in the waist, the deck, in every cabin,
    I flam'd amazement: sometime I'd divide
    And burn in many places; on the topmast,
    The yards and bowsprit, would I flame distinctly,
    Then meet, and join. Jove's lightnings, the precursors
    O' the dreadful thunder-claps, more momentary
    And sight-outrunning were not; the fire and cracks
    Of sulphurous roaring the most mighty Neptune
    Seem to besiege and make his bold waves tremble,
    Yea, his dread trident shake.
Prospero.   My brave spirit!
    Who was so firm, so constant, that this coil
    Would not infect his reason?
Ariel.   Not a soul
    But felt a fever of the mad and play'd
    Some tricks of desperation. All but mariners
    Plunged in the foaming brine and quit the vessel,
    Then all a-fire with me: the king's son, Ferdinand,
    With hair up-staring,—then like reeds, not hair,—
    Was the first man that leap'd; cried, 'Hell is empty,
    And all the devils are here'.

Prospero.   Why, that's my spirit!
    But was not this nigh shore?
Ariel.   Close by, my master.
Prospero. But are they, Ariel, safe?
Ariel.   Not a hair perish'd;
    On their sustaining garments not a blemish,
    But fresher than before: and, as thou badest me,
    In troops I have dispers'd them 'bout the isle.
    The king's son have I landed by himself;
    Whom I left cooling of the air with sighs
    In an odd angle of the isle and sitting,
    His arms in this sad knot.
Prospero.   Of the king's ship
    The mariners, say how thou hast disposed,
    And all the rest o' the fleet.
Ariel.   Safely in harbour
    Is the king's ship; in the deep nook, where once
    Thou call'dst me up at midnight to fetch dew
    From the still-vex'd Bermoothes; there she 's hid:
    The mariners all under hatches stow'd;
    Who, with a charm join'd to their suffer'd labour,
    I have left asleep: and for the rest o' the fleet
    Which I dispersed, they all have met again,
    And are upon the Mediterranean flote,
    Bound sadly home for Naples,
    Supposing that they saw the king's ship wreck'd,
    And his great person perish.   (i. ii. 193)

Again, the thought of 'Jove's lightnings'. And this is closely followed by that of Neptune. Throughout we must observe how Jove and Neptune are twin personifications of the two main aspects of the Shakespearian tempest. A passage I have observed in *Coriolanus* points this vividly. We might, too, observe here the fiery quality of Ariel's 'tempest', recalling *Julius Caesar*; its 'devils' recalling *Macbeth*; and the 'sight-outrunning' lightning, which reminds us of Lear's 'thought-executing fires'. We have, too, as elsewhere, the 'besiege' metaphor. The whole description adds something of agile violence even to our former passages. And, as in the other Final Plays, we see the tempest here to be, in effect, utterly harmless.

Now in this play the themes of sea tempest are inter-woven, as in *Twelfth Night*, with music. The melodies of Ariel, disguised as 'a nymph o' the sea' (i. ii. 301), yet invisible to all save Prospero and himself, lead Ferdinand on to his meeting with Miranda:

Re-enter Ariel, invisible, playing and singing: Ferdinand following.

Ariel's Song.

Come unto these yellow sands,
    And then take hands:
Courtsied when you have and kiss'd
    The wild waves whist,
Foot it featly here and there;
And, sweet sprites, the burthen bear.
    Hark, hark!
                    [*Burthen*: Bow, wow (*dispersedly*).
    The watch-dogs bark:
                    [*Burthen*: Bow, wow (*dispersedly*).
    Hark, hark! I hear
The strain of strutting Chanticleer
                    Cry, Cock-a-diddle-dow.[1]

Ferdinand. Where should this music be? i' the air, or the earth?
It sounds no more; and sure, it waits upon
Some god o' th' island. Sitting on a bank,
Weeping again the king my father's wreck,
This music crept by me upon the waters,
Allaying both their fury and my passion,
With its sweet air: thence I have followed it,
Or it hath drawn me rather. But 'tis gone.
No, it begins again.

Ariel sings.

Full fathom five thy father lies;
    Of his bones are coral made;
Those are pearls that were his eyes:
    Nothing of him that doth fade
But doth suffer a sea-change
Into something rich and strange.
Sea-nymphs hourly ring his knell:
                    [*Burthen*: Ding-dong.
Hark! now I hear them,—Ding-dong, bell.

[1] I follow the *Everyman* edition in the arrangement of this song.

Ferdinand. The ditty does remember my drown'd father.
  This is no mortal business, nor no sound
  That the earth owes. I hear it now above me.

(I. ii. 375)

Observe how the music 'allays' both grief and the 'fury' of the waters: which two are in reality not two, but one. Ariel's first song reveals a richer and richer beauty and a more exact meaning, if we remember our earlier imagery of dances on magic shores beyond turbulent seas. Now we may understand why the 'wild waves', love's antagonists, may be 'whist' with 'kisses'. And if we remember a passage I have quoted from *The Merchant of Venice* wherein a bridal dawn is associated with music, we may find a new precision in the reference to the cock's crowing. And, in the other song, we may recall our other suggestions of the sea's vast bed of treasures torn from life as in Clarence's dream: yet here that pellucid death only turns life itself into new strangeness, newer beauty. Here all Shakespeare's sea and music thought springs into a new and vivid life, creating its own world as a theatre for profoundest vision. But tragedy is stern, too. Ferdinand's eyes, 'never since at ebb', saw the king his father 'wreck'd' (I. ii. 435). Yet, meeting Miranda, he finds a sudden joy:

  My father's loss, the weakness which I feel,
  The wreck of all my friends . . .   (I. ii. 487)

these, he says, and all his present hardships are light burdens in Miranda's presence. Sea grief and final love and union or reunion are throughout blended here in a richer, more musical, and more comprehensive design than in any past play.

A characteristic speech outlines the dangers and tragedies of the sea:

  Gonzalo. Beseech you, sir, be merry; you have cause,
    So have we all, of joy; for our escape
    Is much beyond our loss. Our hint of woe
    Is common: every day some sailor's wife,
    The masters of some merchant and the merchant,
    Have just our theme of woe; but for the miracle,

I mean our preservation, few in millions
Can speak like us: then wisely, good sir, weigh
Our sorrow with our comfort.   (II. i. 1)

'Merchants' again. We remember Antonio's 'theme of
woe' in *The Merchant of Venice*. Here such tragedies are,
as in the Final Plays, magically averted:

> But the rarity of it is, which is indeed almost beyond credit...
> that our garments, being, as they were, drenched in the sea,
> hold notwithstanding their freshness and glosses, being rather
> new-dyed than stained with salt water.   (II. i. 58)

They seem 'as fresh as when we were at Tunis at the
marriage of your daughter who is now queen' (II. i. 97).
But Alonso is comfortless. All that he loves is now divided
or stolen from him by the love-opposing seas:

Alonso.   Would I had never
   Married my daughter there! for, coming thence,
   My son is lost and, in my rate, she too,
   Who is so far from Italy removed,
   I ne'er again shall see her. O thou, mine heir
   Of Naples and of Milan, what strange fish
   Hath made his meal on thee?
Francisco.   Sir, he may live:
   I saw him beat the surges under him,
   And ride upon their backs: he trod the water,
   Whose enmity he flung aside, and breasted
   The surge most swoln that met him; his bold head
   'Bove the contentious waves he kept, and oar'd
   Himself with his good arms in lusty stroke
   To the shore, that o'er his wave-worn basis bow'd,
   As stooping to relieve him. I not doubt
   He came alive to land.
Alonso.   No, no; he's gone.
Sebastian. Sir, you may thank yourself for this great loss
   That would not bless our Europe with your daughter,
   But rather lose her to an African. . . .   (II. i. 114)

This description of Ferdinand is a close replica of that
given of Sebastian to Viola by the Sea Captain in *Twelfth
Night*. Now in Shakespeare's earliest love-passages we

found two varieties of the sea-love antagonism: severance by sea, and loss in sea, with the respective symbols of 'merchandise' and the 'jewel'. Both are present here in Alonso's words. He is separated from his daughter by infinite distances of sea; from his son, drowned 'deeper than e'er plummet sounded' (III. iii. 101), by infinite depths. And we may further observe that Alonso's giving his daughter to an 'African' suggests our numerous other perilous Eastern voyages and the many passages where Siren dangers are associated with oriental shores, where Indian 'beauties' lure man to his peril. Here, too, we may aptly observe the talk about 'widow Dido' and 'widower Aeneas', and the equating of Tunis with Carthage (II. i. 71–85). The great distance (II. i. 117) of Tunis from Italy is stressed by Alonso; and later on, its distance from Prospero's island is further emphasized by Antonio. The new queen of Tunis dwells 'ten leagues beyond man's life' (II. i. 255). She is, in fact, infinitely far; and Alonso and his fleet have undertaken an infinite voyage. In that voyage they were 'sea-swallow'd' (II. i. 259). And Alonso and his company are mazed now in infinite perplexities on the island. Ariel enters, 'invisible, playing solemn music' (II. i. 192). 'Solemn music' again, as in *Cymbeline* and *Henry VIII*. All but Antonio and Sebastian sleep:

> They fell together all, as by consent;
> They dropp'd, as by a thunderstroke.　　　(II. i. 211)

'Thunderstroke'.

Throughout the play we have minor 'tempest' suggestion. It is 'foul weather' for all when the King is 'cloudy' says Gonzalo (II. i. 148). In Sebastian's dialogue with Antonio we have more:

> *Sebastian.*　　　　　　Well, I am standing water.
> *Antonio.* I'll teach you how to flow.
> *Sebastian.*　　　　　　　　　　Do so: to ebb
> 　　Hereditary sloth instructs me.　　　(II. i. 229)

The drama of temptation, treason, and murder of kingly sleep—the *Macbeth* vision repeated—is here controlled

and overwatched by Ariel's music. Also Alonso, with his
lost children, recalls *Lear*, enduring a Lear's grief and
remorse. Here, however, it is ever a sea sorrow:

> he is drown'd
> Whom thus we stray to find, and the sea mocks
> Our frustrate search on land.   (III. iii. 8)

Lear and *Macbeth* are both suggested. That I cannot
prove here. I merely note it the better to observe the effect
of Prospero's and Ariel's actions. We must be prepared
to observe the essences of guilt and grief, tragedy in a
wide sense, in Alonso, Sebastian, and Antonio. Now
Prospero and Ariel appear in turn. There is 'solemn and
strange music':

Alonso. What harmony is this? My good friends, hark!
Gonzalo. Marvellous sweet music!

> *Enter Prospero above, invisible. Enter several strange Shapes,
> bringing in a banquet; they dance about it with gentle actions of
> salutation; and, inviting the King, etc. to eat, they depart.*
>   (III. iii. 17)

But, as they make toward the feast, Ariel interrupts:

> *Thunder and lightning. Enter Ariel, like a harpy; claps his
> wings upon the table; and, with a quaint device, the banquet
> vanishes.*

Ariel. You are three men of sin, whom Destiny,
   That hath to instrument this lower world
   And what is in't, the never-surfeited sea
   Hath caused to belch up you; and on this island
   Where man doth not inhabit; you 'mongst men
   Being most unfit to live. I have made you mad;
   And even with such-like valour men hang and drown
   Their proper selves.
        [*Seeing Alonso, Sebastian, &c., draw their swords.*
                You fools! I and my fellows
   Are ministers of Fate: the elements
   Of whom your swords are temper'd, may as well
   Wound the loud winds, or with bemock'd-at stabs
   Kill the still-closing waters, as diminish
   One dowle that 's in my plume; my fellow-ministers
   Are like invulnerable. If you could hurt,

Your swords are now too massy for your strengths,
And will not be uplifted. But, remember—
For that 's my business to you—that you three
From Milan did supplant good Prospero;
Expos'd unto the sea, which hath requit it,
Him and his innocent child: for which foul deed
The powers, delaying, not forgetting, have
Incensed the seas and shores, yea, all the creatures,
Against your peace. Thee of thy son, Alonso,
They have bereft; and do pronounce by me
Lingering perdition, worse than any death
Can be at once, shall step by step attend
You and your ways; whose wraths to guard you from—
Which here, in this most desolate isle, else falls
Upon your heads—is nothing but heart-sorrow
And a clear life ensuing.

[*He vanishes in thunder: then, to soft music, enter the Shapes
again, and dance, with mocks and mows, and carry out the table.*

Notice the 'thunder and lightning', reminiscent of
Jupiter in *Cymbeline*. Both Jupiter there and Ariel here
represent exactly Destiny. Here we have the thunder of
divine wrath, roused and conditioned by human sin;
there innocent humanity suffering from a tempestuous
fate. And all this thunder and lightning includes the
thunder and lightning which accompanies the Weird
Sisters in *Macbeth*. Tempestuous evil is suggested by all:
which evil may be variously considered the responsibility
of God, man, or the devil. In each instance the tragedy-
tempest association is implicit. Observe here the fine
sea and air imagery; and the suggestion that one sea
tragedy is to requite another. Finally we should note that
human sin has incensed 'the seas and shores' and 'all the
creatures' against man's peace: wherein we find our
tempest-beast association again. Of that I shall say
more shortly. Here we may next observe Alonso's words
after these 'strange' occurrences:

O, it is monstrous, monstrous!
Methought the billows spoke and told me of it;
The winds did sing it to me and the thunder,

That deep and dreadful organ-pipe, pronounced
The name of Prosper: it did bass my trespass.
Therefore my son i' the ooze is bedded, and
I'll seek him deeper than e'er plummet sounded
And with him there lie mudded.   (III. iii. 95)

In *Cymbeline* we found a blending of the 'music' of human love (at the entrance of Posthumus's relations) with the 'thunder' of Destiny at the entrance of Jupiter. Here we have 'solemn music' accompanying the feast, thunder accompanying those accusations which forbid the sinners to partake of it; and, again, 'soft music' after. Thunder is enclosed in music. And, in Alonso's words, the tempests of guilt themselves become music: the winds 'sing', and the 'thunder' is an 'organ-pipe'. The whole incident may be directly related to the Banquet scene in *Macbeth*, wherein a similar guilt is pitted against a feast, and the whole dissolved in the music of tragedy; since, in a final judgement, all Shakespeare's tempests of passion are also a passionate music. Here in Alonso's lines such a thought is poetically explicit. Moreover, Ariel's tempest-stilling music may be directly, on one plane of allegorical reference, considered to suggest the Shakespearian poetry itself. This is our process of poetic actualization carried to its extreme limit. The poetic faculty itself is personified, takes action in a drama whose events are but expanded poetic imagery.

Our tempest-beast association, too, is clearly present in this play. Fierce beasts are powerfully suggested when Sebastian and Antonio try to cover up their guilt:

Sebastian. Whiles we stood here securing your repose,
   Even now, we heard a hollow burst of bellowing
   Like bulls, or rather lions: did't not wake you?
   It struck mine ear most terribly.
Alonso.   I heard nothing.
Antonio. O, 'twas a din to fright a monster's ear,
   To make an earthquake! sure, it was the roar
   Of a whole herd of lions.   (II. i. 318)

These animals are associated both with the murder they

replace and the other tempestuous dangers endured by Alonso. We may note the word 'bellowing' found earlier in *The Merchant of Venice* in Lorenzo's music speech, where animals are tamed by music, but treasonous men have 'no music' in themselves, so that beasts and treasons are associated, as they are here; the 'lions' so often present in tempest-passages; the 'monster', a usual word; and the 'earthquake', as in the *Macbeth* tempest. 'Heavens keep him from these beasts!' says Gonzalo, referring to Ferdinand (II. i. 333). And this incident leads on directly to more such ideas. Throughout Shakespeare the tempest-beasts are to be clearly related to Shakespeare's animal-symbolism as a whole. Animals often suggest the inhuman and bestial qualities in man by association or contrast, just as tempests may suggest either direct natural cruelty or the more cruel behaviour of mankind. All Shakespeare's intuition of the untamed beast in man is here crystallized in the person of Caliban. Now sea monsters are especially abhorrent in Shakespeare, clearly partaking of the tragic violence of both the sea and fierce animals. And it is suggested that Caliban is, in some sense, a sea-monster.[1]

> *Trinculo.* Here's neither bush nor shrub, to bear off any weather at all, and another storm brewing; I hear it sing i' the wind: yond same black cloud, yond huge one, looks like a foul bombard that would shed his liquor. If it should thunder as it did before, I know not where to hide my head: yond same cloud cannot choose but fall by pailfuls.—What have we here; a man or a fish? Dead or alive? A fish: he smells like a fish; a very ancient and fish-like smell; a kind of not of the newest Poor-John. A strange fish! Were I in England now, as once I was, and had but this fish painted, not a holiday fool there but would give a piece of silver: there would this monster make a man; any strange beast there makes a man: when they will not give a doit to relieve a lame beggar, they will lay out ten to see a dead Indian. Legged like a man! and his fins like

[1] I am helped here by Mr. Colin Still, who has noticed this in his book, *Shakespeare's Mystery Play*, which all serious students of Shakespeare should read.

arms! Warm, o' my troth! I do now let loose my opinion;
hold it no longer: this is no fish, but an islander, that hath
lately suffered by a thunderbolt (*Thunder*). Alas, the storm
is come again! my best way is to creep under his gaberdine;
there is no other shelter here about: misery acquaints a man
with strange bed-fellows. I will here shroud till the dregs of
the storm be past.   (II. ii. 18)

More 'tempests'. We might correlate the 'painted' show
monster here, with the picture of a tyrant 'painted upon
a pole' as 'our rarer monsters are' in *Macbeth* (v. vii. 54–
56). Also Macbeth compares himself to a 'bear' fighting
'the course' at the 'stake' (v. vii. 1). That is, the tragic
protagonist at bay is, through the violence of his rage,
imaged as a monster, just as Antony is compared to
an old lion dying (*Antony and Cleopatra*, III. xi. 95).
Of course, this bear-lion contrast exactly points the
different colour and pitch of the two tragedies. Here,
however, the animal-suggestion is rather different. The
Caliban-Trinculo-Stephano plot suggests greed and
drunkenness and all essences bestial, trivial, and vulgar;
the flesh unrefined by spirit. And yet, as so often in
Shakespeare, the beast near to nature shows more
spirituality than the beast that masquerades as man.
Witness the poetry of Caliban's speech, compared with
Stephano's:

> *Caliban.* Be not afeard; the isle is full of noises,
> Sounds and sweet airs, that give delight and hurt not.
> Sometimes a thousand twangling instruments
> Will hum about mine ears, and sometime voices
> That, if I then had waked after long sleep,
> Will make me sleep again: and then, in dreaming,
> The clouds methought would open and show riches
> Ready to drop upon me, that, when I waked,
> I cried to dream again.
> *Stephano.* This will prove a brave kingdom to me, where I shall
> have my music for nothing.   (III. ii. 144)

We may remember again Lorenzo's words on the power
of music to charm even beasts from their nature, and its
clear opposition to 'treasons, stratagems, and spoils'.

Here it temporarily charms Caliban into a fine softening, and is, thus, to be opposed to his bestial and treacherous intents. For these three now proceed to their 'treasons, stratagems, and spoils'. They have many typical Shakespearian vices of the lowest kind: lust (Caliban), greed for spoils (Trinculo and Stephano), and treason against the island's king. They are also drunk. They are representative of all bestiality. Ariel lures them on, repeating exactly the substance of Lorenzo's speech on 'colts':

> Then I beat my tabor;
> At which, like unback'd colts, they prick'd their ears,
> Advanced their eyelids, lifted up their noses
> As they smelt music: so I charm'd their ears
> That calf-like they my lowing follow'd through
> Tooth'd briers, sharp furzes, pricking goss and thorns,
> Which enter'd their frail shins: at last I left them
> I' the filthy-mantled pool beyond your cell,
> There dancing up to the chins, that the foul lake
> O'erstunk their feet.   (IV. i. 175)

We remember Falstaff in *The Merry Wives*. Drunkennes (Ariel notes that his victims were 'red-hot with drinking'), lust, greed, and coarse materiality: all are in Falstaff, and also here. Finally, Caliban and the rest are routed by spirits 'in the shape of' hounds (IV. i. 257) which recall the gnomes in the final Act of *The Merry Wives*. The hounds are really 'spirit' creatures, and we may recall also that hounds are usually musical, beautiful, and aesthetic beasts in Shakespeare. In both plays, the punishment is the same: a mock-drowning, a drenching in liquid filth; undignified punishments given by the spiritual element —Ariel and the hounds—they so sorely lack. So precisely are certain important aspects of the beast-image vividly actualized in *The Tempest*. Caliban is the perfect personification of their significance.

And there is more to observe here. I have noticed that pines, cedars, and oaks occur often in tempest passages. They may either be bent by violent winds, rifted by thunder-bolts, or show their strength by standing

firm. They suggest strength, especially material strength
in or in face of nature, and the cedar may often suggest
the strength of the tragic tempest-battered protagonist in
a wide sense. A stately tree battered by tempests, or
stripped of its leaves in winter, is a usual image for the
tragic fortunes of mortality. This tree-image, then, may
be, in some sense, considered a symbol suggesting strength
and hardness. And its recurrent presence in tempest
passages suggests the cruelty and bitter bleak winds of
nature. It is in this sense that we must read the confine-
ment of Ariel by Sycorax in a pine:

> *Prospero.* . . . And, for thou wast a spirit too delicate
>   To act her earthy and abhorr'd commands,
>   Refusing her grand hests, she did confine thee,
>   By help of her more potent ministers,
>   And in her most unmitigable rage,
>   Into a cloven pine; within which rift
>   Imprison'd, thou didst painfully remain
>   A dozen years; within which space she died
>   And left thee there; where thou didst vent thy groans
>   As fast as mill-wheels strike. Then was this island—
>   Save for the son that she did litter here,
>   A freckled whelp hag-born—not honour'd with
>   A human shape.
> *Ariel.*   Yes; Caliban her son.
> *Prospero.* Dull thing, I say so; he, that Caliban,
>   Whom now I keep in service. Thou best know'st
>   What torment I did find thee in; thy groans
>   Did make wolves howl and penetrate the breasts
>   Of ever-angry bears: it was a torment
>   To lay upon the damn'd, which Sycorax
>   Could not again undo: it was mine art,
>   When I arrived and heard thee, that made gape
>   The pine and let thee out.
> *Ariel.*   I thank thee master.
> *Prospero.* If more thou murmur'st, I will rend an oak
>   And peg thee in his knotty entrails till
>   Thou hast howl'd away ten winters.   (I. ii. 272)

Notice the usual tempest-word 'rage'; the 'pine' and
'oak'; the association of this tree-agony with the tempest

beasts, wolves and 'ever-angry bears'; and the thought of winter. Ariel, himself compact of music and soft airs and warm summery delight, is shown as suffering agonies in the tempestuous world of nature's evil, of wolves and bears, of those hardened tempest-battlers, pine and oak. Ariel's pure music of air and spirit suffers under Nature's hard cruelty. 'Till thou hast howl'd away ten winters.' An eternity of freezing pain. But at the play's end, he sings of summer, ever-living summer, 'under the blossom that hangs on the bough' (v. i. 94). Winter and summer. Another aspect of our tempest-music opposition, recalling Shakespeare's early play, *Love's Labour's Lost*, and its concluding song; and also *The Winter's Tale*.

The Tempest thus contains many of our main elements of imagery: a sea-tempest and a wrecked ship; another land-storm later; supernatural appearances in thunder and lightning. this blending with music; suggestion of fierce beasts, bulls 'bellowing' and lions; a whole series of incidents revolving round Caliban, half fish-monster, half man; and the pine and oak, prisons to Ariel, associated with wolves and bears. Ariel himself is disguised as a 'nymph of the sea', thus forming a contrast with the sea-beast, Caliban: it is the contrast of depths still and translucent (as in *Antony and Cleopatra*) with the mudded turbulence of tragic and tempestuous sea. We have, too, our passage quoted above about merchants and their losses. Alonso and his court have been on an eastern voyage trading in love's merchandise. Moreover, the play is full of names oriental, places mysterious and distant: Argier (I. ii. 261), the 'dead Indian' mentioned by Trinculo, 'men of Ind' (II. ii. 62), the Arabian Phoenix (III. iii. 21–4), Tunis, and Carthage. We have also much talk about strange tales told by travellers returned from romantic adventures:

> When we were boys,
> Who would believe that there were mountaineers
> Dew-lapp'd like bulls, whose throats had hanging at 'em
> Wallets of flesh? or that there were such men
> Whose heads stood in their breasts?   (III. iii. 43)

This recalls Othello's romantic stories about 'men whose heads do grow beneath their shoulders'. We have Ariel's mention of the 'still-vexed Bermoothes' (I. ii. 229). Clearly, *The Tempest* is saturated in thought of sea-adventure, far coasts, amazing discovery. And there is a sea-beauty as well as a sea-terror. Drowned Alonso's eyes are 'pearls', his bones 'coral', all suffers a 'sea-change', all is 'rich and strange' here in spite of apparent wreck and disaster. Even Caliban speaks delight in heavenly riches, 'ready to drop upon him', as he listens to Ariel's music. And 'voices', too, he hears; and Ariel's voice here sings to 'yellow sands', interweaving the sea sorrow and the loss with siren, yet not deceitful, music. We may recall Venus's promise to 'dance on the sands' for Adonis, and Titania's description of how she and the Indian votaress sat and played on 'Neptune's yellow sands'. Thus all our sea and music thought is alive here, miraculously and strangely beautiful. *The Tempest* is Shakespeare's instinctive imaginative genius mapped into a universal pattern; not neglecting, but enclosing and transcending, all his past themes of loss and restoration, tempest and music.

Tempest and music are, indeed, our main themes here. Loss and 'dispersion' in tempest, revival and restoration on the island of music. Moreover, tempest winds and tragedy are set against summer, as in Ariel's song, soft airs and delicate: 'the air breathes upon us here most sweetly' (II. i. 46). The divine visions such as Prospero shows to Ferdinand recall the divine appearances in *Pericles*, *The Winter's Tale*, and *Cymbeline*, and Hymen in *As You Like It*. Iris, Ceres, and Juno appear to bring a bridal blessing. And they speak of country delight, earth's increase, spring, all that is fruitful, beautiful, and kind in nature. And then there is a dance of 'nymphs' and reapers':

> *Iris.* You nymphs, call'd Naiads, of the windring brooks,
>   With your sedged crowns and ever-harmless looks,
>   Leave your crisp channels, and on this green land
>   Answer your summons; Juno does command.

19

Come, temperate nymphs, and help to celebrate
A contract of true love; be not too late.

Enter certain Nymphs.

You sunburnt sicklemen, of August weary,
Come hither from the furrow, and be merry:
Make holiday; your rye-straw hats put on,
And these fresh nymphs encounter every one
In country footing.

*Enter certain Reapers, properly habited: they join with the Nymphs
in a graceful dance.*   (IV. i. 128)

At long last, a union of sea and earth in gentleness,
blessing the bridal union of Ferdinand and Miranda.
Nature's sweetness succeeds tempest. And all is here
finally restored and forgiven. The ship is 'tempest-
tossed' but not lost:

Boatswain. The best news is, that we have safely found
   Our king and company: the next, our ship—
   Which, but three glasses since, we gave out split—
   Is tight and yare and bravely rigg'd as when
   We first put out to sea.
Ariel [*aside to Prospero*]. Sir, all this service
   Have I done since I went.
Prospero [*aside to Ariel*]. My tricksy spirit!
Alonso. These are not natural events; they strengthen
   From strange to stranger. Say, how came you hither?
Boatswain. If I did think, sir, I were well awake,
   I'ld strive to tell you. We were dead of sleep,
   And—how we know not—all clapp'd under hatches;
   Where but even now with strange and several noises
   Of roaring, shrieking, howling, jingling chains,
   And moe diversity of sounds, all horrible,
   We were awak'd; straightway, at liberty:
   Where we, in all her trim, freshly beheld
   Our royal, good, and gallant ship, our master
   Capering to eye her: on a trice, so please you,
   Even in a dream, were we divided from them,
   And were brought moping hither.   (V. i. 221)

So sea sorrow, roaring, and howling are blended with
miraculous survival. Music sounds as mankind find

repentance and recognition. To Prospero's music Alonso
and his companions awake:

> A solemn air and the best comforter
> To an unsettled fancy cure thy brains. . . .   (v. i. 58)

Their 'clearer reason' emerges again:

>   Their understanding
> Begins to swell, and the approaching tide
> Will shortly fill the reasonable shore
> That now lies foul and muddy.   (v. i. 79)

So, to the last, sea-imagery is used to varied effect. Here
the sea is the wide sea of understanding and recognition.
A still sea, calm, prosperous, like the winds and seas that
take these travellers home:

> *Prospero.*   I'll deliver all;
> And promise you calm seas, auspicious gales
> And sail so expeditious that shall catch
> Your royal fleet far off.   (v. i. 313)

So tempests are stilled on the island of song and music.

This last vision encircles all former visions like an arching
rainbow, vaporous and liquid, diaphanous, yet strangely
assured and indestructible. And it contains a description of
magic art necessarily apt to Shakespeare's work as a whole.
The Tempest reflects the whole Shakespearian universe. Its
lord, Prospero, thus automatically speaks as might one
whose magic art had set down the plays of Shakespeare:

> *Prospero.* Ye elves of hills, brooks, standing lakes, and groves
> And ye that on the sands with printless foot
> Do chase the ebbing Neptune and do fly him
> When he comes back; you demi-puppets, that
> By moonshine do the green sour ringlets make
> Whereof the ewe not bites, and you, whose pastime
> Is to make midnight mushrooms; that rejoice
> To hear the solemn curfew; by whose aid,
> Weak masters though ye be, I have bedimm'd
> The noontide sun, call'd forth the mutinous winds,
> And 'twixt the green sea and the azur'd vault
> Set roaring war: to the dread-rattling thunder
> Have I given fire and rifted Jove's stout oak

With his own bolt; the strong-based promontory
Have I made shake, and by the spurs pluck'd up
The pine and cedar: graves at my command
Have wak'd their sleepers, oped, and let 'em forth
By my so potent art. But this rough magic
I here abjure; and, when I have required
Some heavenly music, which even now I do,
To work mine end upon their senses that
This airy charm is for, I'll break my staff,
Bury it certain fathoms in the earth,
And, deeper than did ever plummet sound,
I'll drown my book.   [*Solemn music.*
                                       (v. i. 33)

'Solemn music'. Note here, again, the imagery of sea-shores, and fairy dances 'on the sands'; and the fine tempest-description of winds, sea, sky, thunder; and the 'oak', 'pine', and 'cedar'. Observe the references to Jove and Neptune, the thunder-bolt, the 'roaring war' of 'green' sea ('green' when calm as in *Antony and Cleopatra*) and the azure vault, blackened in tempest. This tempest shuts out the 'noontide sun', as in *Macbeth*; its turbulence is like 'war', its winds 'mutinous'. Then again, emerging from tempests, we have the thought of miraculous resurrection, the theme of all our Final Plays; and then the 'heavenly music'. Such, in short space, is the Shakespearian description of the Shakespearian universe; for on such tempests and music is based the 'rough magic' of Shakespeare's art.

At the end Prospero speaks an epilogue. And here the tempest metaphor is deliberately transposed, given a new, and very personal, sense:

> Gentle breath of yours my sails
> Must fill, or else my project fails,
> Which was to please. . . .   (Epilogue, 11)

From the beginning to the end of Shakespeare's work all 'projects' are associated with sea-adventures; adverse fortune with tempests, but happiness with calm seas and the 'gentle breath' of loving winds. So the poet prays that his work, too, may have a prosperous voyage.

VI

CONCLUSION

SHAKESPEARE'S poetry shows a steady process of simplification. First, we find the weltering disorder of the History Plays, plays whose action is continual conflict and tempest: which tempests are nevertheless interthreaded by themes of peace and music. These we find side by side with the early Romances, plays in which tempests are but the condition through which are attained the dreamland melodies of romance. There music conquers tempests. Then we have the great Tragedies, wherein tempests are exactly bodied forth in plays whose close texture and metaphysical profundity are addressed to minute analysis of disorder in all its forms; and in these plays, too, against tempests sounds still the siren music of peace and love. Here earlier fleeting intuitions are given exact, expanded form, and Shakespeare's characteristic imagery of evil, destruction, suffering, death, and love, is in turn woven with a suitable plot to create single plays. And thence we pass to the Final Plays, wherein the plot is itself Shakespeare's favourite love-imagery embodied in a dramatic story. Poetry becomes strangely active before our eyes, the poetic image usurps the right to direct the plot and action. Poetry thus becomes doubly poetic. And, curiously, the process from the tragedies to *Antony and Cleopatra* and the myths is forecast by Bottom's ranting doggerel in *A Midsummer Night's Dream*:

> The raging rocks,
> And shivering shocks
> Shall break the locks
>   Of prison gates;
> And Phibbus' car
> Shall shine from far
> And make and mar
>   The foolish Fates.   (I. ii. 34)

The sombre plays were plays of tempest and earthquake; and yet their shattering violence itself cleaves that confining pain, breaks it as a shell, bursting the 'prison-gates' of mortality to disclose a newer life in *Antony and Cleopatra* and *Pericles*. In *Antony and Cleopatra* 'Phoebus' car' rises, dispelling the murk of *Macbeth* and the mists of *Lear*, and does indeed mysteriously both 'make and mar' the fates, which are, in that vision, by themselves 'foolish', with great Caesar, 'full fortuned', but 'an ass unpolicied', yet also contribute their part to the wider harmony. There is thus a strange and beauteous revelation, and thenceforward the purest essence of poetic vision is free to take the stage in *Pericles*.

In *Pericles* and *The Winter's Tale* the poet, so long concerned with problems of life and death, now envisions the sister mystery of birth; birth amid the chaotic seas of time, beneath the black thunder of mortality. *Cymbeline* and *The Tempest* are more complex plays, but there too our themes are mainly the ultimate themes of birth, love, God, and the universal mystery of this life which is but a sleep, the greater consciousness in which mortality is but 'such stuff as dreams are made on'; birth, life, and awakening. In *Henry VIII*, too, we have sight of heavenly things beyond mortality; with, again, the blessed Child of mortality's hope on earth. Therefore, though *The Tempest* is not only compacted of all the human themes of the greater tragedies, but also weaves in a final pattern the dominant imagery of all past Plays, thus reflecting the whole Shakespearian universe, yet certain grand simplicities emerge in all the Final Plays out-topping the details of any single human story. After the conflicting values and jostling problems of the past, now all values are eliminated but love, human or divine; all problems but birth and death. And the mighty symbols of Tempest and Music persist antiphonal, charged now with a vaster meaning, more mysterious than nature, more ultimate than humanity. At this last vision we face the systole and diastole of universal things whereby the tempests of time are dissolved in the orchestration of eternity; and the music of the spheres breaks out across the tranquil seas. All words wrong the majesty of that vision; yet we may say that the victory is with love, love which

> is an ever-fixed mark
> That looks on tempests and is never shaken;
> It is the star to every wandering bark,
> Whose worth 's unknown, although his height be taken.
>
> (Sonnet CXVI)

For in love's simplicity the senses are as 'traded pilots 'twixt the dangerous shores' of man's divided being (*Troilus*, II. ii. 64–5). By poetry, too, we may cross the seas of appearance and face that rich reality:

> Was it the proud full sail of his great verse
> Bound for the prize of all too precious you. . . .
>
> (Sonnet LXXXVI)

So perhaps at the last Shakespeare himself, like the sainted King Henry of his youth, found the Indian fairyland of soul-content:

> My crown is in my heart, not on my head;
> Not deck'd with diamonds and Indian stones,
> Nor to be seen: my crown is called content:
> A crown it is that seldom kings enjoy.
>
> (3 *Henry VI*, III. i. 62)

Seldom, indeed—kings of so vast, so turbulent, and tempestuous a spiritual empire as his.

Shakespeare has been presented under numerous titles. I need not list them. I offer instead Shakespeare as a great poet; perhaps the greatest poet. By that I mean, not a writer who is merely facile in the magic turning of fine phrases and the inspired melodies of rhythmic speech; but a poet whose every effect of metaphor and verbal music, of simile and description, stage-direction and symbol, plot and action and personification, are all interwoven, in each play, into one exquisite and significant design; and whose life-work presents a series of single art-forms, together constituting a massive architecture based on the most universal, profound, and potent poetic concepts which the human mind can conceive: the illimitable and awful insecurity of tempestuous sea, its ship-splitting fury, the black engaging waves and rocks and screaming midnight winds, the forked fire and reverberating thunder; and then, again, that spheral harmony in which those multitudinous typhooning seas are stilled, music and light, an awaking splendour across the bright expanse, green slopes and morning airs beyond the printless sand; a dream struck lifeless in the dawn where the voices sing.

And yet tempests are not wholly matters of mysticism and metaphysic: they are really most homely things. And it is in this very ordinariness that their especial power consists. We often speak of the weather in our daily life; we greet each other in terms of the weather; we salute the weather with our attention on first rising in the morning. Why is a sodden day, clouded and foggy, essentially depressing? And why, on a sunny morning, with warmth on the air, when we feel the sun's life tingling our veins, why then is the world of reason reversed by these unreasoning delights? Whence arises our sun-given joy? These things go deeper than our intellects. At another depth we know ourselves kin with bird and butterfly, with tree and hill, with sun and moon and frosty star; and, as these dim or languish with pelting rain or cloud, our spirits, too, moult their feathers in distressful mood. Tempests and all dimming vapours of the sky cut us off from the infinite promise of the firmament. On a clouded day we live parochially, provincially, forgetting that universal metropolis of our heritage. And in such mists arise our dissensions, mistakes, our follies. Thus Oberon obscures the starry welkin with Acheronian fog, so that mortals may be led blindly through the dark; and the stars in *Macbeth* hide their fires, the moon is down, and dark night strangles the 'travelling lamp', the sun. In Shakespeare and in our lives happiness is dependent on light and the infinite sources of light; but tempest, cloud, fog, and all darkness, these set the stage for fear, discord, crime. All evils tremble before the rising sun:

But when from under this terrestrial ball
He fires the proud tops of the eastern pines,
And darts his light in every guilty hole,
Then murders, treasons, and detested sins,
The cloak of night being pluck'd from off their backs,
Stand bare and naked, trembling at themselves.

(Richard II, III. ii. 41)

And dread disorder is heralded by comets or other strange
and disorderly phenomena in the machinery of the skies.
Our little earth is ever interdependent, in Shakespeare,
with the universe that is its home. The man who has no
music in him has thus a spirit 'dull as night' and 'affections
dark as Erebus'. But love ranges the interstellar spaces
and treads their golden fire: so in *Antony and Cleopatra* the
earth and sky are bright with harvest and sun, and the
purpled nights rich with the silver embroidery of moon
and star. These hold the music of creation. Sun and music
and love are all close in Shakespeare.

Now music is the most magic and the most direct of the
arts. And it is the most universal, waking response in
animals, in children, in men. As music enters the mind,
the consciousness is filled with delight that passes words,
or images, or thought itself: so that these either vanish
altogether, or float, as it were, on the rising music, themselves transfigured at that height. In Milton's *Il Penseroso*
music can dissolve the soul 'into ecstasies' and bring
'all heaven' to his eyes. The Shakespearian symbols are
obvious and simple and necessitated by our most ordinary
adventures in flood and rain and cloud, in sunlight and
in music. The human imagination has naturally treasured
such legends as those of Canute, vainly bidding the waves
to abate their usual flood; or of Nero, inhumanly making
music while his city burns.

Shakespeare's poetry demands no esoteric instruction,
nor his symbols any elaborate interpretation. They are
most simple and inevitable. His impressions depend always
on grand simplicities; tempests and music; night and day;
summer and winter. The tempest-music opposition is

interwoven closely with these other suggestions. Observe Gerard Manley Hopkins's line in *The Wreck of the Deutschland*: 'Is the shipwrack then a harvest? Does tempest carry the grain?' The contrast of tempest with all summer delights is likewise implicit in Shakespeare. Tempests blend with cloud and rain, they with fog and darkness generally, thoughts of 'the dead vast and middle of the night', moon-and-star-illumed in *Hamlet*, and utterly black in *Macbeth*. And music ever blends with sun and moon, with flowers, birds, and soft zephyrs. Therefore we pass now to 'seasons'.

Tempests and winter are closely related: hence the tragically impregnated image which I have already quoted from *Love's Labour's Lost*:

> If frosts and fasts, hard lodging and thin weeds
> Nip not the gaudy blossoms of your love. . . .
>
> (v. ii. 811)

And, again, we may remember the two lyrics of spring and winter which conclude the play. Hence also the Duke's speech in *As You Like It*:

> Here feel we but the penalty of Adam,
> The seasons' difference, as the icy fang
> And churlish chiding of the winter's wind,
> Which, when it bites and blows upon my body,
> Even till I shrink with cold, I smile and say
> 'This is no flattery . . .'.
>
> (II. i. 5)

Therefore Hell itself in Claudio's speech is imaged in terms not only of fire but of wind and water:

> . . . and the delighted spirit
> To bathe in fiery floods, or to reside
> In thrilling region of thick ribbed ice;
> To be imprison'd in the viewless winds,
> And blown with restless violence round about
> The pendent world. . . .
>
> (*Measure for Measure*, III. i. 121)

So also in the Norse myths all evil was personified in the Frost Giants hostile to man and his gods. And it is neces-

sary to emphasize again these last Shakespearian quotations. For tempests are not ultimately to be abstracted
from these other suggestions; and the interplay of the
seasons is most important in Shakespeare's work. The
sonnets are crammed with love-imagery of spring and
winter. Winter is 'full of care' (Sonnet LVI); spring
associated with the beauty of youth and love. Therefore,
in *The Winter's Tale*, we have Perdita and her flowers and
all pastoral delights spreading their springtime joy over the
frozen world of Leontes' jealousy and remorse. Summery
effects are scattered widely over Shakespeare's work contrasting with tragedy and grief. Tempests of tragedy are
like things of winter and remind us of all wintry pain, all
bitter-chiding winds and frozen streams. For in winter
nature's heart is frozen and endures its bleak loneliness,
awaiting the fiery lover of spring; or, as the Greeks
imagined, Demeter longing for her Persephone to arise
from the ice-bound Hades of winter. In winter the woods
sadly remember past music, 'bare ruin'd choirs where late
the sweet birds sang' (Sonnet LXXIII): an aeon of endurance
separating that frozen pain from the brimming summer
months which the nightingale filled as with a rich wine of
melody, when his 'wild music' burthened 'every bough'
(Sonnet CII) with song. The Shakespearian imagery is
indeed simple. Like all ancient poems and dramas, like
the ancient religions, yes, and like our own, its symbols
obey the revolving seasons within and from whose ceaseless change man's heart and body derive their more instinctive feelings, in joy or in sorrow. So that human
emotions in Shakespeare are felt as part of a wider joy
and a wider sorrow, the joy and sorrow of the great earth
itself whose visage wanes and spirits droop when deserted
by its own life, the bending eye of its great sun-lover.
Sometimes even the natural process of the season's
alteration is disturbed. In *A Midsummer Night's Dream*
dissension among the fairies makes chaos in nature and
the seasons and creates mistakes and dissension in
humanity. In terms of the vast drama of summer and

winter the Shakespearian drama continually moulds its
language and unrolls its finer truth. Always winter and
tempests are important: one of Shakespeare's latest
myths is named *The Winter's Tale*, and another, *The
Tempest*.

Nor are these Shakespearian symbols unappealing to
other poets. Perhaps the finest passage in Bridges' *Testament of Beauty* is the description of the storm. There is the
famous storm in *David Copperfield*, and the magnificent
tempest-conclusion to *Villette*. One of the noblest visions
in our literature is entitled *Wuthering Heights*, and two of
our finest lyrics, *Lycidas* and Shelley's *West Wind*, sing
respectively the terror and the grandeur of sea or wind.
Spenser, Dryden, Byron, Browning—all have tempests.
Nor is any boast more proud than that of Englishmen who
claim that 'Britannia Rules the Waves'. Indeed, the tempest, especially the sea-tempest, is found throughout the
world's imaginations; often as a symbol of contest and
insecurity, the storm-tossed boat emblematic of man and
his stormy voyage to eternity. The sea in tempest holds a
terror beyond the earth: for then is it churned to a million
billowy hills, lifting, falling, poising the little boat uncertain which way to fall, then sucking it down with
sickening crash, only again to toss it recklessly aloft. And
yet the earth, too, may quake. Earthquake and thunder
are as the terrors of mortality before the awful sceptre of
its God. The earth was thus shaken at the Crucifixion; and
in Greek mythology, Poseidon, god of the sea, is aptly also
the 'earth-shaker'. No symbols are more strikingly awful
than these of sea-tempest and earthquake; and both are
welded close into Shakespearian tragedy. 'Our whole life',
writes Burton in *The Anatomy of Melancholy*, 'is an *Irish
Sea*, wherein there is nought to be expected but tempestuous storms and troublesome waves, and those infinite'
(I. II. iii. 10). His book is full of tempests, the image recurring from page to page. The sea being so hostile in
tempest, many sea adventures were sung by the ancient
poets: as Jason's eastward quest across the seas to win the

magic fleece, or Odysseus' wanderings, with the winds, securely bound in a sack, given to him by their master, Aeolus. All these stories should wake profound responses in our imaginations as they did to a contemporary of Shakespeare, Lord Bacon, who, in his essay on Adversity, recounts how '*Hercules, when he went to unbind Prometheus* (by whom human nature is represented), *sailed the length of the great ocean in an earthen pot or pitcher*'; lively describing Christian resolution, that saileth in the frail bark of the flesh through the waves of the world'. In the tale of Jason, too, we may remember the Siren music that lured mariners to their ruin; and that other Orphean music which had power to keep the ship's course steadily forward on its journey in their despite. Dante loads his *Inferno*, in canto after canto, with imagery of wrecks, tempests, whirlwinds, foul air, mud, bloody rivers, fiery rain, torrents, cataracts, and earthquakes: all these are Shakespearian effects. Many poets seem to have sung the terrors of tempests to the mortal ship which is man's life, as when Milton makes his Samson remorseful of his ignominy:

> How could I once look up, or heave the head,
> Who like a foolish Pilot have shipwrack't
> My vessel trusted to me from above,
> Gloriously rigg'd. . . .   (197)

And elsewhere, in *Samson Agonistes*:

> What Pilot so expert but needs must wreck
> Embark'd with such a steer's-mate at the helm?   (1044)

In *Paradise Lost* the fallen angels are 'o'erwhelm'd with floods and whirlwinds of tempestuous fire' (I. 76). All tragedy is tempestuous, and Job, in the Hebrew story, sees his misfortunes as a tempest:

> Thou tossest me before the wind, I break up under the blast;
> For I know thou wilt house me with death,
>   Where all the living have to dwell.
> And yet a sinking man will stretch his hand,
>   Crying for help in his calamity.[1]   (Job xxx. 22)

[1] Trans. by James Moffat, *A New Translation of the Bible*, Hodder and Stoughton.

So inimical is the sea of fate. Floods and winds are often thus charged with potent hostility in the Bible. In the wide pantheism of Hebrew literature tempests and sea grief are imaged from page to page: especially in the Psalms. Again, Jehovah parted, as the curtains of a portal, the floods of the Red Sea, upcurling them for His chosen people; but withdrew His hand, overwhelming the Egyptian host. The Great Flood itself is remembered as the most terrible act of God. And the sign of God's peace and covenant with man was a rainbow: a rainbow, light refracted in a myriad colours, sweeping across the sky the ethereal music of its blending tints. But, in the day of the New Jerusalem, we are told, in the Book of Revelation, that there will be 'no more sea'. Floods, seas, and winds are enemies to mankind. Time and tide, indeed, await no man's command. But the divine Saviour of mankind may walk upon the waters, and, when the ship is tossed, even the winds and waves obey his authoritative voice.

The most Shakespearian work of recent times is thus a sea story. Nor is this strange. Sea sorrow is deep rooted in Anglo-Saxon literature, and the finest pieces of Old English poetry, *The Wanderer* and *The Seafarer*, sing the terrors of the deep. Joseph Conrad and the Poet Laureate have continued that tradition. 'Tempest' thought is vivid throughout English poetry. But the work I refer to next is the greatest of all sea tales. In Melville's mighty parable his protagonist is embattled against a sea-monster. Mankind, in *Moby Dick*, takes arms against his sea of troubles, as the emissary of humanity, Ahab, lances his harpoon against the inconscient brutality of fate.

And yet Melville, like Shakespeare, passed on; and in his *Pierre* is born a spirit of music, like the music-maidens in Shakespeare, Isabel and her magic guitar. That language is beyond speech, 'eternally incapable of being translated into words; for where the deepest words end there music begins with its supersensuous and all-confounding intimations' (xxi. i). This is Carlyle's 'the inarticulate mystic speech of music' (*Sartor Resartus*, II. v).

And another writer has moulded for us a less tragic figure than Isabel, who also speaks those unearthly melodies that draw the soul from listening mankind: I refer to Hudson's Rima. She is of the land and green glinting forests of the earth, the friend of man and beast, a being of natural sweetness and diaphanous beauty; an angel of nature, girl or bird, with bird-song melody for speech. Like Isabel, she makes sounds beyond speech 'so much higher and more penetrating than any bird music', 'like a tender spiritual music—a language without words, suggesting more than words to the soul'; or like the bell-bird's note, a bell 'not made of gross metal dug out of earth, but of an ethereal, sublimer material that floats impalpable and invisible in space'; again, 'O mystic bell-bird of the heavenly race of the swallow and dove, the quetzal and the nightingale!' (*Green Mansions*, VIII; x). So, too, Isabel's guitar brings to her 'the bird-twitterings in the air' (VI. v). In Shakespeare love is like bird-music, like the lark, herald to the dawn, or the nightingale. Music is the furthest spiritual delight save for love alone; an ethereal, birdlike, winged art, beyond speech. And if poets often blend bird-song with human music, that is partly, too, because the swift flight of birds seems like some intimation of immortality where the duller clods hamper no longer the love and vision that pain man's heart. So Wordsworth images immortality as set beside a sea; and that paradise by the sea is a paradise of sport and child-happiness, again reminding us of Shakespeare's Ariel and his songs; and, next, the poet turns his thought from that dream of immortality to the bird-song and the dance and the music of spring:

> Hence in a season of calm weather
>   Though inland far we be,
> Our souls have sight of that immortal sea
>   Which brought us hither,
>   Can in a moment travel thither,
> And see the children sport upon the shore,
> And hear the mighty waters rolling evermore.

Then sing, ye birds, sing, sing a joyous song,
    And yet the young lambs bound,
    As to the tabor's sound . . .

In Mr. T. S. Eliot's poem *Marina* bird-music calls from the wooded island to the ship wavering in its fog-bound course; and the music of Keats's nightingale becomes an immortality dream sounding in 'faery lands' over 'perilous seas'. The ancient Arabian symbol of immortality is the Phoenix; and, as the Flood subsided, from the Ark a dove was sent, winging its airy course above the waters, divine creature of element strange to man, to bring back tidings of safety to fearful mankind. And both these birds are honoured by Shakespeare in *The Phoenix and the Turtle*, a poem in which is sung love's mystic power to conquer death. Birds, too, are vivid in Shakespeare's love-imagery elsewhere,[1] especially in *Antony and Cleopatra*; and Cleopatra is thus 'my nightingale' to Antony. So that it is usual to find creatures beautiful and feminine, birdlike and musical, in the human imagination, set beside those more monstrous creatures of the deep, or of the swamp, or sometimes of the earth, reptilian or aquatic. The leviathan in the Book of Job is a symbol of God's inscrutable purposes; and in Greek tragedy the Chorus often turns to thoughts of birds and winged freedom in far spaces, desiring liberation from mortality's pain.[2] Grendel is in the Old English myth a grim creature of the swamps; and all the dire monsters of legend come to mind, sea-monsters, chimaeras, hydras, gorgons, dragons. The heroes that slay these are sometimes armed with wings: as Perseus with his winged sandals, or Bellerophon and his aerial steed, Pegasus. Perseus slew first the Gorgon and afterwards a sea-monster in defence of Andromeda. This story of Andromeda, the maid, sacrificed to a monster of the sea, is also repeated in one of Hercules' adventures, a 'virgin tribute', as Shakespeare calls it in *The Merchant of Venice*, there also sacrificed to a sea-monster. Sea-monsters

---

[1] See Appendix A, 'The Shakespearian Aviary'.
[2] For this thought I am indebted to my brother, W. F. Jackson Knight.

oppose love, and all winged purity of the spirit. Cupid has wings, and this ethereal magic of love is well expressed in *Troilus and Cressida*, where Troilus would 'fly' with Cupid's wings across the turgid waters to Cressid. Both slimy sea-monsters and the blessed Albatross are important symbols in Coleridge's sea-poem, *The Ancient Mariner*. In Melville, too, Moby Dick not only sinks the *Pequod*; but that ship itself goes down with a fluttering bird pinned to its mast, drawn under 'with arch-angelic shrieks', so that part of 'heaven' is drawn hell-wards, as when the Angels fell from God. The heavenly Angels are winged; and they are often imagined as offering song and music to God. So, too, Shakespeare imagines the dead as singing in heaven (*All's Well*, IV. iii. 63). And Shakespeare's Angels are also imagined often as winged horsemen: recalling those names I have observed already, Bellerophon and Saint George, heroes either winged or mounted, or both, who are fabled to have slain dragons and gorgons. So, also, in the Shakespearian vision Caliban is a sea-monster, Ariel a winged spirit of the air, delighting to sport on the bat's back, and frolicking with the summer bees. It is as the former intuition of the ass-headed Bottom and Titania, whose fairies invoke Philomel's melody to attend her. And the same thought inspired Plato's vision of man as a charioteer driving two steeds, one bright and fiery and the other ugly and sluggish. It is what Melville imaged in the Epilogue to *Clarel*:

> Yea, ape and angel, strife and old debate—
> The harps of heaven and dreary songs of hell;
> Science the feud can only aggravate—
> No umpire she betwixt the chimes and knell:
> The running battle of the star and clod
> Shall run for ever—if there be no God.

The fiery and the earthy in man: Ariel and Caliban. So also Browning writes of 'finished and finite clods untroubled by a spark' in *Rabbi Ben Ezra*. This very dualism, too, vitalizes Mr. T. S. Eliot's poem of the Hippopotamus paradoxically winging his cumbrous way to

20

heaven, and next performing on a harp of gold. Moby
Dick and Rima are prototypes we do well to consider: in
them we may contemplate the fears and hopes of mankind.

When the sculptor moulds his statue he imposes form
on that which is formless; which form is as 'soul' or 'life'
breathed into stone by his skill. In this way we may
imagine all life as creation imposed on chaos. Chaos is
dark, a vast sea, unutterably dark; formless, and void.
But God says, Let there be Light; and in the seven days
earth and sky and beast and man are formed; and the
waters separated from the earth. Creation is the mastery
of chaos and ocean. And that mastery continues hour by
hour and century by century. Man is the focal point of
this process, planted in the inertia of animal life, yet
agonizingly drawn to angelic harmonies. Thence springs
his tension of pain and suffering, his consciousness and experience of evil. Therefore, though Shakespeare's world is
primarily a world of men, yet his primary symbols, tempest and music, are things unhuman: the one an effect of
nature, subhuman; the other reaching out to infinity and
speaking divine accents, superhuman. We may thus consider successive modes in creation: first, chaos and dark;
next, the sun and moon and stars; the earth; its vegetation
and first amphibious life; its animals; man; his civilization; and, finally, the city of God to which he moves.
This progress is retraced backwards, as I have elsewhere
shown, in Shakespeare's *Timon*. It is a fundamental
sequence in all our thinking. Nor is it without clear
scientific justification. For the earth was once a molten,
formless, weltering chaos; and form and life have since
been imposed thereon. Now again we see the proudly
infinite suggestions of the Shakespearian symbols: since
the Shakespearian rough beasts, the bear and wolf and
sea monsters, suggest qualities which would detain man's
swift ascent, the bestial inertia from which he would
advance. The tug of futurity wrenches him from these,
from his animal kinship, creating tempests: hence tempests and these beasts are always closely associated in

Shakespeare. We may recall the legend of 'Beauty and the Beast'; the beasts in *The Faerie Queen*; and the 'Beast' so vividly important in the Book of Revelation. Tempests and tempest-beasts characterize the present dispensation of conflict.

Sea-tempests suggest the first churning chaos which is the beginning of creation: matter formless, awaiting soul and life. Thus in *Paradise Lost* Chaos is an ocean, where elements are ever battling tempestuously for mastery. And such chaos still too often rules tyrannically in passionate man. Carlyle writes well on this:

> But it is with man's Soul as it was with Nature: the beginning of creation is—Light. Till the eye have vision, the whole members are in bonds. Divine moment, when over the tempest-tost Soul, as once over the wild-weltering chaos, it is spoken: Let there be Light! Even to the greatest that has felt such a moment, is it not miraculous and God-announcing; even as, under simpler figures, to the simplest and least. The mad primeval Discord is hushed; the rudely-jumbled conflicting elements bind themselves into separate Firmaments: deep silent rock-foundations are built beneath; and the skyey vault with its ever-lasting Luminaries above; instead of a dark wasteful Chaos, we have a blooming, fertile, heaven-encompassed World. (*Sartor Resartus*, II. IX)

Creation is thus active in mankind, blending and harmonizing man's passions into a single excellence, directing them towards the kingdom of his heaven. But there are vast seas to be mastered, seas on which only the most impetuous and dauntless navigator of the spiritual world dare once launch his bark. Such a one was Melville:

> Consider all this; and then turn to this green, gentle, and most docile earth; consider them both, the sea and the land; and do you not find a strange analogy to something in yourself? For as this appalling ocean surrounds the verdant land, so in the soul of man there lies one insular Tahiti, full of peace and joy, but encompassed by all the horrors of the half-known life. God keep thee! Push not off from that isle, thou canst never return! (*Moby Dick*, LVIII)

So, in the soul of man, creation and recreation are daily at work; charting new expanses, reclaiming lost land. The poet or prophet is as a Drake or Columbus in his lonely voyage: and on his labour depends civilization and all spiritual advance. So to Wordsworth the statue of Newton is

> The marble index of a mind for ever
> Voyaging through strange seas of Thought, alone.
>
> *(The Prelude,* iii. 62)

For the poet masters the passions by giving them local habitation and form, though they be unruly as the sea and tempestuous as typhoon. Milton, like Shakespeare, in *Samson Agonistes* presents human passions as tempests:

> I see thou art implacable, more deaf
> To prayers, than winds and seas, yet winds and seas
> Are reconciled at length, and sea to those:
> Thy anger, unappeasable, still rages,
> Eternal tempest never to be calm'd. (960)

Similarly, in *Paradise Lost*, Satan and Death confront each other like 'two black clouds with heaven's artillery fraught' (ii. 714).

But all tempests may be, at last, resolved in music. There is music and light in Dante's *Paradiso*. And Shelley writes in his *Prometheus Unbound* (iv. 400) of man in his future chaos-conquering integrity and harmony:

> Man, one harmonious soul of many a soul,
>   Whose nature is its own divine control,
> Where all things flow to all, as rivers to the sea;
>   Familiar acts are beautiful through love;
>   Labour, and pain, and grief, in life's green grove
> Sport like tame beasts, none knew how gentle they could be!
>
>   His will, with all mean passions, bad delights,
>   And selfish cares, its trembling satellites,
> A spirit ill to guide, but mighty to obey,
>   Is as a tempest-winged ship, whose helm
>   Love rules, through waves which dare not overwhelm,
> Forcing life's wildest shores to own its sovereign sway.

All things confess his strength. Through the cold mass
  Of marble and of colour his dreams pass;
Bright threads whence mothers weave the robes their children
    wear;
  Language is a perpetual Orphic song,
  Which rules with Daedal harmony a throng
Of thoughts and forms, which else senseless and shapeless were.

  The lightning is his slave; heaven's utmost deep
  Gives up her stars, and like a flock of sheep
They pass before his eye, are numbered, and roll on!
  The tempest is his steed, he strides the air;
  And the abyss shouts from her depth laid bare,
Heaven, hast thou secrets? Man unveils me; I have none.

Such is the music of perfected man. Shelley's work is full
of tempests and music. The transfiguration of Asia in
the *Prometheus* is accompanied by music. It is the same
with the close of his *Lines written among the Euganean
Hills*. With him, as with Shakespeare, music and love
are all but synonymous. Again, he writes:

No, Music, thou art not the 'food of Love',
  Unless Love feeds upon its own sweet self,
  Till it becomes all Music murmurs of.
                         (A fragment to Music)

And in *Epipsychidion* we have a noble dream of Love's
immortality, in terms of a magic island, music, the quelling
of thunderstorms and earthquake, and the marriage sleep
of earth and ocean. It recalls *The Tempest*. Love's divine
delight is thus continually as music. Tennyson, in
Locksley Hall, so writes of love:

Love took up the glass of Time and turned it in his glowing
    hands;
Every minute, lightly shaken, ran itself in golden sands.
Love took up the harp of Life and smote on all the chords
    with might,
Smote the chord of Self, that, trembling, passed in music out
    of sight.

Such love is the gateway to the Islands of the Blest, set
beyond mysterious seas. Tennyson images his death as

'crossing the bar', adventuring on those infinite waters; and his Arthur is taken in a barge to the 'Island valley of Avilion' where there are no tempests, no rain or hail or snow or blustering wind, but all is springtime meadowy delight. The soul of man progresses from darkness and tempests to music, sunshine, and joy. That joy is truth, such as Lord Bacon so incisively imagined in his essay on Truth:

> The first creature of God, in the works of the days, was the light of the sense; the last was the light of reason; and his sabbath work ever since is the illumination of his Spirit. First he breathed light upon the face of the matter or chaos; then he breathed light into the face of man; and still he breatheth and inspireth light into the face of his chosen. The poet that beautified the sect that was otherwise inferior to the rest, saith yet excellently well: *It is a pleasure to stand upon the shore, and to see ships tossed upon the sea: a pleasure to stand in the window of a castle, and to see a battle and the adventures thereof below; but no pleasure is comparable to the standing upon the vantage ground of truth*, (a hill not to be commanded, and where the air is always clear and serene), *and to see the errors, and wanderings, and mists, and tempests, in the vale below:* so always that this prospect be with pity, and not with swelling or pride. Certainly, it is heaven upon earth, to have a man's mind move in charity, rest in providence, and turn upon the poles of truth.

So the progress of man is as the progress of creation: from chaos and tempest to light and music. And this sequence is everywhere welded into the Shakespearian imaginations.

Man is himself a conscious microcosm of Creation's progress, and can therefore envisage the grand march of time from primal chaos to the celestial city; or, conversely, he so envisages his universe to correspond with his own experiencing mind. Creation is the mastery of darkness and chaos by light and music: a conflict finely imagined in *Macbeth*. Grendel, monster of the inhospitable marshes, is slain in the old myth by Beowulf, a human hero whom some have equated with the Sun-god; suggesting thus the conquest of the weltering morasses by humanity, or by God, rendering them fit for habitation and civilized life. But the sea is often imaged as opposed to man's advance. Hence the importance of Faust's labour in Goethe's poem, the building of a barrier against the encroaching sea. There is rumour of a golden city of delight, purer civilization than any of which we have record, buried under the rolling ocean; and we still wistfully dream the lost music of that Atlantis. Melville has a description which well suits our dreams. Here it is, interesting in his interweaving of sunlight, music, birds, and the heavenly city:

> The land near Cape Horn, however, is well worth seeing, especially Staten Land. Upon one occasion, the ship in which I then happened to be sailing drew near this place from the northward, with a fair, free wind, blowing steadily, through a bright translucent day, whose air was almost musical with the clear, glittering cold. On our starboard beam, like a pile of glaciers in Switzerland, lay this Staten Land, gleaming in snow-white barrenness and solitude. Unnumbered white albatross were skimming the sea nearby, and clouds of smaller white wings fell through the air like snow-flakes. High, towering in their own turbaned snows, the far-inland pinnacles loomed up, like the border of some other world. Flashing walls and crystal battlements, like the diamond watch-towers along heaven's farthest frontier.   (*White Jacket*, xxviii)

Music and light, or fire, are close in our minds. Hence Shakespeare, starting his play of *Henry V*, writes:

> O, for a muse of fire that would ascend
> The brightest heaven of invention!

By music and fire we catch something of our futurity.

But the sea may be an apt symbol of that vast hostility which threatens man's upward endeavour. Regard the dining-saloon of a great liner: the rich food and wines, the flash of silk and gold, the laughter and the coloured lights, the dance, the music; all these planted within the very bosom of ocean, while outside the eternal stars look down on expanses eternal as they, and between one infinity and another the big ship beats onward, bearing a thousand lives as thoughtless of disaster as though the night and stars and unfathomed ocean were not surrounding their little world with an illimitable waste of death. Such is the power of man: he feasts and makes music in the very bosom of death. But consider again. What more potent symbol of human disaster and the littleness of man's civilization may we bring to mind than that of the *Titanic*, sunk in mid ocean, done to death by two of the most hostile forces of nature, freezing cold and engulfing sea, as the great ship was trapped between the iceberg and the Atlantic? Now it is said that in such a depth she would not at first sink to the bottom. Imagine her then, blind floating cumbrous thing, parodying her fatal voyage above, by day, by night, pursuing now her devil's voyage below, the sea swirling through passage and state-room, slashing her rudder from side to side to make the huge leviathan a lunatic thing, charging like some blinded whale, first one way, then another, in the dead vast of ocean; as though some maniac god had seized the universal helm and played at skittles with the stars. Considering these, ask if there is not something profound and moving in man's battle with the waves. Therefore John Donne well imagines Death itself as a tempest:

> He that should first put to sea in a tempest, he might easily think, it were in the nature of the sea to be rough always. He that sees every church-yard swell with the waves and billows of graves, can think it no extraordinary thing to die; when he knows he set out in a storm, and he was born into the world upon that condition, to go out of it again.   (*Sermons*)
>   (Folio III, Sermon 1; 20 Feb., 1617)

To Donne the Christian faith is imagined as music.

Man has, indeed, partially conquered the ocean, and Horace well sang the stalwart bravery of its first pioneers; he now aspires to be victor of the air; but the music of human perfection and peace-in-joy eludes him yet, and till that peace be found the other tempests rage still across uncharted seas. For the tempests of unruly passion still trouble man's estate. Burton, in *The Anatomy of Melancholy*, says:

> So that I may conclude this strong conceit or imagination is *astrum hominis*, and the rudder of this our ship, which reason should steer, but overborne by phantasy cannot manage, so suffers itself and this whole vessel of ours to be over-ruled, and often over-turned.   (I. II. iii. 2)

The opposite of these tempests is music. Toward such music do we bend our hopes, with the prophetic verse of Shelley's *Hellas*:

> And now, O Victory, blush! and Empire, tremble
> When ye desert the free—
> If Greece must be
> A wreck, yet shall its fragments reassemble,
> And build themselves again impregnably
> In a diviner clime,
> To Amphionic music on some Cape sublime,
> Which frowns above the idle foam of Time.   (1000)

'Idle foam'. Civilization is as music. Carlyle, too, so writes of man's advance, his works, his poet-inspired creations:

> Were it not wonderful, for instance, had Orpheus, or Amphion, built the walls of Thebes by the mere sound of his Love? Yet tell me, who built these walls of Weissnichtwo; summoning out all the sandstone rocks, to dance along from the *Steinbruch* (now a huge Troglodyte Chasm, with frightful green-mantled pools); and shape themselves into Doric and Ionic pillars, squared ashlar houses and noble streets? Was it not the still higher Orpheus, or Orpheuses, who, in past centuries, by the divine Music of Wisdom, succeeded in civilizing Man? Our highest Orpheus walked in Judea, eighteen hundred years ago; his sphere-melody, flowing in wild native tones, took captive the ravished souls of men; and, being of a truth sphere melody, still flows and sounds, though now with thousandfold accompaniments, and rich symphonies, through all our hearts; and modulates and divinely leads them. Is that a wonder, which happens in two hours; and does it cease to be wonderful if happening in two million? Not only

was Thebes built by the music of an Orpheus; but without the music of some inspired Orpheus was no city ever built, no work that man glories in ever done. (*Sartor Resartus*, III. VIII)

'The music of wisdom'—or the wisdom of music, that music made by the harmony of man's spiritual estate. Man and his civilization are reciprocally dependent; on human advance the creative purpose, as we know or dream it, necessarily depends.

But this conflict of chaos and creation, tempest and music, is not ultimate; not even while we endure the *Macbeth* darkness and shattering wrench of an evil which would negate creation, not even then is creation's music stilled. There is no chaos, no disorder. 'All things began in order', wrote Sir Thomas Browne, 'so shall they end, and so shall they begin again; according to the ordainer of order and mystical mathematics of the City of Heaven' *The Garden of Cyrus*, v). Again:

> . . . and sure there is music even in the beauty, and the silent note which Cupid strikes, far sweeter than the sound of an instrument. For there is a music wherever there is a harmony, order, or proportion: and thus far we may maintain the music of the Spheres; for those well-ordered motions, and regular paces, though they give no sound unto the ear, yet to the understanding they strike a note most full of harmony. Whosoever is harmonically composed delights in harmony; which makes me much distrust the symmetry of those heads which declaim against all Church-Music. For myself, not only from my obedience, but my particular Genius, I do embrace it: for even that vulgar and Tavern-Music, which makes one man merry, another mad, strikes in me a deep fit of devotion, and a profound contemplation of the First Composer. There is something in it of Divinity more than the ear discovers: it is an Hieroglyphical and shadowed lesson of the whole world, and creatures of God; such a melody to the ear, as the whole World, well understood, would afford the understanding. In brief it is a sensible fit of that harmony which intellectually sounds in the ears of God.   (*Religio Medici*, Part II)

Chaos and disorder and all tempests are but elements of a wider music. So Carlyle writes:

A strange contradiction lay in me; and I as yet knew not the solution of it; knew not that spiritual music can spring only from discords set in harmony; that but for Evil there were no Good, as victory is only possible by battle.

(Sartor Resartus, II. iv)

And again,

Musical: how much lies in that! a *musical* thought is one spoken by a mind that has penetrated into the inmost heart of the thing; detected the inmost mystery of it, namely the *melody* that lies hidden in it; the inward harmony of coherence which is its soul, whereby it exists, and has a right to be, here in this world. All inmost things, we may say, are melodious; naturally utter themselves in Song. The meaning of Song goes deep. Who is there that, in logical words, can express the effect music has on us? A kind of inarticulate unfathomable speech, which leads us to the edge of the Infinite, and lets us for moments gaze into that. (*Heroes and Hero-Worship*, iii)

So music speaks not only to man. It vibrates throughout the whole world of inanimate matter. Though human ears need a machine to express the music and the voices that are broadcast daily from our great cities, that music and those voices would be yet thrilling every inch of English air, in darkness and in tempest, in wind and rain, were there yet no receiver for their notes by the warm comfort of the drawing-room hearth. And, if that be so, what other celestial harmonies may range the universe unguessed to mortality, could we tune our senses to their music? So, too, every tempest contributes its sweeping voice to the mighty orchestra of Shakespeare: within its very fabric is woven its own grander melody.

Nor is the Shakespearian imagination forgetful of music's illimitable appeal: for it tells, in *The Merchant of Venice*, how Orphean music was feigned to draw 'trees, stones, and floods' by its magic,

Since nought so stockish hard and full of rage
But music for the time doth change his nature. (v. i. 81)

And bellowing beasts stand still, 'their savage eyes turned to a modest gaze, by the sweet power of music'. So also it is Caliban who speaks the loveliest music lines in Shakespeare, Caliban distraught to pain by the mystic melodies of Ariel's flute. In everything that has existence the music of creation is ceaselessly at work. Music is creative: it is well known that labouring men can haul a greater weight if they accompany their work with some form of singing or music. In ancient legends we often find cities built to music; and music, too, has been recorded to destroy, as when the sound of trumpets caused the walls of Jericho to crumble; and, indeed, it has been said that all buildings have a corresponding note, to which their fabric will quiver and even fall. Music is a universal power. And so the psalmist imagines all created things to praise their God with music. In rock and beast, in savage and in civilized mankind, it speaks: and the angels themselves know no finer utterance.

> There's not the smallest orb which thou beholdest,
> But in his motion like an angel sings,
> Still quiring to the young-eyed cherubins.
> Such harmony is in immortal souls;
> But while this muddy vesture of decay
> Doth grossly close us in, we cannot hear it.   (v. i. 60)

When people of various tongues are thrown together, they resolve their lonely differences of speech in the common language of song and music. So that we may imagine that all things were created in harmony, and that ever since music is the only true cosmopolitan language and Esperanto of the infinite. It speaks beyond mortality. Therefore music and all infinites of sun and star are ever closely interwoven in Shakespeare. Tempests are but part of creation's wider music: and with a finely inspired intuition the ancient poets imagined the whole universe to swing over in song.

It is often remarked that Shakespeare's world is chaotic as life itself. There is no assured and neat system such as Dante's to lend unity and purpose to the phenomena he presents. There is some truth in this. But just as the world we experience presents both obvious diversity and yet, persistently, unity, whence we derive our term 'the universe', so Shakespeare's world is at the same time both multiple and single. It is both like the work of many men rather than the work of one, resembling Carlyle's 'immeasurable froth-ocean we name literature', and yet it remains uniquely single. Moreover, in its very diversity blended with unity we see not only its blending of single splendour with universal truth, but the very quality which especially differentiates it from the work of other poets: in its very chaos lies its peculiar and distinctive form. Nor is this purely paradoxical. Consider again its tempests of conflict, disorder, and diversity; and its music of concord, love, and unity. Here we may focus the universal profundity of these symbols. For the very same poetic act—the recurrent tempest—which continually points us to the turbulence and jarring discords of this tumultuous world, yet also gives that world its own special and peculiar unity. And not only is the music in Shakespeare's world, which from time to time accompanies themes of love and peace, ever closely related to the tempests through which its delight is attained, but there is that other more universal music itself made of tempests: for those very tempests, those tempestuous passions called from the surging deep, are the very elements of poetry's resolving, passionate, tempestuous music. Shakespearian tragedy is much like the opera so vividly described by D. H. Lawrence in *The White Peacock* (III. i): 'The theatre surged and roared dimly like a hoarse shell. Then the music rose like a storm, and swept and rattled at their feet. On the stage the strange storm of life clashed in music towards tragedy and futile death.' All poetic music is blent of divided words, and conflicting passions, woven into one texture and harmonious design in line, in stanza, act or play; all tempests blent of music, music with music, as often in Shakespeare, when political concord and personal love conflict, creating tempests— and yet again, tempest with tempest, as the tempest-plots of the early Romances with the symbolism of the

Tragedies, to release a yet more indestructible and sublime music, to sound its spheral harmonies in the marriage of tempests and music in the Final Plays. So finely is the Shakespearian world both single and diverse, discordant and harmonious with a discord and a harmony that are one; and yet again, not one but two; and so again resolved into unity. Such is the ever-active drama, static and dynamic, division in unity, of Shakespeare's world.

These symbols go deeper and wider than the seeming ultimates of 'life' and 'death'. For death is but the elongated and antic shadow cast by life; it has no meaning, no relevance, no similitude, to its origin. It is but a sorry caricature, lacking the one dimension of reality. It is a negation, wholly parasitic on the thing it would negate; and, as such, unreal. Thus the dynamic and universal drama of the Christian Trinity does not, and must not, personify the spirit of Negation. Likewise tempests and music, interdependent in their reciprocal action and continual recreation, their blending and withdrawal, the many facets which they present to our contemplation, these are positive; ultimates beyond which the mind can scarcely dream a profounder possibility.

APPENDIX A

THE SHAKESPEARIAN AVIARY

I

BIRD-LIFE is very significantly used in Shakespeare. Such images and impressions occur mainly in direct relation to all essences which may be, metaphorically, considered ethereal and volatile. Bird-life suggests flight and freedom and swiftness: it also often suggests pride. Birds are usually gentle and sweet, and in many instances accompany love; but they may also be evil, as in *Macbeth*, where, however, they yet harmonize with the ethereal and spiritual theme, the swiftness, the dizzying flight. Here, then, I regard a few 'bird' passages in relation especially to the human spirit regarded as that quality in man which is essentially ethereal and aspiring: in this relation we find, particularly, the falcon and the eagle. Next I pass to the lark, bird of dawn, observing its close association with light and music. Thereafter I relate both these strains to more general thoughts of the human spirit, especially to the Shakespearian phrases 'swift thought' and 'apprehension', and then to mythological figures such as Phaethon, Icarus, Cupid, and angels generally. Finally, I pass to *The Phoenix and The Turtle*. But this essay is in no sense exhaustive: it merely indicates certain directions of certain impressions. A comprehensive study of these birds would, however, be most valuable.

II

The falcon is continually used to suggest 'pride'. Now pride may well be either a pleasing or a repellent quality: it may tend towards fine aspiration or insulting insolence. Here it is as insolence:

> This said, he shakes aloft his Roman blade,
> Which, like a falcon towering in the skies,
> Coucheth the fowl below with his wings' shade,
> Whose crooked beak threats if he mount he dies :
> So under his insulting falchion lies
>   Harmless Lucretia, marking what he tells
>   With trembling fear, as fowl hear falcon's bells.
>   (*Lucrece*, 505)

In the same way we hear of Coriolanus's 'soaring insolence'

(*Coriolanus*, ii. i. 270), and Hamlet's 'towering passion' (*Hamlet*, v. ii. 80). Or we may have just a proud confidence:

> As confident as is the falcon's flight
> Against a bird, do I with Mowbray fight.
>
> (*Richard II*, i. iii. 61)

A similar suggestion is probably behind such a passsage as this:

> Now the time is come
> That France must vail her lofty-plumed crest.
>
> (*1 Henry VI*, v. iii. 24)

Richard II is rich in these images: 'How high a pitch his resolution soars!' says King Richard (i. i. 108), fearing Bolingbroke's ambition. He repeats the idea when banishing the two rivals, Bolingbroke and Mowbray:

> And for we think the eagle-winged pride
> Of sky aspiring and ambitious thoughts,
> With rival-hating envy, set on you
> To wake our peace. . . .   (i. iii. 129)

Here the bird is the eagle. The eagle especially harmonizes with the words 'sky aspiring', and often suggests the grand indomitable aspiration of noble mankind toward excellence. Sometimes such aspiration is blameworthy, sometimes it is not; but pure aspiration is at the heart of most of these images, though each be coloured differently by its context. Caesar's ambition likewise receives falcon imagery:

> These growing feathers pluck'd from Caesar's wing
> Will make him fly an ordinary pitch.
>
> (*Julius Caesar*, i. i. 77)

And here is another pride-falcon association:

> Neither the king, nor he that loves him best,
> The proudest he that holds up Lancaster,
> Dares stir a wing, if Warwick shake his bells.
>
> (*3 Henry VI*, i. i. 45)

Wolsey's pride is 'high-blown' in *Henry VIII* (iii. ii. 361). Such towering birds, then, suggest pride of place and ambition. Naturally, they are often associated with kingship. Here, especially, the eagle tends to replace the falcon:

> Yet looks he like a king: behold, his eye,
> As bright as is the eagle's, lightens forth
> Controlling majesty.   (*Richard II*, iii. iii. 68)

A fine bird-passage ends powerfully with a king-eagle association:

> The crow may bathe his coal-black wings in mire,
> And unperceived fly with the filth away;
> But if the like the snow-white swan desire,
> The stain upon his silver down will stay.
> Poor grooms are sightless night, kings glorious day:
>> Gnats are unnoted wheresoe'er they fly,
>> But eagles gazed upon with every eye. (*Lucrece*, 1009)

Again:

> No: know the gallant monarch is in arms
> And like the eagle o'er his aery towers,
> To souse annoyance that comes near his nest.
>> (*King John*, v. ii. 148)

The king of birds is, clearly, an apt associate for the kings of men: partly, at least, because of his sky-aspiring flight, his towering place, as well as his majestic appearance and leonine strength and reputation.

Now the earthly majesty of kings is, as I have elsewhere observed, often associated in the Shakespearian imagination with the spiritual majesty of love. Hence the falcon or eagle image may apply to both equally:

> What peremptory eagle-sighted eye
> Dare look upon the heaven of her brow,
> That is not blinded by her majesty?
>> (*Love's Labour's Lost*, iv. iii. 226)

Or again:

> Upon her wit doth earthly honour wait,
> And virtue stoops and trembles at her frown.
> Then, Aaron, arm thy heart, and fit thy thoughts,
> To mount aloft with thy imperial mistress,
> And mount her pitch.... (*Titus Andronicus*, ii. i. 10)

Observe in this passage the lady's 'wit' and the phrase 'imperial mistress' binding love and majesty, Tamora being actually and metaphorically 'imperial'. 'Pitch' is clearly a 'falcon' word. All this follows directly after Aaron's imagining of Tamora as a 'sun' rising above 'tempests'—I have quoted the passage. All these associations, then, of noble position, love, wit, are close bound with associations of sun, imperial power, and towering birds. Nor must we, of course, be blinded to these significances by remembrance of Aaron's, or Tamora's, iniquity. All this is usual. So in *Twelfth Night* we may find the same pride-love-bird association presented less seriously, as when, during the tricking of Malvolio, we have the words: 'Contemplation makes a rare turkey-cock of him. How he jets under his advanced plumes!' (*Twelfth Night*, II. v. 35). Again,

> *Fabian.* What dish o' poison has she dressed him!
> *Sir Toby.* And with what wing the staniel checks at it!
> (Twelfth Night, II. v. 124)

In the same way, during the similar trick played on Beatrice, we have another falcon-reference:

> Then go we near her, that her ear lose nothing
> Of the false sweet bait that we lay for it.
> No, truly, Ursula, she is too disdainful;
> I know her spirits are as coy and wild
> As haggerds of the rock.　　　(*Much Ado*, III. i. 32)

Here, clearly, 'pride', as contrasted with 'love', is compared to a 'haggerd'. Beatrice herself carries on the metaphor. She will be tame to love:

> And, Benedick, love on; I will requite thee,
> Taming my wild heart to thy loving hand.
> (Much Ado, III. i. 111)

But, though here love and pride may be contrasted—as elsewhere, notably throughout *All's Well* and *Coriolanus*—yet clearly both may be but aspects of the aspiring spirit in man; aspiring, in the one instance usually to material advancement, in the other, to a diviner ambition. We get this idea in a dialogue from *Henry VI*, the 'falcon' leading on directly to thoughts of earthly and heavenly aspiration:

> *King.* But what a point, my lord, your falcon made,
> 　　And what a pitch she flew above the rest!
> 　　To see how God in all his creatures works!
> 　　Yea, man and birds are fain of climbing high.
> *Suffolk.* No marvel, an it like your majesty,
> 　　My lord protector's hawks do tower so well;
> 　　They know their master loves to be aloft
> 　　And bears his thoughts above a falcon's pitch.
> *Gloucester.* My lord, 'tis but a base ignoble mind
> 　　That mounts no higher than a bird can soar.
> *Cardinal.* I thought as much; he would be above the clouds.
> *Gloucester.* Ay, my lord cardinal? how think you by that?
> 　　Were it not good your grace could fly to heaven?
> *King.* The treasury of everlasting joy.

Cardinal. Thy heaven is on earth; thine eyes and thoughts
    Beat on a crown, the treasure of thy heart. . . .

(2 Henry VI, ii. i. 5)

Especially here we may note the line: 'Yea, man and birds are fain
of climbing high.' The whole of Shakespeare's work, indeed, continually emphasizes this quality in man: aspiration. In some form
or another it recurs powerfully in nearly every play, and this
quality is to be related to the eagle and the falcon. The eagle may,
indeed, be related to divine inspiration:

    Was Mahomet inspired with a dove?
    Thou with an eagle art inspired then.

(1 Henry VI, i. ii. 140)

But ambition or pride of some sort is more usual. Pride is in
essence a noble quality. We are faced continually, however super-
ficially blameworthy the ambition concerned may often appear,
with what is one of the most divine elements in man: his aspiring
pride.

Birds are, on the whole, favourites of the Shakespearian
imagination. They suggest fine or sweet qualities usually. Especially
the union of docility and natural strength in the falcon appears to
give it high honours, so that it is ranked beside other such creatures,
hounds and horses; for, though dogs as a whole come off badly,
yet hounds receive very different treatment. Here are all three
together, significantly juxtaposed with girls:

    Somerset. Judge you, my lord of Warwick, then, between us.
    Warwick. Between two hawks, which flies the higher pitch;
      Between two dogs, which hath the deeper mouth;
      Between two blades, which bears the better temper:
      Between two horses, which doth bear him best;
      Between two girls, which hath the merriest eye. . . .

(1 Henry VI, ii. iv. 10)

We may remember the greyhounds and 'milk-white horses trapp'd
in silver' presented to Timon (*Timon*, i. ii. 198, 192). Timon is
fond of hunting (ii. ii. 8). And the similar association of hunting,
hounds, and horses in the Induction to *The Taming of the Shrew* is
also interesting:

    Say thou wilt walk; we will bestrew the ground:
    Or wilt thou ride? thy horses shall be trapp d,
    Their harness studded all with gold and pearl.
    Dost thou love hawking? thou hast hawks will soar

Above the morning lark: or wilt thou hunt?
Thy hounds shall make the welkin answer them,
And fetch shrill echoes from the hollow earth.

(Ind. ii. 42)

Observe how all these are associated with 'morning', the 'lark',
'flowers' (in 'bestrew'), 'gold and pearl'—all positive and happy
images. The baying of hounds is finely imagined in *A Midsummer
Night's Dream* (IV. i. 107–30): here it is honoured by detailed comparison with music, and also, we may note, is associated directly
with dawn and other happy suggestions. Again this links our
falcons with larks: a rather tortuous association perhaps. But a
dawn-hunting association occurs also in the lovely dawn-parting
of *Romeo and Juliet* where a lark is clearly important. The lark's
voice is spoken of as

Hunting thee hence with hunt's-up to the day.

(*Romeo and Juliet*, III. v. 34)

So we find falcons, horses, and hounds somewhat idealized in
Shakespeare. Horses especially are vividly admired, on account of
physical beauty (*Venus and Adonis*, 259–330), faithfulness, as in
the description of 'roan Barbary' in *Richard II* (v. v. 67–94), or
swift warrior-strength:

Come, let me taste my horse,
Who is to bear me like a thunderbolt
Against the bosom of the Prince of Wales:
Harry to Harry shall, hot horse to horse,
Meet and ne'er part till one drop down a corse.

(*1 Henry IV*, IV. i. 119)

Therefore in *Macbeth* the queer acts of a falcon and Duncan's
horses are especially significant: these being especially well-tamed
and orderly creatures. Here is the description:

Old Man.   On Tuesday last,
A falcon, towering in her pride of place,
Was by a mousing owl hawk'd at and kill'd.
Ross. And Duncan's horses—a thing most strange and certain—
Beauteous and swift, the minions of their race,
Turn'd wild in nature, broke their stalls, flung out,
Contending 'gainst obedience, as they would make
War with mankind.   (*Macbeth*, II. iv. 11)

Notice the word 'pride'; and the exquisite appreciation of the horses,
'beauteous and swift'—indeed, it is especially this quality of swift-

ness which our three orders of hunting creatures share: the falcon, hounds (particularly greyhounds), and horses. Horses especially are thus idealized. In our *Venus and Adonis* description we have a fine example of a horse-bird comparison:

> Sometime he scuds far off and there he stares;
> Anon he starts at stirring of a feather;
> To bid the wind a base he now prepares,
> And whether he run or fly they know not whether;
>> For through his mane and tail the high wind sings,
>> Fanning the hairs, who wave like feather'd wings.
>>> (*Venus and Adonis*, 301)

We may observe also Margaret's close association of 'a hawk, a horse, or a husband' in *Much Ado* (III. iv. 55).

Before leaving our birds of aspiration we should see how their close relevance to human qualities is further suggested by a similar Shakespearian use of such mythological figures as Phaethon and Icarus, which is clearly but an extension, both in Shakespeare and in the minds that originally evolved those myths, of the bird-pride association. Here is a clear example:

> Why, Phaethon,—for thou art Merop's son,—
> Wilt thou aspire to guide the heavenly car
> And with thy daring folly burn the world?
> Wilt thou reach stars, because they shine on thee?
> Go, base intruder! overweening slave!
> Bestow thy fawning smiles on equal mates. . . .
>> (*The Two Gentlemen of Verona*, III. i. 153)

Observe the words 'aspire', 'heavenly', 'stars', 'overweening'. Here the loved one (Silvia) is imaged high and remote as the heavenly stars—a usual Shakespearian idea. Hence the lover is guilty of excessive aspiration. Phaethon may also be used in relation directly to kingship (Silvia, I should add, was set high in worldly position, too, the daughter of the Duke who speaks the lines I have just quoted). Richard II compares himself to Phaethon:

> Down, down I come; like glistering Phaethon,
> Wanting the manage of unruly jades.
>> (*Richard II*, III. iii. 178)

Similarly, the story of Icarus and Daedalus is used by Talbot. He addresses his son:

> Then follow thou thy desperate sire of Crete,
> Thou Icarus. (*1 Henry VI*, IV. vi. 54)

Again:

> And in that sea of blood my boy did drench
> His over-mounting spirit, and there died,
> My Icarus, my blossom, in his pride.
>
> (*1 Henry VI*, iv. vii. 14)

'Over-mounting spirit', and 'pride'. Finally Talbot flings out a fine
aspiring and indomitable extravagance; a most typically Shakespearian speech, in which mortal man presents his scornful challenge
to death itself:

> Thou antic death, which laugh'st us here to scorn,
> Anon, from thy insulting tyranny,
> Coupled in bonds of perpetuity,
> Two Talbots, winged through the lither sky,
> In thy despite shall 'scape mortality.
>
> (*1 Henry VI*, iv. vii. 18)

In which short poetic movement all Shakespeare's pride and
aspiration thought is finely and unerringly crystallized and con-
summated.

III

Birds are ethereal, aspiring things; creatures of swift life and
light. Especially is the lark a spirit of dawn and song, of fire and
music. It is a bird of joy:

> The lark, that tirra-lyra chants,
>   With heigh! with heigh! the thrush and the jay,
> Are summer songs for me and my aunts,
>   While we lie tumbling in the hay.
>
> (*The Winter's Tale*, iv. ii. 9)

A bird of merriment and song, happy in the joy-time of spring. The
lark is regularly Shakespeare's 'dawn' bird:

> Stir with the lark to-morrow, gentle Norfolk.
>
> (*Richard III*, v. iii. 56)

And,

> Fairy king, attend, and mark:
> I do hear the morning lark.
>
> (*A Midsummer Night's Dream*, iv. i. 97)

I have lately quoted a passage where, in the Induction to *The
Taming of the Shrew*, Sly is told that he has hawks that will soar
'above the morning lark' (Ind. ii. 46): a passage clearly blending our
lark and falcon imagery. In *A Midsummer Night's Dream* we

might observe that the lark, and dawn generally, are exquisitely
set against the dewy summer night, the moon, and the nightingale's
song ('Philomel with melody . . .'). And this is a usual contrast or
association: the sun-song of dawn and the song of moonlight. The
nightingale and the lark are both music-birds of sweet suggestion.
Often the lark occurs in passages bright with the splendour of dawn:

> Lo, here the gentle lark, weary of rest,
> From his moist cabinet mounts up on high,
> And wakes the morning, from whose silver breast
> The sun ariseth in his majesty;
>> Who doth the world so gloriously behold
>> That cedar-tops and hills seem burnish'd gold.
>>> *(Venus and Adonis, 853)*

The 'gentle' lark. And observe the suggestion of dew in 'moist';
and also the rich metals, 'silver' and 'gold'; 'majesty'; and the
'cedar-tops'. Cedars and pines, so often imaged as withstanding
tempests, may also be more happily associated with dawn:

> But when from under this terrestrial ball
> He fires the proud tops of the eastern pines. . . .
>> *(Richard II, iii. ii. 41)*

'Tops' again—our recurrent tempest-word. Larks wake the
labourer to his day's work:

> When Shepherds pipe on oaten straws
>> And merry larks are ploughman's clocks,
> When turtles tread, and rooks, and daws,
>> And maidens bleach their summer smocks. . . .
>>> *(Love's Labour's Lost, v. ii. 913)*

Notice the idyllic, pastoral happiness here. The lark is a happy
bird, 'merry': to be associated with spring, sunlight, and 'maidens'.
His music is like love's voice:

> Your eyes are lode-stars and your tongue's sweet air
> More tuneable than lark to shepherd's ear,
> When wheat is green, when hawthorn buds appear.
>> *(A Midsummer Night's Dream, i. i. 183)*

His song is ever an apt accompaniment for love:

> Hark, hark! the lark at heaven's gate sings,
>> And Phoebus 'gins arise,
> His steeds to water at those springs
>> On chaliced flowers that lies;
> And winking Mary-buds begin

> To ope their golden eyes:
> With everything that pretty is,
> My lady sweet, arise;
> Arise, arise.   (*Cymbeline*, ii. iii. 21)

A close mesh of joyous and brilliant suggestions. For the lark soars high:

> Look up a-height; the shrill-gorged lark so far
> Cannot be seen or heard.   (*Lear*, iv. vi. 58)

Hence, in our *Cymbeline* passage, it is imaged as singing at 'heaven's gate', blending its music with heavenly fire. The lark is thus afloat on all that is divine, fiery, and ethereal, outreaching and overwinging the dull earth in its upward flight. Often dawn is, in Shakespeare, the bringer of joys, sometimes love-joys. For example:

> Lord, how mine eyes throw gazes to the east!
> My heart doth charge the watch; the morning rise
> Doth cite each moving sense from idle rest.
> Not daring trust the office of mine eyes,
>   While Philomela sits and sings, I sit and mark,
>   And wish her lays were tuned like the lark.
>
> For she doth welcome daylight with her ditty,
> And drives away dark dismal-dreaming night:
> The night so pack'd, I post unto my pretty;
> Heart hath his hope, and eyes their wished sight;
>   Sorrow changed to solace, solace mixed with sorrow,
>   For why she sigh'd and bade me come to-morrow.
>   (*The Passionate Pilgrim*, xiv)

Here again the lark is associated with the nightingale; partly, too, contrasted, in point of 'night' and 'dawn', though, it must be remembered, the nightingale, too, is a love-bird, his music blending with moonlight as the lark's with sunrise. The lark-night contrast is often powerful:

> For night-owls shriek where mounting larks should sing.
>   (*Richard II*, iii. iii. 183)

'Night-owls'. There are evil, as well as sweet birds in Shakespeare, and such are to be powerfully contrasted with the morning lark. 'The night to the owl and morn to the lark less welcome' occurs in *Cymbeline* (iii. vi. 94). Again,

> O gracious Emperor! O gentle Aaron!
> Did ever raven sing so like a lark,
> That gives sweet tidings of the sun's uprise?
>   (*Titus Andronicus*, iii. i. 157)

The raven is an evil bird; like the owl, a *Macbeth* bird. Night and all grim ghostly effects are often expressed together with nocturnal birds, and all prowling beasts of prey. The lark is to be contrasted with these and all coarser birds: 'I took this lark for a bunting' (*All's Well*, II. v. 7). Again,

> What, is the jay more precious than the lark,
> Because his feathers are more beautiful?
>> (*The Taming of the Shrew*, IV. iii. 177)

Or both the nightingale and lark may be contrasted with birds less musical:

> The crow doth sing as sweetly as the lark
> When neither is attended, and I think
> The nightingale, if she should sing by day,
> When every goose is cackling, would be thought
> No better a musician than the wren.
>> (*The Merchant of Venice*, v. i. 102)

There is a somewhat similar passage in *Troilus and Cressida*:

> O Cressida! but that the busy day,
> Waked by the lark, hath roused the ribald crows,
> And dreamy night will hide our joys no longer,
> I would not from thee.   (IV. ii. 8)

Here the night is kind to love, and dawn hostile. Although 'light' effects are very consistently related to love and all joy, yet such a contrast as we have here is clearly possible also. Here the poet uses his crows to point the more unmusical and prosaic qualities of day.

Now a similar situation occurs in *Romeo and Juliet*. I have quoted it before: but it is very important. It should gain fresh and fuller understanding from full quotation in this context:

> *Juliet.* Wilt thou be gone? it is not yet near day:
> It was the nightingale, and not the lark,
> That pierced the fearful hollow of thine ear;
> Nightly she sings on yond pomegranate tree:
> Believe me, love, it was the nightingale.
> *Romeo.* It was the lark, the herald of the morn,
> No nightingale: look, love, what envious streaks
> Do lace the severing clouds in yonder east:
> Night's candles are burnt out, and jocund day
> Stands tiptoe on the misty mountain tops.
> I must be gone and live, or stay and die.

Juliet. Yond light is not daylight, I know it, I:
   It is some meteor that the sun exhales,
   To be to thee this night a torch-bearer,
   And light thee on thy way to Mantua:
   Therefore stay yet; thou needst not to be gone.
Romeo. Let me be ta'en, let me be put to death;
   I am content, so thou wilt have it so.
   I'll say yon grey is not the morning's eye,
   'Tis but the pale reflex of Cynthia's brow;
   Nor that is not the lark whose notes do beat
   The vaulty heaven so high above our heads:
   I have more care to stay than will to go:
   Come, death, and welcome! Juliet wills it so.
   How is't, my soul? let's talk; it is not day.
Juliet. It is, it is: hie hence, be gone, away!
   It is the lark that sings so out of tune,
   Straining harsh discords and unpleasing sharps.
   Some say the lark makes sweet division;
   This doth not so, for she divideth us:
   Some say the lark and loathed toad change eyes;
   O, now I would they had changed voices too!
   Since arm from arm that voice doth us affray
   Hunting thee hence with hunt's-up to the day.
   O, now be gone; more light and light it grows.
Romeo. More light and light; more dark and dark our woes!

                                                    (III. v. 1)

Observe how Romeo's last line deliberately employs the contrast
here of tragedy and light.   Here the lark and nightingale are
clearly contrasted; but both are, powerfully, music birds, and their
presence blends with the richly romantic moment. Notice the
moon reference, 'Cynthia's brow': the moon is continually, and
with obvious aptitude, associated with the nightingale. Which
happens also in Keats's Ode. Indeed, we may remark that Shakespeare's chief music birds, the nightingale and lark, are exactly
those most powerfully honoured by other poets.[1] As usual, Shakespeare's associations are the obvious and universal ones: which makes
interpretation of these imaginations always easy and straightforward,
unless we make difficulties for ourselves. The lark and nightingale are, then, continually used in close relation to love: they are,

[1] We can also, with advantage to our understanding, observe the kind
of bird a poet chooses to address. It was as inevitable that Keats should
write to the nightingale as it was that Shelley should choose the lark. But
this must not be driven too far or we shall be thinking of Wordsworth and
the cuckoo.

indeed, love-spirits, images of the melodies, the sweet pain or fiery aspiration of the human soul. Hence:

> Yet in these thoughts myself almost despising,
> Haply I think on thee, and then my state,
> Like to the lark at break of day arising
> From sullen earth, sings hymns at heaven's gate. . . .
>
> (Sonnet XXIX)

In which we have a fine compression of our lark-love association.

There is, too, a dialogue in *Hamlet* most relevant to my immediate argument:

> *Bernardo.* It was about to speak, when the cock crew.
> *Horatio.* And then it started like a guilty thing
> Upon a fearful summons. I have heard,
> The cock, that is the trumpet to the morn,
> Doth with his lofty and shrill-sounding throat
> Awake the god of day; and, at his warning,
> Whether in sea or fire, in earth or air,
> The extravagant and erring spirit hies
> To his confine: and of the truth herein
> This present object made probation.
> *Marcellus.* It faded on the crowing of the cock.
> Some say that ever 'gainst that season comes
> Wherein our Saviour's birth is celebrated,
> The bird of dawning singeth all night long:
> And then, they say, no spirit dare stir abroad;
> The nights are wholesome; then no planets strike,
> No fairy takes, nor witch hath power to charm,
> So hallow'd and so gracious is the time.
> *Horatio.* So have I heard and do in part believe it.
> But, look, the morn in russet mantle clad
> Walks o'er the dew of yon high eastward hill:
> Break we our watch up. . . .   (*Hamlet*, I. i. 147)

What is 'the bird of dawning'? Usually the phrase is considered to refer to the cock. It may be so. But the lovely line in which the words occur ill suits the cock. The cock in Shakespeare is, indeed, a 'dawn' bird; but his associative value on the whole—if we were to collect a number of cock-passages—would be very different from that of the lark. In this dialogue there is the usual contrast of dawn with the grim and ghostly terrors of night: Shakespeare's night poetry is ever most powerful, from *Lucrece* to *Macbeth*. Remembering our lark passages, we shall perhaps feel inclined to read 'the bird of dawning' in their light.[1]

[1] Since writing this I have been informed by Professor R. S. Knox and

IV

Birds are thus often bright, aspiring, and altogether fine and delicately beautiful creatures in Shakespeare. They are also, very often, especially 'gentle'; and this quality clearly fits them again to associate with love, though it necessarily must not be too closely referred to the pride birds who often accompany a purely worldly ambition. And yet a falcon is tame; and in this tameness joined to speed and strength, the falcon, as I have said, is found associated with horses and hounds. Here is a passage where the falcon is gentle:

> *Juliet.* Hist! Romeo, hist! O, for a falconer's voice,
>   To lure this tassel-gentle back again!
>
> (Romeo and Juliet, ii. ii. 159)

Again, a little further on:

> *Juliet.* 'Tis almost morning; I would have thee gone:
>   And yet no further than a wanton's bird;
>   Who lets it hop a little from her hand,
>   Like a poor prisoner in his twisted gyves,
>   And with a silk thread plucks it back again,
>   So loving-jealous of his liberty.
> *Romeo.* I would I were thy bird.
> *Juliet.*   Sweet, so would I:
>   Yet I should kill thee with much cherishing.
>
> (Romeo and Juliet, ii. ii. 177)

So, too, Adonis is 'like a wild bird being tamed with too much handling' (*Venus and Adonis*, 560). Similarly, birds may suggest nature's innocence, as in the 'martlet' passage in *Macbeth*. In Lady Macduff's dialogue with her son, birds are powerful. We have the 'wren' speech. And also:

> *Lady Macduff.* Sirrah, your father's dead:
>   And what will you do now? How will you live?
> *Son.* As birds do, mother.
> *Lady Macduff.*   What, with worms and flies?
> *Son.* With what I get, I mean; and so do they.
> *Lady Macduff.* Poor bird! thou'ldst never fear the net nor lime,
>   The pitfall nor the gin.
> *Son.* Why should I mother? Poor birds they are not set for. . . .
>
> (Macbeth, iv. ii. 30)

Dr. S. A. Tannenbaum that Q 2 reads 'This bird of dawning'. Also, in answer to a letter in *The Times Literary Supplement*, I have received information from Miss Elizabeth M. Ross, Miss Jane B. Partridge, and Professor C. D. Abbott which shows almost certainly that the cock is the bird referred to. But as others besides myself have felt a difficulty, I leave my text intact.

Birds may be thus purely creatures of gentleness and essential innocence. We may remember, also, Adriana's words in *The Comedy of Errors*:

> Ah, but I think him better than I say,
>   And yet would herein other eyes were worse.
> Far from her nest the lapwing cries away:
>   My heart prays for him, though my tongue do curse.
>
> (IV. ii. 25)

The lapwing occurs also in the lovely lyric melodies and nature atmosphere of *Much Ado* (III. i. 24). There, also, it is to be associated with love; and at the end of that scene we have Beatrice's beautiful line already quoted—'taming my wild heart to thy loving hand' (III. i. 112), a clear falcon-metaphor, its beauty dependent on our immediate understanding of the falcon's pride now sweetly blended with docility.

These few examples may serve further to show why birds are so admirably apt to Shakespeare's love-visions: they are beautiful, aspiring, melodious, and gentle creatures. Hence the birds I have observed in *Antony and Cleopatra*, *Much Ado*, and *A Midsummer Night's Dream*. They are ethereal, spiritual things, to be contrasted with rough beasts and materiality in general. The spiritual is set against the material: especially in *A Midsummer Night's Dream*, where Bottom is humorously associated with song-birds. This is, indeed, but one aspect of our tempest-music opposition. And we may here, in passing, observe how the lark is contrasted with the toad in *Romeo and Juliet*:

> Some say the lark and loathed toad change eyes.
>
> (III. v. 31)

The toad may stand for reptilian, as opposed to ethereal, life. He occurs in the Weird Women's hell-broth enchantments in *Macbeth*. Also in *A Midsummer Night's Dream*, 'Philomel' is invoked to sing Titania asleep, but all ugly forms of life are charmed away: snakes, hedgehogs, newts, blind-worms, spiders, beetles, the worm, and snail (II. ii. 9–24). Thus both the lark and nightingale are to be contrasted with all sluggish and loathsome reptiles. And throughout Shakespeare the musical and ethereal is set against the bestial, the fleshly, the essentially ferocious and material: again Melville's line comes to mind, 'The running battle of the star and clod'. Richard III is compared in turn to a wolf, a hell-hound, a 'rooting hog', a 'bottled spider', a poisonous 'toad', and so on. Birds are usually the opposite of these. Even when they are fierce, they may yet, like the lion, suggest a noble ferocity:

> *Duncan.*   Dismayed not this
> Our captains, Macbeth and Banquo?
> *Sergeant.*   Yes;
> As sparrows eagles or the hare the lion.
>
> (*Macbeth*, I. ii. 33)

Again:

> If you have writ your annals true, 'tis there,
> That, like an eagle in a dovecote, I
> Flutter'd your Volscians in Corioli:
> Alone I did it.   (*Coriolanus*, v. v. 114)

The eagle is important throughout *Cymbeline* both as an imperial bird and the 'bird of Jove'. So fine birds may be things of noble courage or gentleness and sweetness. They are, on the whole, to be definitely contrasted with tempest-beasts of the coarser kind—bears, wolves, sea-monsters, reptiles; though we must clearly see that the lion may be either a tempest-beast on account of his ferocity, or, as in my *Macbeth* quotation, a symbol of courage and nobility to be compared with the eagle.

But to write down man's upward struggle too readily as a beast-bird opposition would be somewhat superficial. As an ultimate statement, that will probably be true. It is Shakespeare's final statement, if we regard his whole work. But on the way we have to encounter a subtle difficulty. The problem of evil is mysterious. We cannot say that evil is to be related to the material only, good to the spiritual. There is a spiritual evil. Birds represent ethereality and volatility, often touching the swift-passing intuitions of beauty and love in man. But, though by intuition we make our most immediate contact with the highest values, we cannot say intuition is always good, and intellect purely a concession to the devil of materiality. For there are evil intuitions. Evil visions in sleep prove the possible immediacy of evil. It is the problem of *Macbeth*: is the evil absolute? Since, then, there is spiritual evil, since there are swift evil intuitions, it is clear that we must not limit ourselves too readily to the most obvious resolution of our human problems into 'bestiality' and 'spirituality'. All this is clearly expressed in Shakespeare.

The faculty which receives swift intuitions in Shakespeare is 'apprehension'. Swift thought I have discussed in 'The Shakespearian Metaphysic' in *The Wheel of Fire*. Here I would emphasize that such 'apprehensions' and swift intuitions may be either charged with paradisal or satanic import: this is our *Antony and Cleopatra–Macbeth* contrast. All thought, but especially any intense mental activity, is 'swift'—passion, madness, love, wit, scorn—all are swift. This I have discussed in my chapter '*Macbeth and Antony and Cleopatra*' in *The Imperial Theme*, and have there given numerous references. Here I would add to my other references and essays on this matter that 'apprehension' is an important word in this relation. Consider, too,

> But his evasion, wing'd thus swift with scorn,
> Cannot outfly our apprehensions.
> > (*Troilus and Cressida*, ii. iii. 123)

Flying or arrow metaphors are usual, sometimes, as here, expressing especially the volatility of wit. We remember Benedick's 'quips and sentences and these paper bullets of the brain' (*Much Ado*, ii. iii. 260), and the archery-imagery throughout that play.. Arrows, being lifeless and mechanic, tend to replace bird-metaphors in this connexion. But this wit-suggestion blends with love, since the loved lady is often keen-witted in Shakespeare. For example:

> The tongues of mocking wenches are as keen
> > As is the razor's edge invisible,
> Cutting a smaller hair than may be seen,
> > Above the sense of sense; so sensible
> Seemeth their conference; their conceits have wings
> Fleeter than arrows, bullets, wind, thought, swifter things.
> > (*Love's Labour's Lost*, v. ii. 256)

Thus thought is bird-like, ethereal, swift: the more passionate or keen spirited it be, the more swift it is. In *Lucrece*, we hear, 'fleet-wing'd duty with thought's feathers flies' (1216). Now *Troilus and Cressida* throughout analyses the meaning of swift realities—especially love. They are considered incapable of inclusion either in action or thought:

> *Cressida.*   Night hath been too brief.
> *Troilus.*   Beshrew the witch! with venomous wights she stays,
> As tediously as hell, but flies the grasps of love
> With wings more momentary-swift than thought.
> > (*Troilus and Cressida*, iv. ii. 12)

Nor can the mind itself hold fully the swift delight of love: such ideas I have observed in my fuller treatment of *Troilus* in *The Wheel of Fire*. Here I will only note Cressida's

> > To be wise and love
> Exceeds man's might; that dwells with gods above.
> > (*Troilus and Cressida*, iii. ii. 163)

Man's 'apprehension' cannot grasp these things fully, cannot be wise at such godlike heights; or, if he can, he becomes divine after the fashion of Cerimon in Pericles, where 'cunning' is said to make a man a god (*Pericles*, III. ii. 27–31). 'Apprehend' is an important word. In one of Shakespeare's most significant passages it occurs twice, neatly juxtaposed with 'comprehend': the difference is important. Theseus speaks, in *A Midsummer Night's Dream* (v. i), on 'the lunatic, the lover, and the poet', all 'compact' of 'imagination'. Whereby we may note that 'imagination' may clearly be evil, since lunacy is close to the troubles of an evil conscience:

> I'll haunt thee like a wicked conscience still,
> That mouldeth goblins swift as frenzy's thoughts.
>
> (*Troilus and Cressida*, v. x. 28)

Now Theseus continues:

> Lovers and madmen have such seething brains,
> Such shaping fantasies, that apprehend
> More than cool reason ever comprehends.
>
> (*A Midsummer Night's Dream*, v. i. 4)

Again,

> Such tricks hath strong imagination,
> That, if it would but apprehend some joy,
> It comprehends some bringer of that joy;
> Or in the night, imagining some fear,
> How easy is a bush supposed a bear!   (v. i. 18)

With which we might compare:

> And the dire thought of his committed evil
> Shape every bush a hideous shapeless devil.
>
> (*Lucrece*, 972)

Which again shows how evil, like love and poetry, may be related to the 'tricks' of 'strong imagination' or 'apprehension'. Now 'comprehension' is clearly to be considered the rationalizing process. Reason cannot properly 'comprehend' the swift 'apprehensions' of the heightened consciousness, which may, as I have said, be either satanic or paradisal, or may refer to territory between these boundaries. 'Wit' is a matter of 'apprehension' at *Much Ado*, III. iv. 68; dullness the reverse of it (*Henry V*, III. vii. 150); though men are 'apprehensive' (i.e. 'spiritual'), Caesar is greater than all others (*Julius Caesar*, III. i. 67). The word stands for 'imagination' at *Richard II*, I. iii. 300; for foreboding at *Troilus*, III. ii. 74–81, where it is associated with Cupid, devils, and cherubins, and is to be compared with the Queen's forebodings in *Richard II* in a scene (II. ii) which I have in *The Wheel of Fire* exactly related to the *Macbeth* vision. 'Apprehension', again, may be used for purely evil and unclean thoughts, as at *Othello*, III. iii. 139. 'Apprehension', indeed, is the finest quality in the human mind by which man enjoys intuitive spiritual perception either of good or evil: it is this that has banished him his Eden. It is the faculty that links man either to the divine or the satanic. Hence Hamlet, in describing the varied excellences of men, concludes: '. . . . In apprehension, how like a god!' (*Hamlet*, II. ii. 326).

Therefore we must be prepared to find evil birds, too, in the Shakespearian Aviary. Clearly, we have only to inspect *Macbeth* to find them. Elsewhere, in *The Imperial Theme*, I have shown that *Macbeth* and *Antony and Cleopatra* enjoy a similarity in opposition; and that this similarity is to be related to the word 'spirit'. I there noted that each play had many examples of ethereal life. In *Macbeth* they are evil, mostly night birds, such as the bat; birds of dark plumage, the crow; of ill omen, the raven; birds of prey, the owl. In *Antony and Cleopatra* we have a very different list—the nightingale, Phoenix, swallow, dove, estridge, eagle. Similarly in *Lucrece*, a poem ever close to the *Macbeth* vision, we find a truly *Macbeth* atmosphere:

> Now stole upon the time the dead of night,
> When heavy sleep had closed up mortal eyes:
> No comfortable star did lend his light,
> No noise but owls' and wolves' death-boding cries.
> > (*Lucrece*, 162)

But in this poem the evil of Tarquin is powerfully opposed to gentle birds. So Lucrece is as a bird killed by his brutality:

> Wrapp'd and confounded in a thousand fears,
> Like to a new-killed bird she trembling lies.   (456)

And the melody of morning birds are a mockery to the settled night of her shame:

> 'You mocking birds', quoth she, 'your tunes entomb
> Within your hollow-swelling feather'd breasts,
> And in my hearing be you mute and dumb:
> My restless discord loves no stops nor rests;
> A woeful hostess brooks not merry guests:
> > Relish your nimble notes to pleasing ears;
> > Distress likes dumps when time is kept with tears.' (1121)

It is unnecessary to point out in detail examples of evil birds: they occur continually in appropriate contexts.

Birds thus suggest the spiritual: usually to be associated with man's upward aspiration, yet occasionally suggestive of an especially spiritual, as opposed to a fleshly, evil.

V

The mysterious problem of spiritual evil in Shakespeare cannot, however, be finally solved here in terms of these birds. I have attempted to answer such questions elsewhere. Finally, we must regard no evil as absolute and the tempest-music opposition—which presents no negation—as fundamental. Therefore now I shall conclude by showing further how Shakespeare's finest visions are presented in terms of swiftness, fire, and music.

Consider Falstaff's speech on 'sack':

> . . . A good sherris-sack hath a two-fold operation in it. It ascends me into the brain; dries me there all the foolish and dull and crudy vapours which environ it; makes it apprehensive, quick, forgetive, full of nimble, fiery and delectable shapes; which, delivered o'er to the voice, the tongue, which is the birth, becomes excellent wit. . . .
>
> (2 *Henry IV*, iv. iii. 103)

Observe here the words 'apprehensive', 'quick' and 'nimble', 'forgetive' (cf. 'In the quick forge and working-house of thought', *Henry V*, v. Cho. 23), 'fiery' and 'wit'. The drink-consciousness here produces swift 'shapes'. The poet's pen also turns vague spiritual forms to 'shapes' (*A Midsummer Night's Dream*, v. i. 16). And this 'drink' speech clearly forms contact with Biron's fine 'love' speech in *Love's Labour's Lost*. For Falstaff tells us:

> . . . So that skill in the weapon is nothing without sack, for that sets it a-work; and learning a mere lord of gold kept by a devil, till sack commences it and sets it in act and use.
>
> (2 *Henry IV*, iv. iii. 123)

Compare Biron's:

> For when would you, my liege, or you, or you,
> In leaden contemplation have found out
> Such fiery numbers as the prompting eyes
> Of beauty's tutors have enrich'd you with?
> Other slow arts entirely keep the brain;
> And therefore, finding barren practisers,
> Scarce show a harvest of their heavy toil:
> But love, first learned in a lady's eyes,

Lives not alone immured in the brain;
But, with the motion of all elements,
Courses as swift as thought in every power,
And gives to every power a double power,
Above their functions and their offices.
It adds a precious seeing to the eye;
A lover's eyes will gaze an eagle blind;
A lover's ear will hear the lowest sound,
When the suspicious head of theft is stopp'd:
Love's feeling is more soft and sensible
Than are the tender horns of cockled snails;
Love's tongue proves dainty Bacchus gross in taste:
For valour, is not Love a Hercules,
Still climbing trees in the Hesperides?
Subtle as Sphinx; as sweet and musical
As bright Apollo's lute, strung with his hair;
And when Love speaks, the voice of all the gods
Make heaven drowsy with the harmony.
Never durst poet touch a pen to write
Until his ink were temper'd with Love's sighs;
O, then his lines would ravish savage ears
And plant in tyrants mild humility.
From women's eyes this doctrine I derive:
They sparkle still the right Promethean fire;
They are the books, the arts, the academes,
That show, contain and nourish all the world:
Else none at all in aught proves excellent.

(*Love's Labour's Lost*, IV. iii. 320)

Observe here the contrast of 'leaden contemplation' and 'slow arts' with the 'fiery numbers' born of beauty; the barren-harvest contrast; the thought of love transcending the brain, the more material intellect; the comparison of it rather with 'all the elements' —that is, water, air, fire; its 'swift' coursing through all the faculties; the eye and eagle reference; love's power of making all the senses more acutely 'sensible', that is, of increasing man's powers of 'apprehension'; the comparison of love-pleasure with wine; its power to give 'valour', here imaged as aspiration too, 'climbing' ever after renown; the comparison of love itself with music, next of love's accents with music; and the clear emphasis on the close connexion existing between love and poetry. So love's eyes hold the true creative 'fire', and thus vitalize books, arts, academes, the whole world. Such is, naturally, the philosophy of the author of *Antony and Cleopatra*.

Now Falstaff and Biron have really said very much the same thing: they both emphasize the added power and vitality and extra-sensitive 'apprehension' of a heightened consciousness. True, the drink-consciousness must be in some sense the lower; but perhaps not to Falstaff. Drink is powerful in the love-visions, *Timon* and *Antony and Cleopatra*. And the impressions in the poet's language are similar. Swiftness, fire, strength are common ideas to both. Both speeches use the verb 'course'—'the sherris warms it and makes it course from the inwards to the parts extreme', and 'courses as swift as thought in every power'. Moreover Biron is attacking, like Falstaff, a philosophy of study and fast:

> Consider what you first did swear unto,
> To fast, to study, and to see no woman;
> Flat treason 'gainst the kingly state of youth. (IV. iii. 291)

Also, Falstaff asserts the power of wine to aid wit and valour; and, Biron asserts the power of love to aid valour, all learning, and especially poetry. Man can thus transcend his mortality for a while. Both speeches emphasize the sluggishness of our normal state— 'slow arts' and 'brain' in the one, and the 'foolish and dull and crudy vapours' of the 'brain' in the other. Such is the godlike 'apprehension' of swift consciousness in its positive and 'delectable' forms. And these impressions are necessarily to be related to our aspiring, singing, and swift birds.

I have noted that these birds are close relations to the horse in Shakespeare. And once, at least, the horse is given a fine apotheosis in terms of such *Antony and Cleopatra* imagery as I have just observed in Falstaff's and Biron's speeches. In *Henry V* the Dauphin praises his horse:

Dauphin. My Lord of Orleans, and my lord high constable, you talk of horse and armour?

Orleans. You are as well provided of both as any prince in the world.

Dauphin. What a long night is this! I will not change my horse with any that treads but on four pasterns. Ça, ha! he bounds from the earth, as if his entrails were hairs; le cheval volant, the Pegasus, chez les narines de feu! When I bestride him, I soar, I am a hawk: he trots the air; the earth sings when he touches it; the basest horn of his hoof is more musical than the pipe of Hermes.

Orleans. He's of the colour of the nutmeg.

Dauphin. And of the heat of the ginger. It is a beast for Perseus: he is pure air and fire; and the dull elements of earth and water never appear in him, but only in patient stillness while his rider mounts him: he is indeed a horse; and all other jades you may call beasts.

Constable. Indeed, my lord, it is a most absolute and excellent horse.

Dauphin. It is the prince of palfreys; his neigh is like the bidding of a monarch, and his countenance enforces homage.

Orleans. No more, cousin.

Dauphin. Nay, the man hath no wit that cannot, from the rising of the lark to the lodging of the lamb, vary deserved praise on my palfrey: it is a theme as fluent as the sea: turn the sands into eloquent tongues, and my horse is argument for them all: 'tis a subject for a sovereign to reason on, and for a sovereign's sovereign to ride on; and for the world, familiar to us and unknown, to lay apart their particular functions and wonder at him. I once writ a sonnet in his praise, and began thus: 'Wonder of nature'—   .

Orleans. I have heard a sonnet begin so to one's mistress.

Dauphin. Then did they imitate that which I composed to my courser, for my horse is my mistress.   (*Henry V*, III. vii. 7)

Observe the words 'volant', 'Pegasus', 'chez les narines de feu'. The horse, in its strength and vitality, is a thing of wings and fire. Hence to ride him is to be like a 'hawk', to 'soar'. This horse is ethereal—'he rides the air'; and, as for the duller element, earth, that is dissolved in music. For this horse is 'pure air and fire', having nothing of the duller elements, 'water and earth': he is a beast, clearly, of music rather than tempest. I have observed that horses, hounds, or hawks are idealized for their speed, vigour, and physical excellence joined to docility: this horse is docile, waiting in 'patient stillness' for his rider to mount. He is, indeed, 'a horse': a high compliment. Observe, too, the 'lark', bird of song and fire, and the 'lamb', creature of white innocence, as in *Macbeth*. Next, he is compared more than once to kingship itself, he is a theme to inspire poetry, and finally associated directly with love—'my mistress'. He is a 'wonder of nature', a phrase recalling the strange and beauteous naturalism of *Antony and Cleopatra*. Indeed, our whole series of impressions are clearly all typical *Antony and Cleopatra* effects. Especially here I would emphasize the hawk and lark, the suggestion of flying ('Perseus' and 'Pegasus'), air, fire, music, and poetry. These are typical Shakespearian effects. Hence, in introducing this play—a theme of brilliance and flashing optimism, heroism and success—Shakespeare writes:

> O for a Muse of fire that would ascend
> The brightest heaven of invention,
> A kingdom for a stage, princes to act
> And monarchs to behold the swelling scene!

> Then should the warlike Harry, like himself,
> Assume the port of Mars; and at his heels,
> Leash'd in like hounds, should famine, sword, and fire
> Crouch for employment.   (*Henry V*, Prologue, 1)

'Fire' again, 'muse', and the idea of ascension to heaven; and also more 'king' effects. Henry V is here imaged as assuming 'the port of Mars': observe the suggestion both of divinity and warlike grace. Warrior prowess is always a powerful value in Shakespeare, second only to love. Finally, we have 'hounds' again. Shakespeare's imagination is curiously consistent. Now these thoughts of the Muse and Mars lead us further. Here they are clearly associated with 'aspiration' effects, and high ardour generally. I pass to a few instances where Shakespeare images direct embodiments of these divine and ethereal essences in terms of myth or religion.

Love's passion twice in *Romeo and Juliet* relates the ardour of its own impatient desire to swift-flying creatures of myth. Here is one:

> Gallop apace, you fiery-footed steeds,
> Towards Phoebus' lodging: such a waggoner
> As Phaethon would whip you to the west. . . .
> 　　　　　　　　　(*Romeo and Juliet*, III. ii. 1)

'Phaethon' again; and again horses and fire. Here is the other—Juliet anxiously awaits the Nurse's return:

> . . . Love's heralds should be thoughts,
> Which ten times faster glide than the sun's beams,
> Driving black shadows over louring hills:
> Therefore do nimble-pinion'd doves draw love,
> And therefore hath the wind-swift Cupid wings. (II. v. 4)

Observe the winged 'nimble-pinion'd doves': I return to 'doves' later. Cupid's swiftness is often mentioned and such thoughts blend with the idea of love's swift consciousness. For example, observe Hamlet's phrase

> . . . that I with wings as swift
> As meditation or the thoughts of love
> May sweep to my revenge.   (*Hamlet*, I. v. 29

This is the same order of image as Troilus's:

> O gentle Pandarus,
> From Cupid's shoulder pluck his painted wings,
> And fly with me to Cressid!
> 　　　　　　　　(*Troilus and Cressida*, III. ii. 14)

Troilus here is 'giddy': expectation is said to 'whirl' him round

(III. ii. 19)—a phrase relevant to my comparison of the *Antony and Cleopatra* vision to a 'swiftly rotating top' in *The Imperial Theme*. All swift thought may 'whirl'. So the passionate Talbot cries:

> My thoughts are whirled like a potter's wheel;
> I know not where I am, nor what I do.
>
> (*1 Henry VI*, I. v. 19)

'These are but wild and whirling words', says Horatio to Hamlet (*Hamlet*, I. v. 133). Now this love-speed imagery closely connected with the mythological god Cupid is frequent. Here is another:

> Love, lend me wings to make my purpose swift. . . .
> (*The Two Gentlemen of Verona*, II. vi. 42)

Again, from *Romeo and Juliet*:

> *Mercutio.* You are a lover; borrow Cupid's wings,
>   And soar with them above a common bound.
> *Romeo.* I am too sore enpierced with his shaft
>   To soar with his light feathers, and so bound,
>   I cannot bound a pitch above dull woe.   (I. iv. 17)

Other examples will, no doubt, be readily remembered. Cupid is, indeed, an important symbol in Shakespeare. He is finely imagined as 'flying between the cold moon and the earth' in *A Midsummer Night's Dream* (II. i. 156): there he is 'all arm'd' and looses a 'love-shaft', a 'fiery' shaft, from his bow. In *Much Ado*, too, we hear of his archery: there the arrows of wit are, so to speak, set against the arrows of love. Hence Benedick is said to have been challenged 'at the bird-bolt' by Cupid's representative (*Much Ado*, I. i. 42).

But winged or heavenly beings are also often imaged as figures of military power and athletic grace in 'port' or action. So King Harry, in a passage I have lately quoted, is thought of as assuming 'the port of Mars'. We might compare Hamlet's:

> See, what a grace was seated on this brow;
> Hyperion's curls; the front of Jove himself;
> An eye like Mars, to threaten and command;
> A station like the herald Mercury
> New lighted on a heaven-kissing hill;
> A combination and a form indeed,
> Where every god did seem to set his seal,
> To give the world assurance of a man. . . .
>
> (*Hamlet*, III. iv. 55)

Observe the words 'grace', 'station', and 'form'. And notice especially the fine image of Mercury, late winged from heaven, light-poised on a mountain top. Mercury is important for our present-purpose. He is a winged god; and he is powerfully imagined by Shakespeare. As messenger god he blends with the concept 'angel'. Consider this significant passage, starting with fine birds and 'young' animals (youth robs these of any coarse suggestion), and next leading up to 'Mercury' and 'angels':

> All furnish'd, all in arms;
> All plum'd like estridges that with the wind
> Baited like eagles having lately bathed;
> Glittering in golden coats, like images;
> As full of spirit as the month of May
> And gorgeous as the sun at midsummer;
> Wanton as youthful goats, wild as young bulls.
> I saw young Harry with his beaver on,
> His cuisses on his thighs, gallantly arm'd,
> Rise from the ground like feather'd Mercury,
> And vaulted with such ease into his seat,
> As if an angel dropp'd down from the clouds,
> To turn and wind a fiery Pegasus
> And witch the world with noble horsemanship.
>
> (*1 Henry IV*, iv. i. 97)

A most important speech. Observe the fine idealizing of soldiership, the vivid pictorial apprehension of the young prince in all his athletic strength and grace of early manhood; and, also, the great imaginative importance attached to horsemanship. Again, as in the Dauphin's praise of his horse, we have fire-imagery; and again, Pegasus—the winged horse of legend that helped to slay the dreaded Chimaera who, with other such, must surely be allowed an honourable place among our tempest-beasts. Finally we see how the Prince is compared with 'feather'd Mercury' and how Mercury is a symbol of active masculine strength seen in terms of grace and beauty. Mercury is apt as a comparison for masculine beauty gilded by the eye of love. Imogen sees Posthumus:

> . . . this is his hand;
> His foot Mercurial. . . .   (*Cymbeline*, iv. ii. 309)

Now this is partly an imagination of a 'warrior' beauty. There is a stress, however, on a 'love' content for the Mercury idea in Cleopatra's

> . . . had I great Juno's power,
> The strong-wing'd Mercury should fetch thee up,
> And set thee by Jove's side.
>
> (*Antony and Cleopatra*, iv. xiii. 34)

And we may have such an impression to outlimn for us a pure 'love' beauty. Romeo speaks of Juliet in terms Mercurial:

> She speaks:
> O, speak again, bright angel! for thou art
> As glorious to this night, being o'er my head,
> As is a winged messenger of heaven
> Unto the white-upturned wondering eyes
> Of mortals that fall back to gaze on him
> When he bestrides the lazy-pacing clouds
> And sails upon the bosom of the air.
>
> (*Romeo and Juliet*, II. ii. 25)

Here an 'angel' clearly develops into a 'Mercury' ('winged messenger of heaven'). Notice how this divine being is, too, a kind of airy horseman, 'bestriding' the clouds. Which recalls Macbeth's agonized imagination of innocent purity, of how Duncan's

> virtues
> Will plead like angels, trumpet-tongued, against
> The deep damnation of his taking-off;
> And pity, like a naked new-born babe,
> Striding the blast, or heaven's cherubim, horsed
> Upon the sightless couriers of the air,
> Shall blow the horrid deed in every eye,
> That tears shall drown the wind.   (*Macbeth*, I. vii. 18)

So finely graced, so noble in action, are Shakespeare's angels, whether to be directly associated with war, love, or innocence. They are often horsemen. Horses, too, are ever beautiful, fiery, athletic things in Shakespeare. Thus, in outlining the varied excellences of men, Hamlet exclaims: 'In action, how like an angel!' (*Hamlet*, II. ii. 325).

So, in Shakespeare's imagery of those excelling qualities in men, his aspiring pride, his soldiership, his love, his athletic grace, beauty of form, all that is 'air and fire' rather than sluggish 'earth and water', we pass from birds, through metaphysical ideas of swift and winged intuitions, to more vivid and concrete embodiments in terms of Cupid, Mercury, and angels. In *The Tempest*, this facet of the Shakespearian imagination clearly receives a final impress in Ariel. Ariel, too, is a spirit of air and fire, of fire and music; yet able to penetrate the earth itself and dive within the sea. He is a spirit of beauty and active grace. He is aptly set beside Caliban. In Ariel we find the consummation of this Shakespearian intuition of winged beauty, air, fire, and music.

23

VI

I have observed instances where birds are metaphorically related to qualities specifically human. There is one instance where what must be considered a specifically human theme is given an exact and comprehensive bird-formulation. I refer to *The Phoenix and The Turtle*. Now our bird-imagery has, clearly, continually suggested the *Antony and Cleopatra* vision. *The Phoenix and The Turtle* is, too, a compressed miniature of the later play. Its theme is the same: the blending of duality in unity, of life and death in love's immortality. This poem has been already—perhaps finally—analysed in respect to its absolute metaphysical significance in Ranjee's *Towards the Stars*.[1] Brilliant as is his treatment, however, the author quite remarkably fails to observe the place of the poem in Shakespeare's work. Indeed, I shall now use, with acknowledgement and thanks, Ranjee's quotations of other Shakespearian 'phoenix' passages for my own purpose: passages he adduces to prove the poem un-Shakespearian.

The phoenix itself is in the 'aspiring' tradition. The bird may suggest man's proud assertion of a vitality outreaching death, like Talbot's 'Icarus' passages. Indeed, our first quotation comes from that very context. Talbot and his son are dead. Sir William Lucy speaks over them with 'a proud commanding spirit' (*1 Henry VI*, IV. vii. 88) as follows:

> I'll bear them hence; but from their ashes shall be rear'd
> A phoenix that shall make all France afeared.
>
> (*1 Henry VI*, IV. vii. 92).

Here is Ranjee's next quotation: but I enclose it in a wider context which I find aptly—for my purpose—includes both 'Phaethon' and the 'falcon'. It is to be observed that all the speakers are vying with each other in 'aspiration':

> *Northumberland.* Yield to our mercy, proud Plantagenet.
> *Clifford.* Ay, to such mercy as his ruthless arm,
>   With downright payment, show'd unto my father.
>   Now Phaethon hath tumbled from his car,
>   And made an evening at the noontide prick.
> *York.* My ashes, as the phoenix, may bring forth
>   A bird that will revenge upon you all:
>   And in that hope I throw mine eyes to heaven,
>   Scorning whate'er you can afflict me with.
>   Why come you not? what! multitudes, and fear?

[1] Reviewed in *The Criterion*, April 1931.

Clifford. So cowards fight when they can fly no further;
   So doves do peck the falcon's piercing talons;
   So desperate thieves, all hopeless of their lives,
   Breathe out invectives 'gainst the officers.

                          (*3 Henry VI*, i. iv. 30)

Notice the close relation of the 'phoenix' to 'heaven'; and again, observe the close Phaethon-phoenix-falcon association. Our next example shows a phoenix-immortality suggestion:

Queen Elizabeth. But thou didst kill my children.
King Richard. But in your daughter's womb I bury them:
   Where in that nest of spicery they shall breed
   Selves of themselves, to your recomforture.

                          (*Richard III*, iv. iv. 422)

There is a sense, of course, in which immortality may be well imaged in terms of time as self-perpetuation either by children or by work and influence: which immortality is part, but not of course the whole, of the full truth expressed by the term. But the phoenix is also a love-symbol: clearly, it finds then apt place in *Timon*: a quotation Ranjee has missed. A Senator speaks thus of Timon:

                          I do fear,
   When every feather sticks in his own wing,
   Lord Timon will be left a naked gull,
   Which flashes now a phoenix.   (*Timon*, ii. i. 29)

Similarly, we find the bird in *Antony and Cleopatra*:

   O Antony! O thou Arabian bird!   (iii. ii. 12)

Timon and Antony, both very similar love-heroes, are thus both compared to the phoenix. So, too, we are not surprised to find the phoenix as a symbol to suit the 'rarity' of Imogen:

   All of her that is out of door most rich!
   If she be furnish'd with a mind so rare,
   She is alone the Arabian bird, and I
   Have lost the wager.   (*Cymbeline*, i. vi. 14)

Here the phoenix suggests primarily faithfulness in love. The phoenix is, indeed, a strange and wonderful bird, its suggestion enclosing all that is finest in spiritual potentiality: aspiration, love, immortality. Its pictorial and mythological beauty associates it with the unicorn—also an immortality-symbol—and here they are together:

                        Now I will believe
        That there are unicorns: that in Arabia
        There is one tree, the phoenix' throne, one phoenix
        At this hour reigning there.   (*The Tempest*, III. iii. 21)

Finally, our grandest example occurs in Shakespeare's grandest
play:

                        . . . but as when
        The bird of wonder dies, the maiden phoenix,
        Her ashes new create another heir,
        As great in admiration as herself;
        So shall she leave her blessedness to one,
        When heaven shall call her from this cloud of darkness,
        Who from the sacred ashes of her honour
        Shall star-like rise, as great in fame as she was,
        And so stand fixed.   (*Henry VIII*, v. v. 40)

The immortality of England's sovereignty is thus nobly symbolized
in terms of the phoenix: it is, indeed, the rarest of Shakespearian
birds.

    As for the turtle-dove, the emotional content here is obvious: it
clearly suggests that element of gentleness which I have observed
as often characterizing Shakespeare's birds. It is, for example, to
be contrasted with the raven in Juliet's line, 'Dove-feather'd raven!
wolvish-ravening lamb!' (*Romeo and Juliet*, III. ii. 76)—a line
following directly after the phrase 'Fiend angelical!', which is
significant. It is contrasted with the griffin (*A Midsummer Night's
Dream*, II. i. 232). Venus, too, is mythologically drawn in her
heavenly car by doves (*Lucrece*, 58; *Venus and Adonis*, 153; *Romeo
and Juliet*, II. v. 7; *The Tempest*, IV. i. 94). The turtle-dove, too,
is proverbial for constant love (*1 Henry VI*, II. ii. 30; *Troilus*,
III. ii. 185). Other passages will come to mind.

    So one of Shakespeare's finest visions is well embodied in *The
Phoenix and the Turtle*. Our bird-references will help our intuitive
understanding of the poem. It is a vision of love's aspiring immortality, upwinging beyond the world of appearance and multiplicity
to the air and fire and music of union, the empyrean of divinity.
But I attempt to do no final justice to the poem here: merely to
observe its birds:

    This is how it starts:

                    Let the bird of loudest lay,
                    On the sole Arabian tree,
                    Herald sad and trumpet be,
                    To whose sound chaste wings obey.

Probably, as Ranjee thinks, the nightingale. The nightingale is, indeed, not only continually present in Shakespeare, but is a universal symbol of sweetly tragic love. Keats wrote an ode on the nightingale. This opening stanza, perhaps, may be best explained by saying that it suggests the quality of the *Romeo and Juliet* vision. The detailed analogy, however, is not close or very valuable. Next, we have *Macbeth*:

> But thou shrieking harbinger,
> Foul precurrer of the fiend,
> Augur of the fever's end,
> To this troop come thou not near!

'Harbinger', 'fiend', 'augur', 'fever'—all call to mind the same words in *Macbeth*; and 'precurrer' also more indirectly recalls the play. Thus are our 'evil' birds to be warded off, as evil forms of life are charmed away from Titania's bower, to give place to Philomel's music. Thus, in a *Cymbeline* stanza,

> From this session interdict
> Every fowl of tyrant wing,
> Save the eagle, feather'd king:
> Keep the obsequy so strict.

I have already observed how the eagle is a bird of grandeur. In *Cymbeline* he is very important, both as the Roman eagle and as Jove's bird, occurring in the Vision of Jupiter:

> . . . the holy eagle
> Stoop'd, as to foot us: his ascension is
> More sweet than our blest fields: his royal bird
> Prunes the immortal wing and cloys his beak,
> As when his god is pleased.   (*Cymbeline*, v. iv. 115)

He occurs in other resplendent passages throughout the play. So all tyrannic birds are to absent themselves; even, perhaps, falcons, in so far as pride may be guilty and earth-bound rather than pure air and fire. Next, we have the swan:

> Let the priest in surplice white,
> That defunctive music can,
> Be the death-divining swan,
> Lest the requiem lack his right.

'Defunctive music', 'death-divining'. Now we are in *The Merchant of Venice*:

> Let music sound while he doth make his choice;
> Then, if he lose, he makes a swan-like end,
> Fading in music.   (III. ii. 43)

Music is truly 'death-divining' in Shakespeare, especially in the final plays. The swan is indeed apt here: symbol of white purity and music-in-death. Next we have the 'crow', often used as a symbol of blackness in Shakespeare, here placed, shall we say, in a *Hamlet* stanza:

> And thou treble-dated crow,
> That thy sable gender makest
> With the breath thou givest and takest,
> 'Mongst our mourners shalt thou go.

And then *Antony and Cleopatra*: .

> Here the anthem doth commence:
> Love and constancy is dead;
> Phoenix and the turtle fled
> In a mutual flame from hence.

'Mutual flame'—fire-imagery is powerful here: so later we have love 'shining' or 'flaming' (33, 35), 'stars of love' (51), 'cinders' (55). And the theme here is clearly the offering up of differentiation, slain on the altar of love: 'twain' is resolved by love into 'one', there are 'two distincts' without 'division' (one of Shakespeare's usual tempest words); 'number' itself is 'slain' (25–8); 'space' and 'distance' are transcended.(29–30); each lover was the very being of the other, the 'self' indeed no longer itself; the 'single', or simple duality of 'nature' was now neither 'one' nor 'two' (33–40). Not merely is dualism transcended into unity, but rather the unity-dualism antinomy is itself transcended. Before such a state, reason fails, 'confounded', as it sees 'division' melted into unity (42), the 'twain', still twain, yet now also a 'concordant one' (45–6), a single music—we remember 'the true concord of well-tuned sounds' in a similar context (Sonnet VIII). Such is the mystery of this love-death intercourse. Even 'truth' and 'beauty' falsify the intuition since 'truth' and 'beauty' are buried with the Phoenix and the Turtle (62–4). They are but mortal categories: yet the very death of 'truth' and 'beauty' creates a third unknown immortality. So fine a mystic paradox vitalizes this bird-song of tragic joy.

Indeed, to Shakespeare, the bird-image is constantly used to suggest the finer harmonies of human aspiration. We remember how the lark was ever as an arrow of flame and song, upcircling to the fire of heaven. And such is the Shakespearian intuition of love:

> Love is a spirit all compact of fire,
> Not gross to sink, but light, and will aspire.
>
> (*Venus and Adonis*, 149)

Therefore in *Venus and Adonis* bird-imagery riots extravagantly. On one page alone there are these fine examples. Venus in her hungry love is as an 'empty eagle':

> Even as an empty eagle, sharp by fast,
> Tires with her beak on feathers, flesh and bone,
> Shaking her wings, devouring all in haste,
> Till either gorge be stuff'd or prey be gone. . . .   (55)

Adonis in love's arms is as a captured bird:

> Look, how a bird lies tangled in a net,
> So fasten'd in her arms Adonis lies. . . .   (67)

Or we have a sea-bird:

> Upon this promise did he raise his chin,
> Like a dive-dapper peering through a wave,
> Who, being look'd on, ducks as quickly in;
> So offers he to give what she did crave. . . .   (85)

I will not look further in this poem: my point is clear enough, and it is time to close. But need we wonder at the birds in *Antony and Cleopatra*? And need we still ask unanswerable questions as to whether Shakespeare 'intended' to put them there?—or was 'conscious' of their presence when he had put them there?

Additional Note (1952): The 'bird of loudest lay' in *The Phoenix and the Turtle* remains enigmatic. The Nightingale was suggested by Dr. A. B. Grosart in 1878; Sir Osbert Sitwell favours the Peacock (see Sir Gurney Benham's articles and Sir Osbert's letter in *The Times Literary Supplement* of 19th and 26th July, 1941 (pp. 352, 359, 364; see also *T.L.S.*, index for 1941, 'Special Articles'). But perhaps the older view favouring the Phoenix itself—'chaste' suggests either phoenix or nightingale—remains the best. The paradox is in character.

(1960): *The Phoenix and the Turtle* has been given an extended study in *The Mutual Flame* (1955).

THE 'HECATE' SCENES IN *MACBETH*

FOR long these generally suspected passages have not seemed to me to fit perfectly into the pattern of our play. My study, too, of Shakespeare's use of music would seem to strengthen that impression: since here music, song, and dances are associated with, presumably, the origin of Evil. But, the more we have reason to believe our old methods of deciding authenticity to be at fault, the more strongly are we forced to accept the authority of the Folio editors. It would be but a poor start to the newer methods I employ, were I to use them to rule out those passages which do not, or seem not to, fit my theories of Shakespeare's symbolisms. Therefore I shall here see what can be made of these passages along the lines of Shakespeare's usual imaginative effects. That is, I inquire what they must mean if they are either Shakespearian, or, though by another hand, yet incorporated in the play by Shakespearian authority.

Hecate enters first at Act III, Scene v:

Thunder. Enter the three Witches, meeting Hecate.

She is, however, mentioned before:

Witchcraft celebrates
Pale Hecate's offerings. . . . (II. i. 51)

Hecate is the goddess of witchcraft and therefore, in this play, she would seem to be the principle of Evil itself. She enters, appropriately it may seem, to 'thunder'. But the thunder must be related not to pure evil, but rather to the discord existing here between these evil spirits. It is a discord within the world of evil. Hecate 'looks angerly' (III. v. 1) on the witches. Next, she speaks a long speech, rebuking the three sisters for their 'trade and traffic with Macbeth'.

Now this speech is not pitched on the weird note that characterizes the prophecies and incantations of the three witches. It has a far lighter, rippling, flow. Indeed, it is very similar to the speeches of other gods or goddesses in Shakespeare: in all we can detect the same apparent faults: almost as though the poet were very deliberately attempting to render an effect pre-eminently supernormal, standing off from the powerful naturalism of his poetic presentations elsewhere. For Shakespeare's normal verse blends the mysterious with the natural so spontaneously, that, if he is to gain an effect preeminently otherworldly, he must in some way fetter his spontaneous utterance. In these passages I feel a certain fettering, impediment, barring the poetic faculty from its usual easy power. The result is, that Hecate, Hymen, Diana, and Jupiter, all have a certain strangeness about them which marks them off from the more firmly actualized figures of the Weird Sisters, the Ghost in *Hamlet*, Oberon, and Puck. And I conclude that this sense we have almost of unreality is part of the intention, I will not say of Shakespeare, but rather of the speeches themselves.

Hecate is clearly not represented as a grim and portentous figure. She is fairy-like, ethereal, a delicate and, presumably, palely beautiful goddess to be strongly contrasted with the bearded and withered ugliness of the Weird Women. To her the prosecution of evil is not a rough act of disorder, no negation, but rather a positive thing of aesthetic delight, a delicate exercise of skill:

> And I, the mistress of your charms,
> The close contriver of all harms,
> Was never call'd to bear my part,
> Or show the glory of our art. . . .   (III. v. 6)

She resents this trafficking of evil with a good man: he cannot appreciate the serene loveliness and fine delight of her mysteries. Therefore,

> And, which is worse, all you have done
> Hath been but for a wayward son,
> Spiteful and wrathful, who, as others do,
> Loves for his own ends, not for you.   (III. v. 10)

The true devotee of evil, that is, should be as free from the clogs of selfish desire as the saint. Macbeth does not love evil for its own sake: he is an imperfect Satanist. And so she would have nothing to do with him. In her, indeed, evil does not appear unpleasant. She is a fairy, floating in air, rising toward the moon, and watching for a 'vaporous drop' to fall to earth:

> I am for the air; this night I'll spend
> Unto a dismal and a fatal end:
> Great business must be wrought ere noon:
> Upon the corner of the moon
> There hangs a vaporous drop profound;
> I'll catch it ere it come to ground. . . .   (III. v. 20)

The imagery is serene. In *Macbeth* we would expect the moon to be obscured: it is not so here. Indeed, our effects suggest rather *A Midsummer Night's Dream*. There are, moreover, some definite reminiscences. 'Acheron' comes at the end of a line in each:

> And at the pit of Acheron
> Meet me i' the morning. . . .   (III. v. 15)

In *A Midsummer Night's Dream* we have

> The starry welkin cover thou anon
> With drooping fog as black as Acheron.   (III. ii. 356)

Here we have the moon vividly imagined: in *A Midsummer Night's Dream* the moon is everywhere important. In that play, the fairies have to accomplish their night's work before morning:

> My fairy lord, this must be done with haste,
> For night's swift dragons cut the clouds full fast
> And yonder shines Aurora's harbinger . . .   (III. ii. 378)

Again:

> But, notwithstanding, haste; make no delay:
> We may effect this business yet ere day.   (III. ii. 394)

'Business'. So, too, Hecate says:

> This night I'll spend
> Unto a dismal and a fatal end:
> Great business must be wrought ere noon. . . .
>   (III. v. 20)

'Dismal' and 'fatal': yet how harmless they are here. There is nothing really terrifying in Hecate. She belongs to the world of *A Midsummer Night's Dream*. Indeed, in that play the fairies actually associate themselves with her:

> And we fairies, that do run
>   By the triple Hecate's team,
> From the presence of the sun,
>   Following darkness like a dream. . . .
>   (*A Midsummer Night's Dream*, v. ii. 13)

And yet, clearly, she blends also with *Macbeth*, in the impressions of 'night', 'dismal', 'fatal'. It was the same with her 'riddles and affairs of death' (III. v. 5)—a lovely phrase carelessly hitting off the *Macbeth* shattering evil as though it were but a paltry thing. Elsewhere she speaks most aptly of Macbeth's future:

> And that distill'd by magic sleights
> Shall raise such artificial sprites

> As by the strength of their illusion
> Shall draw him on to his confusion:
> He shall spurn fate, scorn death, and bear
> His hopes 'bove wisdom, grace and fear:
> And you all know, security
> Is mortals' chiefest enemy.   (III. v. 26)

'Confusion', 'spurn fate', 'scorn death', a final victory over 'grace' and 'fear'. All these are *Macbeth* impressions. And these lines are a most admirable comment on the falling action of the play. And yet again we have more fairylike impressions. There is a stage direction:

> *Music and a song within*: 'Come away, come away', &c.

After which Hecate speaks:

> Hark! I am call'd: my little spirit, see,
> Sits in a foggy cloud, and stays for me.   (III. v. 34)

Similarly, in other passages in the Cauldron scene, generally suspected with the Hecate incidents, we have 'music' (IV. i. 43 and IV. i. 133). These themes of music must be related to the harmony existing in the world of these spirits; but when there is discord between them there is 'thunder', as at Hecate's first entrance. Here music suggests the harmony of absolute evil with itself; which evil immediately appears, in itself, not evil at all. Hecate, and the effects which accompany her, are thus often fairylike. Therefore we may conclude that any important significance to be found in these passages must lie in some direction between the visions of *A Midsummer Night's Dream* and *Macbeth*. I will now indicate whither that must lead us.

In reviewing the imagery of *A Midsummer Night's Dream* I have shown that the play has many typical *Macbeth* effects. There is something fearsome about it—its darkness, its mistakes, and dissensions, its nightmare, its beasts, its reptiles: all these I have already noticed. To requote only one instance: Titania is lulled to sleep with a song invoking Philomel and charming away all evil and ugly forms of life: snakes, hedge-hogs, blind-worms, spiders, beetles, snails (II. ii. 9–24). This touches the evil life-forms in the Cauldron scene of *Macbeth*. But there is, of course, much more; especially we must note the 'nightmarish' quality of each Vision. Now in *A Midsummer Night's Dream* the fairies are, in themselves, delightful beings; but in their clash with mankind they are dangerous. In that play the balance between fairyland and actuality is upset, and this general disorganization is due in each to an unrestful passion for the other. Theseus, we noted, appears to blend the two worlds in himself and thus does not believe in fantastic imaginations, does not see fairies. For he is essentially a noble, good, indeed a Christ-like figure, incorporating imagination in life itself. Now we may apply this philosophy to *Macbeth*. There, too, we have an evil seen in terms of spirit disharmonized with actuality. We have 'naked spirit', as I have called it, as equivalent to evil, not in itself, but rather in that it is disjointed from the shapes and forms of the actual. The actual, similarly, becomes disorganized, shapeless, formless, since it is spirit or soul that creates form of any kind. It is the disjointing of elements, however, rather than the elements themselves, which is evil. Thus we see evil as a condition of disharmony between two elements: neither by itself is actively bad, but rather their separation, division, and therefore conflict, leads to what we call 'evil'. Hence the Weird Sisters, as I have elsewhere clearly shown, are not powerfully and beautifully Satanic. Rather they are symbols of this very disharmony, suggesting both elements in an unpleasant and chaotic mixture. We see them both as spirits, as when they vanish; or as formless, uncouth, and un-natural physical creatures, incongruously bearded hags. Charles Lamb aptly called them 'foul anomalies'. But in Hecate the poet attempts to give an objective image, it would seem, of the purely spiritual quality whose disharmony with human life has caused all the trouble. This, clearly, need not, in fact must not, seem evil at all; the evil being due to its 'traffic' with mankind, or mankind's sight of it in nakedness.[1] The disharmony of the two elements is evil, the elements themselves are not. Hence Hecate is annoyed at this trading and trafficking with the purely human; the dis-harmony is actually as unpleasant to her as it is to mankind, since she knows that a human being cannot be properly harmonized with her art and the ultimate mysteries of fairyland, or wherever she lives. Yet, once the business is started, it has to continue: a deeper law than anything she can control forces conflict and dis-order to run its course to the appointed end in harmony. Hence she helps to further Macbeth's course of crime. So we see that she

---

[1] We may recall the myth of Actaeon, and certain passages of Shelley where he claims to have looked on the naked loveliness of nature. Such vision may cause unrestful aspiration. This is the love of *A Midsummer Night's Dream*, and the imperial ambition of *Macbeth*. Ultimately, these are equivalent.

herself is a creature of music and airy flight, a fairy. But this sweet Satanic music leads to discord when it clashes with the other music of human life.

And here we may, if we choose, quite easily find a place for the music in the Cauldron scene. Macbeth has been shown the music of creation, as the show of Kings passes to 'hautboys': it maddens him, who can have no contact with such life-music, such creative joy in life. For he is dedicate to confusion, and discord. Therefore the witches next torment him by offering him their own—or rather Hecate's—Satanic music. He rejects one world; now he is offered, ironically and mockingly, the other:

> Ay, sir, all this is so: but why
> Stands Macbeth thus amazedly?
> Come, sisters, cheer we up his sprites,
> And show the best of our delights:
> I'll charm the air to give a sound,
> While you perform your antic round;
> That this great king may kindly say,
> Our duties did his welcome pay.
> [*Music. The Witches dance, and then vanish with Hecate.*
>
> (IV. i. 125)

Before Macbeth's entrance we had music:

> And now about the cauldron sing,
> Like elves and fairies in a ring,
> Enchanting all that you put in.
> [*Music and a song:* 'Black spirits', &c.
>
> (IV. i. 41)

Music only occurs, however, when Hecate is present. So at the end Macbeth is offered this music of fairyland or pure Satanism. But he, being a living man, can no more grasp this death-music to his soul than he could the life-music of creation.[1] It is a mockery. The purely spiritual is, to him, an unreality. Awhile the music, perhaps, charms him: then the sisters vanish into their spirit-world. So the maddening music of evil ever vanishes, melts in the hand, leaving bitterness and despair. Macbeth has repudiated the music of life and cannot capture the music of death: set between two musics, he is himself a discord blending with neither. And we are back at the root ideas of the Shakespearian universe—music, tempest, and music.

Such is my reading of these speeches. I have not, in this note,

---

[1] Compare the 'music' incident in *Richard II*, which I analyse at some length in *The Imperial Theme*.

attempted to prove their authority. Rather, assuming for awhile their authenticity, I have tried to see their significance. Should this interpretation be found satisfactory, it may well result in their complete restoration to our confidence. Certainly the Romantic critics accepted them without question. Moreover, if we remember that the Weird Sisters are naturally to be related to the Greek Furies, we immediately find the addition of Hecate, Queen of Evil, almost a necessity. The Furies attend on Hecate in ancient mythology, and Dante respects the tradition (*Inferno*, IX). It seems fairly clear, too, that the author to whom these speeches are usually attributed is unlikely to have written them: they do not look like Middleton's work. Indeed, having regard to Shakespeare's usual method of presenting theophanies—a method which seems almost to aim at an effect of semi-reality only—I can see no good reason for rejecting what I believe to be the only remaining questionable passages of any great length or importance in the Folio.

Moreover, our consideration of Hecate resolves the difficulties I have elsewhere discussed as to the ultimate reality of the *Macbeth* evil. We see Hecate as the embodiment, if such may be imagined, of death absolute, or absolute evil; and, being such, being, that is, an absolute, she is necessarily a creature of harmony and fairy grace, and, therefore, not evil in the usual sense. The Weird Sisters, however, creatures of fog and filthy air, thunder, lightning and tempest, anomalies set between the spirit-world and actuality and variously belonging to either, these represent the essence of disorder, the clash of life and death. And only in such disorganized relations is there, ultimately, any evil at all. We seem, indeed, to have met but another instance where the one element in a play which we most desire to reject is the one stone necessary to complete the mosaic of our pattern, and lead us to a final understanding.

Printed in Great Britain by
Jarrold & Sons Ltd.
Norwich